Tsunami One

Robert E. Rushton

© Copyright 2003 Robert E. Rushton. All rights reserved.

No part of this publication may be reproduced, stored in a retrieval system, or transmitted, in any form or by any means, electronic, mechanical, photocopying, recording, or otherwise, without the written prior permission of the author.

Printed in Victoria, Canada

```
National Library of Canada Cataloguing in Publication

Rushton, Robert E.
     Philosophy organon : Tsunami one & Tsunami two / Rushton.

Includes index.
ISBN 1-55395-857-8

     1. Philosophy.    2. Ethics.    3. Economics.    I. Title.
B995.R883P48 2003              191           C2003-901349-9
```

TRAFFORD

This book was published *on-demand* in cooperation with Trafford Publishing.
On-demand publishing is a unique process and service of making a book available for retail sale to the public taking advantage of on-demand manufacturing and Internet marketing. **On-demand publishing** includes promotions, retail sales, manufacturing, order fulfilment, accounting and collecting royalties on behalf of the author.

Suite 6E, 2333 Government St., Victoria, B.C. V8T 4P4, CANADA
Phone   250-383-6864   Toll-free   1-888-232-4444 (Canada & US)
Fax   250-383-6804   E-mail   sales@trafford.com
Web site   www.trafford.com   TRAFFORD PUBLISHING IS A DIVISION OF TRAFFORD HOLDINGS LTD.
Trafford Catalogue #03-0200   www.trafford.com/robots/03-0220.html

10   9   8   7   6   5   4   3   2   1

PHILOSOPHY ORGANON

Author R Rushton

If it is your desire to have your great grand-children see all the richness of the 22nd Century then you need an all embracing moral, philosophic, and economic Organon from which to work your magic.

Organon: An Instrument Of Thought
In Philosophy Economics and Morality

as they pertain to social production, advocacy groups unions, professional bodies, trade associations and politics operating under current global conditions.

What they positively avoid teaching you to think about in any main stream philosophy, economic or ethics class.

Tsunami One. Philosophy Organon.
Deals with a philosophy which is prerequisite to fully understanding the concepts given in
Tsunami One. Moral Organon
and In
Tsunami Two. Economics Organon

Synopsis Of Content Of Philosophy Organon

Under present day civilization people are being bombarded daily with random facts and fact-less whimsy. Knowledge is being produced at an astounding rate. Nowadays wisdom is lost in a maze of metaphysical flightiness. Where stands the main stream philosophy that puts whimsy into proper perspective, that ties random hard core objective facts together and thus brings forth knowledge of the world as it is - that brings forth objective truth?

Such a philosophy as found herein cannot be detected even in the most prestigious universities tied as they are to obtaining their funding from private for-profit sources. As some produce and all consume, it is from the heart of the producers only that can be found such a objective philosophy.

Citizens, especially working citizens on fees or on salary and wages, who are curious and want to be well informed will find an alternative way of looking at affairs of the globe in these writings that will aid in their navigation through the shoals of contemporary 'logic'.

Philosophy Organon: You will find, in this prose, methodologies laid out on how to obtain objective truth even from some of the most subjective of material. Your mind will be led back to the great philosophers of the past bringing forth their most cogent thoughts and criticizing them. But more significant than the sum total of this past thinking is laid out in this work a guide and a skeletal framework, allowing you to flesh out your own up-to-date reasoning using contemporary sources, categories, and techniques as revealed herein.

The author has also produced a CD-ROM. A fully Searchable Disk. Browse via computer, through name or subject Through >, #, and/or given paragraph number Note: Organon is defined as instrument of thought.

ORGANON

Dialectical and 2020 Materialism

- **CHAPTER 1 >#1**

- 2020 MATERIALIST DIALECTICS >#2

- THE FIRST AND MOST BASIC QUESTION IN ALL OF PHILOSOPHY. >#4

Social and Nature's Laws >#12

Men's Relationship To Reality >#14

- THE ESTATE SYSTEM: UNDERSTANDING MAN'S RELATIONSHIP TO PRODUCTION >#17

The Estate System As It Has Evolved From The Time Of The French Revolution >#19

Two Aspects Of The Basic Question Of Philosophy >#35

Monism, Dualism, Eclecticism and Realism >#38

Philosophers of Materialism >#41

Philosophers of Idealism >#44

The Second Aspect Of The Basic Philosophical Question: Knowability. >#49

- THE SECOND AND MOST BASIC QUESTION IN ALL OF PHILOSOPHY >#61

The subject matter of 2020 Materialist Philosophy >#70

- **CHAPTER 2 >#110**

- DIALECTICAL LAWS OF DEVELOPMENT AND PHILOSOPHICAL CATEGORIES >#111

The Struggle of Opposites >#112

First Law Of Development >#113

Second Law Of Development >#115

Third Law Of Development >#117

- CATEGORIES IN PHILOSOPHY >#119

Category 01: Matter And The Basic Forms Of Its Existence. >#123

Category 02: Motion And The Basic Forms Of Its Existence. >#154

Category 03: Space and Time. >#173

Category 04: Consciousness. >#201

Consciousness And Evolution Of The Forms Of Reflection: >#244

Consciousness, speech. Their origin and interconnection. >#256

Consciousness and Cybernetics. >#275

Category 05: Quality >#287

Category 06: Quantity >#301

Category 07: Proportion >#309

- LAW The laws of transformation of quantitative into qualitative change and visa versa >#329

Category 08: Struggle Of Opposites >#331

- LAW Of The Unity And Struggle Of Opposites: >#363

Category 09: Negation Of Negation >#365

- LAW The Negation of Negation. >#387

Category 10 : The Individual Particular and Universal >#388

Category 11: Cause And Effect >#405

- LAW Causality >#413

Cause and Effect differs from Ground and Consequent. >#420

Category 12: Necessity And Chance >#430

Category 13: Possibility And Reality >#453

Category 14: Content and Form >#468

Category 15: Essence And Appearance >#488

- **CHAPTER 3 >#505**

- **THE NATURE OF HUMAN KNOWLEDGE >#506**

Subject and Object >#522

Practice. The Social and Historical Nature of Knowledge >#53

Knowledge As Intellectual Master Of Reality. The Principles Of Reflection >#545

Language Is The Form Of Existence Of Knowledge. Sign And Meaning >#558

- OBJECTIVE TRUTH >#574

1) The 'subjective truth' flying out of bounds into untruth. >#581

2) The objective truth staying in bounds held there by its tie-in with practice. >#582

3) The lie and the repeating half truth >#583

- Criterion Of Truth And True Knowledge >#598

- **CHAPTER 4** >#612

- **DIALECTICS OF THE PROCESS OF COGNITION** >#613

Levels Of Knowledge: Empirical And Theoretical, Abstract And Concrete. Unity Of Analysis And Synthesis. >#630

The Historical And The Logical Forms Of Reproduction Of The Object By Thought >#649

The Basic Logical Forms Of Thought Are The Proposition, The Concept And The Inference. >#660

Dialectics And Formal Logic >#672

Formation & Development Of Scientific Theory. Intuition >#679

Practical Realization Of Knowledge >#696

Knowledge And Value >#710

- **CHAPTER 5 >#721**

- HISTORICAL 2020 MATERIALISM >#722

The subject-Matter Of Historical Materialism >#733

Laws Of Social Development & Their Objective Character >#747

Peoples Conscious Activity And Its Role In History. Freedom And Necessity >#785

- **CHAPTER 6 >#801**

- MATERIAL PRODUCTION & DISTRIBUTION ARE THE BASIS OF SOCIAL LIFE >#802

Society And Nature, Their Interaction >#805

The Productive And Distributive Forces Of Society And Man's Place In Them. >#854

Production Relations >#889

Dialectics Of The Development Of The Productive Forces And relations Of Production. >#899

- LAW of correspondence of the production relations >#925

- **CHAPTER 7 >#929**

- THE SOCIAL ECONOMIC FORMATIONS, UNITY AND DIVERSITY OF THE WORLD HISTORICAL PROCESS >#930

The Concept Of The Social-Economic Formation >#932

Structure Of The Social-Economic Formations. Basis And Superstructure >#948

Unity and Diversity Of The Historical Process. >#970

The Struggle Between The Estates >#996

- **CHAPTER 8 >#999**

- ORIGIN AND ESSENCE OF ESTATES >#1000

Social Structure And How It Changes >#1020

Estate's Interests and Class Struggle; Forms of Class Struggle and Organization >#1050

For Tsunami One. Moral Organon Contents see beginning of that section

ORGANON
R Rushton
Copyright 1998

CHAPTER 1 >#1

2020 MATERIALIST DIALECTICS >#2

#3   When a man travels into a far concept, he must be prepared to reshape the many things he has learned, and to grasp such understanding as are inherent in the existence of the new concept ; and as **Jack London** said, "...he must abandon the old ideals and the old gods, and oftentimes he must reverse the very codes by which his conduct has hitherto been shaped. To those who have the protean faculty of adaptability, the novelty of such change may even be a source of pleasure; but to those who happen to be hardened to the ruts in which they were created, the pressure of the altered environment is unbearable, and they chafe in body and in spirit under the new restrictions which they do not understand. This chafing is bound to act and react, producing divers evils and leading to various misfortunes. It were better for the man who cannot fit himself to the new groove to return to his own country..."

*****

BASIC PHILOSOPHICAL QUESTION >#4

#5 THE FIRST MOST BASIC QUESTION IN PHILOSOPHY

No matter how diverse philosophical doctrines may be, they all directly or indirectly, take as their theoretical point of departure from the question of the relationship of consciousness to being. Or in other words from the question of spiritual to material or in still other words from the question of subjective to objective.

#6 This basic question of philosophy lies in the fundamental facts of our lives. Yes, there are material phenomena – physical or chemical phenomena, but there are also spiritual and mental phenomena such as consciousness and thought.

#7 **This distinction between thinking and being** enters into any act of human consciousness and behavior. Every individual distinguishes himself from that which surrounds him and is aware of himself as something different from everything else. Thus he sees that no matter what phenomenon he is considering, whether he consciously realizes it or not, can always be placed in the sphere of either the material (Objective) or the spiritual (subjective). And Yet, despite the differences between the objective and the subjective there is a definite connection between them which on closer inspection turns out to be a relation of dependence.

The question then arises; what depends on what? >#8

#9 Which is the cause, and which is the result?
What may be considered primary and what secondary, the objective or the subjective, the material or the spiritual, the object or the subject?

#10 The way philosophers, past, present, and future answer this question split them, or will split them into two great camps. (1) Those who asserted or who will assert the primacy of spirit belong to the camp of idealism, whimsy and myth. (2) Those who asserted, or who will assert the primacy of Nature belong to the camp of the materialist.

#11 All the diverse philosophical schools and trends ultimately adhere either to materialism or idealism, this is why the relationship of the spiritual to the material is the basic philosophical question.

*****

Social and Nature's Laws >#12

#13 The question of the existence of laws of nature, and of social laws, also depends on which we acknowledge as having primacy: matter or spirit. As science has proved, these laws do not depend on human intervention, they exist outside and independently of man's consciousness. Recognition of the laws of nature and society presupposes recognition of the fact that the world exists independently of human consciousness. The idealists (and Theologians) offer quite a different solution to this question. Some of them believe that the world with all its law-governed phenomena is the incarnation of a supernatural world spirit.

Others preceding from the stance of the primacy of the spiritual in relation to the material, maintain that man is directly concerned only with the phenomena of his own consciousness and cannot recognize the existence of anything outside it. Denying the existence of the objective world and regarding objects as combinations of sensations and ideas, these philosophers also deny the objective law-governed nature of phenomena. As they see it, the law of nature and society, the causes of phenomena and processes discovered by science, express only the pattern of phenomena that exists in our consciousness.

*****

Men's Relationship To Reality >#14

#15 Depending on how we answer the basic question of philosophy, we are bound to draw certain definite social conclusions concerning men's relationship to reality, the understanding of historical events, moral principles and so on. If, like the idealists, for example, we regard consciousness, spirit, as primary, as definitive, then we shall seek the source of social evils, which cause great suffering to many in the Fifth-estate (i.e. periodic frustration, anxiety, unemployment, oppression, poverty, wars etc.), not on the character of people's material life (or lack thereof), but on people's consciousness, their errors and wickedness. Such belief gives us no opportunity of determining the main directions in which social life changes.

#16 Apologist philosophers for the First, Second and Third-estates today often attempt to prove that the basic question of philosophy does not exist at all, that it is an imaginary, invented problem.

Some of them believe that the very distinction between the spiritual and the material is relative, if not purely verbal. Thus in the view of Bertrand Russell (1872 1970) it is not at all clear whether anything that is denoted by the terms 'matter' and 'spirit' actually exists. According to Russell the spiritual and the material are merely logical constructs. But all attempts to do away, in one way or another, with the basic philosophical question fall to the ground. They fall because it is impossible to ignore the distinction between thinking and the object of thought (a physical process, for example), between sensation and that which is sensed, which is perceived by the eye, by the ear and so on. The notion of an object is one thing, but the object itself, existing independently of that notion, is quite another.

*****

THE ESTATE SYSTEM: UNDERSTANDING MAN'S RELATIONSHIP TO PRODUCTION >#17

#18 The 'Estate system' was evolving since long before the French revolution. At that time The Estate System was not very well understood, it has evolved to the present time as follows:- (It must be understood that in the present day there are two classes Bourgeois class and salary and wage working class. These are further divided into the Estate System of Domains this in order to give us the tools that facilitate a deeper understanding into the subject at hand.)

The Domains In The Estate System As They Have Evolved From The Time Of The French Revolution >#19

#20 **First-estate:** Those (in their millions) who live off the avails of Religion.

#21 **Second-estate:** Those (in their thousands) who live off the avails of hereditary right, (Leasehold; Nobility).

#22 **Third-estate:** Those (in their hundreds of thousands) who live off the avails of the extraction of value-added. Divided into – Capitalist; who's primary income is from Profit, Stocks, Bonds, Rent, Interest and financial instruments. Bourgeoisie; the little wantabe capitalists who work for themselves in long extended hours for small incomes and identify themselves as capitalists.

They can be further categorized into Small medium and large who's primary income is from shop-keeping and merchandising and the like who hire one, two or more workers. Apparatuchuks; entrenched, bloated, self-aggrandizing, bureaucratic labor and socialist leaders receiving inordinate salaries and perks, the cause of which twists them to eventually identify with, and collaborate with, Third-estate (Capital) against the very Fifth-estate (salary and wage workers) they are elected to represent. Upon this obscenity (and other historical distortions) the Soviet Union did fail. Now then throw in all those politicos who champion all of the above as being the people in the epitome of human progress.

#23 **Fourth-estate:** Those (in their millions) who live off the avails of income from media and entertainment. Divided into Newspapermen (Written word), Electronic men (Electronic word and depiction) Motion Picture Men and entertainers of every sort and description including highly remunerated sports figures.

#24 **Fifth-estate**: (in their billions) Salary and Wage Commodity Producing Labor, the producers of all 'Value-added.' in this world. Those who live by salary, wages, fees and commissions in the production of commodities etc. giving up the value added they produce to maintain all the other Estates. They include Entrepreneurs, Farmers, Proletariat (Students, temporarily unemployed, the infirm and retired people who are willing to participate but due to their historic condition are unable to do so due to their present circumstance in life). The true leaders of the Fifth-estate bind themselves to a life of study, oratory, leading and educating the salary and wage worker, and rejecting bloated pecuniary reward for their efforts:- 'Supeerio', the hero, in the hour of his peoples' distress, sets his own life lower than that of the totality.

#25 **Sixth-estate:** Those (in their millions) who live off the avails of the application of force; policing and military pursuits. (Also Dictators, Terrorists, 'Freedom Fighters' and the like)

#26 **Seventh-estate:** Those (in their hundreds of millions) who live off the avails of Begging, Prostitution, Thievery – all usually referred to as the lumpen-proletariat. The mob etc.

#27 Broadly speaking
First-estate, Religion; Society ruled by Theocracy

#28 Second-estate (Feudal); Society ruled by Monarchy

#29 Third-estate with the aid of the Forth-estate; Society ruled through a parliamentary 'democracy', (4 seconds in the poling booth then 4 years of dictatorship in the parliaments) what we may refer to here as the Triptocracy

#30 Fifth-estate; with the aid of an enlightened free Fourth-estate: Society ruled through a parliamentary democracy with grass roots input into it by referendums and recalls which body in turn has a seat in the UN or some body like the UN:- Pentocracy

#31 Sixth-estate; Society ruled by the police, military and martial law, usually a Dictatorship.

#32 Seventh-estate; Society ruled by the mob – Ochicracy.

#33 Then there are all the other permutations:- Caudillismos, Tyrannies, Anarchy, Apparatuchuks and more.

#34 **Ratiocination:** the process of logical reasoning and **Iteration:** the action or a process of iterating or repeating: as a procedure in which repetition of a sequence of operations yields results successively closer to a desired result. These together with **Dialectics**:- di.a.lec.tic n [ME dialetik, fr. MF dialetique, fr. L dialectica, fr. Gk dialektike, fr. fem. of dialektikos of conversation, fr. dialektos] (14c) 1: logic 1a(1) 2 a: discussion and reasoning by dialogue as a method of intellectual investigation; specific: the Socratic techniques of exposing false beliefs and eliciting truth b: the Platonic investigation of the eternal ideas 3: the logic of fallacy 4 a: the Hegelian process of change in which a concept or its realization passes over into and is preserved and fulfilled by its opposite; also: the critical investigation of this process b (1) usually plural but singular or plural in construction: development through the stages of thesis, antithesis, and synthesis in accordance with the laws of dialectical materialism (2): the investigation of this process (3): the theoretical application of this process esp. in the social sciences (4) usually plural but sing. or plural in Construction a: any systematic reasoning, exposition, or argument that juxtaposes opposed or contradictory ideas and use. seeks to resolve their conflict b: an intellectual exchange of ideas 6: the dialectical tension or opposition between two interacting forces or elements. These aspects of thinking enter into the well stocked armory of 2020 Materialist Philosophy.

*****

Two Aspects Of The Basic Question Of Philosophy >#35

#36 **THE FIRST And Second ASPECTS of the basic question of philosophy;** The <u>first</u> aspect is the question of the essence, the nature of the world, and the <u>second</u> is the question of its knowability.

#37 Let us consider the first aspect. **'Idealism'**, as we have seen, proceeds from the assumption that the material is a product of the spiritual. **'Materialism'** on the contrary, begins from the assumption that the spiritual is a product of the material.

Monism, Dualism, Eclecticism and Realism >#38

#39 Both idealism and materialism are of a monistic character, that is to say, they proceed from one definite principle. In one case the material is taken as primary and definitive; in the other, it is the spiritual that is primary. But there are some philosophical theories that proceed from both principles; these theories assume that the spiritual does not depend on the material, or the material on the spiritual. Such philosophical theories are called dualistic. Dualism in the final analysis usually leans toward idealism. Some philosophers try to combine the propositions of idealism with those of materialism and visa versa. This philosophical position is known as eclecticism. Still others deny any adherence to either materialism or idealism and call themselves 'realists'. They recognize the existence of a reality independent of the cognizing subject, but do not regard it as material. Analysis of such 'realism' shows that this theory is either eclectic or idealist in character, that is to say, it attributes any reality independent of cognition to God, the absolute spirit, supernatural being, and so on.

#40 Both materialism and idealism have traveled a long road of development and have many varieties.

*****

Philosophers of Materialism >#41

#42 **The first historical form of materialism** was the materialist philosophy of slave-owning society. This was a spontaneous, naive materialism, which expressed in ancient Indian philosophy (the philosophical school of the 'Charvaks'), and in its most developed form in ancient Greece (mainly the atomistic doctrines of Democritus (b c. 460 BC d c. 370 BC) and Epicurus (341 270BC). It is noted that the line of Democritus stands in bold contrast to the idealistic line of Plato.

#43 In the age of its emergence, the Third-estate gave us a materialistic interpretation, as opposed to the first and second estate's feudal relgio-idealistic world outlook. This materialist world outlook was most vividly expressed in the works of the English philosophers Francis Bacon (1561 1626) and
Thomas Hobbes (1588 1679),
the Dutch philosopher Spinoza (1632 1677),
the French materialists La Mettrie (1709 1751),
Holbach (1723 1789),
Helvetius (1715 1771), and
Diderot (1713 1784).
In the 19th century this form of materialism was developed in the works of Ludwig Feuerbach (1804 1872),
The Russian revolutionary democrats
Aleksandr Herzen (Ivanovich) (1812 1870),
Vissarion Grigoryevich Belinsky (1811 1848),
Nikolay Gavrilovich Chernyshevsky, (1828 1889), Nikolay Aleksandrovich Dobrolyubov (1836 1861)
The highest form of modern materialism is
Dialectical and Historical 2020 Materialism.

*****

Philosophers of Idealism >#44

#45 Among the varieties of idealism mention must be made of
Objective Idealists
Plato (427 347 BC)
Hegel (1770 1831) according to which the spirit exists outside and independently of the consciousness, independently of matter, independent of nature, as a kind of 'world reason',

'world will' or 'unconscious world spirit', which supposedly determines all material processes.

#46 **Subjective Idealists**
Aristotle (364 322 BC)
George Berkeley (1685 1753)
Ernst Mach (1838 1916)
Richard (Heinrich Ludwig) Avenarius (1843 1896).

#47 Subjective idealists assert that objects which we can see, touch and smell do not exist independently of our sensory perceptions and are merely combinations of our sensations. It is not difficult to see that the subjective idealist, if he follows this principle consistently, must arrive at an absurd conclusion. Everything that exists, including other people, adds up to no more than my own sensations. It follows, then, that only I exist. This subjective idealist conception is known as 'solipsism'. Needless to say, the subjective idealists constantly try to avoid solipsistic conclusions, thus disproving their own initial proposition. Berkeley, for instance, maintained that for an object to exist it must be perceived by a person otherwise it does not exist; (The famous tree falling in the forest does not make a sound unless there is someone there to hear it. This proposition is pure hog-wash as a recording device near the tree will soon prove that the sound did exist even if Berkeley, or anyone else, was not there to hear it at the precise moment of its fall. The recording devise sound can be played back at a later time, not only that, but this methodology also proves that sound is material in nature.) Nevertheless he tried to prove that beyond the limits of sensations there was God and our sensations were only signposts by means of which God communicated his will to us. The development of the sciences overthrows the idealist assertion that the world is based primarily on the supernatural, on the spiritual.

#48 **All materialists, proceeding from scientific knowledge**, regard the spiritual as a product of the material. This is a correct point of view, but this stance must be enhanced by a 'dialectical' method of its proof in the study of matter. The spiritual is a product of the 'development' of matter, a property of highly organized matter. This means that the spiritual does not exist always and everywhere, but that it arises only at a definite stage of development of matter and is itself subject to historical change.

*****

THE SECOND ASPECT Of The Basic Philosophical Question: Knowability. >#49

#50 All consistent and conscious advocates of philosophical materialism defend and seek to substantiate the principle of the knowability of the world. They regard our knowledge, concepts and ideas as reflections of objective reality. Only a minority, who are not consistently materialist, tend to deny the possibility of obtaining reliable objective knowledge -- these latter are known as agnostics. (from the Greek - no knowledge).

#51 As regards idealism, some of its exponents did adopt the position that the world was knowable (for example, the objective idealist Hegel, who nevertheless regarded knowledge, not as a reflection of objective reality, but as the world spirit's cognition of itself). Other idealists maintained that in cognition we are concerned only with our own sensations, perceptions and cannot go beyond the limits of the cognizing subject. (the subjective idealists Berkeley, Mach, Avenarius and others). And yet another Group rejected in principle the possibility of knowing anything that exists outside and independently of the human consciousness (Immanuel Kant (1724 1804), Friedrich Nietzsche (1844 1900)).

#52 Agnostic philosophers quite often attempt to adopt an intermediate position between materialism and idealism, but veer in the end towards idealist denial of the external world and the objective content in human concepts and ideas. The characteristic feature of modern idealism is that, unlike classical idealism, most of its supporters take the stand of agnosticism.

#53 Once we understand the meaning and significance of the basic question of philosophy, we are able to find our way amid the diversity of philosophical doctrines, trends and schools that have succeeded one another in the course of thousands of years. There are only two main streams in philosophy: Objectivism and Subjectivism; Materialism and Idealism. This means that any philosophical doctrine, no matter how original, is ultimately either materialist or idealist in substance.

#54 The struggle between materialism and idealism is closely connected with the struggle between science and religion, materialists, as a rule, rejects the religious explanation of the world and provides the theoretical basis of atheism. The atheist sees that a people's belief in fantasy and whimsy does not 'usually' harm either the world or its 'believers', it is only when these religions war amongst themselves that great harm can come to the human race. Religion can also be used as a mask for all manner of chicanery.

#55 Idealism is closely bound up with religion and beneath them both, in the present era, philosophy lies in chains. Subjective idealism, which usually claims that sensory perceived objects are no more than the sensations of the individual, nevertheless quite often recognizes the existence of a supersensory, supernatural first cause, that is to say, the existence of God. On the other hand, the 'world reason' of the objective idealists is, in fact, a philosophical pseudonym for God. It would be wrong, however, to identify idealism with religion, because idealism is a system of erroneously conceived theoretical views that have taken shape in the course of the contradictory development of knowledge. (Also in the study of human knowledge it would be wrong to assume that materialist philosophy has not had its certain social and epistemological roots.)

#56 When we speak of the epistemological roots of idealism, we mean a one sided approach to cognition, the exaggeration or even absolutisation of one of the aspects of this intricate, many-sided, and internally contradictory process. In pointing out the epistemological roots of idealism, we point out that idealism is not a meaningless jumble of words but a distorted reflection of reality, that is connected with certain peculiarities and contradictions in the process of cognition.

#57 The contradictions we encounter in cognitive activity take many forms. They may be contradictions between thinking (concepts) and the sensory reflection of reality (sensations), between theory and practice and so on. The epistemological roots of idealism lie in the fact that a particular side of cognition or a particular proposition is exaggerated or absolutised to such an extent that it ceases to be true and becomes an error. Thus, some idealist, eager to stress the active character of thinking, arrive at the conclusion that it has a creative force which is independent of matter. The subjective idealists, proceeding from what we know of the qualities of things by means of our sensory perceptions, infer that only our sensations are known to us and they are the only thing we can know anything about.

#58 Certain social conditions are needed to turn the possibility of the emergence of idealism into reality, to turn certain individual errors of cognition into a philosophical system. This comes about when the errors in cognition correspond to the demands of certain estates and social groups, and are supported by them. The social conditions required to bring about idealism are: contradiction between manual and mental work, the appearance and development of estates. The ideologists of these classes, who treat manual labor with contempt, are deluded into thinking that mental activity is the determinative factor in the existence and development of society.

#59 Reactionary Estates have an interest in seeing that the development of cognition does not undermine the idealist and religious superstitions in a society that is made up of countervailing estates. The need of one estate to preserve itself is quite often the reason why certain individual idealist mistakes occur in the process of cognition become reinforced and harden into definite systems of beliefs.

#60 The theological and philosophical are different forms of social consciousness. Theological arguments are based on blind faith, while philosophy appeals to the reason and seeks to furnish logical proof for its propositions no matter how subjective or objective they may be.

*****

SECOND MOST BASIC QUESTION IN PHILOSOPHY
>#61

#62 **Dialectics and Metaphysics:** Whereas the question of the relationship of thinking to being is the first and paramount question of philosophy, the second most important philosophical question is the question of whether the world and the universe is in a changeless state or, on the contrary, is constantly changing and developing.

#63 Metaphysics is defined as the area of knowledge that lies beyond physical reality. Metaphysicists (Theologians, subjective and most objective idealists) believe that the cosmos, world and society etc. are in a changeless state. (or at least, they believe, that if there have been changes to society in the past we are now living in the epitome of the best possible world that could ever be. i.e. Third-estate and the triptarchy rules all.)

#64 Dialecticians believe that the cosmos, world and society are in a changing and developing state. Dialectics considers things, their qualities and relationships, and also their mental reflections, concepts, in their interconnection, in motion: inception, in their contradictory aspects in their appearance, development and disappearance.

#65 Ignorance of dialectics was a weakness in previous materialist philosophers. It was this that made it difficult for them to evolve a consistent materialist view of the world, and particularly of society. In their understanding of social phenomena these philosophers, despite their hostility to the idealist interpretation of nature, themselves strayed into idealist positions.

#66 The conscious application of dialectics allows us to make correct use of concepts, to take into consideration the interconnection of phenomena, their contradictoriness, change-ability, and the passing of one contradiction into another. Only the dialectical-materialist approach to the analysis of the phenomena of nature, social life and consciousness reveals the actual which govern them and the motive forces of their development, making it possible to foresee the future and to discover effective means of molding it according to human design. The scientific dialectical method of cognition is a revolutionary method, because acknowledgement of the fact that everything changes and develops implies the necessity for abolishing all that is obsolete and that impedes social progress.

#67 The method of cognition diametrically opposed to the dialectical method is known as the Metaphysical method. The advocates of this method consider objects and phenomena in isolation from one another, as things that are essentially immutable and devoid of internal contradictions. The metaphysics sees the relative stability and definiteness of an object or phenomena, but underestimates their capacity for change and development. The metaphysical mode of thinking denies the objective existence of contradictions, that is to say, it asserts that they are to be found only in thought, and then only when thought is concerned with error. (But having said that, the philosopher must recognize that there are also two aspects to metaphysics the sigma metaphysical and the omega metaphysical for which see definitions.)

#68 In early materialism at the first stages of its existence (i.e. Ancient Greece) was originally connected with naive dialectics, but subsequently, under the influence of many factors, particularly the limitations of the natural sciences of its day, it acquired a metaphysical character. On the other hand, dialectics was developed not only by the materialists but also by certain outstanding exponents of idealism (i.e. Hegel)

#69 The history of dialectics may be divided into the following basic stages:

1) The spontaneous naive dialectics of the ancients
Democritus (c. 460 BC c. 370)

2) The dialectics of the Renaissance

Bruno, Giordano, original name FILIPPO BRUNO, byname IL NOLANO (1548 1600)

3) The idealist dialectics of the German classic philosophers
Kant
Johann Gottlieb Fichte, (1762 1814)
Friedrich Wilhelm Joseph von Schelling, (1775 1854)
Hegel.

4) The dialectics of Vissarion Grigoryevich Belinsky (1811 1848),
Aleksandr (Ivanovich) Herzen, HERTZEN(1812 1870)
N(ikolay) G(avrilovich) Chernyshevsky, (1828 1889)

5) The Neo-materialist
Karl Marx
Frederick Engels
V.I.Lenin
Ernst Haeckle
G.M. Gak and others
2020 Materialism

*****

THE SUBJECT MATTER OF 2020 MATERIALIST PHILOSOPHY >#70

#71 Unlike Third-estate philosophy, dialectical 2020 Materialism is base on the firm foundation of modern science and progressive social practice. Third-estate philosophers usually oppose philosophy to science, assuming that philosophy cannot and by its very nature should not be science. "Philosophy as I shall understand the word," writes Bertrand Russell, "is something intermediate between theology and science. Like theology, it consists of speculation on matters as to which definite knowledge has, so far, been unascertainable; but like science, it appeals to human reason rather than to authority, whether that of tradition or that of revelation. All definite knowledge – so I should contend – belongs to science; all dogma as to what surpasses definite knowledge belongs to theology, but between theology and science there is a No Man's land, exposed to attack from both sides; this no man's land is philosophy."

#72 The forgoing description fully applies to modern idealist philosophy, which is closely inter-linked with religion. But besides such philosophy there is also the consistently scientific philosophy of iterative dialectical and historical materialism.

#73 Every specialized science investigates qualitatively definite laws -- mechanical, physical, chemical, biological, astronomical, economic, and so on. There is no science, however, that studies laws that apply equally to the phenomena of nature, the development of society, and human thought. It is these universal laws that form the subject matter of 2020 Materialistic philosophy – the most general laws of the motion and development of nature, of human society and thought.

#74 The study of the laws and categories of the universal dialectical process forms the heart of a new world outlook and furnishes a general method of scientific cognition of the universe, and takes a specific form in every specialized science.

#75 Every science makes use of certain general concepts (categories) for example of 'causality', 'necessity', 'law' 'form', 'content' etc. Specialized sciences naturally do not study these categories, but use them as ready-made forms of thinking. Thus chemistry investigates the laws of the chemical process, and biology, the laws of life. Only 2020 Materialist and historical philosophy investigates law as the essential connection between categories, phenomena and universality in all its infinitely varied forms.

#76 In the specialized sciences we also have to do with concepts whose content is restricted to the given sphere of research. The basic concepts of political economy, for instance, are commodity, money (Labor token) and capital. Philosophical categories, unlike those of the specialized sciences, are the most general concepts which are used directly or indirectly in any science. No scientist, whether he is a naturalist, historian, economist, or literary scholar, can do without such most general concepts as law, regularity, contradiction, essence and phenomenon, cause and effect, necessity and chance, content and form, possibility and reality.

The philosophical categories express the most general connections between the phenomena and at the same time are stages in cognizing the world around us, generalize the historical experience of man's investigation of the world; they are the very instruments of thought.

#77 Of course the study of philosophical categories is no substitute for studying specific processes. 2020 Materialism is a guide to cognition in the most diverse fields of reality, but it does not replace and cannot replace these specialized sciences and the specific research methods they employ -- The sequence is usually (Thesis - Purpose - Apparatus - Method - Observation - Conclusion). (Antithesis - Purpose - Apparatus - Method - Observation - Conclusion) (Synthesis and a new upward spiral, (or coil) of investigation and so on)

#78 2020 Materialism does not offer ready made solutions to the questions that are studied by the specialized sciences;

rather it arms them with a scientific philosophical world outlook, a general scientific methodology.

#79 A Characteristic feature of old philosophy and even more so of contemporary Third-estate philosophy is that it divorces the science of thinking (logic) from the theory of knowledge (epistemology) and separates both of these from the theory of existence (ontology). 2020 Materialism rejects this metaphysical opposition and provides grounds for the principle of the unity of dialectics, logic and theory of knowledge. This means that materialist dialectics, that is to say, the theory of development in its fullest and most balanced form, also comprises a theory of cognition and the logical forms by means of which this historical process takes place. The laws of cognition, of thinking are the reflection of the general laws of being in the human consciousness.

#80 There are, of course, quite definite distinctions between dialectics, logic and the theory of knowledge within their general unity. These distinctions between the individual components of dialectical 2020 Materialism are relative.

#81 Historical 2020 Materialism is an inseparable part of 2020 Materialistic philosophy. Without it the dialectical materialist world outlook could not possibly exist.

#82 The structure of 2020 Materialist philosophy is complex, all the more so because life constantly reveals new targets of research, hitherto unknown problems, and thus introduces changes in the subject matter of philosophy, placing in the foreground now one aspect, then another and so on. 2020 Materialistic philosophy today is a system of philosophical disciplines, an integral world and cosmic outlook which is at the same time a theory of knowledge, logic and a general sociological theory.

#83 The experience of history shows the effectiveness of philosophy, that is to say, its significance in theory and practice, depends largely on the extent to which it embraces the whole ensemble of human knowledge. Science and philosophy have always benefited by learning from each other. Many ideas that formed the foundations of contemporary science were first advanced by philosophy.

#84 One has only to mention the brilliant insights of Leucippus (5th century BC) and Democritus concerning the atomic structure of matter. One could also cite the idealist philosopher Rene Descartes' (1596 1650) concept of the reflex and the principle which he formulated of the conservation of motion (the constant of the multiplication of mass by velocity). The idea of the existence of molecules as complex particles consisting of atoms was developed on the general philosophical plane in the works of the French philosopher Pierre Gassendi (also spelled Gassend (1592 1655), and also by the Russian Mikhail Vasilyevich Lomonosov, (1711 1765). It was the philosophers who formulated the idea of the development and general interconnection of phenomena, the principle of the material unity of the world. And to this day materialism has changed its form with every new great discovery in natural science.

#85 Comparatively recently the adherents of one of the most widespread trends in modern Third-estate philosophy, neo-positivism were maintaining that science had no need of philosophy whatever, that modern natural science itself could answer philosophical questions without resort to philosophy. As for any purely philosophical problems not studied by natural science, the neo-positivists maintained that they were pseudo-problems, that is to say, they had no scientific meaning. This approach to the question of the relationship between philosophy and natural science has today been condemned even by the neo-positivists, because it turned out to be of no use in principle to natural science, which itself asks philosophy to answer questions.

#86 Natural science today is strongly influenced by integrating tendencies, it is seeking new general theories, such as general theory of elementary particles, a general picture of the development of vegetable and animal world, a general theory of systems, a general theory of control, DNA, ecology, society, economics, law and so on. Generalizations at such high levels can be made only with a flourishing philosophical culture.

#87 A constant and increasing intrinsic need is felt in various scientific fields to examine the logical apparatus of knowledge. The need to understand the character of a theory and the means by which it is built up. The need to analyze the relationship between empirical and theoretical knowledge. The need to provide initial concepts of science and the methods of learning truth. All this, too is the task of philosophical inquiry.

#88 The scientist with no philosophical training quite often makes glaring philosophical and methodological mistakes, particularly when assessing new phenomena. Philosophy takes revenge on those natural scientists who neglect it. Scientists who became addicted to spiritualism led them into mysticism for example.

#89 The most eminent natural scientist of modern times constantly stress the tremendous orientational significance of a philosophical world outlook in scientific enquiry. Max Planck (1858 1947) said that the scientist's world outlook would always determine the direction of his research. Louis de Broglie (1892 1987) pointed out that the split between science and philosophy that occurred in the 19th century harmed both philosophy and natural science. Max Born

(1882 1970) always stressed that physics was only viable when it was aware of the philosophical significance of its methods and results. According to Albert Einstein (1879 1955), the contemporary physicist is obliged to devote far more attention to philosophical problems than were those of previous generations owing to the difficulties presented by his own science.

#90 The whole dramatically conflicting picture of modern social life places tremendous demands on philosophy. The philosophies underlying the humanities as well as science and technology are coming to the fore again and again.

#91 In this situation of intense ideological conflict those who work in specialized fields of knowledge and are not armed with a scientific world outlook and method will find themselves powerless to resist the impact of Third-estate ideology and fall prey to idealist philosophy and theology.

#92 All spheres of present-day life: the productive forces, science, technology, economic, relationships between estates, national, international, intellectual, culture and everyday life, are in the throes of a revolutionary change. Man himself is changing.

#93 What has caused this revolution which is transforming the whole world and all aspects of human life?

#94 In what way are the various aspects of this worldwide revolutionary process connected and interdependent?

#95 What are its directions and motive forces?

#96 What may be the social consequences of the scientific and technological revolution (STR) that we are witnessing today?

#97 Is national and social oppression eternal?

#98 Where is mankind heading?

#99 Why do the tremendous forces created and set in motion by human beings often turn against them?

#100 Where should we seek the sources of local and world wars and the threat of thermonuclear disaster?

#101 How can wars be abolished?

#102 How can the labor token (money) be protected?

#103 How can the environment be protected?

#104 What are the objective scientific rules of law as opposed to subjective theological canon and triptarchy law?

#105 Not a single specialized science, no matter how great its significance, can answer these and other vitally important questions of how we look on the world and our fellow man, and the answers to them are to be found not in theology or in idealist philosophy. They can only be found in 2020 materialist philosophy.

#106 2020 Materialism regards social progress, the changes occurring in modern society from the standpoint of how they relate to the emancipation of mankind from all oppression.

#107 Philosophical world outlooks must be placed and must adhere to one or other of the principal philosophical parties – either the materialist and objective, or the Idealist and subjective. This is a real fact in the history of philosophy. Materialism and Idealism are the two warring parties in philosophy. Descartes said "I think therefore I am." But if we take, for example the, Acropolis and its Parthenon, built by human labor, then in rebuttal to Descartes we may say for them "We, (the Acropolis and the works that stand upon it) do not think but still here we are!"

#108 The Fifth-estate's struggle with all other estates is not confined to the economic or political sphere, it acquires a special intensity at turning points in history. The present epoch is marked by the most profound social transformation ever known in the history of mankind.

#109 Third-estate apologists and ideologists usually acclaim political neutrality in matters of theory they say they stand above the practical political interests of all estates social groups and parties, and thus represent knowledge for the sake of knowledge, they maintain that partisanship is incompatible with the scientific approach. They champion the every man for himself syndrome and destructive competition. They sneer at cooperation as is embodied in the social nature of man.

*****

CHAPTER 2 >#110

DIALECTICAL LAWS OF DEVELOPMENT AND PHILOSOPHICAL CATEGORIES >#111

The Struggle of Opposites >#112

First Law Of Development >#113

#114 There is an interconnection and interaction between the quantitative and qualitative aspect of an object thanks to which small, at first imperceptible, quantitative changes, accumulating gradually, sooner or later upset the proportion of that object. And then evoke fundamental qualitative changes which take place in the form of leaps and whose occurrence depends on the nature of the objects in question and the conditions of their development in diverse forms. (i.e. Historical leaps may take decades, years, months, or days, atomic explosive leaps may take nanoseconds)

Second Law Of Development >#115

#116 All things, phenomena and processes possess internal contradictions, opposing aspects and tendencies that are in a state of interconnection and mutual negation. The struggle of opposites gives an internal impulse to development, leads to building up of contradictions, which are resolved at a certain stage in the disappearance of the old and the appearance of the new. (Of the billions of opposites one might mention a few in passing; plus minus, up down, in out, male female, matter energy, war peace and so on.

Tsunami One.   Philosophy Organon

Third Law Of Development >#117

#118 The law of negation of negation is a law whose operation conditions the connection and continuity between that which is negated and that which negates. For this reason dialectical negation is not naked 'needless' negation, rejecting all previous development, but the condition of development that retains and preserves in itself all progressive content of previous stages, repeats at a higher level certain features of the initial stages and has in general a progressive, ascending character. (i.e. cultural revolutions which under the pretext of struggle against the old destroy the precious, hard won gains of the past have nothing in common with fifth-estate objectives.

*****

CATEGORIES IN PHILOSOPHY >#119

#120 With the help of categories philosophy studies and registers the most general properties, connections and relationships between things, the laws of development that operate in nature, society and in human thought. Categories, in the sense of universal forms of scientific thought, arose, developed, and are still developing, on the basis of social practice. They reflect the reality, the properties and the relationships of the objective world that exists outside us.

#121 The categories of neo-materialist and historical dialectics are a summing up of the knowledge, a generalization of the experience of cognition and practice, of the whole previous history of mankind. They are the nodal points of cognition, the stages by which thought penetrates to the essence of things.

#122 One cannot obtain a correct understanding of a particular category merely by analyzing it as such, that is, in isolation from other categories. In objective reality everything is interconnected, is in a state of general interaction. Categories are so interconnected that they can be understood only as elements in a definite system of categories.

*****

Category 01: Matter And The Basic Forms Of Its existence.
>#123

#124 One result of the historical development of science, and social historical practice has been to prove the materiality of the universe, its un-createability and indestructibility. Its eternal existence in time and infinity in space, its inexhaustible self development, which necessarily leads, at certain stages, to the emergence of life and of sentient beings. Through them matter becomes capable of knowing the laws of its own existence and development. What then are the basic properties of matter, the forms of its existence? What general laws of development may it be said to possess?

#125 The philosophic understanding of matter: In the world around us we observe countless numbers of diverse objects and phenomena. Have they anything in common? What is their nature? On what are they based? The various attempts to answer these questions led historically to the concept of the substance of all things. Substance was understood as the universal primary foundation of all things, their final essence. While objects and phenomena might appear and disappear, substance could neither be created nor destroyed, it merely changed the form of its existence, moving from one state to another. It was the cause of itself and the basis of all change, the most fundamental and stable layer of reality.

#126 The very shaping of philosophy as a form of social consciousness is related to the appearance of the idea of substance and the unity of the world around us, the law governed interconnection of the phenomena of reality.

#127 In their materialist theories the philosophers of the Milesian school in ancient Greece elevated concrete forms of reality to the rank of substance. For Thales (c 6th cent. BC) substance was water, for Anaximenes (c 545 BC) it was air, for others it was earth, and these substances were thought to be capable of turning into one another. In the philosophy of Heraclitus (c 540 470 BC) substance was fire, which formed the sun, stars and all other bodies, and determined the eternal changing of the world. For Anaximander (c 611 547 BC) substance was an infinite and indefinite material which he called 'aperion', eternal in time, inexhaustible in structure and constantly changing the forms of its existence.

#128 None of these notions, however, gave expression to the idea of non-contradictory form. Not one of the four first principles possessed the required universality and stability, and the idea of 'apeiron' was too vague and allowed too many interpretations. The atomic theory of substance proposed by Leucippus (5th Century BCE) and Democritus (5th Century BCE) and subsequently developed by Epicurus (3rd Century BCE) and Lucretius (1st century BCE) was free of these defects. This theory allowed the existence of primary elementary particles called atoms, which could neither be created nor destroyed, were in constant motion, and differed from one another in weight, form and disposition in bodies. It was thought that the differences in the number of atoms composing them, by differences in their shape, mutual disposition and velocity. The number of atoms in the universe was infinite, their vortices formed stars like the sun, and also planets, and certain favorable combinations of atoms resulted in the emergence of living beings and man himself.

#129 Atomic theory was the first to propose in a concrete and definite form the 'principle of the conservation of matter' as the principle of the indestructibility of atoms. It was this concrete-ness and definiteness in expressing the idea of conservation of material substance that was to give atoms a place in all subsequent materialist theories. From the idea of the conservation and absoluteness of matter there necessarily followed the thesis that the universe was eternal and infinite, **that matter is primary in relation to mind, to human consciousness, and that all phenomena were in some way dependent on laws.** Belief in the materiality of the universe and the obedience of all phenomena to certain laws of nature gave the supporters of atomic materialism confidence in the boundless potentialities of man's reason, in his ability to find consistent explanations for all phenomena.

#130 In the philosophy and natural science of modern times atomic theory was further elaborated in the works of Newton, Gassendi, Boyle, Lomonosov, Hobbes, Holbach, Diderot and other thinkers. It provided the basis for explanations of the nature of heat, diffusion, conductivity, and many chemical phenomena. It contributed to the 'corpuscular theory of light.' But while science was still undeveloped, there were many phenomena that atomic theory was unable to explain; nor could it be deduced from the assumed properties and laws of motion of atoms the specific features of living organisms and a multitude of other phenomena of nature and society. It must be admitted that even in contemporary science the majority of known phenomena still have no causal and structural explanations. In contrast to atomic theory there appeared various idealist theories that elevated divine will, universal reason, absolute spirit and so on to the rank of the universal substance. These theories separated the mental attributes of the human brain from the brain itself and set them up as the Absolute, as Universal Reason, creating matter, space and time. But this idealist and closely related religious understanding of substance made no progress in solving the question of the essence of the universe because they merely substituted one unknown for another, even more mysterious unknown.

#131 Neither idealism nor religion ever provided a natural, rational explanation of the universe and for many factions of uncritical and unthinking people they merely created the illusion of such an explanation. On the other hand, the materialist philosophers always set out to explain phenomena by natural causes and see them as a result of operation of objective laws of the motion of matter. 2020 Materialism means understanding nature and the world as they are, without supernatural additions, that is to say, with the greatest degree of objectivity and authenticity possible for their historical time.

#132 Science has proved the soundness of this approach and as science advanced, the limitations of the metaphysical method of thought that dominated the minds of many scientists became increasingly apparent. The mechanistic picture of the universe that had prevailed in the natural science of the 17th to 19th centuries had absolutized the known mechanical laws of motion, the physical properties and states of matter. They were applied both to the microcosm and to all the conceivable space-time scales of the universe. The unity of the world was understood as homogeneity and uniformity of structure, as an endless repetition of the same stars and planets and other forms of matter, obeying eternal and immutable laws of motion. It seemed that absolute truth was not far away, that the fundamental laws of the universe had been revealed and only technical difficulties prevented scientists from deducing all properties of matter.

#133 But nature turned out to be far more complex than many physicists and philosophers had thought. In the second half of the 19th century Faraday and Maxwell established the laws of change of qualitatively new form of matter – the electromagnetic field, and these laws proved incompatible with those of classical mechanics.

#134 The turn of the century saw a new series of discoveries: radioactivity, complex chemical atoms, electrons, the dependence of mass on velocity, and quantum mechanics. It was established that some laws of mechanics did not apply to the structure of the atoms or the motion of electrons, and the space-time properties of bodies were shown to be dependent on their velocity. The mechanical picture of the universe and the metaphysical understanding of matter were thrown into a state of crisis. The radioactive disintegration of atoms was interpreted by them as the 'disappearance' of matter, the conversion of matter into energy.

#135 But matter is a philosophical category denoting the objective reality which is given to man by his sensations, and which is copied, photographed and reflected by our sensations, while existing independently of them.

#136 This definition of matter is organically connected with the materialist answer to the basic problem of philosophy. It indicates the objective source of our knowledge as matter, and not that matter is unknowable. At the same time, unlike previous philosophical systems, dialectical 2020 materialism does not reduce matter merely to certain 'forms', to particular substances, sensuously perceptible bodies, and so on. Matter embraces the whole infinite diversity of the objects and systems of nature, which exist and move in space and time and possess an inexhaustible variety of properties. Our sense organs can perceive only an insignificant part of these actually existing forms of matter, but thanks to the construction of increasingly powerful instruments and measuring apparatus people are constantly extending the frontiers of the known world.

#137 For any material formation to exist it must be objectively connected and interacting with them, be an element in the general process of change and development of matter.

#138 The concept of matter as objective reality characterizes matter together with its properties, forms of motion, laws of existence, and so on. But this does not mean that every arbitrarily selected fragment of objective reality must be matter. It may also be a concrete 'property' of matter, a certain law or form of its motion, inseparable from matter and yet not identical to it. In the structure of objective reality we must distinguish concrete material objects and systems (forms of matter), the properties of these material systems (general and particular), the forms of their interaction and motion, and laws of existence possessing varying degrees of universality. Thus, motion, space, time, the laws of nature possess objective reality, and yet they cannot be regarded as matter. Matter exists in the form of an infinite variety and diversity of concrete objects and systems, each of which 'possesses' motion, structure, connections, interactions, space-time and many other general and particular properties. Matter does not exist outside concrete objects and systems, and in this sense there is no 'matter as such' understood as a primary and structure-less substance. In dialectical 2020 Materialism the concept of substance has undergone radical changes in comparison with the way it was understood in previous philosophy. Dialectical 2020 Materialism recognizes the substantiality of matter, but only in the sense that matter (not consciousness, not absolute spirit, not divine reason etc.) is the one universal basis, the substratum for the various properties, connections, forms of motion and laws. But there is also no grounds for allowing the existence of any primary structure-less substance within matter itself, as the deepest and most fundamental layer of reality. Every form of matter (including micro objects) possesses a complex structure, a variety of internal and external connections, and the ability to change into other forms. (a good example in the natural world is Metamorphosis and so on)

#139 The 'essence' of things, or 'substance' is also relative. It expresses only the degree of profundity of man's knowledge of objects. And while yesterday the profundity of man's knowledge did not go beyond the atom, and today goes beyond the atom and DNA, Dialectical 2020 Materialism insists on the temporary, relative, approximate character of all these milestones in the knowledge of nature gained by the progressing science of man. The mico-particles are as inexhaustible as the atom, just as the cosmos is as inexhaustible as the galaxy. A scientific theory can be only an open-ended system of knowledge with unlimited prospects of development.

#140 Objects or things are sometimes regarded as the sum of their various properties. Matter may also be regarded in the same way, but it must not be reduced merely to its properties. The latter never exist by themselves, without a material substratum; they are always inherent in certain definite objects.

#141 Matter always has certain organization; it exists in the form of specific material systems. A system is an internally (or externally) ordered plurality of interconnected (or interacting) elements. The connection between the elements of a system is always more powerful, stable and intrinsically necessary than the connection between any of its elements and the environment, and the elements of other systems. The internal ordered-ness of a system is expressed in the set of laws governing the connections and the interactions between the elements. Each law expresses a certain order or type of connection. The structure of a system is the sum of the internal connections between its elements and also the laws of these connections. Structure is an indispensable element of all existing systems.

#142 The concept of system and element are correlative. Any system may be an element of an even larger system. Similarly an element may be a system if we are concerned with its structure, with deeper structural levels of matter. But this correlativity of concepts does not mean that systems have been invented by man merely as a convenient means of classifying phenomena. Systems exist objectively, as ordered integral formations.

#143 The range of present day knowledge of matter extends from ten to the minus fifteen cm (the core of the nucleon) to ten to the thirty cm (20 million light years. All matter within these limits i.e. all known matter, possesses a structural organization. Tentatively one may identify the following basic types of material systems and the corresponding structural levels of matter.

#144 In inanimate nature we recognize elementary particles (including anti particles) and fields, atomic nuclei, atoms, molecules, aggregates of molecules, macroscopic bodies, geological formations, the earth and other planets, the sun and other stars, local groups of stars, the Galaxies, and the metagalaxies which are in infinite numbers of systems in an infinite universe.

#145 In animate nature, biosystems, interorganic and super organic. The former includes the DNA and RNA molecules, as vehicles of heredity, complexes of protein molecules, cells (consisting of subsystems (neural, blood circulation, digestive, gas exchange, etc.) and the organism as a whole. Superorganic systems including families of organisms, colonies, various populations – species, biological communities, geographical landscapes, and the whole biosphere.

#146 In society, the types of intersecting systems are also numerous; the family, various groups (production staffs, teaching bodies, research teams, sports teams etc.) communities, associations and organizations, parties, classes, estates, states, systems of states and the whole of international united and un-united nations.

#147 This is very general and far from complete classification because at every structural level large numbers of additional interpenetrating systems based on various forms of connection and interconnection of their elements may be identified.

#148 The factors determining the integrity of systems are constantly becoming more complex as matter ascends in its spiral development. In inanimate nature the integrity of systems is determined by the nuclear (in atomic nuclei), electromagnetic and gravitational forces of their connections. A system may be accounted integral if the energy of the interaction between its elements 'exceeds' the total kinetic energy of these elements plus the energy of external influences tending to destroy the system. Otherwise the system either does not come about or disintegrates.

#149 In animate nature, integrity is determined not only by these factors, but also by information processes of connection and control, self regulation and reproduction at various structural levels.

#150 The most accurate and detailed classification of the basic forms of matter is that based on types of material systems and corresponding levels of matter. There is also widespread classification of forms of matter according to fundamental physical properties. This classification begins with 'substance', comprising all particles, macroscopic bodies and other systems possessing finite rest mass. Then comes objectively existing 'anti-substance', comprising anti-particles (anti-protons, positrons, anti-neutrinos etc) (i.e. in the struggle of opposites) these are sometime incorrectly called anti-matter. Atoms and molecules made up of anti-particles may in the absence of ordinary forms of substance be stable and form microscopic bodies and even cosmic systems (anti-worlds). In these bodies the laws of motion and development of matter would be the same as those that pertain in the world around us.

#151 In addition there are what may be termed 'insubstantial' forms of matter – electromagnetic and gravitational fields, and also neutrinos and anti-neutrinos of various types, none of which possess finite rest mass.

#152 Field and substance should not be opposed to each other because fields exist in the structure of all substantial systems and help to hold them together.

#153 The dialectical 2020 Materialist theory of matter and the forms of its existence provides a methodological foundation for scientific research, for the elaboration of an integral scientific world view and the interpretation of scientific discoveries consistent with reality. It is constantly extending its vision and insight with the advance of scientific knowledge, which seeks an ever fuller and deeper reflection of the laws of the existence of matter.

*****

Category 02: Motion, The Basic Forms Of Its Existence. >#154

#155 As we get to know the world around us, we see that there is nothing in it that is absolutely stationary and immutable; everything is in motion and passing from one form into another. Elementary particles, atoms and molecules move within all material objects, every object interacts with its environment, and this interaction is bound to involve motion of some kind or another.

#156 Any body, even a body that seems stationary in relation to the earth moves together with it around the sun, and together with the sun in relation to other stars of the Galaxy, which in turn moves in relation to other stellar systems, and so on.. Nowhere is there absolute equilibrium, rest and immobility; all rest and equilibrium are relative, are actually a state of motion. The stability of a body's structure and external form depends on the interaction taking place in space and time is motion; conversely, all motion includes the interaction of the various elements of matter.

#157 Taken in its most general form, motion means the same thing as change, as any transition from one state to another. **Motion is the universal attribute, the mode of existence of matter. Nowhere in the world can there be matter without motion, just as there can be no motion without matter.**

#158 This important position may be proved by the rule of contraries. Let us suppose the existence of a certain form of matter possessing no motion whatever, internal or external. Since interaction involves motion, this hypothetical matter could have no external or internal connections or interactions. But in that case it would be structure-less and devoid of any elements because without interacting the latter could not unite with each other and produce this form of matter. Nothing could arise out of this hypothetical matter because it would have no connection or interactions. It would be totally unable to reveal its existence in relation to any other bodies because it would have no power to influence them. It would possess no properties because every property is the result of internal and external connections and interactions. And finally, it would in principle be unknowable to us since all cognition of external objects can take place only through their influence on our sense organs and the scientific instruments used to enhance them. We should have no reason to suppose the existence of such matter because if we add up all these 'non-features' we get pure nothing, a fiction that has absolutely no correspondence with reality. Consequently, if any possible objects of the external world possess certain properties or structure, reveal their existence in relation to other bodies and may in principle be cognized, all this is the result of their intrinsic motion and interaction with the environment.

#159 Since it is inseparably bound up with motion and possesses intrinsic activity, matter does not need any external, divine 'first push of a so called unmoved mover' to set it in motion (the metaphysical concept of an unmoved mover was at one time maintained by certain metaphysical and religious philosophers, who regarded matter as an inert mass). These philosophers identified mass with matter, then mass with energy, and eventually drew the conclusion that matter and energy were the same thing.

#160 The spirit of energism persists in the reasoning of some contemporary scientists, who on the basis of E=MC squared (where E == energy, M = mass, C = the velocity of light infer the equivalence of matter and energy. The conversion of particles and anti-particles (when interacting) into photons is regarded as the destruction of matter and its conversion into 'pure energy'. In reality, however, photons, or quanta of an electromagnetic impulse, but are a particular form of matter in motion. Matter is not destroyed but passes from one form to another in a process strictly conforming to laws of the conservation of mass, energy, electrical charge, impulse, moment of impulse and some other properties of micro-particles.

#161 Energy in general cannot exist separately from matter and is always one of the most important properties of matter. Energy is a quantitative measure of motion expressing the internal activity of matter, the ability of material systems to perform certain work or bring about changes in the external environment on the basis of internal structural changes. In this case from a bound state (corresponding to the rest mass) energy passes into active forms, for example the energy of irradiation.

#162 Nature confronts us with innumerable qualitatively differing systems, each of which possesses its own, specific kind of motion. Only a small number of these motions, which may be subdivided into a series of 'basic' forms of motion, are known to present day science. These are the modes of existence and functioning of material systems at the corresponding structural levels. The basic forms of motion include sets of processes that obey general laws.

#163 The basic forms are Mechanical (change of place or space). Physical (electromagnetism, gravitation, heat, sound etc,) Chemical (conversion of the atoms and molecules) Biological (metabolism in living organisms) and Social (Social change and also thought processes). These classifications of motion proceed from the principle that higher forms of motion cannot be qualitatively reduced to lower forms.

#164 In the last hundred years science has discovered a great number of new phenomena in the microcosm and the macrocosm; the motion and mutations of elementary particles, processes in atomic nuclei, in stars, in supersolid states of matter, expansion of the Metagalaxy, and so on.

#165 We must also mention the forms of motion of macroscopic bodies: heat, processes of crystallization, changes in aggregate states, structural changes in solids, fluids and gases and plasma. The geological form of motion comprises complex of physico-chemical processes connected with the formation of various minerals, ores, and other substances in conditions of high temperature and pressure. In the stars there appear such forms of motion as self supporting thermo-nuclear reactions and formation of chemical elements (particularly during explosions of new and supernova stars). With cosmic bodies of great mass and density such processes as gravitational collapse and conversion to supersolid states may take place. This happens when a body's gravitational field becomes so powerful as to prevent all particles of matter and electro-magnetic radiation from escaping (the so called 'black holes'). On the scale of the microcosm we are witnessing a grandiose expansion of the Metagalaxy, which appears to be a stage in the form of motion of this gigantic material system. Each structural level of matter has its own forms of motion and functioning of the corresponding material system.

#166 The forms of motion in animate nature comprise processes occurring both within living organisms and in super-organic systems. Life is the mode of existence of protein bodies and nucleic acids which consists of metabolism, in the constant exchange of substances and energy with the environment, the living organism recreates its structure and functions, and keeps them relatively stable. This metabolism leads to the constant self-renewal of the cellular composition of tissues.

#167 Life is a system of forms of motion and comprises processes of interaction, change and development in super-organic biological systems – colonies of organisms, species, bioceonoses, biogeoceonoses, and the whole biosphere.

#168 The highest stage of development of matter on earth is human society with its inherent social forms of motion. These forms constantly become more complex as society advances. They comprise various manifestations of peoples purposeful activity, all social changes and forms of interaction between various social systems – from man to the state and society as a whole. A manifestation of the social forms of motion may be seen also in the processes of reflection of reality in thought, which are based on syntheses of all the physico-chemical and biological forms of motion in the human brain.

#169 All forms of motion of matter are closely interconnected. This interconnection reveals itself primarily in the historical development of matter and in the emergence of higher forms of motion on the basis of the relatively lower forms on the spiral. Thus the human organism functions on the basis of interaction of the closely related physico-chemical and biological forms of motion (is forced onward and upward, not only by the immediate history behind it but by the 'recent' history on the spirals (coils) below it.) while at the same time human beings are individuals, and collectively they form the social forms of motion.

#170 In studying the interrelations of the forms of motion it is important to avoid separating the higher from the lower forms or mechanically reducing the one to the other. If one separates them there is no possibility of explaining the origin and structural peculiarities of the higher forms. On the other hand, ignoring the specific qualities of the higher forms of motion and crudely reducing them to lower forms leads to mechanicism and oversimplification.

#171 Knowing the relationship between the forms of motion provides an important clue to the material unity of the world, the specific features of the historical development of matter. Studying matter is largely a question of studying the forms of its motion and if we could know all about motion we should also know about matter in all its manifestations. But this process is infinite.

#172 Discovery of the laws governing the interrelationship of the forms of motion guides us towards knowledge of the essence of life and other higher forms of motion, towards modeling the functions of complex systems, including the human brain, and technological systems of increasing complexity. Scientific and technical advance opens up boundless prospects in this direction.
*****

Category 03: Space and Time. >#173

#174 All the objects in the world around us possess certain dimensions, extension in various directions, move in relation to one another or, together with the earth, in relation to other space bodies. Similarly all objects arise and change in time. Space and Time are universal forms of the existence of all material systems and processes. No object exists outside space and time, just as space and time cannot exist by themselves, outside matter in motion.

#175 We often look upon space and time as universal conditions of the existence of bodies. This approach does not lead us into error as long as we are dealing only with concrete bodies and systems. Every body or system exists and moves in the spatial structure of an even larger system –

the Galaxy and so on. The emergence and the whole cycle of development of the smaller system manifests itself as a time stage in the development of any of the subsystems comprising it.

#176 But this notion of space and time as conditions of existence becomes untenable when we move on to a consideration of matter as a whole. If we accepted it, we should have to acknowledge that besides matter there also existed space and time in which matter was somehow 'immersed'. In the past this approach led to conceptions of absolute space and time as the external conditions of the existence of matter (Newton). Space was regarded as an infinite void containing all bodies and not depending on matter, and absolute time as a steady flow of duration in which everything appeared and disappeared, but did not itself depend on any process in the universe.

#177 Scientific advance has exploded these notions. No such absolute space consisting of an infinite void exists. Everywhere there is matter in certain 'forms' (substance, field and so on), and space is a universal property (attribute) of matter. Similarly there is no absolute time. Time is always indissolubly connected with motion and the development of matter. Space and time exist objectively and independently of consciousness, but not independently of matter.

#178 Space is the form of existence of matter that expresses its extent and structure, the coexistence and interaction of elements in various material systems.

#179 Time is the form of the existence of matter characterizing the duration of the existence of all objects and the sequence in which states of matter replace each other.

#180 All properties of space and time depend on motion and the structural relations in material systems must be inferred from them. Of the properties of space and time we may single out the 'universal' which manifests itself at all known structural levels of matter, and the 'particular' and the 'individual', which inhere universal properties are inseparably linked with the other attributes of matter and the dialectical laws of its existence. They are of paramount importance for philosophy.

#181 The main universal properties of space comprise extent, which signifies the location in relation to one another of various elements (sections, volumes), the possibility of adding to any given element some other element or of reducing the number of elements. Space without extent would exclude all possibility of quantitative change in its elements and also any structure of material formations. The fact that there are coexisting and interacting elements in material systems, is what gives the internal space of such systems extension. So extension is organically connected with the structure of systems.

#182 The universal properties of space also include its inseparable connection with time and the motion of matter, and the dependence of structural relations in material systems.

#183 Unity of continuity and discontinuity is inherent in space (or rather, the spatial properties of matter). Discontinuity is relative and reveals itself in the separate existence of material objects and systems, each of which has certain dimensions and limits. But material fields (electromagnetic, gravitational, etc.) extent continuously throughout all systems. The continuity of space also reveals itself in the spatial movements of bodies. A body moving towards a certain place passes through the whole infinite sequence of elements of length between them. Thus another feature of space is its cohesion; there are no gaps in it. Space is three dimensional, a fact that is organically connected with the structural nature of systems and their motion.

#184 The extension of space is closely related to metrical relations, which express the specific connections of spatial elements, the order and qualitative laws of these connections. The metrical relations of the plane, the sphere, the pseudosphere (a figure that looks like a gramophone horn) and other surfaces are expressed in various types of geometry . Euclidean and non-Euclidean (Lobachevsky, Riemann). Possession of certain metrical properties is one of the universal characteristics of space.

#185 Of the universal properties of time (or rather temporal relations in material systems) we should mention its continuous connection with the extent and motion of matter, its duration, asymmetry, irreversibility, non cyclical nature, unity of continuity and discontinuity, cohesion, and dependence on structural relations in material systems.

#186 Duration is the consistency of the existence of material objects, their conservation in a relatively stable form. Since the speed of change of any process is finite, duration is formed by the occurrence of one moment of time after another. It is similar to the extension of space and results from the conservation of matter and motion. This conservation also conditions the cohesion of time, its continuity, which is universal and absolute. Discontinuity is characteristic only of the existence of concrete qualitative states of matter, each of which appears and disappears, passing into other forms. But the elements of matter of which they consist (elementary particles for example) may not appear or disappear in this process but merely change their connections, forming different bodies. In this sense the discontinuity of the lifetime of matter is relative, while the continuity is absolute. This fact is expressed in the laws of the conservation of matter and its primary properties.

#187 The asymmetry or one-directionality of time indicates that it changes only from the past to the future, that such change is irreversible. In space one can move in any direction. In time movement toward the past is impossible; (excepting of course, that if by some 'miracle' one could travel outward from an event, at say twice the speed of light, one would be able at some point, to look back at the past flowing toward him at the speed of light.) all change occur in such a way that it brings about the next, future moment in time. States or cycles that have already occurred can never be absolutely and fully repeated. All cycles are relative and express only the fact that processes are more or less repeatable. But in every cycle there is always something new and time is always irreversible. This irreversibility of time is determined by the asymmetry of cause-effect relations, the general irreversibility of the process of the development of matter, in which new possibilities, qualitative states and trends are always appearing.

#188 The development of science in the 20th century has thrown new light on the connection of the properties of space and time with material processes. The theory of relativity has proved that as the velocity of bodies increase their dimensions relatively decrease in the direction of their motion and that all processes in them tend to slow down (in comparison with their speed in a state of relative rest). A slowing down of processes also occurs under the influence of very powerful gravitational fields created by large accumulations of substance. As a result, the spectral lines of radiation emitted by objects known as 'quasars' (quasi-stellar objects) are shifted to the red side of the spectrum.

#189 The influence of gravity gives rise to the 'space curve', due to the effect of the distortion of light rays in gravitational fields. It is possible for the mass and density of a system to become so great that light rays begin to move in a closed circuit in its immediate vicinity. Such an effect would occur, for example, if the whole mass of the sun were concentrated in a globe 2.5 km in diameter.

#190 In the 20th century similar phenomena have been observed in the Galaxy due to the effect of gravitational collapse (catastrophically rapid contraction of substance). At first it was assumed that such objects or phenomena (predicted in theory and known as 'black holes') were absolutely closed because they did not emit any radiation. But it later became clear that they created a static gravitational field and absorb interstellar dust and gas from surrounding space. When particles of matter fall on such super-dense objects they clash with each other causing powerful electromagnetic irradiation, which is measured by instruments on earth. This proves once again that there is no ground for assuming the existence of absolutely closed systems in space.

#191 The universal properties of space and time also include their infinity. Since matter is absolute, uncreatable and indestructible, it exists eternally. Any assumption that time is finite, that it must have a stop, end or wall leads to religious conclusions about the creation of the world and time by the unmoved mover God. This concept has been totally disproved by all the findings of science, practice and philosophical theology (or Xotheology the study of all religions, their subjective content, and their objective impact on mankind)

#192 The infinity of time should not be understood as unlimited monotonous existence in certain similar forms and states. Matter has always been and always will be in an unfailing state of development, which implies the endless appearance of qualitatively new forms, states, tendencies and laws of change. The infinity of time has not only a qualitative aspect, (unlimited duration) but also a qualitative aspect, connected with the historical development of matter and its structural inexhaustibility.

#193 In the social life of our time we observe an acceleration of development and, today an ever increasing number of scientific and technical discoveries, together with social change associated with the dominance, development, and withering away of estates and their associated economic basis is in progress.

#194 There is nothing in the world that is not a certain state of matter, one of its properties, a form of motion, a product of its historical development, that is not ultimately conditioned by material causes and interactions. Man himself is the most complex of all known material systems and the manifestations of his activity, including the higher forms of mental reflection and creation, have material origin and depend on social relations.

#195 Dialectical 2020 Materialism offers a scientific and integral explanation of nature and society and provides a methodological basis for the investigation in depth of all past and of all new and hitherto unknown phenomena. But the unity of the world cannot be reduced merely to the homogeneity of its physio-chemical composition or to the fact that all phenomena obey certain known physical laws. Owing to the operation of the universal law of the passing of quantitative into qualitative changes, each specific quality exists within certain limits, in finite time scales. It cannot be extrapolated to infinity. So every specific scientific theory has a limited sphere of application. The truth is always concrete and every scientific theory must of necessity be an open-ended system of knowledge (see dissertation on truth #581).

#196 Matter is infinitely diverse in its manifestation. As space time scales change (increase or decrease) at certain stages there inevitably occur certain qualitative changes in particular properties, in forms structural organization, in the laws of the motion of matter. Many laws of the microcosm differ in quality from the laws of macroscopic phenomena and on the gigantic scale of the universe there are states and processes of matter the theory of which has yet to be evolved.

#197 Nevertheless, despite all the qualitative diversity and structural inexhaustibility of matter, the universe is one. This unity manifests itself on in the infinite cosmic scale in the absoluteness, substantiality and eternal nature of matter and its attributes. In its the mutual connection and conditioning of all material systems and structural levels, in the natural determination of their properties, in the interchanging multiplicity of forms of matter in motion, in the correspondence between the universal laws of the conservation of matter and its basic properties.

#198 The unity of the world also reveals itself in historical development of matter, in the emergence of more complex forms of matter and motion on the basis of relatively less complicated forms. And finally, it finds expression in the operation of universal dialectical regularities of existence, which may be observed in the structural development of all material systems.

#199 The homogeneity of the physico-chemical composition of bodies, the universality of their quantitative laws of motion, the similarity in the structure and functions of systems, the resemblance of properties, which make it possible to model complex systems and processes on the basis of simpler phenomena for the purpose of discovering fresh information about the world are local manifestations of universal unity.

#200 The dialectical 2020 Materialist theory of matter and its forms of existence is the foundation of 2020 Materialist philosophy, the basis of its integrated monistic world outlook. It is of great importance as a method of modern science and helps us to integrate, sciences, geopolitical, economic and social conception of the world as moving and developing matter.

*****

Category 04: Consciousness. >#201

#202 Man possesses the wonderful gift of consciousness, of mind, with its ability to reach back into the distant past, or probe the future, its world of dream and fantasy, its ability to penetrate into the realm of the unknown, What is consciousness? What are its origins and peculiar features?

#203 Man began to ponder the riddle of his consciousness a very long time ago. For many centuries the best minds of mankind have tried to discover the nature of consciousness, have wrestled with the questions of how inanimate matter at some stage in its development engenders animate matter, and how animate matter engenders consciousness. What is the structure and function of consciousness? What is the mechanism of the transition from sensation and perception to thought, from the sensuously concrete to the abstractly theoretical? How does the consciousness link to the material physiological processes that occur in the cortex? These and many other closely related problems remained for a long time beyond the bounds of strictly objective scientific research.

#204 Various idealist and religious interpretations of the phenomena of consciousness is a manifestation of a certain non-material substance – the 'soul', which is allegedly immortal and eternal, independent of matter in general and of the human brain in particular, and lives a life of its own. Unable to explain the natural causes of dreams and fainting, of death and of various cognitive, emotional and volitional processes, the ancients arrived at false conclusions about these phenomena. Dreams, for instance, were interpreted as the impressions of the 'soul' leaving the body during sleep. The 'soul' also no longer resided in the body that it quitted in death and went to reside in 'heaven': Some believing that it returned to earth in someone else's after life. The soul's of animals, insects, microbes and other living matter were, for some reason, believed to be non-existent. These naïve fantastic beliefs were further developed and acquired a theoretical 'substantiation' and consolidation in various idealist philosophical and theological systems. Any idealist system was bound in one way or another to proclaim consciousness (reason, idea, spirit) an independent supernatural essence, not only independent of matter but even creating the whole material universe and controlling its motion and development.

#205 **In contrast to these various idealist beliefs 2020 Materialism proceeds from the fact that consciousness is a function of the human brain the essence of which lies in the reflection of material reality.** At the same time the problem of consciousness has turned out to be extremely difficult for materialist philosophers and psychologists as well.

#206 Some materialists, baffled by the problem of the origin of consciousness, came to regard it as an attribute of matter, as its eternal property, inherent in all its forms, higher and lower. They declared all matter animate. This belief has been called hylozoism (from the Greek hyle – matter, and zoe – life.)

#207 Dialectical 2020 Materialism proceed from the fact that consciousness is an attribute not of any matter but of highly organized matter. Consciousness is connected with the activity of the human brain, with the specifically human social way of life. Consciousness can never be anything but consciously apprehended existence, and people's existence is the real process of their life.

#208 Dialectical 2020 Materialism's concept of consciousness is based on the principle of 'reflection', that is, the mental reproduction of outside objects in the brain of the individual in the form of sensations, perceptions, representation, propositions, inferences and concepts. (And it is to be noted that any reflection is more or less distorted by the degree of 'polish' of the mirroring surface.) It is that the content of consciousness is ultimately determined by surrounding reality and its material substratum, and the senses immersed in this reality are the vehicles to the brain.

#209 In the course of evolution animals acquired the ability to mentally reflect external influences only when they developed a nervous system. The improvement of the mentality of animals under the influence of their changing way of life was closely connected with the development of their brain. Man's consciousness arose and is developing in close connection with the rise and development of the specifically human brain under the influence of rational work activity, social relations and intercourse. The brain is the organ of consciousness understood as the highest form of the mental reflection of reality. The human brain is an extremely sensitive nervous apparatus consisting of a vast number of nerve cells. The total has been estimated by some researchers at 15 trillion. Each of these cells is in contact with the others, and all of them together with the nerve endings of the sense organs form a highly intricate network with countless connections.

#210 The human brain has an extremely complex 'hierarchical' structure. The simplest forms of reflection, analysis and synthesis of external influences and regulation of behavior are performed by the lower sections of the central nervous system – the spinal cord the medulla oblongata, the middle brain and the diencephalon while the more complex forms are controlled by the higher sections, above all, by the cerebral hemisphere. Excitations evoked by the actions of external agents on the sense organs travel along the nerve fibers to various parts of the cortex of the cerebral hemispheres. The 'subcortical' apparatus of the brain is the organ of extremely complex forms of activity transmitted by heredity, i.e. inborn or instinctive activity. This part of the brain performs an independent function in the lower vertebrates and tends to lose its independence in the higher vertebrates, the mammals and particularly in man.

#211 The interaction between the organism and the environment, and also between various parts of the organism and between its own organs, is effected with the aid of reflexes. That is, reactions of the organism evoked by irritation of the sense organs and performed with the participation of the central nervous system. Reflexes are classified in two basic groups – unconditioned and conditioned. Unconditioned reflexes are inborn, inherited reactions of the organism to the influence of the external environment. Conditioned reflexes are reactions of the organism acquired in the process of life activity; their character depends on the individual experience of the animal or human being. The theory of the reflex activity in the brain was developed by many scientists in various countries particularly those in Russia i.e. Pavlov and others.

#212 The brain is an exceptionally complex functional system. To understand its functioning correctly we must combine the data obtained from study of separate nerve cells with research into the external behavior of the individual. No feeling, sensation or impulse can occur outside the physiological processes in the brain.

#213 The idea that the human brain is the organ of thought arose in earliest times and is today generally accepted in science. Even in modern times, however, some idealist 'philosophers' contest the proposition that consciousness is a function of the brain.

#214 Consciousness is a product of the brain's activity, and it arises only thanks to external influences reaching the brain through the sense organs. The sense organs are the 'apparatuses' that reflect, and inform the organism of, changes in the external environment, or within the organism itself. They may therefore be divided into external and internal organs. The external sense organs are the senses of sight, hearing, smell, taste, touch – skin sensitivity. The signals that reach the brain from these sense organs carry information about the quality of things, their connection and relationships. The sense organs and their corresponding nerve transformations taken together were called by Pavlov 'analyzers'. The analysis of the influence of the environment begins in the peripheral part of the analyzer – the receptor (nerve endings), where some particular type of energy is singled out from all the multiplicity of types of energy influencing the organism. The highest and most subtle analysis is achieved only with the help of the cortex. Excitation of the sense organs only produces sensations, becomes a fact of consciousness when it reaches the brain.

The cortical physiological processes are the necessary material mechanisms of reflective mental activity, of the phenomena of consciousness.

#215 The physiological mechanisms of mental phenomena are not identical to the content of the mind (mentality, psyche) which is the reflection of reality in the form of, ideal (idea) images.

#216 Dialectical 2020 Materialism is opposed to the primitive interpretation of the essence of consciousness by the advocates of 'vulgar materialism' (C Vogt, L Buchner, J Moleschott and others) which reduces the consciousness to its material substratum – the physiological neural process occurring in the brain. Every natural scientist is bound to reach the conclusion, wrote Carl Vogt, that "all the abilities that are called psychical (Seelenthatigkeiten) activity are in fact only motions of the cortical substance or, to express it somewhat more bluntly, thought is in almost the same relationship to the cortex as bile is to the liver…" This is the sense in which Vogt sees consciousness as something material.

#217 It is a great mistake to identify consciousness with matter. This is obviously false. That both thought and matter are real i.e. exist is true. But to say that thought is material is to make a false step, a step towards confusing materialism and idealism. No less fallacious is the dualistic concept of 'psycho-physical parallelism', according to which psychical and material (psychological) processes are absolutely, heterogeneous essences, between which there is a great gap. Some advocates of this concept have assumed that the correspondence which we observe between physiological and physical processes is ordained by some God.

#218 Consciousness is not a special essence divorced from matter. But the image of the object created in the human brain cannot be reduced to the material object itself, which exists outside the subject, the knower. Nor can it be identical with the physiological processes that occur in the brain and generate this image. Thought, consciousness are real things. But they are not objective realities they are something subjective, ideal.

#219 **Consciousness is the omega subjective image of the objective world**. When we speak of the omega subjectivity of an image, we have in mind the fact that it is not a distorted reflection of reality, but something ideal, that is – something material has been transformed and reprocessed in the brain of the individual – a thing in a person's consciousness is an image, and the real thing is its prototype, its model. The fundamental distinction between the material and the adherents of idealistic philosophy consists in the fact that the 2020 Materialist regards sensations, perceptions, idea and images in the mind of man generally, as images of objective reality outside that mind. The world is the movement of this objective reality reflected by our consciousness. To the movement of objects and matter outside me there is an omega subjective movement, of ideas, perceptions, ideas and images inside me.

#220 The emergence, functioning and development of consciousness is intimately linked with man's acquisition of knowledge of certain objects or phenomena. The way in which consciousness is and in which something is for it, is knowing. Something comes 'to be' for consciousness insofar as the consciousness 'knows' this something. Consciousness would be impossible if man did not have a cognitive relation to the objective world. At the same time when we speak of consciousness, we are mainly interested in its spiritual activity, as an ideal phenomenon that differs qualitatively from the material. Cognition is the activity of the consciousness directed towards reflection of the surrounding world.

#221 Not all of man's mental activity is conscious. The concept of psyche, the mental, is wider than the concept of consciousness. Animals have mentality but no consciousness. A child's mental life begins as soon as he is born, before it has yet acquired consciousness. When a person falls asleep and sees fanciful scenes, these are physical phenomena but they are not consciousness. And even when a person is awake not all of his mental processes are illuminated by the light of consciousness. Life demands of a person not only conscious forms of behavior, but unconscious ones that relieve him of the need to alert his consciousness when this is necessary. Unconscious forms of behavior are based on hidden recording of information concerning the properties and relationships of things. The range of the unconscious is fairly wide, embracing sensations, perceptions and representations (images) when they proceed outside the focus of consciousness, and also instincts, skills, intuition and orientation.

#222 The problem of the unconscious has always been the subject of acute controversy between materialism and idealism. One of the most widespread theories of the unconscious is that of the Austrian psychiatrist Sigmund Freud. Freud investigated many aspects of the unconscious, revealed its place and role in mental illness. But Freud incorrectly maintained the consciousness is determined by the unconscious, which he regarded as highly charged complex of instinctive urges. According to Freud, the structure of the personality, its behavior, character and also all human culture are determined ultimately by people's inborn emotions, by their instincts and drives, whose inner core is the sexual instinct.

#223 2020 Materialism rejects these irrationalist notions of man's mental life, which exaggerate the role of biological factors. 2020 Materialism asserts that the guiding principle in human behavior is reason, consciousness and unlike the animals, the normal human being is governed by conscious mental activity with consciousness being an integrated system of diverse but closely connected cognitive and evotional-volitional elements.

#224 The initial sensory image, the most elementary fact of consciousness is sensation, by means of which the subject comes into direct contact with objective reality. Sensation is the reflection of individual properties of objects during their immediate action on the sense organs. Singling out the reflection of quality as the main factor in sensation – the very first and most familiar to us is sensation, and in it there is inevitably also quality and this is also expressed in speech: when we name any sensation, what we have in mind is precisely the quality given in the sensation – red, blue – sweet, spicy – loud, soft, -- rough, smooth – good, bad odor and so on.

#225 Sensation is the conversion of the energy of external irritation into a fact of consciousness. The loss of the ability to feel must inevitably entail the loss of consciousness.

#226 Whereas sensations reflect only the separate qualities of things, the thing as a whole, in the unity of the various sensorily reproduced properties is reflected in perception. A person's perception usually includes apprehension of objects, their properties and relationships. For this reason **the character of perception depends on the level of knowledge that a person possesses and on his interests.**

#227 The process of sensory reflection is not confined to sensation and perception. A higher form of sensory reflection is 'representation'. This is imaginal knowledge of objects that we have perceived in the past but are not acting on our senses at the given moment. Representations, or images, arise as the result of the perception of external influences and their subsequent retention in the memory.

#228 The images with which man's consciousness operates are not restricted to the reproduction of what is sensorily perceived. A person may creatively combine, and with relative freedom, create new images in his consciousness. The highest form of representation is productive, creative 'imagination'.

#229 Owing to its relative freedom from immediate influence of the object and its generalization of the total evidence of the senses into a single conceivable image, representation is an important stage in the process of reflection, which moves from the sensation to thinking. Dialectical 2020 Materialism acknowledges the qualitative difference between representation and thought but does not divorce them from each other. Is sensuous representation 'closer' to reality than thought? Both, yes and no. Sensuous representation cannot apprehend 'movement as a whole', it cannot, for example, apprehend movement at a speed of 300,000 km per second, but thought does and must apprehend it.

#230 Theoretical thinking, which takes the form of 'concepts, propositions and inferences', is a reflection of the essential, law governed relationship of things, Some aspects of the world that are inaccessible to sense perceptions are open to thought. On the basis of the visible, tangible, audible, and so on, we are able, thanks to our ability to think, to penetrate into the invisible, intangible and inaudible. By means of thought we make the dialectical transition from the external to the internal, from phenomena to the essence of things, processes, and so on. While it is the highest form of reflective activity, thinking is also present at the sensory stage; as soon as a person senses or perceives something he begins to think, to apprehend the results of sensory perceptions.

#231 Consciousness is not only the process of cognition and its result – knowledge; it is also an emotional experience of what is cognized, a certain evaluation of things, qualities and their relationships. Without emotional experiences which help to mobilize or inhibit our energies, It is impossible to have certain relationships to the world for it is well known that there has never been, nor can there be, any human search for truth without human emotion.

#232 The mainspring of peoples behavior and consciousness is need – man's dependence on the external world, the individual's subjective demands on the objective world, his need for such objects and conditions as are essential to his normal life activity, his self-assertion and development.

#233 Yet another important aspect of consciousness is 'self-consciousness'. Life demands of a person that he should know not only the external world but also himself. In reflecting objective reality man becomes aware not only of this process but also of himself as a feeling thinking being, aware of his ideals, interests, and moral make-up. He singles himself out from the surrounding world and is aware of his attitude to that world, of what he feels and thinks and does. A person's becoming aware of himself as an individual is, in fact self-consciousness. Self-consciousness forms under the influence of social life, which demands of a person control over his behavior and responsibility for his actions.

#234 Consciousness exists not only within the individual. It becomes objectivized and enjoys a supra-personal existence

– in the discoveries of science, in the creation of art, in legal and moral standards and so on. All these manifestations of the social consciousness are a necessary condition for the formation of the personal, individual consciousness. The consciousness of each individual person absorbs knowledge, beliefs, faiths and evaluations of the social environment in which he lives.

#235 Man is a social being. Historically formed rules of thinking, standards of law and morality, aesthetic tastes and so on mould a person's behavior and thinking, make him a representative of a certain way of life, level of culture and psychology. If man is social by nature, he will develop his true nature only in society, and the power of his nature must be measured not by the power of the separate individual but by the power of the society. Mental abilities and qualities are formed in the process of a person's life in society and are determined by specific social conditions.

#236 A person becomes a conscious being, rises to the level of personality, to the heights of contemporary thought only in the course of social development.

#237 A basic principle of the dialectical 2020 Materialist's interpretation of consciousness is the acknowledgement of the inseparable connection between consciousness, activity and practice (dynamic, exertion, routine, work etc.)

#238 Consciousness and the objective world are opposites that form a unity. The basis of this unity is practice. People's sensuously objective activity, which are expressed in labor, the struggle between Estates, scientific experimentation and so on. It is these activities that make it necessary to reflect reality in human consciousness. The need for consciousness that gives true reflection of the world lies, consequently, in the conditions and needs of social life itself.

#239 Although consciousness is a function of the brain, it is not the brain but the person, acting as the subject of transforming activity, as the maker of history, that is aware of reality. Consequently; The essence of human consciousness cannot be revealed by proceeding only from the anatomical, physiological properties of the brain. The emergence, functioning and development of consciousness is possible only in society, on the basis of people's practical activity.

#240 In influencing us the objective world is reflected in the consciousness and becomes ideal. In its turn, consciousness, the ideal, is transformed by means of practical activity into reality, into the real.

#241 Consciousness is characterized by an active creative attitude to the external world, to oneself, to human activity. The activeness of consciousness can be seen in the fact that a person reflects the external world purposefully, selectively. He reproduces in his head objects and phenomena through the prism of the knowledge he has already acquired – his representations and concepts. Reality is recreated in human consciousness not in the dead form of a mirror-like reflection, but in a creatively transformed state. Consciousness is capable of creating images that anticipate reality. It has the ability to foresee.

#242 Man's brain has evolved in such a way as not only to receive, preserve and produce information, but also to draw up a plan of action and put it into effect through active direction. Human action is always designed to achieve an ultimate result, that is, a certain aim. Any significant action on the part of the individual represents the solution to some important problem, the realization of some intention. The succeeding stages of the process of action and activity as a whole are more or less clearly coordinated inasmuch as the whole process is predetermined by its goal, its plan.

Speaking of the distinction between human wage and salary commodity producing labor-activity and the behavior of the animals. It is that man not only changes the form of what is given in nature; he also realizes his own conscious goal, which, as a law, determines the means and character of his actions – actions which must be subordinate to his will. The aim which a person strives to achieve, is that which must be created, that which does not yet exist in reality. It is the ideal model of the desired future. Human action has as its precondition two closely connected processes. One of them is the setting of the goal, that is envisaging, the anticipation of the future, which proceeds from cognition of the relevant connections and relationships of things, and the other is the programming, the plan of action that should lead to realization of the goal.

#243 The setting of goals, that is, the foreseeing of the purpose for which a person carries out certain actions, is an essential condition of any conscious act. However the essence of the matter is not accounted for by its 'aim', but by its 'realization'. The realization of the aim presupposes the application of means, that is, of what is created and exists for the sake of the aim. Man creates things which nature did not produce before him. The design, scale, form and properties of the things that man has transformed and created are dictated by human needs and goals; they embody human ideals and plans. The fundamental vital meaning and historical necessity of the emergence and development of consciousness lie precisely in the creative and regulative activity designed to transform the world and make it serve the interests of man and society. Wo/man's consciousness not only reflects the objective world, but creates it, for the world does not satisfy men and women and they decide to change it by their labor activity.

Consciousness And Evolution Of The Forms Of Reflection: >#244

#245 The ability of the human brain to reflect reality is a result of the prolonged development of highly organized matter. Some philosophical and psychological conceptions erroneously assert that the puzzle of the emergence of consciousness from its biological preconditions is made clear by the fact that only man is recognized as possessing mental faculties. This idea goes back Descartes, who assumed that animals are merely complex machines. Exactly the opposite position is held by those who believe that not only animals but all nature is animate (Robinet and others). Between these two extreme concepts there is an intermediate position of "biopsychism', according to which intelligence, mental activity, is a property only of living matter. Ernst Haeckel and others)

#246 Dialectical 2020 Materialism rejects both the idea of the universal animism of matter and the idea that intelligence is inherent only in man. Nor does it share the position of 'biopsychism'. Dialectical 2020 Materialism proceeds from the fact that 'mental reflection of the external world' is the property of matter that appears at a high level of development of living beings when a nervous system is formed.

#247 When considering the sources of consciousness in its clearly expressed form sensation is associated only with the higher forms of matter. Reflection as a general property of matter is conditioned by the fact that objects and phenomena are in universal interconnection and interaction. In acting on one another they produce certain changes. These changes take the form of 'traces', which register the peculiarities of the acting object or phenomenon. The forms of reflection depend on the specific nature and level of structural organization of the interacting bodies. The content of reflection, on the other hand, is expressed in what changes take place in the reflecting object.

#248 The correlation between the results of reflection and the reflected object may be expressed in the form of isomorphism and homeomorphism. Isomorphism means a similarity between certain objects, the kind of resemblance in their form and structure that we find, for example, in photographs or approximate reflections, for example as on maps. An isomorphous reflection is a close reproduction of the original.

#249 Reflection is inherent in matter at all stages of its organization, but the highest forms of reflection are connected with living matter, with life. What is life? Life is a specific, complex form of the motion of matter. Its important attributes are irritability, growth, and procreation. These are based on the exchange of substance, on metabolism. Metabolism is the essence of life. It involves a certain material substratum (In the conditions on earth, consumption and creation of proteins, DNA, nucleic acids and so on)

#250 Life is primarily a process of interaction between the organism and its environment. On our planet it takes the form of countless different organisms, from the simplest to the most complex, such as man. In the process of biological evolution the increasing complexity of the structures and patterns of behavior of organisms is accompanied by a similar sophistication of the forms of reflection. Reflection, the forms which it assumes in various organisms directly depend on the character and level of their behavior, their activity. As their activity becomes more complex, living organisms acquire sense organs and develop a nervous system. At the same time their very activity depends on the regulative influence of reflection.

#251 The initial, elementary form of reflection inherent in all living organisms is irritability. This is expressed in the selective reaction of living bodies to external influences (light, change in temperature and so on). At higher levels of evolution of living organisms irritability passes into a qualitatively new property – sensitivity, that is the ability to reflect the individual proportions of things in the form of sensations.

#252 Reflection achieves a higher level in vertebrates, which acquire the ability to analyze complexes of simultaneously acting irritants and to reflect them in the form of perception – an integrated picture of the situation. Sensations and perceptions, as was said earlier, are images of things. This implies the appearance of elementary forms of mental activity, mentality as a function of the nervous system and a form of reflection of reality.

#253 Usually a distinction is made between two closely connected types of behavior in animals; instinctive, inborn behavior, which can be inherited, and individually acquired behavior. Animals possess the ability to reflect the biologically significant properties of objects of the environment (that is to say, properties that help them to satisfy their need for food, to avoid danger, and so on).

#254 The perfecting of this ability leads to the formation of various complex forms of behavior. In the higher animals, such as the apes, they are expressed in the ability to discover circuitous routes to a goal, in the use of various objects as tools, and so on. In short, what we call in everyday terms animal 'intelligence'.

#255 The high level of development of mental activity in animals shows that man's consciousness has its biological preconditions and that there is no unbridgeable gap between man and his animal ancestors; in fact, there is a certain continuity. This does not mean, however, that their mental activity is of precisely the same quality.

*****

Consciousness and speech. Their origin and interconnections. >#256

#257 Consciousness and speech originated with the transition of our ape-like ancestors from the appropriation of ready made objects with the help of their natural organs, to grasping, to the making of artificial tools, to labor, to human forms of life activity and to the social relationships that grow up on its basis. The transition to consciousness and speech represents a great qualitative leap in the development of the psyche, of mental activity.

#258 The animals' mental activity helps them to orientate themselves in a changing environment and adapt themselves to it, but they cannot deliberately and systematically transform the world that surrounds them. Labor, understood as a goal-orientated activity, is the basic condition of all human life and the formation of consciousness. The various forms of constructive labor of the past and now in this new age wage and salary commodity producing labor is the prime basic condition for all human existence, and this to such an extent that, in a sense, we have to say that labor created man himself. The initial form of labor is the process of making tools out of wood, stone, bone and so on, and producing the means of existence with their help. Some animals also have the ability to use various objects as tools. For example, apes sometimes pick up a stone to break nuts with, or they may use a stick to catch a bait, and so on. Although not a single ape has ever made itself the most primitive tool still they may be taught to do man's will, as can dogs and other animals.

#259 About a million years ago our ape-like ancestors lived in the trees. Changing conditions brought them down from the trees onto the ground. In this new situation they had to make systematic use of sticks etc as a means of defense from beasts of prey, and also for the purpose of attacking other animals. The need for the systematic use of tools compelled them gradually to pass on to the processing of materials that they found in nature to the production of the tools themselves. All this led to a substantial change in the functions of the forelimbs, which adapted themselves to more and more new operations and became the natural instruments of labor.

#260 As it developed in the process of work activity the hand brought improvements to the whole organism including the brain. Consciousness could arise only as a function of a sophisticated brain, formed under the influence of labor and speech. Work activity and the development of the brain also improved man's sense organs. His sense of touch became more and more accurate and subtle, his hearing acquired the ability to distinguish the finest shades and similarities of sounds in human speech, his vision grew ever more perceptive. The eagle sees much further than man, but the human eye sees considerably more in things than does the eye of the eagle.

#261 The logic of practical action was registered in the brain and there turned into the logic of thought, giving rise to the ability to set goals.

#262 At first man's awareness of his actions and surroundings was limited to sensuous images, their combination and primitive generalization. Consciousness was at first only awareness of the immediately perceived phenomena in the environment, the immediate connection to other people. As the forms of work and social relationships became more complex, however, man acquired the ability to think in the form of concepts, propositions, and inferences that reflected the ever more profound and diversified connections between the objects and phenomena of reality.

#263 The origin of consciousness is directly connected with the birth of language, of articulate speech which expresses people's images and thoughts in material form. Like consciousness speech could only take shape in the process of work, labor which demanded the coordinated actions of several people working together, and which they could not perform without close contacts and constant intercommunications.

#264 Speech was preceded by a long period of the development of the sound and motor reactions in animals. It is well known that animals have a need for sound communication but animals have no need for speech communication. The little that even the most highly developed animals need to communicate to each other does not require articulate speech.

#265 The activity of speech is performed with the aid of language, that is, a definite system of means of communication. There are various forms of speech: oral, written and internal soundless invisible speech, which is the material form of consciousness when man says something 'to himself'.

#266 The basic units of speech are words and sentences. Words are a unity of meaning and sound. The material aspect of the word (sound, written symbol) denotes an object and is a sign. The meaning of the word, on the other hand, reflects the object and is a vehicle of a complete thought or proposition.

#267 It is language that helps us to make a transition from living contemplation, from sense perception to generalized, abstract thinking. Every word (speech) already 'universalizes' by objectivizing our thoughts and feelings on speech, presenting them to ourselves.

#268 Philosophers have for long been deeply interested in the origin of consciousness and speech, which has evoked much controversy. Some thinkers treated speech and thought as exactly the same thing, maintaining that reason is language. Others divorced consciousness from speech and believed that thinking could be performed without language, that language was a product of thought.

#269 2020 Materialism treats consciousness as being in close connection with language and speech, neither thought nor language in themselves form a realm of their own they are only manifestations of actual life. Just as language does not exist without thought, thought does not exist without language. The separation of thought from language, on the one hand, inevitably makes a mystery of consciousness by depriving it of the material means of its formation and realization. And, on the other, such a dissociation leads to the interpretation of language, of speech, as a self contained essence divorced from the life of society and the development of culture.

#270 Consciousness and speech form a unity, but it is an internally contradictory unity of diverse phenomena. Consciousness 'reflects' reality while language 'denotes' it and expresses thoughts. When clothed in the forms of speech, thoughts and ideas do not lose their unique qualities.

#271 In speech our representations, thoughts and feelings are clothed in a material sensually perceptible form and thus pass from our own personal possession into the possession of other people, of society. This makes speech an effective instrument with which some people can influence others and with which society can influence the individual.

#272 Whereas in animals the experience of the species is passed on by the mechanism of heredity, which makes their progress extremely slow, in people experience and the various methods of influencing the environment are largely passed on through the instruments of speech. In addition to the biological factor – heredity – man has evolved a more powerful and also direct means of passing on experience – the social means, thus tremendously accelerating the rate of progress of both material and intellectual culture.

#273 It is thanks to speech that consciousness takes the shape and develops as a social phenomena, as the intellectual product of social life. As a means of human intercourse, of the exchange of experience, knowledge, feelings and ideas, speech links not only the members of a given social group or generation, but also different generations. Hence the continuity of historical epochs.

#274 Idealist philosophers and theologians maintain that consciousness develops out of its own internal sources or by some god and can be understood only in its own terms. Dialectical 2020 Materialism, on the other hand, proceeds from the fact that consciousness cannot be regarded in isolation from the other phenomena of social life. Consciousness is not isolated, it develops and changes in the process of the historical development, first of local and then of global society. Although consciousness has its origins in the biological forms of mental activity, it is not a product of nature, but a socio-historical economic phenomenon. It is not the brain as such that determines what sensations, thoughts and feelings a person may have. The brain becomes the organ of consciousness only when a person is drawn into the maelstrom of social life. When he acts in conditions that feed his brain with the juices of historically evolved and developing culture and compel him to function in a direction set by the demands of social life, and orient him towards posing and solving problems necessary to man and society.

*****

Consciousness and Cybernetics. >#275

#276 A substantial contribution to our knowledge of the nature of reflection and consciousness has been made by cybernetics, the science of intricate self-regulating dynamic systems. Such systems include living organisms, organs, cells, biological communities, society and certain technical devices, all of which have the ability to receive information, to process and memorize it, to act on the feed-back principle and to regulate themselves on this basis.

#277 What is information? What relation does it bear to reflection? There is no consensus on this question. Some scientists are inclined to treat information and reflection as the same thing, while others assume that these concepts are closely related but not identical.

#278 In the process of reflection there is bound to be some transmission of information, that is to say, a transmission from one object to another of a certain pattern (structure, form), on the basis of which one may assess certain attributes, or properties of the acting object.

#279 Specific information processes occur at every level of the organization of matter. Exchange of information takes place even in inanimate nature, but there it is never deciphered. The ability not only to receive but to make active use of information is a fundamental property of animate matter. The adaptive functions in animal, their behavior, and the control that goes with it, would be unthinkable without information. In cybernetics control is the programmed regulation of the actions of one system (controlled) by another (controlling). Thus the brain is a controlling system, while the organs of movement form the controlled system.

#280 Information is passed on by means of certain signals, that is, any material processes (electrical impulses, electromagnetic modulation, smells, sounds, colors, and so on). A signal can convey information because it possesses a certain structure. Information is the content of the signal.

#281 Information signaling is the principle on which all computers are based. The appearance of the computer with its ability to process vast quantities of information for man has highlighted the problem of whether it is possible to model through the help of machines, the problem of the similarities and differences between the processes occurring in modeling machines and the human brain. For instance, there are machines that can 'identify' visual images.

Admittedly they can 'identify' only the limited class of objects that have been fed into them in the process of their 'teaching' or even 'self teaching'. The fundamental difference between human perception and the 'identifying' function of the machine is that in the first case the result is a subjective image of the object, and in the computer it is a code of various features of the object that it needs for performing certain tasks. The computer has not yet evolved to the point where it is immersed in the efficiency of the electro-chemical 'wash', historically conditioned, labor-adapted, objective omega-subjective orientation of the gray matter that is the human brain.

#282 The most practical results so far achieved have been in the modeling of memory. Machines have been built that can memorize information at very high speeds, store it in their 'memory' for any length of time and faultlessly reproduce it. The 'memory' of such machines is capacious, but machine 'memory' differs essentially from human memory. In the human brain the memory is organized on the basis of a conceptual system of references that enable it to select the information that it needs without going through every item in succession. The conceptual organization of knowledge and not the speed of the physiological processes involved is what gives the human memory its rapidity of recall. A person memorizes information not by storing it mechanically but through a comprehended goal-orientated process.

#283 The modeling of certain aspects of thought activity is no less impressive in its results than the modeling of perception and memory. At present there are machines that can perform such intellectual operations as proving geometrical theorems, translation from one language to another, or playing chess.

#284 Cybernetic machines are extremely effective for modeling the characteristically human ability of formal logical thought. But human consciousness is by no means confined to such thought. The human brain has a dialectical flexibility and accuracy in solving problems that are not conditioned by any rigid system of formal rules.

#285 We must remember that man's ability to think is shaped by his assimilation of a historically accumulated culture, by his education and training, and by the performance of certain activities with the aid of means and devices created by the society that he is born into. The richness of a man's inner world depends on the richness and diversity of his social connections. Therefore, if we wished to model the whole human consciousness, its structure and all its functions, it would not be enough to reproduce only the structure of the brain. We should have to reproduce the logic of the whole history of human thought, and consequently repeat the whole historical path of human development and provide it with all its needs, including political, moral, aesthetic, work and other needs.

#286 Man has evolved as a conscious being in the course of social development, and so the insights to man and his consciousness are not so much problems of natural science, and certainly not just a problem of cybernetics, but require philosophical and sociological insights. Thus examination of the question of consciousness, its specific features, its connection with the external world, with the brain and speech confirms the correctness of the Dialectical 2020 Materialist proposition that consciousness is essentially of a reflective and socio-historical character.

*****

Category 05: Quality >#287

#288 Dialectics is not just a matter of asserting that everything develops. What we have to do is to understand the mechanism of this development scientifically. In the present age of astonishing scientific advance and great social transformation no one ventures to deny the principle of development. On the contrary, everyone 'agrees' with it. But this 'agreement' is sometimes of a kind that makes for distortion of the truth.

#289 There exist various views on and approaches to the principle of development. From the vast array the two most essential conceptions, one which expresses the scientific, dialectical theory, and the second an unscientific, anti-dialectical theory.

#290 In the second conception of motion, self-movement – its driving force, its source, its motive, remains in the shade (or its source is made external – God – subject etc.).

#291 In the first conception the chief attention is directed precisely to knowledge of the source of self-movement.

#292 The second conception is lifeless pale and dry.

#293 The first alone furnishes the key to the 'leaps', to the 'break in continuity', to the 'transformation into the opposite', to the destruction of the old and emergence of the new.

#294 The distinguishing feature of the dialectical conception of development lies in the understanding of development not as a simple quantitative change (increase or decrease) of what exists, but as a process of disappearance, destruction of the old and emergence of the new. This process is demonstrated in the law of the transformation of quantitative changes into qualitative changes and visa versa.

To find out what this law is all about we must examine a number of categories such as property, quantity, quality and measure.

#295 Getting to know an object begins with the external, direct impressions we have when we see it in the process of interaction with other objects. Nothing can be known about it without such interaction. (For example in the shoe business, amongst others, quality is measured by three characteristics –durability, utility and emotional appeal as compared to its competitors' product. Note that comparison is required.) And it is this interaction that reveals the properties of things, which once known, provide the clue to the things themselves. Metal for instance, has such properties as density, compressibility, heat and electrical conductivity, and so on. One might conclude from this that a thing is nothing more than the sum total of certain properties, so that to know a thing we merely have to established what those properties are. But this conclusion would be premature. No matter how important the properties of a thing, when it comes to describing it, the thing cannot be reduced to its properties.

#296 For instance, a number of properties of third-estate rule change in the course of its development. The old third-estate in certain countries takes over the first and second estates. It eventually obtains almost full rule over all other estates, especially the fourth-estate, subsequently even the peasants and farmers are pushed into the fifth-estate and the third-estate holds sway over it all. In the final stage the third-estate takes over the global role of 'managing' all estates for the purpose of extracting as much global 'value added' that is possible for its own use. In this process it creates boom, bust and unmitigated competition to its own detriment and to the detriment of all estates. This state of affairs continues until there is a qualitative change that bursts the 'frustration' 'anxiety' 'every man for himself' 'gun mentality' asunder and a new state of affairs comes into being. The future peoples that are historically connected with this new state of affairs will then alleviate the problems of the old order and bring about a new order.

#297 Consequently the properties of an object are a manifestation of something more essential which characterizes the object itself. This more essential something is the object's 'quality'. Quality is what defines an object as one thing and not another. It is what accounts for the amazing diversity of the real world. "Quality as Hegel says, "is above all, a direct determinacy identical with being…a thing is what it is thanks to its quality and in losing its quality, it ceases to be what it is." Quality is something more than mere totality of even essential properties, because it expresses the unity, the integrity of a thing, its relative stability, its identity with itself. (For example, on a shallow basis, it may be argued that technological progress is really nothing but the quality of educational improvements in human beings and the machines they operate.)

#298 Quality is closely connected with the 'structure' of an object, that is to say, with certain form of organization of the elements and properties of which it is composed, thanks to which it is not merely the sum total of the latter but their unity and wholeness. The conception of structure tells us why the change or even the loss of some or other of the thing's properties does not always mean or may not directly change the quality of a thing. (going back to the shoe example the durability may remain the same even though the material of construction may change.) Another example – in the capitalist mode of production embodies the interconnection of all aspects, elements and properties implied in its private property nature, in the relationship between capital and wage & salary commodity producing labor. This is what determines its quality, and until the structure of the connection between the means of production and the producers changes, capitalism will not cease to be what it is. It is this kind of change and comparison that is ignored by the third-estate Triptocracy and their apologists, who try to identify changes in certain properties in the expropriation of value-added with a fundamental qualitative change. (as an example of this the wage and salary commodity producing worker in advanced countries may be made to feel he is a member of the third-estate by virtue of his owning some stock shares or by the small equity he may hold in his house and so on.)

#299 In the very definition of quality we are at once confronted with the dialectics of the object, the thing. Whenever we define the quality of a thing, we relate it to something else and consequently set limits to its existence. Beyond these limits it is not what it was, but something else. This means that the quality of a thing is identified with its finiteness.

#300 If we state that objects have the same quality, it means that they are the same. They may, of course, possess different properties, but qualitatively they are identical. Since they are identical in quality, they differ from one another only in quantity. There may be more or less of them, they may differ from one another in volume, size and so on. In other words, the qualitative identity of objects is the precondition for understanding their other aspect – the quantitative aspect. Hegel says that quantity is 'sublated quality', that is, the analysis of things as qualities inevitably leads us to the category of quantity. This is quite natural because quality and quantity cannot exist separately. We separate them artificially only for the sake of knowledge but, having done so, we restore the connection. (i.e. the reader may think about how the price of desks and their number can be compared to the price of cars and their number by the quality and quantity of labor embodied in the manufacture of them.)

*****

Category 06: Quantity >#301

#302 The category of Quantity demands abstraction from the qualitative diversity of things. According to the general law of knowledge we must first investigate the qualitative difference between things, and then their quantitative regularities. The latter allow us to obtain a deeper knowledge of the essence of things. For example, science was for long unable to understand the cause of qualitative difference of colors – i.e. green, violet and so on. The explanation was found only when it was established that difference of color and intensity depends on the quantitatively different length and frequency of electromagnetic waves.

#303 Commodities are the 'cell' of the capitalist mode of production. Commodities differ as to use-value, that is that they satisfy different needs of the consumer. The salary and wage labor which produces qualitatively different commodities also has special characteristic qualities; it is the concrete labor of the architect and the carpenter, the engineer and the welder, the teacher, and his product - the graduated student, the confectioner, the shoemaker and so on. But if these are only differences in commodity-producing salary and wage labor, how can we effect an exchange of, say shoes and tables? This exchange is made possible because commodities are not only the product of concrete labor, but also of the 'abstract labor' characteristic of commodity production, wage and salary work is the expenditure of human energy, mental and manual. It is this qualitatively identical labor that allows us to compare the most divers commodities and to exchange them. Such labor can be distinguished in terms of quantity; consequently, various goods can be exchanged in various proportions. (for example let us say that the labor token equivalent (money) of two thousand shoes can be exchanged for one car and so on.)

#304 From what has been said it is clear that the quantity is an expression of the similarity, the identity of things, thanks to which they can be increased or decreased, added up or divided, and so on. Quantity is therefor embodied in size, in number, in the degree and intensity of development of certain aspects of an object, in the rate of flow of certain processes, in the space-time properties of phenomena. The more complex the phenomena become the more complex are their quantitative parameters, and the more difficult they are to analyze in terms of quantity.

#305 The essential difference between quantity and quality is that one can change certain quantitative properties of an object without its undergoing any significant changes. For instance, one may raise the temperature of water, that is, without changing its aggregate state. This means that the quantity of a thing is not closely connected with its state as its quality. In the analysis of quantitative relationships one can, within certain limits, ignore the quality of objects. (i.e. in the case of water this relationship ceases when the heat content is raised to such a high level as to turn it from water at a given pressure and temperature into steam at the same pressure and temperature.) The wide application of quantitative mathematical methods in many sciences investigating qualitatively different objects is based on this peculiarity of quantity.

#306 Changes of quantity, however, are in external relationships to a thing only within certain limits for each particular thing. Sometimes even the smallest departure beyond these limits leads to fundamental qualitative change in the thing. Any changes in quantity, of course, have their effect on the state of a thing, its properties. But only quantitative changes that have reached a certain level are connected with fundamental changes of quality.

#307 The dependence of quality on quantity may be traced in the qualitative diversity of atoms, for example. Every kind of atom is defined by the number of protons in its nucleus, in other words, by its atomic number in the periodic system of elements. One proton more or one proton less and we have a qualitatively different kind of atom.

#308 Thus the quality of thing is inseparably linked with a certain quantity. This connection and interdependence of quality and quantity is called 'proportion'.

*****

Category 07: Proportion >#309

#310 The category of proportion expresses the kind of relationship between the quality and the quantity of an object that obtains when its quality is based on a definite quantity, and the latter is the quantity of a definite quantity. It is the changes in the interrelationships, changes of proportion, that explain the mechanism of development. Hence development should be understood not as motion within certain fixed and immutable limits, but as replacement of the old by the new, as an eternal and ceaseless process of renewal of what exists. At a certain stage quantitative changes reach a level of when the former harmony of quality and quantity becomes disharmony. At this point the old qualitative state must yield to the new.

#311 The transformation of quantitative into qualitative changes goes hand in hand with the reverse process: new quality gives rise to new changes of quantity. Thus the fifth-estate mode of production will be freed of the fetters of the third-estate usurpation of 'value added' and its subsequent squander on stock schemes and boom and bust and unmitigated requirement for growth and more growth in advanced countries and squalor and more squalor in backward countries.

#312 Quantitative changes occur constantly and gradually. Qualitative changes takes place in the form of a break in the gradualness. This means that development, since it is the unity of quantitative and qualitative change, is at the same time the unity of continuity and discontinuity – life and development in nature include both slow evolution and rapid leaps, breaks in continuity.

#313 If we deny development as the unity of the two forms (quantity and quality), then we must accept one of the two possible but equally incorrect concepts of the world. Either we must regard all the richness of the world, the diversity of the phenomena of inorganic and organic nature, the multitudinous varieties of plants and animals, and man himself, as having always existed and as changing only in quantity. Or else we must assume that all this was by some magic miracle suddenly brought into being. Both these notions have been held in the history of science and philosophy, (the latter notion being also held by theologians), but these notions have been overthrown by the whole course of advancing knowledge and historical practice.

#314 Both views have also become widespread in social theories. All the reformist theories in the wage and salary sector are based on the one sided exaggeration of continuity, of the quantitative gradualness of development from which it is argued that out of triptocracy will come a pentocracy by means of the gradual accumulation of more humanistic attributes in society. These are the reformist (and food bank-ists and homeless shelter-ists. Freedom 55-ists). Don't get us wrong, we applaud the humanistic efforts of these particular '-ists'. But they do not get at the root of the problem of poverty, frustration etc. they only gloss it all over and thus they become apologists for third-estate expropriation of value-added.)

#315 In contrast to the reformists the anarchists and elements of the new right completely deny the significance of quantitative, continuous forms of development and recognize only social cataclysms and rebellions. (brought about by individual acts of terrorism bombings etc.) Assuming that social conditions can be changed only in this way, they fall prey to political adventurism and disregard the objective conditions that are essential for revolutionary leaps forward.

#316 All qualitative changes take place in the form of leaps. A certain process ends in a leap, which denotes the moment of qualitative change of an object, the breakthrough, the critical stage in its development. In the general thread of development a new knot is tied. Triptocracy creates its own grave digger, itself creates the elements of a new system, yet at the same time without a 'leap' these individual elements change nothing in the general state of affairs and do not effect, for example the rule of third-estate capital.

#317 Leap is a form of development that occurs much quicker than the form of continual development. It is the period of most intensive development, when the old and obsolete are transformed and make way for new, higher stages of development. Thus, social revolutions give tremendous impetus to the development of the material and spiritual life of societies. The same significance is attached to 'leaps' in science, which denotes new and important discoveries.

#318 Development thus proceeds as the unity of continuity and discontinuity (the dialectic between them), when one measure yields to, or is transformed into another.

#319 The qualitative differences in the forms of motion of matter – mechanical, physical, chemical and others – are regarded by science as the 'nodal points' in the process of the gradual differentiation of matter. Such 'breaks in continuity' are discrete (discontinuous – packets) states of matter at various structural levels (elementary particles, nuclei, atoms, molecules and so on) Evolutionary gradualness and revolutionary (leap-like) forms in their unity constitute a law of social development.

#320 Changes of quantity are transformed into qualitative changes in various ways, depending on the specific conditions in various spheres of reality. The concrete forms of this transformation, this leap from one state into another, are studied by the specialized sciences. Philosophy helps us to find our way in this great variety of forms, without claiming, however, that these forms give an exhaustive picture, since life is always richer than any theory.

#321 The typical and most general forms of leaps of qualitative transformations are as follows. (1) comparatively rapid and sharp transformations of one quality into another when the object as a stroke or series of strokes undergoes fundamental qualitative change. (2) gradual qualitative change, when the object changes elements by means of the gradual accumulation of quantitative changes, and only as the result of such changes passes from one state into another.

#322 What determines these different forms? Why does the leap take place now in one form and now in another? The answer to these questions is to be sought above all in the particular features of the developing objects themselves.

#323 Nature and natural processes offer a multitude of examples when leaps and transformation from one quality to another take place in the form of rapid changes. Such are the qualitative transformations of elementary particles, chemical elements, chemical compounds, the release of atomic energy in the form of atomic explosions, and so on. On the other hand, there are objects in nature whose qualitative changes into other more complex and perfect objects involve very long processes and can occur, as a rule, only gradually. Such are the qualitative changes of some species of animals into others. Usually the two qualitative poles in such transformations, are linked by many intermediate forms.

#324 But however gradually a process of qualitative change proceeds the transformation to the new stage is a leap in spite of all gradualness the transition from one form of motion to another always remains a **leap**. This is what distinguishes gradual qualitative changes from the gradual quantitative changes. The latter, while changing certain individual properties of a thing do not affect its quality up to a certain point.

#325 It would be wrong to regard the gradualness of qualitative changes, as if these changes simply accumulate in number until they oust the old quality entirely. In reality this process is much more complex. It is not simply the arithmetical addition of the elements of the new quality, but a path of gradual perfection. It is of gradual, sometimes imperceptible qualitative changes, a path that presupposes profound structural changes in the old quality, a number of intermediate stages and steps in the ascent to the ultimate result, that is to completion of the leap.

#326 The forms of this leap depend not only on the nature of the object but also on the conditions in which the object is placed. Thus in the condition of natural radioactivity the disintegration of certain substances, uranium for example, proceeds extremely slowly; half-life is about ten to the nine years. But the same process of disintegration during the explosion of an atomic bomb takes place almost instantaneously because of chain reaction.

#327 Historical experience has shown that qualitative changes, leaps, also take place in social development. Social revolutions, which have in the past and will in the future radically transform the life of society.

#328 What has been said allows us to draw a general conclusion concerning the essence and significance of the law of transformation of Quantitative into qualitative changes and visa versa.

*****

LAW
The laws of transformation of quantitative into qualitative change and visa versa >#329

#330 This law states that – **There is an interconnection and interaction between the quantitative and qualitative aspects of objects thanks to which small, at first imperceptible, quantitative changes, accumulating gradually, sooner or later upset the proportion of that object and evoke fundamental qualitative changes which take place in the form of leaps (Eureka! effect) and whose occurrence depends on the nature of the objects in** question and the conditions of their development in diverse forms.

*****

Category 08: Struggle Of Opposites >#331

#332 The contradiction between quality and quantity is only one of the manifestations of the general law that internal contradictoriness is inherent in all things and processes, and that this is the source and motive force for their development. Thus the study of contradictions is the nucleus of dialectics.

#333 The two major concepts of development are sharply opposed particularly over the question of contradictions. This opposition runs right through the history of philosophy and is still a characteristic of philosophy today.

#334 Many modern third-estate apologist philosophers flatly deny the dialectically contradictory essence of phenomena. They assume that only our 'thoughts' may be contradictory, while objective things are free from all contradictions.

#335 The contradictions of thought or, as they are sometimes called, 'logical contradictions' certainly do occur, they are the result of logical inconsistency, logical error. When we make contradictory statements about one and the same thing considered at the same moment and in the same relation (for instance, "the table is round" and "the table is not round") such contradictions of ideas is impermissible. The appearance of such contradictions in scientific theories testifies to their incorrectness or incompleteness. At the same time contradictions of ideas may conceal objective contradictions in phenomena themselves of which we are not yet aware. It is such objective contradictions that the opponents of dialectics refuse to acknowledge.

#336 The world knows of no absolutely identical things or phenomena. When we speak of the similarity or identity of certain objects, their very similarity presupposes that they are in some way different, dissimilar, otherwise there is no sense at all in comparing them. This implies that even a simple outward comparison of two objects reveals the unity of identity and difference: every object is simultaneously identical to another yet different from it. In this quite simple sense identity is not abstract but a concrete identity containing within it an element of difference – identity with itself requires difference from everything else as its compliment.

#337 The difference in an object is not only a difference in relation to another object but also a difference in relation to itself, that is, the given object, no matter if we are comparing it with something else or not, contains an instantaneous difference in itself. For example, a living being is a unity of identity and difference not only because it is similar to and dissimilar from other beings, but also because in the process of living it denies itself, or, to put it simply it is moving toward its own end, its death.

#338 When dialectical theory maintains that an object simultaneously exists and does not exist, that it contains within itself its own non being, this must be understood in only one sense. An object is a unity of stability and changeability, of the positive and the negative, of what is dying out and what is entering life and renewal and so on.

#339 The means that every object, every phenomenon is a unity of opposites. What this important proposition implies above all is that opposite aspects and tendencies are inherent in all objects. Internal contradictions are an inseparable property of the structure of any object or process. Moreover, every object or group of objects has its own specific contradictions which have to be discovered by concrete analysis. But mere acknowledgement of the internal contradictoriness of phenomena does not fully explain the concept of the unity of opposites. It is very important to take into consideration the character of the connection and interaction between opposites and their structure. This structure is such that each of the aspects of the whole is entirely dependent on its opposite for its existence and this duality is not confined merely to their external relationships. The interconnection, interdependence and inter-penetration of opposite aspects, properties and tendencies of the developing whole are an essential feature of any unity of opposites.

#340 But the interdependence of opposites is only one of the specific features of dialectical contradiction. Another of its vital aspects is 'mutual negation'. Because the two aspects of the whole are opposites they are not only interconnected but also mutually exclusive and mutually repellent. This factor is expressed in the concept of the struggle of opposites. (i.e. up down, in out, plus minus, male female, coin - tails heads, and infinite numbers of other such opposites and so on)

#341 In its generalized form this concept comprises all kinds of mutual negation of opposites. In some cases, particularly in social life and partially in organic nature, this mutual exclusion of opposites is literally expressed in the term 'struggle'. Such, for example, is the struggle during warfare and the struggle for the use of 'value-added' (Money - Labor tokens) between members of estates and the whole of estates in society. (In our own age the Triptocracy's supremacy over the Pentocracy and the resultant struggle.)

#342 In inanimate nature the term 'struggle of opposites' applies chiefly to the action and counteraction, attraction and repulsion, and so on. But no matter what concrete forms this struggle assumes, the main thing is that the dialectical contradiction implies also an element of mutual negation of opposites, and this negation is an extremely important element, because the 'struggle of opposites' is the motive force, the source of development.

#343 What has been said about each of the elements of dialectical contradiction – the elements of 'unity' and 'struggle' of opposites – allows an important conclusion – The <u>unity</u> of opposites is conditional, temporary, transitory, relative. The struggle of mutually exclusive opposites is absolute, just as development and motion are absolute. This means that the struggle of opposites naturally results in the disappearance of the existing object as a certain unity of opposites and the appearance of a new object with a new unity of opposites inherent in that particular object.

#344 The essence of the dialectical contradiction may be defined as an interrelationship and interconnection between opposites in which they mutually assert and deny (inhibit) each other, and the struggle between them serves as the motive force, the source of development. This is why the law in question is known as the law of the unity and struggle of opposites.

#345 This law explains one of the most important features of dialectical development: motion, development takes place as self-development. This concept is highly relevant to materialism. It means that the world develops not as a result of any external causes (say, divine first impulse – the unmoved mover) but by virtue of its own laws, the laws of motion of matter itself.

#346 The dialectical theory that motion or development of nature is in fact self-motion, self-development, explains why many contemporary philosophers are so vehement in their attacks on the proposition of the contradictory essence of things. Development understood in this way leaves no room for a mythical mystical force on which the livelihood of so many of them depend. (receiving crumbs from Triptocracy's table.)

#347 Some philosophers recognize contradictions, for example the contradictions in the Triptocracy and its economic arm capital residing in big banks and unmitigated competition with its inherent anxiety, with its boom and bust reverberations, they try to minimize them and gloss them over. In this field there are many different angles of approach, but the anti-dialectical meaning remains one and the same.

#348 Postulating that internal contradictions are inherent in all things and processes and comprise the motive force of self development of nature and society, 2020 Materialist dialectics explains how this process takes place.

#349 Contradictions are not something immobile and immutable. Once they have arisen, specific contradictions develop and pass through definite stages. A phenomenon cannot disappear and be replaced by another phenomenon until its contradictions are revealed and fully developed, because only in the process of such development are the preconditions for the leap into the new qualitative stage created.

#350 This process has two basic stages (1) the stage of development, of the unfolding of the contradictions inherent in an object; (2) the stage of resolution of these contradictions.

#351 When it first begins to develop, contradiction is in the nature of a slight difference. This difference then deepens into a manifest contradiction, whose opposite sides are less and less able to remain in the framework of the former unity. At this stage of development the contradiction becomes a dynamic relationship driving toward resolution.

#352 This process can be shown for example in the development of the fetus in animals and humans. A better example can be given however – that is in the development of present-day global society. In striving for maximum profit in unmitigated competition the Triptocracy are compelled to develop what is in essence, global social production. But the more social production becomes globalized, the more it enters into contradictions with the third-estate's private ownership of the means of production and capital distribution. Thus the means of production that it uses to extract an extraordinary amount of 'value-added' – amounting to trillions upon trillions of labor tokens that wash around the globe daily seeking a safe place to nestle, seeking a safe place to hide. (but there is no such place, it's an illusion.)

#353 The second stage, the resolution of the contradiction, is the natural culmination of the process of the development and struggle of opposites. Whereas the whole previous process takes place within the framework of unity, the interconnection of opposites, the stage of the resolution of contradictions signifies the removal of this unity, its disappearance, which coincides with a fundamental qualitative change in the object.

#354 2020 Materialist dialectics attaches great importance to the study of resolution of contradiction. No wonder then, that in the hands of genuinely progressive forces, and particularly the entrepreneurs, wage and salary workers. It serves both as a powerful instrument of cognition, and highlights the place that the UN (or some body such as it) will take in the revolutionary transformation of the world.

#355 The character of contradictions, their forms of development and means of resolution cannot be the same in both inorganic and organic nature, in nature and society, and in different social formations. Dialectics does not claim to provide the 'catalogue' of all possible contradictions. Its task and the task of 2020 Materialists is rather to point out the strategy of approach to the study and manipulation of phenomena for the enhancement of man's time upon this earth, and possibly even in the cosmos. What the specific contradictions of a particular object are and how they are resolved are questions that must be decided by scientists in the appropriate fields of knowledge. At the same time it would be wrong to assume that these highly general laws and concepts formulated by 2020 Materialist dialectics do not develop and become more concrete under the influence of new facts and in new conditions. This can be seen from the category of contradiction itself.

#356 The emergence of the Pentocracy (fifth-estate) to the global stage demands that this category should be expressed in more specific terms. Under Pentocracy contradictions will have a different character it is pointed out that contradiction and antagonism are not one and the same thing. Under Triptocracy antagonism reigns, under 'true' Pentocracy contradictions remain but antagonisms disappear.

#357 What is the difference between internal and external contradictions? There are theories in philosophy that reduce contradictions merely to the relation between things and forces that are external to one another, to the clash between them. These are mechanistic theories, 'theories of equilibrium', which regard things as being in a state of rest, free of internal contradictions, and, consequently, deny the dialectical understanding of motion as self motion, self development.

#358 Any object, being a relatively independent system, has its own internal contradictions, which are in fact the basic source of its development. The difference between several such object's external contradictions are closely connected with its internal contradictions, and interact with them. If we regard an object as an element of a larger system which includes other objects, the contradictions of the given, larger system become an internal contradiction, that is, a contradiction within the larger system. (i.e. contradiction within contradiction)

#359 The law of the unity of opposites is of tremendous importance in our search for knowledge. The condition for the knowledge of all processes of the world, their real life, is the knowledge of their unity of opposites. The question of how to express in human concepts motion, change and transition from one state to another is a crucial question that throughout the history of philosophy and science has been a challenge to the best minds and continues to challenge them today.

#360 According to certain theories human concepts can give only static reflections, snapshots of changing things, and this is seen as setting a limit to knowledge. Hence the conclusion is drawn that there must always be antagonism between objects and the knowledge of them, and that only a certain inexplicable immediate feeling (mystical intuition) can express motion.

#361 Dialectics has shown that true, concrete thought thinks in terms of contradictions that grasp the opposing sides of phenomena in their unity. It is capable of seeing not just one aspect of a contradiction and registering it in a rigid, static concept, but all aspects of contradiction, and not only their arrangement, but their connection, their interpenetration. This means that concepts must be as dialectical, that is, as mobile, flexible, plastic, interconnected and interpenetrating as the objects they reflect.

#362 Human concepts should embody in an ideal form the real contradictions, connections and interpenetrations of opposites, their transmutation, and so on.

*****

LAW

The Law Of The Unity And Struggle Of Opposites: According to this Law all things, phenomena and processes posses internal contradictions, opposing aspects and tendencies that are in a state of interconnection and mutual negation: the struggle of opposites give an internal impulse to development, leads to the building up of contradictions, which are resolved at a certain stage in the disappearance of the old and the appearance of the new. >#363

#364 Of course knowledge of this law helps us to understand the processes at work in the world, and to see what is obsolescent and what will replace it.

*****

Category 09: Negation Of Negation >#365

#366 We shall now deal with yet another important question of the doctrine of development. Is there any tendency that governs the direction of the infinite process of development? If so, then what is it? This question is also central to the struggle between various philosophical conceptions and theories and forms the subject of fierce controversy (particularly in its relation to social development)

#367 In pre 2020 Materialist philosophy there were cyclical theories which recognized the ascending development of society, but which assumed that on reaching its highest point society would be thrown back to its initial position and development would begin all over again. Such a theory was maintained by Giovanni Vico. The ideologist of the progressive bourgeoisie upheld the view that society was developing constantly, although they also regarded the third-estate system as the peak of its progress. (at the time of the French revolution they only recognized the first three estates) Later such philosophers as Oswald Spengler for instance, put forward various pessimistic theories which assumed the inevitable destruction of bourgeois society to be the end of all social development.

#368 When considering the transformation of quantitative into qualitative changes and the struggle of opposites, we saw that an essential part of the process of development is played by 'negation'. Qualitative transformation is possible only as the negation of the old state. The contradictoriness of things signifies that they contain their own negation.

#369 Negation is an inevitable and logical element in all development. In no sphere can one undergo a development without negating one's previous mode of existence. Nothing new could come about without this element. But what is negation? In ordinary consciousness the concept of negation is associated with the word 'no': to negate is to say 'no' to reject something, and so on. There can certainly be no negation without rejecting something. But dialectics regards negation as a part of development, and therefore this concept has a far deeper meaning than in ordinary usage. Negation in dialectics does not mean simply saying no, or declaring that something does not exist, or destroying it in any way one likes. **The essence of dialectical development lies in the fact that it is a mode of negation that conditions further development.**

#370 Dialectical negation has two essential features (1) It is a condition and factor of development, and (2) it is a factor in the connection between new and old. The first means that only the negation that serves as the precondition for the emergence of certain new, higher and more perfect forms is 'positive negation'. The second means that the new as the negation of the old, of what has gone before, does not merely, destroy, does not leave behind it a 'desert', but merely 'sublates' the old. (i.e. mother and daughter; father and son.)

#371 The term 'sublation' expresses the meaning and content of dialectical negation: the previous state is simultaneously negated and preserved. It is preserved in a dual sense. First, without previous development there would be no foundation for the new forms. Second, everything that is preserved from the previous stage of development passes to the next stage in a substantially different form. Thus, certain forms of mental activity which developed in the animals have been passed on to man in a 'sublated' form, and in man they have been transformed on the basis of the features that are peculiar to man (work activity, the ability to think, and so on)

#372 Development, however, is not confined to a single act of negation. Even if certain positive elements are preserved in the first negation, it is still the complete opposite of what was negated. The relationship between the initial form and the first negation is a relationship of two opposed forms. What happens next, after the first negation has produced a new form that is opposite of the previous form? This can be illustrated by tracing the development of some specific object from beginning to end.

#373 At the very beginning of its development social production assumed a form in which the workman was united with his means of labor, that is the instrument of labor belonged to the producer himself (bow, arrow and plow). There came a time the (first negation) when this became a brake on further progress in production and the means of labor became separated from the person who worked them. After a long history of slavery a new and better form arrived. (another negation). A complex development simply put is that the slave states were divided up. And the former slaves obtained a small plot of land while, under feudalism, the feudal lord retained the vast majority of land and tools of production came into the hands of the feudal lord. When this mode of production and living became a further brake on development there was another negation. When production achieved its full development under capitalist third-estate conditions the wage and salary commodity-producing workers have been almost completely deprived of the ownership of productive land and also tools of production. Thus we see in, political economy, and in history a trail of negations, and negations of negations This negation of negation can be shown to be at work in other objects and phenomena.

#374 This is dialectical negation, when an object achieves its unity, it itself logically prepares its own negation. The object has completely exhausted itself and has to give way to a new and higher form. This is another negation on the infinite road of negations. The previous negation gives way to the next negation and for this reason is known in philosophy as negation of negation.

#375 From the above example we see the necessity for the 'younger' negation, or the new stage of negation, depends on the following; the initial form and that which negates it are opposites, they contain an abstract one-sidedness which must be overcome for further development to take place. Hegel was therefore right when he defined the 'younger' (second) negation, that is to say, the negation of negation as the synthesis that overcomes the 'older' (first) abstract, untrue elements, taking 'abstract' and 'untrue' in the sense of their one-sidedness and incompleteness.

#376 Here we come to yet another important feature of the negation of negation. In the concluding stage of the whole coil of development, at the stage of the younger (second) negation, certain features of the initial form from which development began are inevitably restored.

#377 This dialectical character of development is vividly manifested in the development of knowledge. For instance, in the process of research into the nature of light, the idea was first advanced that it was a stream of light corpuscles or particles. Then the diametrically opposed theory of waves was put forward. The physics of the 20th century had to face the fact that neither of these views was a true explanation of reality. "We have two contradictory pictures of reality," said Einstein. "separately neither of them fully explains the phenomena of light, but together they do." In other words, the contradiction between two one-sidedly contradictory views was resolved by their higher synthesis in a new theory which regarded light as the unity of corpuscular and wave properties. From assertion to negation from negation to 'unity' with the asserted – without this dialectics becomes empty negation, a game, or skepsis.

#378 The effect of the law of the negation of negation is that development moves not in a straight line but in a spiral (coil), so that the ultimate point coincides with the point of departure, but at a higher level, each younger higher coil denoting a more developed state. This is the sense in which we use the term coil of development.

#379 The process of the negation of negation is often expressed in the terms 'thesis' (initial point of development), 'antithesis' first negation and 'synthesis' (second negation), which form a trinity that expresses the essence of development. The result is that the law of the negation of negation is often reduced to a purely formal and external device by means of which all the richness and complexity of the objective development is arbitrarily subordinated to a rigid scheme. Even Hegel an idealist, himself prone to schematize, protested against such understanding of dialectics, saying that the trinity is only a superficial, external aspect of the mode of cognition. 2020 Materialist dialectics is fundamentally opposed to any such formalistic approach or schematization. Like any other law of dialectics, the law of the negation of negation does not impose any schemes, it merely guides inquiry in the right direction.

#380 Analysis of the law of the negation of negation now allows us to answer the question we asked above, about whether any objective law-governed tendency exists in the endless replacement of some phenomena by others, any tendency that determines the course of development.

#381 Development is in fact, a chain of dialectical negations, each of which not only rejects the previous links, but also preserves all that is positive in them, thus concentrating more and more in the further, higher links, the richness of development as a whole. The infinity of development lies not in the infinite arithmetical addition of one unit to another, but in the emergence of new and higher forms which create within themselves the preconditions for further development. Hence the general law-governed tendency of development, from the simple to the complex, from the lower to the higher, the tendency of progressive, ascending motion.

#382 A characteristic feature of the process of the negation of negation is its irreversibility, that is, development that as a general tendency cannot be motion in reverse, from higher forms to lower forms, from the more complex to the less complex. This is due to the fact that every new stage, while synthesizing in itself all the richness of the previous stages, constitutes the foundation for even higher forms of development.

#383 In relation to the world as a whole, to the infinite universe, it would be wrong, of course to speak of one line of development, of the progressiveness of all development. In relation to individual systems however, or their elements, the tendency to ascending development is clearly observable. But there must be no over simplification in our understanding of progressive development. Like any dialectical process, it is realized in contradictions, through the struggle of opposites. Progress in some forms is accompanied by regress in others. Every ultimate form that results from ascending development creates the preconditions for its own negation. Progression itself is realized in the struggle of opposing tendencies and makes its way only through a forest of intersecting lines of development. Certain of these lines may lead backwards instead of forwards and thus express an element of regression. In short, progression must not be understood sigma-metaphysically, as a smooth process without deviations and zigzags. This fact is particularly relevant to social development, which is an arena for various classes and parties pursuing their own interests and fighting for their own aims. (i.e. the regression of Hitler Germany, the regression taking place today by 'Super Nationalism' and Super Religion and the so called 'ethnic' cleansing in Palestine, Africa, and the Bulkans, privatization of public property and so on. But overall there is an undercurrent of progress in the world despite these setbacks.)

#384 One must not forget that the law of the negation of negation operates in different ways in different conditions and in different objects. Every kind of thing therefore has a peculiar way of being negated in such a manner that it gives rise to a development and it is just the same with every kind of conception or idea.

#385 In social life and under the aegis of the UN or an organization like it the dialectical negation of the old and the assertion of the new will be characteristically a matter of consciously dealing with problems as they arise. Dealing with problems on a planned basis and under control of nations with grass roots daily democracy. The majority of which will have evolved by revolution or by evolution into Pentocracies. The old third-estate and its Triptocracy, its global depredation, devastation, death and anxiety causing ways will gradually disappear just as the first and second estates are despised and disappearing in the affairs of thinking men in our day because of their irrelevancy in human affairs. Only in this way can man save and preserve the greatest values of the material, intellectual and culture accumulated by previous development.

#386 It must be noted that so called 'cultural revolutions' which under the pretext of struggle against the 'old' destroy the precious, hard won gains of the past have nothing to offer the Pentocracies of the future.

LAW
THE NEGATION OF NEGATION >#387

The law of the negation of negation is a law whose operation conditions the connection and continuity between that which is negated and that which negates. For this reason dialectical negation is not naked 'needless' negation, rejecting all previous development, but the condition of development that retains and preserves in itself all the progressive content of previous stages, repeats at a higher level certain features of the initial stages and has in general a progressive, ascending character.

*****

Category 10 : The Individual Particular and Universal >#388

#389 The first thing that comes to mind when we consider the world around us is it variable quantitative and qualitative diversity. The universe is a unity but it exists in the form of a totality of various things, phenomena and events that possess their own individual, unique attributes. The existence of separate objects and phenomena divided from one another in space and time and possessing individual qualitative and quantitative definition is characterized by the category of the individual. This category expresses that which distinguishes one object from another that is inherent only in a given object. (a quart of milk - a gallon of milk; a litter of water - a cubic metre of water; a short war - a protracted war; a sensate being - an insensate being & so on)

#390 Any object or process is only an element in some integrated system. Not a single thing or phenomenon exists by itself. Nothing can arise or remain in existence or even change without being connected with a large number of other things and phenomena. (the milk is connected to the cow which is connected to the feed which is connected to the soil and of course all millions of systems, digestive, physiological, psychological, agricultural, transportation and so on that go into the production & distribution of milk.)

#391 The universality of the properties and relationships of things is expressed in the category of the universal. This category reflects the similarity of the properties, the aspects, of an object, the connection between the elements, the parts, of a given system and also between different systems. The universal may take the form of a definite class or group, which may be registered, for example in such concepts as 'crystal', 'animal', 'man', and so on.

#392 The universal does not exist before or outside the individual, just as the individual does not exist outside the universal. Any object is a unity of the universal and the individual. The particular is a kind of connecting link between the individual and the universal. For instance, production in general is an abstraction. It stresses what is universal and inherent in production in all epochs. At the same time this universal can be broken down into millions of divisions. It exists both as something particular and as something individual.

#393 The universal is not introduced into the individual from the sphere of pure thought. Both difference and unity are inherent in the objects and events of the real world. They are both objective indivisible aspects of being. Any one thing is both different from all other things and at the same time in some respect resembles them, possesses certain properties in common with other things.

#394 We cannot take a single step without encountering the unity of universality and difference; there is dialectics in the simplest phrases i.e. 'Jane is a woman', 'Fido is a dog', 'the individual is the universal'. Consequently, the opposites (the individual is opposed to the universal) are identical: the individual exists only in the connection that leads to the universal.

#395 The universal and its relation to the individual is given different interpretations in different philosophical systems. The sigma-metaphysical and theological 'philosophers' usually divorced the individual from the universal and counterposed them to each other. In the Middle Ages the so called nominalists maintained that the universal had no real existence, that it was merely names, or words, and that only individual things with their properties and relationships actually existed. The Realists, on the contrary, assumed that the universal existed in reality as the spiritual essence of things, that it preceded individual objects and could exist independently of them.

#396 The problem of correlating the individual and the universal cries out for solution. When it comes to the laws of the historical process. Some thinkers try to assert that the sphere of social existence is 'unique', and that all relationships in it are inimitably individual. No law can be established for that which does not repeat itself, and on this basis the low-governed nature of the historical process is rejected.

#397 Is this position valid? No. In all their concreteness individual events actually do nearly repeat themselves. Every war, for example, taken in all its individuality, is unlike any other war. But in this unique individuality of concrete events there is always something universal; their essential qualities, the types of internal and external connection. The fact that the Second World War was not like the Greco-Persian wars is no obstacle to the sociological sturdy of various types of war, even though, in their cyclical nature, there are things that never quite repeat themselves exactly.

#398 In no way does the universal level down the individuality of events. It only testifies to the fact that this unique individuality is the concrete form of manifestation of the essentially universal.

#399 The individual thing owes the concrete form of its existence to the law governed system of connections within which it arose and exists as a qualitative entity. The individual is 'dominated' by the universal. This 'power' of the universal is not something supernatural. It is not hidden in certain forces that stand above the individual things but in a system of interacting individual things, where each thing is poured into the 'cup' of the universal, revives it, enriches it, and also partakes of its vital juices. While existing and developing according to the laws of the universal, the individual at the same time serves as a precondition of the universal. This is the case for example, in the development of animate nature. Through its individual changeability an organism acquires some new and useful attribute. This individual attribute may be passed on by heredity and in time become an attribute not of one individual but of a number of individuals, that is, an attribute of a variety within the framework of a given species. This variety may later become universal – generic. Diametrically opposed processes take place in the development of organisms, when a certain generic attribute begins to die out or atrophy. Such an attribute becomes an attribute of only a few organisms, and then appears only as an exception – in the form of atavism. In this case the universal becomes the individual.

#400 The action of the universal as law is expressed in the individual and through the individual. But such a law cannot be applied to the world as a whole. In this case one cannot say that the universal arises from the individual or vise versa. Both universal and individual form a unity. While it appears to create the universal, the individual itself at the same time arises and moves according to definite laws. The individual exists only in the connection that leads to the universal, every individual is connected by thousands of transitions with other kinds of individuals, things, phenomena and processes etc.

#401 A correct appreciation of the dialectics of the individual, particular, and universal, is of tremendous importance both in the field of knowledge and its practical application. Science is concerned with generalizations and operates with general concepts, and it is this which arms us with foresight in our practical activities.

#402 Scientific research may take two paths: the path from the individual as the point of departure of thought to the particular and from the particular to the universal, and also the path from the universal and general to the particular and from the particular to the individual. In fact all real, exhaustive knowledge consist solely in raising the individual thing in thought from individuality into particularity and from this into universality, in seeking and establishing the infinite in the finite, the eternal in the transitory. The form of universality is the form of self-completeness, hence of infinity; it is the comprehension of the many finites in the infinite.

#403 Appreciation of the dialectical interaction of the individual, particular and universal arms us with a method of knowing the phenomena of social life.

#404 There are those in philosophy and politics who absolutize the individual and the particular, when this is applied in individual countries it leads to national self isolation, provincialization of its peoples as opposed to the international interest. No less dangerous is dogmatism, the essence of which lies in absolutizing general truths.

Category 11: Cause And Effect >#405

Cause = the producer of an effect.
Effect = something that is produced by an agency or cause.

#406 The concept of cause and effect have evolved in the process of social practice and cognition of the world and the cosmos. In them thought reflects the vital laws of the objective world, knowledge of which is necessary for man's practical activity. When a person finds out the causes of phenomena and processes he is able to influence them, to recreate them artificially to bring them to life or prevent their appearance. Ignorance of the causes and the conditions that evolve phenomena render a person helpless. And conversely, knowledge of causes offers people and society the opportunity of taking effective action.

#407 Cause and effect are related concepts. A phenomenon that brings into being another phenomenon is, in relation to that phenomenon, its cause. The result of the action of cause is effect. Causality is an internal connection between phenomena in which whenever one exists the other must necessarily follow. For example, the heating of water is the cause of its turning into steam and in this process there is a leap (latent heat absorption) from one state -- water -- into another state -- steam.

#408 Cause precedes effect in time. But this does not mean that every previous phenomenon is in a causal relationship with the phenomenon that follows it. Night precedes morning, but it is not the cause of morning. One must not confuse causal connection with the temporal sequence of phenomena. The superstitious person will sometimes say that the cause of a war was a comet or a solar eclipse, or some other natural or social phenomenon that occurred before the outbreak of war.

#409 Cause should be differentiated from occasion. Occasion is an event which immediately precedes another event and makes it possible, but does not necessarily engender or determine it. The connection between occasion and effect is external, superficial and inessential.

#410 The causal connection of phenomena is objective and universal in character. All phenomena in the world, all changes and processes must be induced by certain causes. There is no such thing as a causeless phenomenon, nor could there be. Every phenomenon must have its cause. We are able to detect the causal connection of phenomena with varying degrees of accuracy. The causes of billions of phenomena are still unknown to us, but the causes objectively exist. Thus medicine has not yet fully discovered the cause of cancer, but this cause exists and will eventually be discovered.

#411 There is intense conflict between materialism and idealism over the question of causality. The materialists acknowledge objective causal connection of phenomena that is independent of both will and consciousness, and its more or less accurate reflection in the human consciousness. Idealist philosophers and theologians on the other hand, either deny the causality of all phenomena of reality or deduce causality not from the objective world, but from the action of imaginary supernatural forces.

#412 The proposition that all phenomena are causally conditioned, expresses the law of causality. Philosophers who acknowledge this law and apply it to all phenomena are called determinists. Philosophers who deny the law of causality are called indeterminists.

*****

LAW
Causality >#413

The law of causality states that all phenomena of nature and society be explained through natural causes, this rules out any possibility of their being due to supernatural forces.

#414 The history of Philosophy tells us that the English philosopher David Hume (1711 1776) denied the objectivity of causal connection. Hume's proposition that we obtain our knowledge of the causal connection of phenomena from experience is correct, but the rest of his argument goes off on the wrong track. Hume reduced experience to sigma-subjective sensations and denied that they possessed any objective content. In experience we observe that one thing follows another, but , according to Hume, in the first place we have no ground for believing that the former may be the cause of the latter, and secondly, there are no grounds, proceeding from past and present experience, for drawing conclusions about the future. Hume's conclusion boils down to the following: Causality is merely a sequential, habitual connection of sensation and idea. And predicated on this basis is an expectation of that connection. Thus Hume holds that our past experience gives us grounds for expecting that in future friction will give rise to heat, but we have not and cannot have any assurance of there objectivity and necessity of this process.

#415 Proceeding from the data of science, dialectical 2020 Materialism asserts that <u>practice</u> is the proof of the objectivity of causality.

#416 Kant did not agree with Hume that causality was merely a habitual conjunction of sensations. Kant recognized the existence of causal connections as necessary in character, though not in the objective world but in the mind. He did not attribute this to experience; causality existed as a priori, innate category of intellect, on the basis of which various perceptions were linked together into a proposition.

#417 The idealistic views of Hume and Kant on causality are reproduced in various versions by neo-Kantians and also by the positivists particularly the Machists. Ernst Mach asserted that there is no cause and effect in nature, but that all forms of causality spring from our subjective desires. This view of Hume on causality is repeated by Bertrand Russell, who regards the concept of cause as a pre-scientific generalization serving only as a guide to action. The only difference between Hume and Russell in their interpretation of causality is. That according to Russell the law of causality is based not on habit, as maintained by Hume, but on an animal faith which has become deeply embedded in the language. Russell said, 'Belief in the external causation of certain kinds of experience is primitive, and is, in a certain sense, implicit in animal behavior'.

#418 Many contemporary idealist philosophers insist on the idea that the word 'cause' should be excluded from philosophical terminology. Causality, in their view, is as obsolete as monarchy. The law of causality is replaced by the law of functional connection; thus they assert that one must not say that a phenomenon A causes phenomenon B: But one must say that A and B depend on each other.

#419 One can envisage all kinds of dependencies, in the form of functional connection. The relationship of cause and effect may also be envisaged in the form of functional dependency, effect being a function of cause. However this obscures everything that really conditions effect, which is another real phenomenon. The idealists dissolve causality into functional dependency on the pretext that science is not interested in how phenomena arise, or whether there is any dependency between phenomena (or quantities) which can be expressed by definite formula. But this is a fallacious point of view. Knowledge of real causal connections is the basis of people's practical activity. Knowing cause, we can evoke phenomena desirable for society or, on the contrary combat those that are undesirable or harmful.

Cause and Effect differs from Ground and Consequent. >#420

Ground = rational or factual support for one's position or attitude.
Consequent = anything that follows upon something else without a causal relationship.

#421 Some idealists substitute for causal connection the logical connection of 'ground and consequent'. But there is a distinction between the two. Ground in formal logic is any idea from which another idea follows. For example, if one has the idea (ground) that there is a god then follows the (consequent) idea that there is an unmoved mover. If one has the idea (ground) that there is only a spiritual universe then follows the idea (consequent) 'I think therefore I am.' (but in material philosophy that is an absurd statement implying that it is thinking that creates material! It is that in the material universe there is the rock and there is the amoebae etc. - they cannot think but there they are!)

#422 Causality, on the other hand is the connection not of ideas in an inference, but the connection between real phenomena, one of which evokes the other. The principle of causality is attacked by some physicists. They maintain that modern physics has disposed of the idea that all phenomena have a cause of their existence. They believe there is no causal conditionality in microprocesses. Not a single micro-particle, for example, the electron obeys the law of causality; each one chooses its path freely from the various possibilities. The reason given is the uncertainty relation. It is true that whereas in the macroprocesses one can simultaneously define both the position and the velocity of a body, the position and velocity of a micro-particle cannot be simultaneously defined with unlimited accuracy. This law of motion of the micro-objects discovered by physicists does not fit in with the notion of causality that was characteristic of 17th and 18th centuries. It has become known in history as Laplacian determinism (Pierre Simon de Laplace (1749 1827)).

#423 The Laplacian, or mechanistic, form of determinism arose from the external, mechanical motion of micro-objects, and assumes the possibility of simultaneous exact knowledge of coordinates and impulse. In describing the processes at work within the atom we encounter the special properties of particles (simultaneously corpuscular and wave), and here the former concepts of coordinates and impulse evolved for macro-objects are not applicable in the microcosm. But from the principle of the uncertainty relation in the microcosm it does not follow that we should deny causality. The law of causality maintains only one thing: all phenomena have a cause. Just how causality operates in certain concrete cases, whether it is possible to define simultaneously the coordinates and velocity of the particles with an unlimited accuracy, is another question whose solution involves a knowledge of the concrete properties of the respective objects.

#424 Modern physics provides rich factual material confirming the universality of the law of causality and the diversity of forms in which it is manifested. Thus knowing the angle at which the electron and positron collide (in certain conditions they turn into two photons) and also their velocities, one can predict the path of motion of the two photons, Surely this proves the existence of causality in the microcosm. Micro-processes obey certain laws, they follow a certain sequence.

#425 The cause produces the effect, but the effect may also influence the cause and change it. From history it is known that the development of the merchant class caused a certain effect on the development of feudalism. The development of merchant capital was the cause of, and had the effect of, the undermining of the aristocracy. And it aided the further development of capitalism and thus the undermining of serfdom and creation of a proletariat this further accelerated the development of capitalism and so on.

#426 From psychiatry, the patient may interact with the psychiatrist so that in the course of therapy both psychiatrist and patient may be changed by the experience. Thus from every walk of life and in every material association these cause and effect relationships abound.

#427 The interaction of cause and effect implies their constant influencing each other, with the result that both cause and effect are modified. Interacting forces and factors are not of equal value, of course, it is the task of science to reveal decisive, determining causes in the system of interacting forces.

#428 The interaction of cause and effect is influenced by the surrounding phenomena, which are summed up in the term conditions. Conditions are phenomena that are necessary for the occurrence of a certain event, but do not themselves induce it. Thus a pathogenic organism may cause illness, depending on the condition, that is upon the state of health of the person it attacks. Some of these conditions may encourage the effect, while others may prevent it. Depending on the conditions, one and the same phenomenon may be engendered by different causes, and on the contrary, one and the same cause may produce different effects.

#429 Despite their diversity, the causal interconnections of phenomena do not account for all the wealth of connections in the universe. Scientists, historians, economists, lawyers, politicians, engineers, generals, labor leaders and so on cannot confine themselves to studying only the causal interconnections of phenomena; they must study phenomena in all the diversity of their law-governed connections.

*****

Category 12: Necessity And Chance >#430

#431 As we have seen, the law-governed connections and relationships of things are essential and necessary. Necessity is the stable, essential connection of things, phenomena, processes and objects of reality conditioned by the whole preceding course of their development. The necessary stems from the essence of things and, given certain conditions, is bound to occur. A distinction should be drawn between necessity and inevitability. Not everything that is necessary is inevitable. Necessity is inevitable when all other possibilities have been ruled out and there is only one left.

#432 But does everything that happens in the world occur of necessity? No, there are also chance events. Chance is what under certain conditions may occur or may not occur, may happen in a certain way or may happen otherwise.

#433 The Theologian's view of the world holds that everything in the universe, in the life of society and of the individual, is preordained by God or by fate, or by a world spirit, whose blind force is irreversible. They promote the cult of the individual in that they say that all is preordained and one can only obtain one's relief from the anxieties of this world in heaven. Belief in fate, in predestination, is known as fatalism.

#434 Ignorance of dialectics usually leads to an antithesis between necessity and chance, one of which is supposed to exclude the other. Democritus asserted, for instance, that everything occurs only through necessity. People he said invented the idol of chance so that they could use it as a pretext for their own unreasoning. Nearly all philosophers who deny chance identify it with the absence of cause. Hence the fallacious conclusion that since everything has its cause, chance is impossible. It is alleged that we describe those phenomena whose cause we cannot discover or predict as chance phenomena, whereas these phenomena in themselves are, in fact, not accidental but necessary. Spinoza believed, for instance, that there is nothing accidental in nature, that all is determined by natural necessity. The French materialists of the 18th century also asserted that everything occurs of absolute necessity and there is no chance in the world at all. "Out of whole of life," said Holbach, "there is a line that we (each and every one of us), at Nature's bidding, must draw on the surface of the globe without any possibility of deviating from it for a single moment."

#435 The absolutizing of necessity and denial of chance follow logically from the mechanistic world outlook. Its most characteristic expression was in the stand taken by Laplace "All phenomena," he wrote, "even those that are so insignificant as to appear independent of the great laws of nature are as necessary an effect of them as the revolutions of the sun. When one is ignorant of the bonds that unite them to an entire system of the universe, one makes them depend on ultimate causes or on chance, according to whether they happen and proceed with regularity or without any apparent order; These imaginary causes have successively receded with the boundaries of our knowledge and disappear entirely in the face of sound philosophy, which sees in them nothing but the expression of an ignorance of which we ourselves are the true cause."

#436 However, necessity, if absolutized, turns into its opposite. Rejection of chance, the French materialists of the 18th century reduced necessity to the status of chance. Holbach asserted that a monarch's suffering from indigestion, or a woman's whim are sufficient causes to make men go to war, to lay cities in ruins, to spread starvation and infection and create misery and grief for many centuries to come.

#437 Present day positivists deny the existence of necessity in nature and society. Thus according to L Wittgenstein (1899 1951), there is only logical necessity -- the necessity that one statement must follow another. Moreover, logical necessity does not reflect any objective laws but stems from the nature of language.

#438 Metaphysical thinking gives rise to a false alternative: either the world is dominated by chance, in which case there is no necessity, or else, there is no such thing as chance and all that occurs is inevitable.

#439 In reality necessity does not exist in 'pure form'. Any necessary process occurs in a multiplicity of accidental forms.

#440 The main difference between necessity and chance is that the appearance and the existence of the necessary is conditioned by the essential factors, whereas chance events are usually conditioned by the inessential factors.

#441 It would be wrong to think that phenomena can only be either necessary or accidental. The dialectics of necessity and chance lies in the fact that chance is a form of the manifestation of necessity and its compliment.

#442 Accidents can, in the course of development, become necessity. Thus, the law governed attributes of one or another biological species appeared at first as accidental deviations from the features of another species. But these accidental deviations established themselves and accumulate, and the necessary qualities are more or less fixed in the DNA coil and form the necessary qualities of a new organism. This quality change will depend upon the fittest 'society' of such organized individuals (quantity) to survive and this 'society' will itself not be static but will also evolve in a like manner over time.

#443 The factor of chance has never remained outside the field of vision of scientific knowledge, even when chance events are abstracted as something of secondary importance. The fundamental aim of knowledge is to reveal what is governed by law, what is necessary. But it does not follow from this that the accidental belongs only to the field of our subjective notions and should therefore be ignored in scientific research. Through the analysis of various accidental individual facts science moves on to the discovery of what lies at the bottom of things, of a certain necessity.

#444 Application of the dialectics of necessity and chance is an important factor in correct, practical creative activity. A good many discoveries in science and inventions in technology have been made thanks to lucky coincidence. However well calculated our actions, something is always left to chance. The development of production and science tends to take man out of the power of unfortunate accidents.

#445 Here are some examples: If you buy a lottery ticket it does not follow that you are bound to win a prize. Winning something in a lottery is a typical example of chance event. There is 'almost' certain necessity that someone will win a prize, this certainty is made up of all the participants 'taking a chance' in the lottery. On an historical basis let us take the peoples making up a social milieu. Let us take for example the peoples of slave societies of the past - Egypt, Greece and Rome etc. Many imperceptible chance changes in some of those societies led to the necessity of achieving a better (i.e. feudal) society, and so too, within feudal society, millions of chance changes led to the necessity of a capitalist society. What follows is not yet exactly clear to us as, but many see the necessity for change; in the bowls of this society billions of chance changes (especially in the bank and money (labor-token) systems) will eventually lead to the necessity for a new society.

#446 The distinction between statistical and dynamic laws, which plays a large part in science, is based on appreciation of the influence of chance.

#447 Dynamic laws are a form of necessary causal connection in which the interrelation between cause and effect is univalent; in other words, if we know the initial state of one system we are able to predict its future development. Thus, the prediction of solar or lunar eclipses is built on calculation of the dynamic laws of the movement of celestial bodies.

#448 Statistical laws, unlike dynamic laws, are the dialectical unity of necessary and chance attributes. In this case the subsequent states that follow from the initial state are not unique and can be predicted only to a certain degree of probability.

#449 The concept of probability is closely connected with the concept of uncertainty. Uncertainty arises when there is a choice to be made from several objects. Probability and the measure of uncertainty have a quite simple interdependence: the less the probability of choice the greater the uncertainty.

#450 A characteristic feature of statistical laws is the fact that they are based on chance that has a certain stability. This means that they are applied only to large groups of phenomena as accumulation of gas molecules, for example, obey statistical laws. The motion of an individual molecule in relation to the laws that prevail in the whole group is accidental, but from this intermingling of chance movement of individual molecules there is formed a necessity that manifests itself not completely, or perhaps not at all, in each individual case.

#451 There is also a law of large numbers, which expresses the dialectics of the necessary and the accidental. This law runs as follows: The combined effect of a large number of accidental factors produces, under certain , rather common, conditions, results almost independently of chance. In other words, the amassing of a large number of individual cases, phenomena, leads to the leveling of their accidental deviations in one direction or another and in the formation of a definite trend, of something law-governed. This trend or law is called statistical.

#452 Manifesting itself in a mass of individual phenomena, statistical law with its specific interrelation of cause and effect, of necessity and chance, of individual and universal, of whole and parts, of possibility and probability, constitutes the objective basis on which the application of statistical methods of research is based.

*****

Category 13: Possibility And Reality >#453

#454 The category of possibility and reality occupy an important place in the well-stocked armory of modern theoretical thinking. Like all other categories of dialectics, they reflect the universal connections and relations of things, the process of their change and development.

#455 Nothing can come from nothing and the new can arise only from the womb of the old. The existence of the new in its potential state is, in fact, *possibility*. A child comes into the world. She possesses a great number of potentialities -- the possibility of sensing, feeling, thinking and speaking. Given the right conditions, the possibility becomes *reality*. By reality in the broad sense of the term we mean everything that actually exists, in embryo, in maturity, and in the state of passing away. This is a unity of the individual and the universal, the essence and the diverse forms of its manifestation, the necessary and the accidental. In the narrower sense we mean by reality a realized possibility -- something that has come about, something that has developed. There is nothing in the world that is not either a possibility or a reality, or 'on the way' from one to the other.

#456 The process of development is the dialectical unity of possibility and reality. Possibility is organically linked with reality. The possible and the real interpenetrate one another.

After all, the possible is one of the forms of reality in the broad sense of the word; it is internal potential reality.

#457 Reality has priority in the interconnection between the categories of possibility and reality, although possibility precedes reality in time. But possibility itself is only one of the elements of that which already exists as reality.

#458 While emphasizing the unity of possibility and reality we must at the same time bear in mind the difference between them. The possibility of a person knowing all in the philosophy behind any science – law, engineering, medical, welding, carpentry, teaching or any other practice for example in their entirety differs essentially from the fulfillment of this possibility in reality.

#459 There are various kinds of possibility. Possibility may be 'universal' or 'individual'. A universal possibility expresses the preconditions of the general aspects of individual objects and phenomena, thus we can say that every particular (individual) thing is, as it were, at a crossroad, facing two ways. 1) 'life' facing backward toward something – birth; and 2) 'life' and facing forward toward something – death. A universal possibility is conditioned by the laws of development of reality. While an individual possibility depends on the specific conditions of existence and action of these general laws. i.e. Jane; birth; development and decay, every individual possibility is unique.

#460 Possibilities may be real (concrete) or formal (abstract). We call a possibility real if it expresses the law-governed, essential tendency of development of the object in question, and if the necessary conditions for its realization exist in reality. A formal possibility expresses an inessential tendency of development of the object while the necessary conditions for its fulfillment are not present in reality. Only formal grounds can be given in its favor. This example from Hegel gives insight into this formal aspect of possibility. "It is possible that the Sultan of Turkey will become Pope, because he is a man, and as such, may be converted to Christianity, may become a Catholic priest, etc."

#461 Formal possibility does not in itself contradict objective laws. In This sense it differs fundamentally from impossibility, that is, from that which cannot, in principle, under any condition be realized. For example, no one can make a perpetual motion machine, because this contradicts the laws of the conservation of energy. In both theoretical and practical activity it is extremely important to be able to distinguish the possible from the impossible.

#462 A formal possibility may be regarded as a possibility only in the abstraction from all other possibilities. Any amount of formal possibility fail to become reality. For example third-estate ideologists assert, for instance, that in the conditions of capitalism any poor man may become a millionaire. But this is a formal possibility because millions of poor men remain poor and might even become beggars before one becomes a millionaire. Not only that, but many millionaires become poor men in the unremitting and incessant competition and lack of cooperative effort brought about by globalization of the world economy. (It might be noted that at the end of the 20th century 1.5 Billion people live in abject poverty; in industrial countries there are 125 million people who live below the poverty line;, these grim statistics can be enumerated ad nauseum but are too lengthy for this particular work.)

#463 The difference between real and formal possibility is to a certain extent relative. A perfectly real possibility may be lost or remain objectively unrealized because of certain circumstances. It then becomes a formal possibility. At the same time a formal possibility may turn into a real possibility. For example, the possibility of manned space flight was at one time only formal, but now has become real.

#464 Possibility precedes reality in time. But reality, as a result of previous development, is at the same time a starting point of further development. Possibility arises in the given reality and is fulfilled in a new reality.

#465 As hidden tendencies expressing the different directions in the development of an object, possibilities characterize reality from the standpoint of its future. All possibilities are 'aimed' at realization and possess a certain direction. But this orientation on the future does not signify that, as the fatalists assert, the final result of any process in the world is predestined from the very beginning and is utterly inevitable. Dialectical 2020 Materialism proceeds from the fact that development is not the unfolding of a ready made collection of possibilities, but a constant process of generation of possibilities within the framework of reality, and their conversion into a new reality.

#466 Like everything in the world possibilities develop: some of them grow, others wither away. Certain conditions are required for a possibility to become a reality. There is a substantial difference between the process of realization of a possibility in nature and its realization in human society.

#467 In nature the realization of a possibility occurs on the whole spontaneously, not so in human society. History is made by people, so a great deal depends, consciousness and initiative in the process of realization of the possibilities invested in social development. And under third-estate domination every one wills their own destiny and out of it comes that which no one wills.

*****

Category 14: Content and Form >#468

#469 Any object of reality is a unity of content and form. Content cannot just exist in the world by itself; it must have some kind of form.

#470 By content is meant the composition of all the elements of an object, the unity of its properties, internal processes, connections, contradictions and trends of development. For example, the content of an organism is not merely the sum total of its organs but the whole actual process of it life activity proceeding in a certain form.

#471 By form is meant the mode of external expression of content, the relatively stable definiteness of the connection of the elements of content and their interaction, the type and structure of content.

#472 Form and content constitute a certain relationship between features of an object that are not only different but opposed to one another. Moreover, the division of an object into form and content exists only within the framework of their inseparable unity, and their unity exists only as something internally divided.

#473 There is no unbridgeable gap between form and content. They may pass into each other. For example, thought is an ideal form of reflection of objective reality and at the same time makes up the content of neuro-physiological processes.

#474 Form is not something external which is superimposed on content. For example, a fluid in a state of weightlessness and left to itself acquires a spherical form. The most splendid idea cannot produce a work of art if it is not clothed in a corresponding artistic form, in artistic images, which in this case has even further content – the artistic labor (and her whole conscious life and past labors) embodied in the particular work of art.

#475 Form is a unity of the internal and external. As the means of connection of the elements of content, content is something internal. Form constitutes the structure of the object, and becomes as it where the outward manifestation of the content. As in the example in labor there is a means of connecting one form with another form (i.e. Houses with Automobiles, Pyramids with Greek columns and so on) by means of the labor content contained within them. (This particular illustration brings in the whole economic structure behind – money, use-theory and labor-theory of value, value-added "surplus-value" which lies outside of the present scope of discussion see Economic Organon)

#476 Another example; the internal content (other than labor) of a work of art is primarily the theme, the means of connection of the artistic images and ideas that make up its external form, the sensually perceived appearance of the work, its outward presentation.

#477 Forms differ according to the degree of their universality. A form may be the means of organization of an individual object, a class of objects or an infinite number of objects.

#478 The problem of the correlation of form and content has been treated in various ways by various philosophical schools. According to Aristotle, content and form exist in the beginning as something independent of each other and only subsequently, when something takes shape, do they enter into close connection. According to the idealist Aristotle, the primary form, or form of forms, is God.

#479 In third-estate bourgeois philosophy the relationship of form and content is usually distorted, in the sense that form is divorced from content and absolutized. i.e. the outward form of a man with a house and auto and other outward manifestations of form, in this case wealth, when the content of it all is sought out this particular man may be wealthy or he may be near bankruptcy, so too, such an analysis may be carried out for the whole of national or even global society.

#480 The absolutizing of form leads to abstractionism in art where often, not always, there is little skill and hardly any labor involved in its content. In these cases form becomes a self sufficient value under the social milieu created to foster such art. (i.e. throwing paint on a canvass in the slipstream of a jet engine and so forth.)

#481 Form and content are opposites making up a unity. Their inseparable unity manifests itself in the fact that certain content is 'clothed' in a certain form.

#482 Content is the primary aspect; the form of organization depends on what is organized. Content is not formed by some external force it forms itself. Between form and content there exists internal contradictions. The emergence, development and overcoming of these contradictions are one of the most essential and universal expressions of development through the struggle of opposites.

#483 The categories of form and content are crucial to the understanding of the dialectics of development. A form that corresponds to content promotes and accelerates the development of content. There must, however, come a time when an old form ceases to correspond to the change in content and begins to act as a brake on the further development. A conflict arises between form and content.

Which may be only resolved by the breakdown of the obsolete form and the appearance of a new form that corresponds to the new content. This new form exerts an active influence on the content and promotes its development.

#484 The unity of form and content presupposes their relative independence and the active role of form in relation to content. The relative independence of form is expressed, for example, in the fact that it may lag a little way behind the development of content. A change of form is a recognition of the connection within the object. This process takes place in time, is realized through contradictions and collisions; for example in the conditions of antagonism the developing new content is in struggle with the forces of reaction and eventually the new content will result, in the end, by manifesting itself in a new form.

#485 When form lags behind content they cease to correspond to each other. Let us suppose that the aims of society (its form) correspond to its production relations (its content) during the ascending period of development there is no lag. Now let us suppose under developing circumstance that the aims of society change but the production relations remain frozen in a previous era then there is a lag in content vis-a-vis form.

#486 The relative independence of form and content is also expressed in the fact that one and the same content may take various forms. But one and the same form may have different content. A Corinthian Greek column, for example, may take the same labor content to construct as a Ionic Greek column. Or conversely two similar Ionic Greek columns may have a differing labor content. Also in another example the laws of phenomena that are different in nature may be expressed by the same formula. i.e. C speed of light.

E (energy) = MCsquared, but also M (mass) = E/Csquared – same content – different form.

#487 Appreciation of the interconnection between content and form and their relative independence is particularly important in practical activity. Flexible forms in any struggle constitute one of the most important tasks of people today.

*****

Category 15: Essence And Appearance >#488

#489 Essence and appearance are categories expressing different aspects of things, stages of knowledge, different depths in our understanding of an object. Human knowledge proceeds from the external form of an object to its internal organization. Knowledge of an object begins with determining its external properties, the relationship of things in space. Getting to know their causal and other profound law-governed relationships and properties leads to the disclosure of essence. The logic of development of knowledge and the needs of social practice have compelled people to draw a strict distinction between what constitutes the essence of an object and what the object appears to be to them.

#490 Dialectical 2020 Materialism proceeds from the fact that both essence and appearance are universal objective characteristics of things.

#491 What is meant by knowing the essence of an object? This means that we have understood the cause of its origin, the laws of its existence, the internal contradictions and tendencies of development inherent in it, and its determining properties.

#492 The essence of the third-estate's mode of control over production is private ownership of public production. The third-estate holds, at the present stage of history, the first, second, fourth and sixth and seventh-estates in a thrall. All this in order to hold the fifth-estate's public production of surplus-value for the third-estate's own private use.

But historically the mass of people in the fifth-estate is growing in people numbers while all other estates are shrinking. (except the seventh-gangster-hikikomori-estate which is also growing). Thus we have at one poll a huge number of people with little or no capital whilst at the other pole we have a few number of people with huge capital.

#493 The essence of any process may be revealed in various degrees. Our thinking moves not only from appearance to essence, but from the less profound to the more profound essence.

#494 The category of essence expresses the special reality which constitutes, as it were, the 'foundation' of an object, something stable, and fundamental in its content. Essence is the organizing principle, the nodal point of connection between the basic features and aspects of an object.

#495 The category of the universal is closely linked with the category of essence. That which constitutes the essence of a definite class of objects is at the same time their universality.

#496 Essence is what is important, determining (necessary) in an object. When we speak of essence, we have in mind something that proceeds according to law or as Lenin (1870 1924) put it "...law and essence are concepts of the same kind, or rather, of the same degree, expressing the deepening of man's knowledge of phenomena, the world...". For example Mendeleyev's (1834 1907) Periodic Law reveals the essential internal connections between the atomic weight of an element and its chemical properties.

#497 Essence and law, however, are not identical. Essence is wider and richer. For example, the essence of life lies not merely in any one law, but a whole complex of laws. When describing the essence of an object, we use categories close to the category of essence but not identical with it: the individual in the many, the universal in the individual, the relatively stable in the changeable, the internal, the law governed.

#498 And what is 'appearance'? Appearance is the outward manifestation of essence, the form of its expression. Unlike essence, which is hidden from man, appearance lies on the surface of things. Essence as something internal is contrasted to the external, changeable aspect of things. When we talk of appearance as something external and essence as something internal, we have in mind not a relationship in space, but the objective significance of the internal and external for characterizing the object itself. Appearance cannot exist without that which appears in it, that is without essence. Here too, we see a transition, a flow from one to the other: the essence appears. The appearance is essential. There is nothing in essence that does not appear in some way or another. But appearance is more colorful than essence, if only for the reason that it is more individualized, involving a unique totality of external conditions. In appearance, the essential is connected with the unessential, the accidental.

#499 Essence reveals itself both in the mass of phenomena and in the individual, essential phenomenon. In some phenomena essence shows itself completely and 'transparently', while in others it is veiled.

#500 Essence and appearance are related categories. They are characterized through one another. Whereas essence is something general, appearance is individual, expressing only an element of essence. Whereas essence is something profound and intrinsic, appearance is external, yet richer and more colorful; whereas essence is something stable and necessary, appearance is more transient, changeable and accidental, like the appearance and disappearance of clouds in the hidden essence (invisible moisture) of the clear atmosphere around them.

#501 The difference between the essential and the unessential is not absolute but relative. For instance, at one time it was considered that essential property of the chemical element was its atomic weight. Later this essential property turned out to be the charge of the atomic nucleus. The property of atomic weight did not cease to be essential, however. it is still essential in the first approximation, essential on a less profound level, and is further explained on the basis of the charge of the atomic nucleus.

#502 Essence is expressed in its many outward manifestations. At the same time essence may not only express itself but also disguise itself in these manifestations. When we are in the process of gaining sensory knowledge of a thing, phenomena sometimes seem to us to be not what they are in reality. The seemingness is not generated by our consciousness. It arises through our being influenced by real relationships in the objective conditions of observation. Those who thought the sun rotated around the earth took the seeming appearance of things for the real thing. Under present conditions, when a person works he produces his own subsistence and he is paid for this but the hidden thing is that that same person produces added value (surplus value) which only his employer sees. The added values of all global production are now washing around the globe in billions of billions of labor tokens (money). Unattached from whence they came, manipulated by super-bankers and speculators, they restlessly seek a safe haven, looking for a safe place to nestle. So what seems to be – Persons receiving full salary or wages for what they produce is not the real case, not the essence, of things.

#503 Thus to obtain a correct understanding of an event, to get to the bottom of it, we must critically test the evidence of immediate observation, and make a clear distinction between the seeming and the real, the superficial and the essential.

#504 Knowledge of the essence of things is the fundamental task of science. Someone once said that the history of science shows that knowledge of essence is impossible without considering and analyzing the various forms in which it is manifest. At the same time these various forms cannot be correctly understood without penetrating to their foundation, there essence.

*****

CHAPTER 3 >#505

THE NATURE OF HUMAN KNOWLEDGE >#506

#507 What is knowledge? What are its basic forms? By what laws do we proceed from ignorance to knowledge, from one knowledge to another deeper knowledge? What is truth? What is its criterion? By what means or methods is truth arrived at and error overcome? These and other philosophical questions are considered by the theory of knowledge, or epistemology.

#508 Materialist Dialectics Is The Theory Of Knowledge That Springs Forth From The Fifth-estate.

#509 The problems of the theory of knowledge arose with philosophy itself. In Greek philosophy analysis of the nature of knowledge began with Democritus, Plato, Aristotle, the Epicureans, the Skeptics and the Stoics. They were followed in modern times by Bacon, Descartes, Locke, Spinoza, Leibnitz, Kant, Diderot, Helvetius, Hegel, Feuerbach, Herzen, Chernyshevsky and other thinkers, who made important contribution in this field.

#510 The problem of knowledge occupies a central place in neo-materialist philosophy. Dialectical 2020 Materialism reveals the lack of substance in the philosophical theories that deny or doubt man's ability to obtain objective knowledge of nature or social reality. Despite the differences between them these theories may be characterized in general as philosophical and epistemological skepticism, to use the ancient Greek term, or agnosticism, a term that arose in the middle 1800's.

#511 The ideas of philosophical skepticism were enunciated by the Greek philosophers Pyorrhea (c365 c275 BCE), Carbides (c214 c129 BCE) and Aenesidemus (1st century BCE). These early skeptics reached conclusions that truth was in principle unobtainable on the grounds that opposite, mutually exclusive opinions are expressed on every question. They argued that neither sense perceptions nor the rules of logic offered any possibility of knowing things, and that all knowledge was no more than belief or opinion. In modern times the arguments of the ancient skeptics were revived and developed by a number of thinkers, most notably the Scottish 18th century philosopher David Hume, who maintained that all knowledge was, in essence, non-knowledge. "The most perfect philosophy of the natural kind only staves off our ignorance a little longer," He said, "as perhaps the most perfect philosophy of the moral or metaphysical kind serves only to discover a larger portion of it..." Hume recommended faith and force of habit rather than knowledge as the basis for practical action.

#512 Kantianism is the next variety of agnosticism. Kant produced a detailed analysis of the cognitive process, its separate elements: the senses, intellect and reason. This analysis was an important contribution to the theory of knowledge. But the direction and general conclusion of all his theoretical reasoning are incorrect. Kant revealed the complex and contradictory world of knowledge, but he divorced it from the things of the real world. "...Of what they (things) are in themselves," he wrote, "we know nothing, we know only their appearance, that is, the notions they evoke in us, acting on our senses."

#513 Kant is right in saying that knowledge begins with experience, with sensation. But experience as he understands it, instead of bringing man into contact with the world of things themselves, separates him from it because Kant presumes the existence in the consciousness of a priori knowledge, i.e. forms of sensation and intellect that exist prior to and independently of experience. According to Kant, knowledge is built up not out of that which is given by experience but out of these a priori forms. Apriorism brings him to an inescapable agnosticism.

#514 Agnosticism does not disappear when we come to the philosophy of the 19th and 20th centuries. It was accepted by various schools of bourgeois philosophy, particularly, the positivists and such varieties of positivism as Machism and the related philosophy of pragmatism. Recent third-estate apologist philosophy has contributed nothing original to the premises of agnosticism; it merely reproduces Kant or Hume, and more often than not presents a mixture of the two as the latest thing in philosophy.

#515 How does agnosticism treat the basic trends in philosophy – materialism or idealism? It would be an oversimplification to assume that all idealist philosophers are agnostics. Descartes, Leibnitz (1646 1716), Hegel and others were not. Hegel, as Engels observes, "...overthrew agnosticism ..insofar as this was possible from an idealist standpoint." But the idealist criticizes agnosticism inconsistently, makes concessions to it in a number of fundamental questions. On the other hand not every agnostic is a determined, consistent advocate of idealism. Often he tries to occupy a compromise position in the struggle between materialism and idealism. For the materialist the 'factually given' is the outer world, the image of which is in our sensations. For the idealist the 'factually given' is sensation, and the outer world is declared to be a 'complex of sensations', but the agnostic does not go on either to the materialist recognition of the reality of the outer world, or to the idealist recognition of the world of our sensations.

#516 Agnosticism, as a theoretical conception of knowledge which divorces the content of our sensations, perceptions and concepts from objective reality, i.e. rejects the objective content of those sensations, is idealism when it comes to solving the second aspect of the basic question of philosophy. Admittedly, not everyone who call himself an agnostic actually is an idealist. Some naturalists such as Thomas Huxley (1825 1895), who in the 19th century introduced the term agnosticism, declared themselves agnostics thus disguising their natural scientific materialism.

#517 The attitude of agnosticism to dialectics and metaphysics is equally contradictory. Agnosticism interpreted the dialectical contradictions of human knowledge subjectively. It is true that an element of skepticism is essential to the process of cognition. Since the days of the Greeks skepticism has contained a certain dialectical element. The skeptics often perceived the richness, complexity and contradictoriness of the progress of knowledge towards truth. But agnosticism absolutizes the mobility and relativity of knowledge and its skepticism acquires a negative bias. The agnostics are content to assert the relativity of knowledge, its contradictoriness, and refuse to proceed any further towards the laws of the objective world: The separation of subjective dialectics (motion of knowledge) from the objective dialectic (motion of matter) is the basic epistemological source of agnosticism.

#518 Agnosticism was rightly criticized as soon as it appeared. Its opponents were quick to point out the contradictory nature of its statements and the absurdity of its ultimate conclusions. But in this criticism there was often more wit than solid argument. The agnostic concept of knowledge arises as a reflection of the contradictory nature of the process of acquiring knowledge. But agnosticism also reflects the position of certain estates in society, their world view. To overcome agnosticism we have therefore to solve the complex problems of the theory of knowledge and to overcome, to expose and to eradicate the agnosticism's social roots. Neither the old contemplative materialism nor idealist dialectics can cope with this problem. It can be solved only on the basis of materialist dialectics, which is also the theory of knowledge of 2020 Materialists.

#519 The basic assumptions of the dialectical- 2020 Materialist theory of knowledge are:-
1) Things exist independently of our consciousness, independently of our sensations, outside us.
2) There is definitely no difference in principle between the phenomenon and the thing in itself, and there cannot be any such difference. The only difference is between what is known and what is not yet known.
3) In the theory of knowledge, as in every other sphere of science, we must think dialectically, that is, we must not regard our knowledge as ready made and unalterable, but must determine how knowledge emerges from ignorance, how incomplete, inexact knowledge becomes more complete, more exact.

#520 The theory of knowledge owes fifth-estate thinkers two things that have changed epistemology fundamentally (1) the extension of materialist dialectics to the sphere of knowledge; (2) introduction into the theory knowledge of 'practice' as the basis and criteria of true knowledge. 2020 Materialist dialectics has put an end to the isolation and separation of the laws of thought from the laws of the objective world, because it is the science of the most general laws of motion both of the external world and of human thought. There are the two sets of laws which are identical in substance, but differ in their expression insofar as the human mind can apply them consciously, while in nature and also up to now for the most part in human history, these laws assert themselves unconsciously.

#521 The subjective dialectics of cognition is thus the reflection in the process of cognition of the objective reality of the objective laws intrinsically inherent in dialectics. The basis of this cognitive process is social practice.

*****

Subject and Object >#522

#523 Knowledge does not exist in a person's brain as something primordial, it is acquired in the course of his life and is the result of cognition. The process of man's acquisition of new knowledge is called cognition.

#524 In order to understand the essence, the laws of cognition one must decide who is the subject, that is, who is the knower. This would seem to be no great problem; naturally the subject of cognition is man. But, in the first place, the history of philosophy tells us that there have been thinkers who believe that it is fundamentally impossible for man to know the essence of things, and thus rule the subject of 'knowledge' out of existence. And secondly, some thinkers and natural scientists assert that cognition and, in particular, theoretical thinking can be done not only by people but by machines they build such as computers. And finally, it is not enough merely to assert that man is the subject of cognition; one must find out what makes him the subject.

#525 Ludwig Feurebach criticized the idealist notion that the subject of cognition is consciousness or self-consciousness, correctly noting that consciousness is inherent in man alone. For Feurerbach man was a corporeal being, living in space and time and possessing by virtue of his link with nature the ability to know reality. It would seem that in his concept of cognition Feuerbach had in mind an essentially natural concrete human being. However, it turns out that in Freuerbach's theory man is only a natural and not a historically developing social being.

#526 How does man acquire his concrete, real essence? Man possesses the inherent properties of a natural being including sensory perception, but he creates his second, social nature – culture, civilization. By means of labor he creates himself, not simply assimilating the objects of nature, but changing them in accordance with his needs. Man can do this only because he is a social being, in definite relations with his own kind. Man is no abstract being encamped outside the world. Man is the world of man, the state, society. Outside society there is no man, and consequently, no subject of cognition either. (also think about the infinite number of other planets in the infinite universe with other cognitive thinking beings that have evolved upon them)

#527 But one is quite entitled to ask, surely it is not all mankind, society as a whole, that gets to know things, but separate individuals. Of course society cannot exist without individuals, who think, produce, possess their own features and abilities. But these individuals can be the subjects of cognition only thanks to the fact that they enter into certain social relations with one another and acquire the instruments and means of production and transportation accessible to them at a given level of social organization.

#528 Thus the process of cognition is determined by the historically conditioned structure of man's cognitive abilities, the level of development of cognition, which in turn is determined by the existing social conditions. by asserting that consciousness, reason does not depend on actual individuals organized in society objective idealism made a mystery of the specific feature of cognition that it is a social process. Taking the overall result of human activity enshrined in forms of consciousness, idealism presented it as an independent essence moving according to its own logic.

#529 The process of cognition, however needs not only a subject, but also an object with which the subject (man) can interact. Man himself, the subject of cognition, can be judged by what becomes the object of his cognition and practice. For example, in the time of Galileo (1564 1642) and Newton (1642 1727), the electron, although it existed in reality, did not come within the range of human knowledge. Man was not capable of discovering it and making it an object of his thoughts and actions.

#530 Only by knowing the level of development of society can we infer what object of nature will become an object of human cognition. For example, social practice is now at such a level that exploration of space is gradually entering the sphere of human activity.

#531 Man is forever bringing new phenomena of nature into the orbit of his being, turning them into objects of his activity. In this way the human world is made wider and deeper. Criticizing Feurebach's concept of reality – he does not see that the sensuous social world around him is not a thing given direct from all eternity, remaining ever the same, but the product of industry and of the state of society.

#532 Thus, a considerable number of the objects of cognition are phenomena of nature transformed by human beings. These objects of cognition are to a certain degree dependent on human practical activity. This activity creates culture, an element of which is knowledge.

*****

Practice. The Social and Historical Nature of Knowledge >#533

#534 An indispensable condition on which knowledge depends is the influence that the objects of nature and social processes exert upon man, but this process is based on the impact that man himself makes on objective reality. Knowledge develops through people's intervening in objective phenomena and transforming them. We can understand the essence of human cognition only by deducing it from the peculiarities of this practical interaction of subject and object.

#535 Mankind and nature are two qualitatively different material systems. Man is a social being and acts in an objective way. His possession of consciousness and will exerts a substantial influence on his interaction with nature, but this interaction does not thereby lose its material essence. Man acts with all the means at his disposal, natural and artificial, on the phenomena and things of nature, transforming them and at the same time transforming himself. This objective material activity of man is known as practice.

#536 The concept of practice is a fundamental theory of knowledge. Despite the hype of third and fourth-estate apologists, movie makers and what not to the contrary, social production by the vast majority of the worlds population is the most important form of human practical activity. But practice cannot be confined entirely to the sphere of production. If it is, man becomes merely an economic being, satisfying by means of his labor his need for food, clothing, habitation, transportation and so on, and his consciousness becomes purely technical in character. Practice in the broadest sense, comprises all the objective forms of man's activity; it embraces all aspects of his social being, in the process of which his material and spiritual culture, including such social phenomena as the fifth-estate's struggle for recognition and the development of art and science.

#537 In his production, labor activity, man treats nature not as an animal does, obtaining only what it and its offspring immediately require; man is a universal being, he creates things by his own yardstick according to emerging and developing aims.

#538 All forms of man's objective activity are built on the foundation of labor, production and distribution, and it is these forms that engender such phenomena as knowledge of things, processes, and the laws of objective reality. Initially, knowledge was not separated from material production: the one was part of the other. As civilization developed, however, the production of ideas broke away from the production of things, and the process of cognition became a relatively independent intellectual activity. This subsequently gave rise to the opposition between theory and practice, the contradictions of which are the subject matter for study by 2020 Materialists.

#539 In analyzing the interrelations between theoretical activity and practice, we shall see the dependence of theory on practice and at the same time its relative independence. **The dependence of knowledge on practice explains to us the social and historical nature of knowledge.** All aspects of cognition are connected and determined by society. The subject of cognition is man in his social essence, the object is a natural object or a social phenomenon which emerges in their ideal form thanks to cognition or people's practical material activity.

#540 From nature man has inherited certain biological factors on which the functioning of consciousness depends; these are the brain and a fairly well developed nervous system. But man's natural organs have changed their purpose and function in the process of social development. Thus the hand is not only the organ of labor, it is also the product of labor. It is thanks to social activity that the sensory organs, the brain and hands, have acquired the ability to create such marvels as pictures and statues, the beauty of edifices to religion and to commerce etc. that fill mans world. Even these are made more beautiful by the compositions of great masterpieces in literature, music, science and philosophy that further enhance man's delight in it.

#541 It follows from the social nature of knowledge that the development of knowledge is caused by the changes in man's objective activity, in his social needs, which determine the aim of knowledge, its target, and stimulate people to strive for ever deeper theoretical mastery of knowledge.

#542 The relative independence of cognition allows it to anticipate the immediate demands of practice, to foresee new phenomena and actively influence production, commerce and other spheres of human life. For example the theory of the complex structure of the atom arose before society had consciously set itself the goal of making practical use of atomic energy.

#543 That knowledge foretells practice is due to the development of social practice, on the one hand, and specific laws of knowledge, on the other. The connection between knowledge and the practical tasks that the individual and mankind as a whole set themselves is often of a complex and indirect nature. For example the results of contemporary mathematical research are mainly applied in other branches of science, such as physics and chemistry, and only afterwards in engineering and the technology of production and transportation.

#544 Of course, there is always the possibility of theoretical activity becoming divorced from practice. In the field of cognition this may lead to its becoming a closed-circuit system without any outlet in human practice. The systematic application of knowledge to practice is, therefore, a guarantee of its objectivity, of its ever-deeper penetration into the essence of the things and processes of objective reality.

*****

Knowledge As Intellectual Master Of Reality. The Principles Of Reflection >#545

#546 The result of the process of cognition is knowledge. The concept of knowledge is extremely complex and full of implications. Many epistemologists have concentrated on one or another aspect of knowledge and presented this aspect as expressing the whole nature of knowledge. This one sidedness has led to the exclusion of major factors comprising the very essence of knowledge with the result that some concepts of knowledge are incomplete and even misleading.

#547 The first definition of knowledge establishes its place in the process of social life. In knowledge man masters an object theoretically, transfers it to the plane of the ideal. Knowledge is ideal in relation to the object outside it. It is not the knowable thing, phenomenon or property itself; it is a form of assimilation of reality, man's ability to reproduce things and processes in his thoughts, aims and desires, to operate with their images and concepts.

#548 This means that knowledge, since it is ideal, exists not in the form of sensuously material things or their material copies, but as something opposite to the material, as a moment or aspect of the objective interaction of subject and object, as a form of man's activity. As something ideal, knowledge is interwoven with the material, in motion of the nervous system, in the signs created by man (words, mathematical and other symbols, etc.)

#549 This is what gives rise to the ideas through which man intellectually masters objects and creates images of things and processes which exist or may exist.

#550 If we say that the specific nature of knowledge lies in the grouping of ideas, we must also pose the question of their content, their relationship to objective reality. The dialectical-materialists the 2020 Materialist say this in general terms – The ideal is nothing else than the material world reflected by the human mind, and translated into forms of thought.

#551 **The relationship between knowledge and objective reality is expressed in the concept of reflection.** This concept was proposed by philosophy in ancient times. The 2020 Materialists have developed and enriched it with new content. But in some cases in the past the materialists gave the process of reflection a mechanistic coloring; reflection was regarded as the influence of objects on man, whose sense organ, the brain registered their imprint, their form, like wax.

#552 Why is such a concept as reflection needed? When discussing the content and source of knowledge, how and in which form it is connected with objective reality, we cannot uphold the position of materialism without understanding knowledge as a reflection of the things, properties and laws of objective reality.

#553 2020 Materialism in the theory of knowledge proceeds from recognition of the existence of an objective reality independent of man's consciousness, and in the knowability of that reality. Recognition of objective reality, which forms part of the content of knowledge, is directly connected with the concept of reflection. Knowledge reflects the object; this means that the subject creates forms of thought that ultimately produce properties and laws of the given object, that is to say, the content of knowledge is objective. (but as in any reflection, such as a mirror for example, where the image may be more or less distorted by the fineness or lack thereof in the irregularities of the surface; so too in human reflection where the astute reflectionist may see much further and finer than one who is not refined in the intricacies of the matter under reflection.)

#554 The idealist theory of knowledge shirks the concept of reflection and attempts to substitute for it such terms as "correspondence" presenting knowledge not as an image of objective reality but as a sign or symbol replacing it. 2020-materialists firmly protest against this because signs and symbols may quite possibly indicate imaginary objects, and everybody is familiar with instances of such signs or symbols. The idealist themselves, such as Ernst Cassirer (1874 1945), the neo-Kantian, make no secret of the reasoning for their dislike of the concept of reflection. Defending the concept of knowledge as a symbol in relation to the object, he wrote: "Our sensations and ideas are symbols, and not reflections of objects. From an image we demand a certain likeness to the reflected object, but we can never be sure here of this likeness."

#555 The idea of knowledge as reflection is today opposed by philosophers of various schools. Some reject reflection as allegedly a concept of 'metaphysical materialism' (an oxymoron if there ever was one). But 2020-materialism proceeds from the recognition of the activeness of the 'subject in the process of the practical and theoretical mastering of the object'. Thus it can be seen that the theory of reflection is presented by these philosophers as the basis of dogmatism, but true reflection of reality rules out dogmatism and catechism.

#556 Of course, reflection, seen as a lifeless copying of existing things and processes and considered apart from the subjective, actively creative influence of man, cannot serve as a characteristic of knowledge. Knowledge can be an instrument of transformation of the world only when it is objective and active, practically orientated reflection of reality. Knowledge is the mastering of objectively existing reality, it has reality as its content, that is, it reflects the properties and laws of phenomena and processes existing outside it. Without such reflection subjective activity cannot be creative, cannot produce necessary things and is no more than a fruitless exercise of the will. In other words, denial of the fact that knowledge is reflection strips knowledge of its objective content.

#557 Thus the 2020-materialist's theory of knowledge is a dialectical-materialist theory and reveals the nature of knowledge, basing it on the principle of reflection; it endows the concept of reflection with new content, extending it to include people's sensuously practical, creative activity. Knowledge is the coincident reflection of reality, tested by social practice. It is a form of human activity determined by the attributes and laws of the phenomena of objective reality, that is to say a means of purposeful and creatively active reflection of an object.

Tsunami One.   Philosophy Organon
*****

Language Is The Form Of Existence Of Knowledge. Sign And Meaning >#558

#559 Knowledge is ideal as a reflection of material reality and must be distinguished from that reality. But it does not exist outside the world it reflects, it must assume a specific material form of expression. Man as an objective being acts only objectively, and his knowledge also exists in objective form. One may operate with knowledge only in so far as it takes the form of 'language', a system of sensorily perceptible objects, a system of 'signs'. The idea of a thing, its image, cannot be conveyed to someone else except by means of 'language'.

#560 This link between knowledge and its existence in the form of language was noted by philosophers in the 1800's. The 'mind' is from the outset afflicted with the cares of being 'burdened' with matter, which here makes its appearance in the form of agitated layers of air, sound in short, of language. Language is as old as consciousness, language is practical, real consciousness that exists for other men as well, and only therefore does it exist for me.

#561 On the surface, knowledge takes the form of a system of signs denoting an object, event, action, etc. That which the sign denotes is its meaning. Sign and meaning are indivisible: there can be no sign without meaning and vice versa.

#562 A distinction must be made between linguistic and non-linguistic signs, the latter including signals, markings, and so on. Knowledge exists in linguistic signs, whose meaning is contained in cognitive images of the various phenomena and processes of objective reality.

#563 There is no intrinsically necessary, organic link between the sensorily perceived object, acting as a sign, and its meaning. One and the same meaning may be attached to different objects performing the function of a sign. Moreover, artificial formations, created for a special purpose – symbols – may also act as signs.

#564 The development of knowledge has brought into being a highly ramified system of artificial symbolic language (for example the symbol language of mathematics, chemistry, and so on.) These languages are closely connected with the natural languages, but are a relatively independent system of signs, (such a system of signs may be universal and are thus capable of crossing language barriers). Science more and more often and effectively resorts to the use of symbols as a means of expressing the results of cognition.

#565 Symbolism is widely used by certain philosophical schools to defend idealistic notions. Indeed, if knowledge exists in the form of a system of signs, and the role of these signs is more and more often performed in modern science by symbols, the idealist interpret this as confirmation of their concept that knowledge is a symbol and not the reflection of reality. Thus neo-positivists constantly stress the idea that the adoption of artificial language by science has entailed a loss of objectivity in knowledge. "The new physics," writes the idealist Phillip Frank, "does not teach us anything about 'matter' and 'spirit' but much about semantics. We learn that the language by which the 'man on the street' describes his daily experience is not fit to formulate the general laws of physics." Of course, physics has its own language, which is unlike any natural national language, but it creates such language not in order to move away from the process it studies, but to investigate them more deeply and thoroughly.

#566 Knowledge is becoming increasingly symbolical in its form of expression, and scientific theory often appears in the form of a system of symbols, but the importance of these symbols and equations is that they give a more accurate and profound reflection of objective reality. It is not the symbols themselves that are the result of knowledge, but their ideal meaning, whose content is the things processes, properties and laws studied by the given science. It is not the symbols in Einstein's formula $E = m$ (c squared) that are knowledge; knowledge is the meaning of the symbols that comprise this formula and the relationship between them expresses one of the laws of physics – the connection between energy and mass; that is, it provides real knowledge.

#567 Admittedly, it is not always easy to decide the meaning, that is, the class of objects, to which certain symbols and theories as a whole refer. The time has passed when all knowledge was, in effect, self-evident and a definite sensuous image or object could be perceived in every concept. It is no accident therefore that we are now urgently confronted with the problem of interpretation, the elucidation of the theories expressed by a more or less formalized symbolic language.

#568 The very term 'interpretation' has acquired a non-traditional meaning. It now signifies not only scientific explanation, implying a search for laws and causes of phenomena (science has never relinquished that task and it is still the most important element of scientific research). But also the logical operation of defining the cognitive significance of abstract, symbolic systems in different fields of knowledge and establishing the possible empirical content and sphere of application both of the individual terms (symbols) and statements (expressions) of theory, and of theory itself as a whole.

#569 The logical thinking of the 20th century had been much concerned with the questions involving the interpretation of abstract theoretical systems. At first glance this would not seem to be an intricate task. We have a certain scientific theory with its own specific language; in order to understand the theory we must reduce its language to another language, a more universal and formalized one, for example, the kind of language provided by modern formalized logic. In general such comparisons of two languages is extremely fruitful because it allows us to test scientific theory by rigorous linguistic criteria, to establish its non-contradictoriness, the accuracy of the terms used, and so on. But this method cannot be used to elucidate the 'objective' sphere of theory, that is, its cognitive significance and objective content.

#570 There is another means of interpreting scientific theory; this is to compare its language with the language of observation, of experiment, to seek not only the abstract objects behind the terms and expressions of theory, but also the empirical, sensuous objects that can be actually observed. This operation, known as empirical interpretation, allows us to relate the abstract theoretical system to the phenomena of objective reality. (i.e. the whole of ship building rules have been built up over many centuries; theoretical thinking going into new designs and then the empirical adjustment to the rules as experience is gained in the actual operation of the vessel at sea, failures noted, new formula devised which are subsequently tested off in practice and so on). But even the empirical interpretation does not solve the whole crucial problem – the elucidation of the whole cognitive significance of the theoretical system One and the same theory may be interpreted through different experiments which, even taken together cannot replace the knowledge it contains of the laws of phenomena.

#571 Some schools of contemporary philosophy, notably logical positivism, assume that knowledge is built up of two elements – the rules of operating with linguistic signs and the total evidence of sense perception. Therefore, say the neo-positivists, scientific theory can be interpreted only by linguistic means of formal logic or by reduction to the language and consequently to our sensory images. The untenablilty of these neo-positivist concepts lies in the fact that, in analyzing the language of science, they ignore the content of knowledge, whereas Kant, even in his day, convincingly showed that knowledge is independent of the form it is given by the process of cognition. This implies that, to understand theory and grasp its cognitive significance, to understand the knowledge of objective reality it contains, we must not confine ourselves to interpreting it by means of the language of formal logic and empirical observation, but include it in the general process of development of knowledge and of human civilization in general.

#572 By this means we can understand the part played by theory in intellectual development, in the intellectual mastery of the phenomena and processes of objective reality, and where it is leading human thought and activity. In this revealing of the cognitive significance of theory a tremendous part is played by the categories of philosophy.

#573 **From the above the conclusion may be drawn that knowledge is the spiritual assimilation of reality essential to practical activity. Theories and concepts are created in the process of this assimilation, which has creative aims, activity reflects the phenomena, properties and laws of the objective world and has real existence in the form of a linguistic system.**

Tsunami One.   Philosophy Organon
*****

OBJECTIVE TRUTH >#574

#575 For practical activity we need knowledge that reflects with the greatest degree of fullness and accuracy the objective world as it exists in itself, independently of man's consciousness and activity. Here we are confronted with the question of the truth of knowledge. What is truth? How is it possible? Where are the criteria by which we can separate true knowledge from the untrue or the false?

#576 Long standing tradition that goes back to the philosophy of ancient times tells us that truth is what corresponds to reality. But this definition is so broad that it has often been accepted by mutually exclusive philosophical schools both materialists and idealist. Even the agnostics agree with it, while putting their own interpretation on the terms 'correspondence' and 'reality'. The agnostics say they are not against knowledge in general, but against knowledge as the reflection of things and processes as they exist in themselves. So the general conclusion is that all philosophers have believed the attainment of truth to be the aim of knowledge and have recognized its existence.

#577 For these reasons the 2020 Materialist philosophy, which differs qualitatively and quantitatively from all preceding philosophical theories cannot rest content with an abstract definition of truth; it has to go further. 2020 Materialism has developed a more concrete concept of objective truth, which means knowledge whose content does not depend on a subject, does not depend either on the individual or on mankind as a whole.

#578 As we have noted, there can be no knowledge, and consequently no truth, independent of man's practical activity. This is where the objective idealist are wrong in their conception of taking truth beyond the sphere of man and mankind into some transcendental world.

#579 But on the other hand truth is only truth inasmuch as it possesses objectivity, a content that accurately reflects objective reality. Thus, such statements as "the electron forms part of the structure of the atom of any element." or the "Fifth-estate is a relatively growing power in the world while all other estates in relation to it are dwindling', are objective truths because their content is taken from objective reality. They are the state of things that exist independently of the consciousness of the people who seek to know it.

#580 Objective truth expresses the dialectics of subject and object. On the one hand, the truth is subjective it is a form of human activity; on the other, it is objective because its content does not depend either on the individual or on mankind as a whole. But it must be emphasized that in the minds of men such as religious and other idealists a 'subjective truth' exists and the whole subject of truth may be visualized as follows:-

Where ub = upper bound into untruth region.   lb = lower bound.
    at = absolute truth
    st = subjective truth = --
    ot = objective truth = ++
    ht = half truth (repeating half truths a specialty of 4E)
    l = lie

Tsunami One.   Philosophy Organon

1) The sigma subjective 'truth' flying out of bounds into the untruth and whimsical regions. >#581

```
              --              --st
ub _____ --____ -- _____--___ --___
            --          --
                 --           --
at _____ -- _____at
                              --
lb_____--___
                                 --
```

2) The objective truth staying in bounds held there, in the objective region, by its tie-in with practice. >#582

```
ub _____
                        ++
at ___++___    __++__    __++___    ++__    ++___
         ++          ++            ++ ++
lb _____
```

3) The lie and the repeating half truth falling into the lower bounds of complete and utter falsehood >#583

```
ub_____

at__ _____
      l ht
lb __l __ht_____
       l     ht
       l     ht
```

#584 Why is it necessary to consider subjective truth, half truths and lies when considering truth as a whole? To answer this question one must take the view that subjective 'truth' has led to great works in mankind, witness the great edifices and works of art dedicated to religion. As a relevant digression consider the following:-

Turning the Subjective into the Objective

Is there any condition where a subjective
truth can be made more objective?
May I paint a picture for you where you
might gain insights into this phenomenon?

Can you suppose for a minute that
a certain employer of men (and
ladies too of you so wish)
has an employee evaluation process? (EEP)

Is there not a certain
condition where subjective truth
can be brought more in line with
objective truth in such an EEP process?

Let us suppose for example
that you are such an employer
of men and those men are 'EEPed'
by other men in your organization.
(EEPors and EEPees)

Is it not that only one EEP about
the man tells very little about him?
(but tells a lot about the EEPor)

But is it not also that it is possible

Tsunami One.   Philosophy Organon

to have several EEPors give EEPs in
isolation from one another but all arriving at a
similar conclusion about a given EEPee.

Then is it not that the combined documents
will give a good profile of the EEPee?

And is it not also that this combined
subjective method will arrive at a
closer approximation to the objective
truth than a single isolated EEP?

Is This method universal in scope?
For example; can all Jews EEP, as
it were all Muslims, or visa versa?
Will this method lead to an objective
result in this case?

Can, for another example, all Catholics
EEP all Protestants, or visa versa,
and an objective result be achieved?

Is it that I must shout No! and
again, No! for is there not busted
mirrors and holy smokes 'round about?

The student is urged to think about other
ways that the subjective might,
under certain circumstance,
be brought more into line with the objective.

Prime amongst the subjective should be the
Moral aspects of life.
Think about abortion, suicide, euthanasia.
These will be discussed in the Moral Organon.

#585 As for half truths, when repeated several times a half truth is tantamount to propaganda which in itself has had a very large impact on the social practice of mankind.

#586 Denial of objective truth takes various forms. By refusing to accept the existence of a reality independent of consciousness subjective idealism also denies the objective content of human knowledge, objective truth. Pragmatism deduces truth from practice, understood as subjective activity designed to achieve utility. Bertrand Russell, a prominent figure in British neo-positivism, believed truth to be a form of faith. "...It is in fact primarily beliefs that are true or false; sentences only become so through the fact that they can express beliefs." Russell sees truth as a belief, but one that is not confirmed by fact. The question of what constitutes a fact that confirms belief is left open; it may be some external association, and so on. In other words, the objectivity of the content of knowledge as the decisive moment of truth does not figure in this theory.

#587 Objective truth is not something static. It is a process that includes various qualitative states. Dialectical materialism draws a distinction between absolute and relative objective truth.

#588 The term 'absolute truth' is used in philosophical literature in various senses. It often implies the notion of complete and ultimate knowledge of the world as a whole. This is truth in the last instance, the ultimate realization of the strivings and potential of human reason. But is such knowledge attainable? In principle man is capable of knowing everything in the world, but in reality this ability is realized in the process of the practically infinite historical development of society. 'The sovereignty of thought is realized in a series of extremely unsovereignly-thinking human beings" Each result of human knowledge is sovereign (unconditionally true), inasmuch as it is a moment in the process of cognition of objective reality, and unsovereign as a separate act, inasmuch as it has its limits which are determined by the level of development of human civilization. Therefore the desire to achieve absolute truth in the last instance at all costs is like going on a wild goose chase.

#589 Sometime the term 'absolute truth in the last instance' is used to describe factual knowledge of individual phenomena and processes the authenticity of which has been proved by science. Such truths are also sometimes called eternal: 'Leo Tolstoy was born in 1828', birds have beaks', 'chemical elements have atomic weight'.

#590 Do such truths exist? Of course they do. But everyone who would limit cognition to the achievement of such 'game show' knowledge would not get very far, for if mankind ever reached a stage at which it should work only with eternal truths, if it worked with results of thought which possess sovereign validity and an unconditional claim on truth, it would then have reached the point where the infinity of the intellectual world both in its actuality and in its potentiality had been exhausted. And thus the famous miracle of the counted uncountable would have been performed.

#591 Science has developed through overthrowing various assertions that claimed to be absolute but turned out to be true only for their time (for example 'the atom is indivisible', 'all swans are white' and so on). Actual scientific theory quite often contains an element of the untrue, the illusory, which is revealed by the subsequent course of cognition and the development of practice.

#592 But do we not then set foot on the perilous path of denying objective truth? If in the process of cognition a moment of illusion is discovered in what was thought to be true, if the opposition between true and false is relative, then perhaps there is no general difference between them? This, is the argument of the Relativists, who absolutize the relativity of knowledge. By eliminating the opposition between truth and error they come to the conclusion that truth turns ultimately into error and that the history of science is thus merely the replacement of one error by another.

#593 At this point it would do well to reiterate the definition of metaphysical: (metaphysical adj 1: of or relating to metaphysics 2 a: of or relating to the transcendent or to a (purported) reality beyond what is perceptible to the senses b: supernatural 3: highly abstract or abstruse; also: theoretical 4 often cap: of or relating to poetry esp. of the early 17th century that is highly intellectual and philosophical and marked by unconventional imagery.) But 2020 Materialism recognizes two metaphysical states the sigma and the omega for which see definitions.

#594 Relativism is correct in one respect -- its recognition of the fluidity, the mobility of all that exists including knowledge, but the Relativists metaphysically divorce the development of knowledge from objective reality. 2020 Materialism and the dialectics thereof certainly does contain relativism but it is the relativism that recognizes the 'objective' relativity of all our knowledge, that the limits of approximation of our knowledge of truth are historically conditioned.

#595 2020 Materialism's theory of knowledge, while opposing both the Dogmatists and the Metaphysical Relativists, acknowledges the existence of both absolute and relative truths, but in doing so it establishes their interconnection in the process of achieving objective truth. To be a 2020-Materialist is to acknowledge objective truth – truth not dependent upon the metaphysical whims of man or mankind.

#596 Absolute truth exists because in our objectively true knowledge there is something that is not overthrown by the subsequent course of science, but only enriched with new objective content. At the same time at any given moment our knowledge is relative; it reflects reality truly in the main, but not completely, and only within certain limits and with further movement of knowledge it becomes more accurate and more profound.

#597 In ancient Greece a geometry was developed that is known to science as Euclidean geometry. Is it true or not? We may define it as an objective, absolute-relative truth, because its content is drawn from the spatial relationships existing in objective reality. But it is true only up to a certain point, that is, while it remains abstracted from the curvature of space (regarded in Euclidean geometry as zero). As soon as space is considered with a positive or negative curvature, scientists have recourse to non-Euclidean geometry (Lobachevsky's or Reimann's), which have extended the limits of our knowledge and contributed to the development of geometrical knowledge – along the path that leads us ever deeper into objective truth.

*****

Criterion Of True Knowledge >#598

#599 In seeking objective truth, people experience a need for a criterion to help them distinguish it from error.

#600 This would appear to be quite simple. Science yields objective truth and people have worked out many ways of proving and testing it. But this is not the whole story. Proof in the strict sense of the term is the deduction of one knowledge from another, when one knowledge must necessarily follow from another – thesis from arguments. (theory - purpose - apparatus - method - observation - conclusion - thesis - antithesis - synthesis - new theory - and so on). Thus in the process of proof knowledge does not go beyond its own sphere, but remains as it were, confined within itself. This is what has given rise to the idea of the existence of a formal criterion of truth, when truth is established by collating one set of knowledge with another.

#601 The so call theory of 'coherence', which had been much publicized in the 20th century by the neo-positivists, proceeds in general from the proposition that no other criterion exists, and that truth itself is the agreement of one set of knowledge with another set of knowledge. This is established on the basis of the formal logical law of inadmissibility of contradiction. But formal logic can guarantee us the truth of a deduced statement only if the premises from which it follows are true; A follows from B, B follows from C, and so on ad infinitum.

#602 But from where, we may ask, do we obtain the general principles, the axioms and even the rules of logical deduction that form the basis of any proof? This question was asked by Aristotle. If we follow the theory of coherence, we can only accept them as conventional agreements (conventions) and thus write off all attempts to establish the objective truth of knowledge, thereby submitting to subjectivism and agnosticism in the theory of knowledge.

#603 The history of philosophy records various approaches to the problem of the criterion of true knowledge. Some philosophers saw the solution in empirical observation, in the sensations and perceptions of the individual. Of course, empirical observation is one of the means of testing knowledge. But in the first place, not all theoretical concepts may be tested by direct observation. Secondly, the empiricism of observation alone can never adequately prove necessity i.e. it does not follow from the continual (apparent) rising of the sun in the morning that it will rise again tomorrow. But knowledge that lays down laws must contain in itself both necessity and universality.

#604 Of course, scientific practice does sometimes test statements and theories by sensory experience. But this cannot serve as the ultimate criterion of truth because from one and the same theory there may follow quite different consequences that can be tested experimentally. The fact that one such consequence, or several of them taken together, correspond to experience still does not guarantee the objective truth of the whole theory. Besides, not all propositions of science can be tested by direct recourse to sensory experience. This is why even the neo-positivists, who champion the principle of 'verification' (Testing knowledge by comparing it with the data of experience, observation and experiment), have felt its unreliability as a general criterion of the truth of knowledge, particularly when dealing with scientific theories that possess a large degree of universality. To rescue the principle of verification, they go on inventing ever wider interpretations of the concept of 'experimental verifiability', on the one hand, while limiting the sphere of its application (not all true ideas can be tested experimentally, etc.), on the other. Some of them have proposed that verifiability should be replaced by falsifibility, that is the attempt to find experimental data that refute rather than confirm the theory.

#605 Disproving what appear to be facts are of course, essential to science, particularly as a means of establishing the limits of applicability of a given theoretical system. But this method cannot be used to prove an objective truth.

#606 If empirical observation is not a criterion, then perhaps, general principles, axioms, the rules of logical deduction, etc. may be regarded as true simply because they are clear and obvious, that is to say, their truth is self-evident and requires no proof, since the opposite would be simply unthinkable. But modern science is essentially critical and cannot rely either on faith or self-evidence, and paradox is common in its statements.

#607 2020-Materialism has solved the problem of the criterion of truth by showing that it lies ultimately in the activity which is the basis of knowledge, that is social historical practice. The question whether objective truth can be attributed to human thinking is not a question of theory but a practical question, man must prove the truth i.e. the reality and power, the this-worldliness of his thinking in practice.

#608 What gives practice its strength as a criterion of truth? The criterion of true knowledge must possess two qualities. First, it must undoubtedly be sensuous and material in character, it must take man out of the field of consciousness into the world of objects, because it is the objectivity of knowledge that must be established. Second, knowledge, particularly the laws of science, has a universal character, and the universal and infinite cannot be proved by one individual fact or by any number of them taken together. Man's practical activity, the nature of which is intrinsically universal, possesses this special feature.

#609 A person 'definitely' grasps objective truth only when the notion becomes 'being-for-itself' in the sense of practice. Moreover, in practice the universal acquires the sensuously concrete form of a thing, a process, and so it has in itself 'not only the dignity of universality, but also of immediate actuality'. in other words, in practice the objectivity of knowledge which is universal in character acquires the form of sensuous authenticity. This does not mean, of course, that from the standpoint of 2020-Materialists epistemology every concept, every act of knowledge must be directly tested in practice, in production or some other form of human activity. In reality the process of proof takes the form of deducting one set of knowledge from another, that is, the form of a logical chain of reasoning, some of whose links are tested by application in practice. But does not this suggest the idea that besides practice there exists criterion based on the logical apparatus of thought, on the collation of one set of knowledge with another? Of course, the forms and laws of logical deduction do not depend on separate acts of practical activity, but this does not mean that they are in general unconnected with practice and not engendered by it. The practical activity of man had to lead his consciousness to the repetition of various logical figures thousands of millions of times in order that these figures could obtain the significance of axioms.

#610 Practice is not a fixed state, but a process formed of individual elements, stages and links. Knowledge may overtake practice of one historical period or another. There may be not enough available practice to establish the truth of the theories that are advanced by science. All this indicates the relativity of the criterion of practice.

#611 But this criterion is simultaneously absolute because only on the basis of practice of today or tomorrow can objective truth be established. The criterion of practice can never, in the nature of things, either confirm or refute any human idea completely. This criterion too is sufficiently 'indefinite' not to allow human knowledge to become absolute, but at the same time it is sufficiently definite to wage a ruthless fight on all varieties of idealism and agnosticism. As it develops practice overcome its limitations as a criterion of knowledge. Developing practice cleanses knowledge of all that is false and urges it on to new results that human kind needs.

*****

CHAPTER 4 ># 612

DIALECTICS OF THE PROCESS OF COGNITION ># 613

#614 Cognition takes place as a passing from ignorance to knowledge, from one knowledge to another, deeper knowledge, as movement towards objective, ever fuller truth with more and more facets. This process is made up of a multitude of elements and aspects that have a necessary connection with one another. As epistemology, materialist dialectics explains what is meant by cognition and reveals the interaction of its basic components, their role in the attainment of truth.

#615 Philosophy long ago single out the two elements that make up cognition. These are the 'sensory' (sensations, perceptions and representations) and the 'rational' (thought in its various forms, concepts, propositions, inferences, hypotheses, theories). This at once gave rise to the question: what is the significance of these elements in the origin and development of knowledge? How are they related? There have been of course many different answers to these questions.

#616 The adherents of sensationalism assume that the decisive role in cognition belongs to the sensory element, to sensations and perceptions. Here we have a sound idea because it is indeed only through sensations that a person is connected with the external world. The first premise of the theory of knowledge undoubtedly is that the sole source of our knowledge is sensations. But the nature of man's sensations and perceptions, their role in cognition, may be understood in different ways.

#617 Idealist sensationalism (Berkeley, Hume, the Machists) regards sensations and perceptions as the ultimate reality that we can know; it either repudiates the existence of reality outside cognition or dismisses the question of the source of sensations and perceptions as absurd. Moreover, the idealist often try to make capital out of the actual contradictions in the sensory reflection of reality. (every reality is distorted more or less by its reflection, just as is made evident by the relative true-ness to the eye that beholds those reflections of the room sent forth by a mirror or by the polished surface of a bent samovar).

#618 The 'physiological' idealism that emerged in the 19th century with its narrow interpretation of physiological data about the sense organs assumes that an external stimulus only gives an impulse to sensation but in no way determines its content. The content depends on the 'intrinsic energy' of every sense organ (i.e. according to them the sense organ does not perceive the object, the object perceives the sense organ – a completely non-sensical point of view.) If the problem is stated in this way sensations are virtually isolated from the external world and their content is interpreted as something subjective. A subjectivity which can at best perform the role of a symbol, a hieroglyph in relation to the objects of the external world, and this conclusion obviously leads to agnosticism.

#619 At the other extreme we have the view of sensations known as 'naive realism'. Its adherents assume that things and processes existing outside the human mind are exactly the same as what man feels and perceives. The individual and his nervous system allegedly play no part in forming sensations.

#620 In reality the sense organs do influence the formation of sensations. A sensation is a subjective image of the objective world. If color is a sensation only depending upon the retina then light rays falling on the retina produce the sensation of color. This means that outside us, independently of us and of our minds, there exist a movement of matter, let us say of waves of a definite length and a definite velocity and a definite packet. This wave-packet which, acting upon the retina, produce in man the sensation of a particular color – This is materialism; matter acting upon our sense-organs produces sensation. Sensation depends on the brain, nerves, retina etc., on matter organized in a definite way.

#621 As the source of human knowledge sensations and perceptions are to be trusted. Within certain limits they give us notions of the external world that correctly reflect reality. This coordination between sense data and the external world is the result of the evolution of living beings, their adaptation to the environment.

#622 But although sense data provide the source of knowledge, they are not its whole content. The thesis of sensationalism proclaimed by John Locke (there is nothing in the reason that was not originally in the senses), expresses the sigma-metaphysical-narrowness that bears the name 'empiricism' From the standpoint of empiricism knowledge not only takes its source from sensations and perceptions; it never goes beyond them. To thought, empiricism grants only the role of summing up, arranging the data of experience, which is understood as the totality of man's sensations and perceptions. The empiricism of the materialist philosophy of the 17th and 18th centuries was progressive inasmuch as it encouraged experimental research and helped to rid knowledge of speculative scholasticism. Subsequently, however, empiricism became one source of agnosticism and various kinds of superstition. This was because in its contempt for theoretical thought it led science to operate with obsolete concepts or, as someone remarked...this resulted in some of the most sober empiricists being led into the most barren of all superstitions, into 'modern' spiritualism.

#623 Contemporary empiricism takes the form of neo-positivism or logical positivism. Although not opposed to thought in general, it allows it only in the form of logical calculus (logical proof, operations and signs). The neo-positivists try to find and single out in modern science certain initial elements (statements and terms) which can be related to immediate sense data. These data are taken as the basis of knowledge, all other knowledge being reduced either to this basis or to logical rules of deduction, which are conventional i.e. a matter of agreement between scientists. The whole course of development of science has convincingly demonstrated, however, that knowledge cannot be reduced to the two elements of experimental and logical signs. It embraces the whole complex, synthesizing activity of human reason.

#624 Whereas the empiricists exaggerate the role of sensory reflection the representatives of another school known as 'rationalism' absolutize the role of thought in cognition. In opposition to the sensory contemplation of the empiricists the rationalists (Descartes, Spinoza and others) advocate super sensory, allegedly independent of sense data 'pure thought' able to deduce new knowledge logically, unsupported by experience. They advanced the concept of 'intellectual intuition' by means of which the reason, by passing the data of the senses, could gain direct knowledge of the essence of things and processes. This belittled the role of sensory experience. Experience henceforth only gave impetus to thought or served merely to corroborate speculative deductions. Logically developing these concepts, some rationalists (Descartes) arrived at the idea of the existence of 'innate knowledge' specifically in the form of fundamental concepts of mathematics and logic. Declaring these 'innate' ideas to be absolute truths, the rationalists tried to deduce from them the basic content of scientific knowledge.

#625 The 'apriorism' of Kant is a somewhat toned down, diluted form of rationalism. According to Kant, knowledge springs from two sources (1) the data of sensory perceptions that provide the content of knowledge and (2) the forms of sensuousness and intellect which are a priori (independent of experience). Kant is quite right in assuming that knowledge arises as a result of the synthesis of the sensory and the rational, but he divorces these two elements from each other. Sensory perceptions are connected with the influence on the sense organs of 'things-in-themselves', which are independent of the consciousness, whereas the rational forms of cognition (categories) are rooted in the priori pre-experience abilities of the intellect. Thus having correctly understood the categories (most general concepts) as forms of cognition Kant failed to see that they are such only because they reflect the true relationships and forms of the objective world. The forms of thought do exist independently of specific, individual experience, but they have arisen and developed on the basis of the sensuously objective activity of mankind as a whole. Kant was wrong in treating them as forms that are innate in man.

#626 Cognition begins with the living, sensory contemplation of reality. Man's sensory experience (sensations, perceptions, representations or images) are the source of knowledge linking him with the external world. This does not mean that every individual act of knowing begins with experience. Knowledge is not inherited in the biological sense, but it is passed on from one generation to another. There are forms of knowledge that theoretically generalize the experience of previous generations and these forms are independent of the 'particular experience of each individual'.

#627 Knowledge is not only that which is provided by the sense organs. With the help of various forms of thought it goes beyond the bounds of sensory images. Even such simple judgement as 'the rose is red' is a form of the connection between sensations and perception on the basis of the concepts of flowers, their coloring etc. Without concepts a person cannot express in language his sensory experience. This is why there is no such thing as 'pure' sensory contemplation. In man it is always permeated with thought. Nor is there any such thing as 'pure' thought, since the latter is always connected with the sensory material, even if only in the form of images and signs.

#628 Living sensory contemplation of reality may be regarded as direct only in the sense that it links us with the world of things, their properties and relationships, but it is conditioned by previous practice, by the existence of formed language, and so on. No knowledge can be acquired without previously digesting the results of sensations.

#629 Thus knowledge is unity of the sensory and the rational reflection of reality. Without sensory representation, images, man can have no real knowledge. Many of the concepts of modern science, for example, are extremely abstract, and yet they are not entirely free from sensory content not only because they owe their origin in the final analysis to human experience and their inclusion in the results and course of man's intellectual development.

*****

Levels Of Knowledge: Empirical And Theoretical, Abstract And Concrete. Unity Of Analysis And Synthesis. >#630

#631 The sensory and the rational are the basic elements of all knowledge. But in the process of cognition we may distinguish different level, qualitatively unique stages of knowledge that differ in their fullness, depth and range, in the means by which their basic content is achieved, and in the form of their expression.

#632 Here we find such levels as the 'empirical' and the 'theoretical'. By the empirical we mean a level of knowledge whose content is basically obtained from experience. (from observation and experiment i.e. the construction of a ship is based upon the past experience and observation of such a structure under severe sea states and failures and weaknesses noted and their findings brought to bare on new better structures for the future.) In a similar manner such empirical methods may be used in psychological medicine and so on.) Thus it is subjected to a certain amount of rational and theoretical treatment, that is expressed in a certain language. At this level of knowledge the object of cognition is reflected in those of its properties and relationships that are accessible to sensory contemplation. For example, in modern physics even elementary particles are accessible to empirical cognition. In a cloud chamber or in a powerful accelerator particles are sensually perceived by the researcher in the form of photographs of their tracks, and so on. The results of these observations and measurements are registered in a certain language. The data of observation and experiments are the empirical basis on which theoretical knowledge is built. So much importance is attached to obtaining these data that in certain sciences a division of labor has occurred with the result that one group of scientists may specialize in experimental research, while another engages mainly in theoretical study. It is no accident that we speak today of experimental physics, biology, physiology, psychology, etc. Experiment is being ever more widely applied in the social sciences as well.

#633 Theoretical cognition is on a different level from the empirical. At the theoretical level the object is reflected in its connections and laws, which are discovered not only by experiment but through abstract thinking. The task of theoretical knowledge is to resolve the visible, merely external movements into true intrinsic movement. In theoretical knowledge the sensory provides a certain basis and form of expression (a system of signals) for the results obtained by thought.

#634 In any field of science we encounter theories in which knowledge not only goes far beyond the bounds of sensory experience, but sometime contradicts the sensory data (i.e. the sun around the earth – or the earth around the sun question of the ancients). This contradiction is dialectical; it disproves neither the theoretical postulates, nor the empirical data. Take for example Einstein's theory of relativity, quantum mechanics, Lobachevsky's geometry and much else. Experience tells us nothing about the constant velocity of light; when Max Planck proposed that light is emitted in quanta, in packets, there was no experimental confirmation of this fact; when Lobachevsky (1793 1856) proposed the axiom 'through a point that is not on a given straight line there passes at least two straight lines that are in the same plane as the given line and do not cross it.' he did not base his proposition on any visual conceptions of space; in fact, he contradicted those that existed.

#635 The empirical and the theoretical levels of knowledge are closely interconnected. First, theoretical constructions arise from generalization of previous knowledge, including that which is obtained through observation and experiment. This, of course, does no imply that all theories come directly from experience; some of them take ready existing concepts and theories as their point of departure. But if we take not separate theories but theoretical knowledge as a whole, it is of course directly or indirectly connected with empirical knowledge.

#636 Theoretical knowledge can and should anticipate experimental data. Theoretical physics produced the idea of the existence of ant-particles long before they were experimentally detected. But it would be a mistake to assume that in this case there was nothing for observation and experiment to do but record the results of theory. When scientists discovered the positron in cosmic rays, this was a brilliant experimental confirmation of the quantum equation invented by the British physicist Paul Dirac (1902 1984), which implied the existence of an electron with two opposite electrical charges, negative and positive. But empirical observations also corrected Dirac, who held that the particle symmetrical to the electron was not a positron but a proton.

#637 Thus the development of knowledge presupposes constant interaction of experiment and theory. Absolutization of either is disastrous to the development of science. Even so, it is theory and not experiment that is the goal of science; scientific development depends not so much on the quantity of empirical data as on the quantity and quality of the well founded theories it produces. Present day research in many fields of both natural and social sciences, having accumulated considerable empirical material, is experiencing a need for new fundamental theories on the basis of which it would be possible to generalize and systemize this material and move on from there.

#638 The level of knowledge is determined not only by the means by which it is attained, experimental or theoretical, but by how the object is reflected -- in all its connections and manifestations or in only one aspect, although perhaps a very important one. From this standpoint knowledge is classified as concrete or abstract.

#639 In principle, knowledge seeks to become concrete, that is to say, many sided, embracing the object as a whole. But this very concrete-ness may be of different kinds. In a person's sensory experience an object may be given in many connections and relationships, and therefore sensory concrete-ness is limited in content: it does not give man an exhaustive knowledge of a phenomenon or it laws.

#640 To rise to a higher level of concrete-ness one must first view the object or group of objects from one particular angle, having eliminated the others by abstraction. In this sense thinking may be regarded as a means of knowing reality through abstraction.

#641 'Abstraction' is very important means of reflecting objective reality through thought. Abstraction brings out the essential in any given relationship. Moreover, by singling out any particular property or relationship, thought can abstract itself even from the things and phenomena to which their properties and relationships belong. Thus we arrive at the qualities of 'white-ness', 'beauty', heredity', 'electrical conductivity', and so on. Such abstractions are known in logic as abstract objects.

#642 In the process of abstraction thought does not confine itself to singling out and isolating a certain sensually perceptible property or relationship of an object. (if so abstraction would not overcome the defects of sensory concrete-ness.), But abstraction tries to lay bare the connection hidden from and inaccessible to empirical knowledge. Thus 'immersion in abstraction' is a means of knowing the object more profoundly. "Thought proceeding from the concrete to the abstract – provided it is correct – does not get away from the truth but comes closer to it. The abstraction of matter, of law of nature, the abstraction of value, etc. in short all scientific (correct serious, not absurd) abstractions reflect nature more deeply, truly and completely. Modern science, which has made abstraction the main instrument for penetrating the essence of things and processes, confirms this fact.

#643 But no abstraction is all powerful. It is the means by which human thought singles out individual properties and laws in the object. By means of abstraction the object is analyzed in thought and broken down into abstract definitions. The formation of these definitions is the means of attaining new concrete knowledge. This movement of thought is known as the ascent from the abstract to the concrete. In the process of this ascent the object is reproduced by thought in its entirety. Such a process first described by Hegel.

#644 **Movement from the sensuously concrete through the abstract to the concrete in thought is a law of the development of theoretical knowledge.** The concrete in thought is the most profound and meaningful knowledge. For example in economic relations one may begin his analysis with abstract definitions of commodities and go on from there to build a picture of the third-estate's economic and political relations to other estates.

#645 Truth cannot be objective if it is not concrete. If it is not a developing system of knowledge, if it does not constantly enrich itself with new elements expressing new aspects and connections of the object and deepening our previous scientific ideas. In this sense truth is always a theoretical system of knowledge that seeks to reflect the object as a whole.

#646 The movement from sensuously concrete through the abstract to the concrete in thought which takes place on the basis of practice includes such operations as analysis and synthesis. To abstract a phenomenon or object we must split it up mentally into its properties, relationships, parts, stages of development, and so on. On the other hand, the construction of the concrete in thought proceeds on the basis of synthesis, the unifying of the various properties and relationships discovered both in the given object and in other objects. For example, modern science has reduced the emission of solar energy and the thermonuclear reaction to a single principle.

#647 This combination in thought of various phenomena, aspects and properties is itself made possible by objective laws. Thought can bring together into a unity only those elements of consciousness in which or in whose real prototypes this unity already existed and now, at the given historical juncture, is laid bare before us.

#648 Knowledge cannot make any real step forward by only analyzing or only synthesizing. Analysis must precede synthesis, but analysis itself is possible only on the basis of what has been synthesized; the link between analysis and synthesis is organic and intrinsically necessary.

*****

The Historical And The Logical Forms Of Reproduction Of The Object By Thought >#649

#650 Reproducing an object in thought in all its objectivity and concrete-ness means cognizing it in development, in history. So among all the various means of attaining knowledge two methods are outstanding: the historical and the logical.

#651 The historical method involves tracing the various stages of development of objects in their chronological sequence, in the concrete forms of their historical manifestation. Let us say, for example, that we have to reproduce the development of the modern estates system. The historical method requires that we should begin the description of the process from its inception and development in certain countries of Europe and America with numerous details and concrete forms that express both the universal, the necessary, and the particular, the individual, and even the accidental. This method has its merits, inasmuch as it attempts to present the historical process in all its diversity, including its unique and individual features.

#652 But to reveal the history of an object, to single out the main stages of its development and basic historical connection one must have a theoretical concept of the object, of its essence. The other method – the logical method – does in fact aim at reproducing in theoretical form, in a system of abstractions, the essence, the main content of the historical course. This kind of inquiry begins with an examination of the object in its most developed form.

#653 The logical method has its merits and certain advantages over the historical. In the first place, it expresses the object in its most essential connections; secondly, it provides simultaneously an opportunity of knowing its history. The point where this history begins must also be the starting point of the train of thought, and its further progress will simply be the reflection, in abstract and theoretically consistent form, of the historical course. Though the reflection is corrected, it is corrected in accordance with laws provided by the actual historical course, since each factor can be examined at the stage of development where it reaches its full maturity, its classical form. Thus the logical method reflects in theoretical form simultaneously both essence of the object, the necessity and the laws and also the history of its development because in reproducing the object in its highest, most mature form. Such form must include its previous stages, sublated, as it were, we thus also arrive at a knowledge of the main, the basic stages in its history.

#654 The logical method is not merely a speculative deduction of one concept from another. It is also based on reflection of the real object, but only at the essential points in its development, and not necessarily following the temporal and perceptible connection between these points, as it appears on the surface.

#655 In the political economic sphere – for example in 'Capital', the writer proceeded on the basis of the logical method of inquiry. He does not expound the history of capitalist production relations in a systematic, chronological way; he examines the present economic structure in its mature, classic form, However he simultaneously give the history of the system and the analysis of the concepts summing it up. We can see this from any concept that we care to choose as an example. In this way the logical sequence in the changing forms of value (elementary, expanded, general, money, labor-token) reflects their replacement in the course of history.

#656 The historical and logical methods of research are closely interconnected. On the basis of the unity of the historical and the logical one can, as required, make a special study either of the history of development of an object or of its contemporary structure.

#657 The historical method of research is absolutely justified when its goal is study of the history of the object itself. Even here, however, unity of the logical and historical i.e. our study of the history of the object in all its diversity, with all its zigzags and accidents, should be our guiding principle leading us to an understanding of the object's logic, its laws, the basic stages of its development. Not only does logic lead to history; historical research itself proceeds from certain concepts generalizing history and embracing the essence of the objective inquiry.

#658 The logical reproduction of the object in thought proceeds in certain forms. Knowledge is the reflection of nature by man. But it is not a simple, not an immediate, not a complete, reflection. But it is the process of a series of abstractions, the formation and development of concepts and laws. Here there are actually objectively, three members (1) Nature, (2) Human Cognition, (3) the form of reflection of nature in human cognition, and this form consists precisely of concepts laws and categories.

#659 The form of thought is the pattern by means of which objective reality, the object in its historical development, is reflected in a system of consistent, interconnected abstractions. Abstractions differ not because one deals with a particular object of nature or society while another deals with another such object, but because they have different functions in thought. These various patterns of thought have been shaped by the goals of man's search for knowledge, and it is thanks to them that an object may be known comprehensively, in its actual parts as a whole.

*****

The Basic Logical Forms Of Thought Are The Proposition, The Concept, And The Inference. >#660

#661 The traditional meaning of proposition in logic is a thought that affirms or denies something about something: 'hydrogen is a chemical element', 'a commodity has value' A proposition reveals all the characteristics features of the thought in question. The process of thinking begins when we pick out certain individual attributes and properties of objects and make certain elementary abstractions. All real knowledge takes the form of propositions or systems of propositions. Even the expression of the results of living, sensory perception in rational form acquires the form of a proposition. For example 'this house is bigger than that.'

#662 Any proposition reveals the connection between the particular and the universal, between identity and difference, the accidental and the necessary, and so on. The fact that identity contains difference within itself is expressed in every sentence, where the predicate is necessarily different from the subject. 'the lily is a plant,' 'the rose is red', (note the difference 'a rose is a rose' = a tautology) where, either in the subject or in the predicate there is something that is not covered by the predicate or the subject that from the outset identity with itself requires difference from everything else as its compliment is self-evident.

#663 Cognition leads logically to the singling out of the universal and the essential in the object under consideration, that is, to a concept, which sums up this or that stage in the cognition of the object and expresses the knowledge attained in concentrated form. Human concepts are not fixed but eternally in movement, they pass into one another, they flow into one another, otherwise they do not reflect either living life or inanimate matter. The analysis of concepts, the study of them, the art of operating with them always demands study of the movement of concepts, of their interconnection, of their mutual transitions.

#664 Revealing the dialectics of the movement of concepts means discovering the laws of their development. The development of concepts procedes in two main directions: (1) new concepts arise reflect the objects and phenomena which have become the target of theoretical inquiry; (2) old concepts are concretized and raise to a higher level of abstraction. The rethinking, clarifying and enrichment of the basic concepts that form the categories of a given science are of particular importance. Revolutions in science are accompanied by radical upheavals in its fundamental concepts, by changes in the content of the old concepts and emergence of the new one that change the system and method of the thought of scientists. (and eventually at some stage the whole population comes to see the new concepts and embraces them.)

#665 No concept can exist outside its definition, in the process of which it is aligned with another, wider concept. Revealing the essence of an object entails revealing the general. However, to have a concept it is not enough merely to point out what is general. So definition always involves stating to what immediate species the object belongs, i.e., a more general concept, and also indicating the 'special features' of the species in question. For example, the concept of 'stars' may be defined at an early period in history as follows; 'Stars are natural celestial bodies that emit light.' and at another more advance period as follows: 'Stars are natural celestial bodies that emit light as well as many other electromagnetic waves.'

#666 There can be no concept or even any thought processes as such without 'inferences'. Inferences are the means by which we obtain new knowledge on the basis of previously established knowledge without resorting to the experiences of the senses. Inference is the only process by which we deduce certain propositions (conclusions) from other judgements (premises); it is thus a system of proportions. Inference expresses the ability of theoretical thought to go beyond the bounds of what is given by direct sensory experience, observations and experiments. If man were unable to acquire new knowledge through inference, he would for example, never have been able to calculate the distance from Earth to other celestial bodies. He could not tell what the stars are made of, or penetrate into the world of the atom and the elementary particles of which it consists. A conclusion is drawn from certain premises, but it does not merely repeat them; it produces something new, something that enriches knowledge.

#667 Propositions, concepts and inference are interconnected; if one changes the others must change also. This interdependence shows itself in the process of thought, which includes (1) definitions of the properties of the object (proposition) (2) summing up of previous knowledge, formation of scientific concepts, (3) transition from one, previously attained set of knowledge to another (inference).

#668 All these elements exist in scientific theory, which is relatively self contained and yet sufficiently broad system of knowledge describing and explaining a certain group of phenomena. Propositions form the principles and statements of theory, concepts are its terms, and the various inferences are the means of obtaining knowledge through deduction.

#669 The function of theory is not only to systemize the results obtained by cognition, but to point the way ahead to new knowledge.

#670 Theories in science may be of different kinds depending on the object which they reflect, on how wide the range of phenomena they describe, and on the means of proof that they use. An unusual form of theory is the so-called 'metatheory' that is the theory about theory.

#671 The emergence of metatheories and metasciences is something new and characteristic of the development of knowledge in the 21st century; it is evidence of an interest in the structure, the ways of building theory and its development. The process of integration of theories, the creation of 'unifying theories', is also characteristic of the present day. The combination of theories that have been evolved at different times to explain different things into a single new theory with different principles is proof of the movement of knowledge along the path of objective truth. Even theories created by different sciences are now being combined. The solution of the problems connected with metatheories, with the combination and integration of theories, demands further intensive elaboration of logic.

*****

Dialectics And Formal Logic >#672

#673 Logic studies the forms of thought. It is traditionally supposed to have been founded by Aristotle, who first collated and systemized the problems that later became known as the problems of logic. In modern times great contributions to the development of logic was made by Francis Bacon and other philosophers. By the 17th and 18th centuries a branch of philosophy had taken shape known as traditional or classical, formal logic. Its laws included the laws of proof, and it regarded the forms of thought as the principles of being itself.

#674 Formal logic was further developed on the one hand by new means of logical analysis and, on the other, by the study of new forms of proof suggested by the development of scientific knowledge. Various systems of mathematical symbols were evolved for solving logical problems; the use of formal logic in mathematics particularly for proposes of proof led to a development of formal logic itself. This was how the variety of formal logic, known as symbolic or mathematical logic, arose. Today this form of logic is used primarily to analyze synthetic, formalized languages; it studies their syntax and semantics. Logical syntax formulates the rules of the construction and transformation of linguistic expressions only from the formal standpoint, without taking into consideration their content; logical semantics analyze linguistic systems in order to discover the meaning of their elements.

#675 The formal logical analysis of theoretical knowledge has produced great results. Cybernetics, for example, would be impossible without this method of analyzing knowledge on the basis of synthetic, formalized languages. This method allows us to analyze existing knowledge, suitably rearrange it, express it in a system that is as strictly formalized as possible and transfer certain functions of human thought to a computer. Analysis of knowledge by means of formal logic leads to the production of new knowledge by helping to identify certain missing elements and links that are needed for the construction of a strictly formalized theory and indicating where they are likely to be found.

#676 Logic developed not only through separating formal logic as an independent science, which later evolved into symbolic logic with a specified subject-matter and method of study. The study of the forms and methods of theoretical thought leading to objective truth also developed within the framework of philosophy. Continuing this line of development, materialist dialectics has emerged both as a theory of knowledge and as dialectical logic. Dialectical logic arose as a continuation and development of previous logical theories. It does not deny the importance of formal logic, but seeks to define its true place in the study of scientific knowledge

#677 Dialectical logic does not exist and cannot exist outside materialist dialectics, because it reveals the significance of the most general laws of development of the objective world for the movement toward truth. It thus investigates the extent to which the content of knowledge coincides with the object of inquiry, the extent to which knowledge approaches truth. Differing in quality from formal logic, dialectical logic does not consider the forms of thought only from the standpoint of their structure; it also is interested in their concrete content. It considers them not a rigid, isolated form, but in their interconnection, in motion and development. Whereas formal logic concentrates mainly on the analysis of established theories, dialectical logic reveals the logical principles of transition to new knowledge and studies the formation and development of theories.

#678 The basic demand of dialectical logic are as follows (1) examination of all facets of an object, (2) examination of the object in its development, in its self movement. (3) a full 'definition' of an object must include the whole of human experience (i.e. history). (4) dialectical logic holds that truth is always concrete, never abstract.

*****

The Formation And Development
Of Scientific Theory. Intuition >#679

#680 2020 Materialist dialectics studies the movement of scientific knowledge, singling out its forms and laws, the fundamental concepts and principles by which thought arrives at objective truth. The fundamental concepts and principles in science are the result of people's creative activity. But what is scientific creativity? Does the scientist's creative activity follow any particular laws or is it absolutely free and untrammeled by any of the demands of logic? Of course creativity, as we have seen, is influenced by a large number of factors that do not fall within the scope of logic, but at the bottom it still represents the activity of human reason, that is, it is rational and consequently the object of logical analysis.

#681 Scientific research begins by stating the problem, generally it follows the line, as has been stated before:- Theory, purpose, apparatus, method, observation, conclusion, thesis, antithesis, synthesis, new theory and so on up the ubiquitous limitless spiral (coil). The notion of 'problem' usually implies an unknown quantity or quality and the term may be preliminarily defined as that which is not known to man and should be known. This rather incomplete definition contains the important factor – the factor of the obligation to know, i.e. the goal, that which gives direction to inquiry.

#682 However, it will be readily be appreciated that the distance between the unknown and the obligation to know is rather considerable. There is much that man does not know and, in principle at least, nothing that he would not like to know. So he must decide what he does not know but is capable of knowing at the given stage of his development.

This in itself requires a certain amount of knowledge, and so a problem – paradoxical as it may sound – is concerned not merely with the unknown, but with knowing what is unknown.

#683 Problems emerge from the needs of man's practical activity, in the form of certain desire for new knowledge. Science has to reach definite level of development to acquire the necessary and sufficient grounds for posing certain problems. For example, man's desire to explore the universe has now made its first steps.

#684 To state a problem we must have some preliminary, even if incomplete knowledge of how it is to be solved. The correct statement of the problem, the definition of the real need for new knowledge that can be satisfied in the given circumstances, takes us a good half of the way toward attaining new knowledge.

#685 But in both stating a problem and, even more so, in solving it we must have facts. The term 'fact' is used in various senses. We speak of something that has happened (process of objective reality) as a fact; we also speak of knowledge of that something as a fact. What interests us at the moment is the fact in the second meaning of the term. What knowledge can be called factual? Primarily it is the knowledge obtained by empirical means i.e. by means of observation and description of the results. Theory must be built only on the basis of the data of experience. But, as we have already noted, in building theory we must proceed from authentic knowledge, no matter whether it was obtained empirically or by reasoning (theoretically).

#686 To state and solve a problem, to test the propositions made, we must already have some knowledge whose objective truth has been firmly established. This authentic knowledge also provides part of the factual basis of the enquiry. The facts of modern science are made up both of results of empirical scientific observation and of laws whose reliability has been established in practice. Authenticity is the essential condition for the qualification of knowledge as fact. So facts are often called stubborn things; they have to be accepted whether we like them or not. All the other attributes of a fact, its invariability, for instance, that is, its relative independence of the system of which it forms a part, are derived from its authenticity. A fact is that which has been proved to be objectively true and remains so no matter in what system it is included. Hypotheses and conjectures may collapse and fail to stand the test of practice, but the facts on which they are based, remain and pass on from one system of knowledge to another.

#687 Conjecture is a preliminary proposition that has not yet been fully investigated. Conjecture is a proposition whose logical and empirical foundations have not yet been explained. For example, the preliminary idea of Rutherford and Soddy concerning radioactive decay was only a conjecture that was subsequently developed by further research to the level of a scientific hypothesis.

#688 How do conjectures arise? Why does one particular idea and not another occur to the scientist? The reply to these quite reasonable questions is that one cannot ignore the concept of intuition.

#689 New ideas that change our former notions arise, as a rule, not through strictly logical deduction from previous knowledge and not as simple generalization of experimental data. But new ideas arise as a kind of leap in the movement of thought, by its immediate connection with practical activity, which impels thought to seek new results beyond the bounds of what can be perceived by the senses and argued on strictly logical lines. (in the material world too the leap is evident, i.e. water turning into steam by the application of sensible heat, there is a period where latent heat is absorbed by the water prior to its 'leap' into steam.)

#690 But this is not to say that intuition is independent and arises out of nothing. It gets its first push from the previous level of empirical and theoretical knowledge of the object. The abilities and experience of the thinker, his whole way of thought, are rather important in this respect. His intuition may be influenced by various episodes in his life, and the influence of these chance factors, the speed and suddenness with which the idea comes, sometimes look like 'inspiration'

#691 The history of scientific discoveries abounds in legends about the incidents that are supposed to have sparked off brilliant intuitions. We have heard of 'Newton's apple', 'Mendeleyev's dream' and so on. But while not denying the possibility of such incidents, we must see behind every such case of intuition the effort of human thought, its constant and stubborn search for solution to the problems it has posed. Intuition furnishes in concentrated form the experience of the previous social and individual intellectual development of mankind. There is nothing mystical about it, its immediacy is relative, and intuitively suggested theoretical propositions are afterwards tested by logical processes, as a result of which the original conjecture is either discarded as unfounded or acquires the form of a scientifically based hypothesis.

#692 The transition from the conjecture to hypothesis entails finding arguments that, as Einstein put it, turn 'the miracle into something knowable.' this is where logic, without which intuition would be left in mid-air, comes into its own. Existing knowledge is mobilized and new facts are sought that can turn the conjecture into a hypothesis. Thus a new fact is observed which makes impossible the previous method of explaining the facts belonging to the same group. From this moment onwards, new methods of explanation are required – at first based on only a limited number of facts and observations. Further observational material weeds out these hypotheses, doing away with some and correcting others, until finally the law is established in a pure form.

#693 A hypothesis is knowledge based on supposition. The substantiation and proof of a hypothesis presupposes a search for new facts, the devising of experiments, and analysis of any previous results that have been obtained. Sometimes several hypotheses that are 'tested' by various means are advanced to explain one and the same process. Simplicity and economy, though supplementary in determining the most authentic theoretical system, are also of importance in choosing hypothesis. Thought must take the most rational, clear and simple path in its approach to the problems of reflecting reality and all the richness of it interconnections. All other things being equal, preference must be given to the hypothesis that achieves the goal in the clearest, simplest and most economical way. But economy and simplicity are only contributing factors in our choice between hypotheses of equal value; they are not criteria of the truth of the hypothesis. The only criterion of that is practice in all its diversity. The substantiation and proof of a hypothesis turn into theory.

#694 Theory is not something absolute, it is a relatively complete system of knowledge that changes course in the course of its development. A theory is changed by adding to it new facts and the concept that expresses them, and by verifying its principles. A time comes, however, when a contradiction is discovered that cannot be solved in the framework of the existing theory. This crucial moment can be detected by concrete analysis. Its arrival heralds the transition to a new theory with different and more exact principles.

#695 Between a new and old theory there are complex relations, one of which is expressed in the **Principle Of Correspondence.** According to this principle, a new theory acquires its right to exist when previous theories turn out to be limited cases. For example, classical physics is now a limited, particular case of modern theories. This principle expresses simultaneously both continuity and development of knowledge. If the objective truth of a theory has been established, this theory only limits the sphere of its application. The rules of transition from new theory to old can be defined. The inclusion of one theory in a wider, more general theory helps to establish authenticity.

*****

Practical Realization Of Knowledge >#696

#697 As we have seen, knowledge arises and develops on the basis of man's practical activity and serves it inasmuch as it creates the prototype of thing and processes that man needs and can create. So knowledge must eventually be practically realized in some way or another. But for this it must be shaped accordingly and acquire the form of an idea.

#698 In philosophical literature the term 'idea' is often used in the broad sense as any thought, any knowledge regardless of its form; concept, proposition, theory, and so on. **There is however, a more exact meaning of the term idea. An idea is a thought that achieves a high degree of objectivity, fullness and concrete-ness while at the same time having a practical purpose.**

#699 Thus in order to be realized knowledge must become an idea that combines three factors (1) Concrete, integrated knowledge of an object, (2) the urge for practical realization, for material embodiment, and (3) purpose and program of action, the subject's plan for changing the object. Such are the ideas of science through which production is reorganized and deep-going changes occur in society. Thus we speak of the idea, of the 'estate system' in political and economic matters in the world, the idea of space exploration, the idea of cancer cure and so on. (Estate system - first brought forth by ancient philosophy but made more concrete during the French Revolution and refined in subsequent History.)

#700 Ideas are put into practical effect with the help not only of material means (tools instruments of labor) but also of man's spiritual energies (will emotion and so on. The world does not satisfy man and man decides to change it by his activity.) This human determination is based on the knowledge given to man by his intellect, his thought. But the latter must be in accordance with the will to change the world. The determination to act in accordance with an idea must mature and in the process much depends on the individual's belief in the truth of an idea, in the necessity of acting in accordance with it, in the real possibility of its being transformed into reality.

#701 Belief or conscious faith in the rightness of one's actions based on knowledge is not ruled out by 2020 Materialism but we do oppose the substitution of blind faith, catechism or habit for knowledge. 2020 Materialism opposes fanatical faith. It draws a strict distinction between faith that comes from objective knowledge, and the blind subjective idealist faith in dogma on which religion and third-estate philosophy is based. (especially the ideas of private ownership of public property, the extraction of value-added for private use with the subsequent requirement for predatory banks, unmitigated growth, destructive competition, every man for himself, the impoverishment of the peoples and the ecology of the globe.) A person who acts without believing in the truth of the ideas that he wishes to put into practice is deprived of the will, purpose and emotional drive that are needed for success. Not a single brilliant idea can be born or a single brilliant project realized without human enthusiasm, without a man's reason being influenced by the whole gamut of his feelings. Scientific knowledge must become personal conviction giving the individual the determination to take action designed to change the existing reality.

#702 The process of the practical realization of ideas, their conversion into the world of objects that confronts the individual is known in philosophy as 'objectification.'

#703 Objectification has two aspects (1) the social, and (2) the epistemological. The social aspect of objectification involves finding out the relationship between the object created by man's labor and the man himself, as in the case of alienation, for example which will be discussed later. Considering objectification from the epistemological stand-point involves asking whether the object obtained in practice corresponds with the idea that was to be realized. When we put an idea into practice we solve the question of its objective truth and do away with all the illusory in it. This process may reveal certain discrepancies between the idea and its realization. Discrepancies arise either because of the 1) imperfection of the idea. Or 2) the lack of sufficient knowledge and means of realizing it. Or 3) the absence of the necessary material and spiritual means of realizing it. Or 4) because of the absence of the necessary material and spiritual means and conditions for its complete fulfillment in objective reality. Thus objectification sums up one cycle of research and reveals a new one. Finally the object obtained in practice is analyzed from the standpoint of its correspondence with man's rational aims.

#704 The reasonable, the rational is not primordially given, is not a property of nature; it is the product of man's historical development, his labor and thirst for knowledge. The only bearer of reason is man who through work and other forms of practice, introduces reason into the surrounding world and influences nature by realizing his practical, scientific, ideas and aims.

#705 Since practice as an objective historical process is, on the one hand, subordinated to man's goals expressed in his ideas and on the other hand, goes beyond them in creating something new, practice is always both rational and irrational. (i.e. the practice of just war is rational while the practice of unjust war is irrational, hence the huge psychological problems and one-sided-truths (propaganda) required to keep up the tempo of a people engaged in an unjust wars.)

#706 In contrast, to irrationalism, which absolutizes the irrational element of life, divorces it from the rational, regards it as the dominant tendency of all development, 2020 Materialism recognizes the irrational as the opposite of the rational and quite often as an accompanying factor in the rational. There is no eternal irrational, but there may be something irrational in a given set of historical conditions. But the irrational as a subsidiary, unforeseen result of our activity does not remain forever. Irrationality is finally overcome by subsequent knowledge and practice.

#707 Knowledge itself as a factor in human activity may also be evaluated in the categories of the rational, since it follows logic, certain established forms of reason. At the same time it quite often goes beyond these forms and cannot be explained by them, that is to say, it contains an element that can be overcome only by changing logic itself, by restocking its armory with new forms and categories of thought. Irrationalism concentrates attention on this irrational residue of knowledge which, has not yet been explained in the existing forms of reason, regards it as the true essence and thus creates a distorted notion in the course of cognition.

#708 The rational as the main stream of development of knowledge exists in two forms; (1) Ratiocination, and (2) Reason. Ratiocination means operating with the forms of thought, with abstractions according to a set program or pattern, without going into the method itself, its limits and possibilities. Ratiocination divides the whole, the one, into mutually exclusive opposites, but cannot embrace them in the unity of their interpenetration. The specific features of ratiocination are best seen in an algorithm (Iteration). The system of rules for performing various computations of an exact nature in which each stage determines the next, the whole process being divided into separate steps and the instructions for dealing with them provided in the form of a combinations of symbols. This means that algorithmic operations can be preformed by computers. Ratiocination is essential to theoretical thought; without it thought would be vague and indeterminate. It makes thought systematic and rigorous, seeking to turn theory into a formalized system. But it is not ratiocination that constitutes the characteristic feature of human thought. This is expressed by reason itself.

#709 As distinct from ratiocination, reason uses concepts with an awareness of their content and nature, and therefore reflects things and processes in a purposeful, creatively active way; reason is the instrument of transforming activity, of creating a world that answers to the needs and essence of man. Human reason seeks to reach out beyond the bounds of the already formed system of knowledge, to create a new system in which man's goals are expressed with greater fullness and objectivity. Whereas the characteristic feature of ratiocination is analysis, reason is characterized by synthesis, which is human creative ability taken to its highest level. Human knowledge is the unity of ratiocination and reason, from the heights of which objective reality is understood and the ways of the rational transformation are determined

*****

Knowledge And Value >#710

#711 The practical realization of ideas takes place in culture, material and spiritual, in things, works of art, standards of morality, and so on. So how are ideas related to man's social needs? People begin, not from a purely theoretical relationship to the objects of external nature, but from the mastering of them they give these objects a special (generic) name. This is because they know the ability of these objects to serve their needs satisfactorily – they may call these objects goods or in some other way, which means they are practically using these object, that is they are useful to them.

#712 The philosophical problem of value arose out of the growing understanding of this attitude to the objects of the external world as the means of satisfying human needs. The point is not whether the material and spiritual objects man creates and also the phenomena of nature that serves the needs should be given certain names, whether they should be called 'goods', 'values', or something else or classified in some other way. The real question is the nature of value, its relationship to the subject and object, to knowledge, and so on.

#713 The objects of nature, of our material and spiritual culture have the ability to satisfy man's needs, to serve his aims, Hence they can and should be approached from the standpoint of value. How do objects acquire this ability?

Does it come from nature or from man, from his special gifts and abilities? If we say that value lies only in objects, we endow them with the intrinsic properties of serving man and his aims. But we know that nature and its objects existed long before man himself came into being. On the other hand, we cannot simply say that an object may satisfy man's material and spiritual needs, regardless of its intrinsic qualities. If grain did not contain certain necessary substances it would not be food, it would be of no use to man.

#714 2020 Materialistic philosophy regards value as a social and historical phenomenon and an element in the practical interaction of the subject and the object. The social world is not something extraneous to the material, natural process. The product of human labor is a continuation of nature. Thus value is a property of objects that arise in the process of social development, and at the same time it is also a property of the objects of nature that have been included in the process of labor, of everyday life and that are the life-element of human reality.

#715 Certain third-estate philosophical schools (who laud and condone the third-estate's private appropriation of the fifth-estate labor's 'value-added' to a product) divorce the value approach to objects and phenomena from their objective, scientific investigation. In point of fact, however, the scientific and value approaches to the objects of reality can be separated only in abstraction, for certain strictly defined purposes.

#716 The scientific approach seeks to register our knowledge of an object as it exists outside us and outside mankind in general, and to give a clear definition of knowledge itself, that is, of objective truth.

#717 The value approach, on the contrary, seeks in considering both the object itself and its reflection to concentrate attention on the human relationship, to evaluate everything from the standpoint of the object's intrinsic ability to satisfy human needs.

#718 The social impact of the appropriation of value-added is devastating on appropriators (expropriators) as well as the fifth-estate itself. This appropriation causes anxiety in all estates. The every man for himself syndrome permeates all estates and the value-added component of global production – held in a few third-estate hands – washes around the globe seeking a safe place to nestle, but there is no such safe place in the every person for itself world. (Last 7 words carefully chosen.)

#719 The value approach considers not knowledge in its pure form, but the embodiment of knowledge in the material and spiritual culture that serves man and his aims. The value approach plays a great part, for example, in the moral or artistic consciousness, whose specific attitude to the objective world it largely expresses.

#720 At the same time in real human activity, both objective and spiritual, the two approaches (the objective scientific approach and the value approach) are combined and cannot exist without each other; they flow from one source -- man's practical relationship to objective reality.

*****

CHAPTER 5 >#721

HISTORICAL 2020 MATERIALISM >#722

#723 **Historical 2020 Materialism As A Science:** Historical materialism has its own specific subject matter – the most general laws of development of human society. This makes it relatively independent as a general sociological theory, as the scientific historical basis of a global brotherhood.

#724 Pre 2020 Materialism was inconsistent and limited. It was unable to apply the principles of philosophical materialism to the study of social life and history and in this field held subjective idealist views.

#725 Certain social and theoretical preconditions were required before historical materialism could come into being. It was ushered in by the logical development of the progressive social, political and philosophical thought. But social conditions also played a part in revealing the possibility of discovering the laws of social life.

#726 The acceleration of social development, the kaleidoscope change from the English, and especially the French (1789 1794) third-estate revolutions, the extreme aggravation of first and second estates verses the third-estate, the extreme contradictions between them and the emergence on the scene of the fourth and fifth estates were the social preconditions that favored the appearance of historical materialism.

#727 The great events that took place at the end of the 18th and in the first half of the 19th centuries showed that society was by no means a monolith. The show that it was but a living social organism subject to change and obeying in its existence and development certain objective laws that were independent of the human will and consciousness.

#728 The chaos and arbitrariness that had previously reigned in views on history and politics have now been replaced by an integral and harmonious scientific theory. The theory which shows how, in consequence of the growth of the formerly advanced sectors of the third-estate and lately of the productive force of the highly evolved sectors of the fifth-estate, it can be shown that out of one system of social life another and higher develops.

#729 The most general laws discovered by dialectical materialism operates in society, but here they take a specific form. If we wish to know the laws of development of human society, it is not enough to know the general principles of philosophical materialism and the laws of dialectics; we must also study the specific forms in which they take effect in history and in social life.

#730 It is only in a society with an antagonistic structure that the law of the unity and struggle of opposites takes the form of a struggle between the various estates. And in what great diversity of forms and trends has this struggle taken place over the various historical epochs.

#731 The dialectical method, applied to society, and the method of historical materialism are, in essence, identical concepts. When applied to society, the dialectical method becomes concrete. This means that in addition to general philosophical categories we must have such purely sociological categories as social existence and social consciousness, material and ideological relationships, the productive forces and the production relations, the mode of production, the socio-economic formation, the basis and the superstructure. social classes, Estates, Nations, Inter-nations and so on. These categories sum up the major laws of social existence and socio-historical knowledge.

#732 Just as Darwin put an end to the view of animal and plant immutability so the classical materialists put an end to the view of society being a mechanical aggregation of individuals. Such an aggregationist view allows of all sorts of modifications at the will of the 'authorities' or elected representatives and the government. Classical materialists put an end to that thinking and made a science of social formations – showed that the economic formations of society are a sum total of given production relations and the development of such formations are a process of natural history. (For it is all rather like Lawrence's 'Rocking Horse Winner' everywhere the walls whisper "there's never enough money.")

*****

The subject-Matter Of Historical 2020 Materialism >#733

#734 Human history and society is, in its essence and structure, the most complex form of existence of matter. It is a specific, qualitatively unique part of nature, in a certain sense opposed to the rest of nature. This interpretation of the interrelationship between society and nature fundamentally distinguishes historical materialism both from idealism, which in most cases creates an antithesis between society and nature, and from a metaphysical materialism, which does not recognize the qualitative difference between them.

#735 Giovanni Vico (1688 1744), the Italian philosopher wrote that the history of society differs from the history of nature in that it is made by people, and only people, whereas in nature phenomena and processes take place of themselves, as a result of blind impersonal, spontaneous forces. The fact that society is the scene of action of people possessed of minds and wills, who set themselves certain goals and fight to achieve them, has in the past and even now in our own time is a stumbling-block for sociologists, economists, and historians. Many of whom seek to study the essence, the fundamental causes of social processes and phenomena. Some of them, absolutizing the specific nature of social and historical events, metaphysically oppose the natural sciences, which study general, recurrent phenomena and processes, to the historical sciences, which are allegedly concerned only with the individual and unique. Thus in the 19th century certain German philosophers representing one of the schools of Neo-Kantianism (H Rickert, W Windelband) believed there must exist two different and even opposite methods of cognition. The so called nomothetic, or generalizing method, which is applied by the natural sciences, and the ideographic, or individualizing method (concerned only with individual, unique events), which is used by the historical sciences.

#736 But such a sigma-metaphysical counterpoising of the natural sciences to the social sciences is far-fetched and unjustifiable. We are no more likely to find in nature than in history of society two phenomena that are absolutely identical (for example, two animals of a species or two leaves on one and the same tree). On the other hand, in society, in history, besides the specific and the individual there is also the general. This general manifests itself in the instruments of production, the productive forces, the economic activity, in the social relationships, in the political and spiritual life of various countries and peoples that are at the same stage of historical development. It is by detecting these general features that we are able to discover the laws of social life.

#737 It might be supposed that since social events and processes are the result of peoples own activity, it should not be so difficult to understand them as it is to understand the phenomena of nature. And surely it ought to be easier for man and society to establish their power over social relationships than to subjugate the colossal forces of nature that are hostile to man. But this picture is incorrect, as human history and the history of science show.

#738 In the first half of the 19th century the natural sciences of society was still only in embryo. Step by step mankind was getting to know the laws and forces of nature and bringing them under control. But it turned out to be a far more difficult task to discover the true nature of human society and its laws. Even more difficult and prolonged was the task of mastering the social laws and processes and bringing them under the control of society. The possibility of solving these problems came with the creation of 2020 Materialism, with its insights into the estates system operating in society and how the fifth-estate's salary and wage workers physical numbers, in absolute terms, are ever increasing. (The other estates in relative terms are ever decreasing due to historical factors the contents of which are under discussion herein.)
Along with this phenomenon, the third-estate, although dwindling in physical numbers, has been able to amass a disproportionate share of the worlds labor-tokens in the form of capital.

#739 The fourth-estate (media) is largely controlled by the third-estate. But an interesting recent phenomena – in the creation of an 'internet' – it has come about that the fourth-estate no longer can control the minds of men as it once did, for the net is free to publish anyone's works – kooks, as well as the serious minded. The result of all this is that everyone on the net wills his own outlook and out of that comes that which no one wills.

#740 Human society, social phenomena and process are studied by various sciences, each of which studies only a certain aspect of social life, one or another type of social relationship or phenomena (economic, political, ideological)

#741 Historical 2020 Materialism deals, not with the separate aspect of social life, but with its general laws and the driving forces of its functioning and development. It deals with social life as an integrated whole, the intrinsic connections and contradictions of all its aspects and relations, first of all, the relations of social existence and social consciousness. Unlike the specialized sciences, historical 2020 Materialism studies, first and foremost, the most general laws of the development of society, the laws of the rise, existence and motive forces of the development of social-economic formations – the rise of the estates system.

#742 The general sociological laws, which concern all historical epochs operate in each definite economic formation of society, in each epoch, in a specific way. Therefore, if we wish to obtain a correct idea of the character and essence of general sociological laws, we must study their specific functions in the various historical epoch in the various formations. (i.e. Tribalism, Slaveism, Feudalism, Capitalism, Socialism, Militarism, Gangism, Gangsterism – all forms at work in society in today's world, and so on.) Thus the concept of 'general sociological laws' includes the intrinsic connections and relations that are characteristic of the most general laws of economic formations of society.

#743 Historical 2020 Materialism also differs from the science of history. Historical science implies study of the history of countries and peoples, of events, in their chronological sequence. Historical 2020 Materialism, on the other hand, is a general theoretical, methodological science. It studies not one particular people, or one particular country, but human society as a whole, considered from the standpoint of the most general laws and driving forces of its development.

#744 Historical 2020 Materialism combines both theory and method in one. It furnishes the dialectical materialist solution to the basic, epistemological question of social science – the question of the relationship between social being and social consciousness. It tells us about the most general laws and driving forces of society and is therefore a scientific general sociological theory. For this reason historical 2020 Materialism is both an effective method of studying the phenomena and processes of social life, and a method of revolutionary action. Only with its help can the historian, the economist, the student of law or art find his way amid the complexities of social phenomena. It gives the political leaders of the fifth-estate a guiding principle a golden thread for investigation and understanding of the specific historical situation.

#745 Political economy and historical materialism especially the labor theory of value and historical 2020 Materialism which will become the mainstay in fifth-estate struggles for democracy free of fourth and third-estate half truths and propaganda. Propaganda that is used for the continuance of unremitting competition that bring with them deep going anxiety and fear culminating in the 'me only syndrome' that permeates today's society. Fifth-estate peoples reject all of that they want cooperation and brotherhood.

#746 Historical 2020 Materialism will also become highly relevant to concrete social research. When employing mathematical methods or methods of polling, interviewing, circulating questionnaires and so on, one must have a firm footing in the general sociological theory of 2020 Materialism. Historical 2020 Materialism will give us an objective basis for scientific orientation in historical events, enable us to know and understand them, to predict them scientifically, and to see the prospects and trends of social development, thus providing the theoretical basis for action.

*****

The Laws Of Social Development And Their Objective Character >#747

#748 In the social production of their existence, men inevitably enter into definite relations, which are independent of their will, namely relations of production appropriate to a given stage in the development of their material forces of production. The totality of these relations of production constitutes the economic structure of society, the real foundation, on which arises a legal and political superstructure and to which correspond definite forms of social consciousness. The mode of production of material life conditions the general process of social, political and intellectual life. It is not the consciousness of men that determines their existence, but their social existence that determines their consciousness. At a certain stage of development, the material productive forces of society come into conflict with the existing relations of production or – this merely expresses the same thing in legal terms – with the property relations within the framework of which they have operated hitherto.

#749 As global productive forces develop under third-estate's direction, this estate is in the position to siphon off all the 'value-added' produced by the fifth-estate. Driven on by unremitting competition the third-estate is in constant fear of losing this capital (capital produced by purloined value added) either to that of competition or to the more fiendish forces of global overproduction with its resultant collapse of markets. The anxiety produced in all estates including the third-estate itself during this process is acutely felt by all men. Thus this form of development of global productive forces leads all inter estate relations to turn into fetters.

#750 Then begins an era of social revolution these revolutions once masked by nationalist aims turned into the wars of the past – the forces at the helm turned these local disruptions into the nationalistic chauvinistic and religious wars of the past. While these still go on the Globe has entered a new era.

#751 In the past nationalist chauvinistic trends were acerbated by localized media (fourth-estate) spilling fourth half-truths and silence on other matters of great import. Third-estate media giants controlled the press and naturally letters to the editor were carefully screened so that their content fit in with third-estate aims.

#752 In the course of new developments, and globally speaking, this grip of third-estate over the fourth-estate is falling away. (although there are some notable exceptions) The Internet, now in its infancy, gives all little men the potential of airing his views to his fellow man. Every man airing his sole view on the internet wills his own outlook on things, and as we have previously observed, out of it will come an over-view that no man wills.

#753 A great Internationalism is taking shape the UN, reviled by reactionary forces in the past is still strengthening and giving a global outlook on things. Nationalistic aims are now scrutinized by that august body and it is not now so easy for a nation to hide its misdemeanors from the global community. (Although it must be observed in all honesty that there are certain forces working clandestinely internally within its boundaries that want to overthrow it.)

#754 The changes in the economic foundation lead sooner or later to the transformation of the whole immense superstructure. In studying such transformations it is always necessary to distinguish between the material transformation of the economic conditions of production and the philosophic conditions. The economic conditions can be determined with the precision of natural science. But it is harder to comprehend the legal, political, artistic, philosophic and ideological forms in which men become conscious of this conflict and fight it out. Just as one does not judge an individual by what he thinks about himself, so one cannot judge such a period of transformation by its consciousness. But on the contrary, this consciousness must be explained from the contradictions of material life, from the conflict existing between the social forces of production and the relations of production.

#755 No social order is ever destroyed before all the productive forces for which it is sufficient have been developed, and new superior relations of production never replace older ones before the material conditions for their existence have matured within the framework of the old society.

#756 Mankind thus inevitably sets itself only such tasks as it is able to solve, since closer examination will always show that the problem itself arises only when the material conditions for its solution are already present or at least in the course of formation.

#757 In the past social laws were generally treated in the same way as the laws of the mechanical, physical or biological processes occurring in nature. The specific features that characterize social life, which created by people with intellect and will-power, were thus ignored.

#758 The natural historical process is a process that is as necessary and objective, a much governed by law, as the natural processes: it is a process that not only does not depend on people's will and consciousness. At the same time, unlike the processes of nature, the natural historical process is a result of the activity of people themselves. At first glance this proposition appears to imply a logical contradiction. How can we reconcile the fact that the historical process is created by people possessing consciousness and will, setting themselves certain tasks and goals, with the fact that history obeys certain necessary, objective laws that do not depend on human will and consciousness?

#759 This contradiction can be explained if we remember that people, particularly large groups of people – nations, estates parties etc. in pursuing their aims, in being guided by certain interests, ideals and desires, at the same time always live under certain objective conditions that do not depend on their will and desire. And these ideals and desires ultimately determine the direction and character of their activity, their interests, ideas and aspirations.

#760 In complete accord with the materialist world outlook, Historical 2020 Materialism proceeds from the proposition that social existence is primarily in relation to social consciousness. Social consciousness is a reflection of social existence at that given epoch in history. It may be more or less a correct reflection or it may be false. It is not social consciousness or the ideas of some political leader that determines the system of social life and direction of social development, as the idealists assume. On the contrary, it is social existence that ultimately determines social consciousness, the ideas, aspirations and aims of individuals and social classes and the estates to which they belong. What, then, is implied by the concept of 'social existence' of

'Estates' which holds such an important place in historical 2020 Materialism?

#761 In philosophical 2020 Materialism the category of existence is regarded as identical with the concept of matter, of nature. Accordingly, social existence is understood as the material life of society, its production and reproduction. Social existence is comprised of social production of people themselves, the system of social relations that arises in the process of the production of material goods i.e. the production, or economic, relations, and other forms of human community.

#762 Social existence is primary because it is independent of social consciousness; social consciousness is secondary because it is a reflection of people's social existence.

#763 The question is sometimes asked: how are we to understand the independence of social existence from social consciousness? Do not people themselves create their means of production? Is not the distinguishing feature of human labor people's own purposeful activity? Do not people themselves establish their relations with one another in the process of production?

#764 True, people themselves build their social life. But not always and not everywhere do they build consciously. Of course, they perform every single act of building, modifying, transporting and production consciously. But it does not follow from this that they are always conscious of the character of the social relations into which they enter in this process, of how these relations are changing, or what the social consequences of these changes are. Driven on by vital necessity, people work, produce, consume goods and exchange the results of their actions, and the economic relations thus formed do not depend on their conscious choice or desire, but on the level of social production they have achieved.

#765 What is more, people's will, aims, desires and aspirations, conditioned by their social or personal interests, embodied in their actions and making their appearance on the stage of social life, clash, interweave and come into contradiction with one another with the result that the desired is only rarely achieved. History is made in such a way that the final result always arises from conflicts between many individual wills, of which each in turn has been made what it is by a host of particular conditions of life. Thus there are innumerable intersecting forces, an infinite series of parallelograms of forces, which give rise to one resultant – the historical event. This may again itself be viewed as a power, which works as a whole unconsciously and without volition. For what each individual wills is obstructed by everyone else, and has been already observed, what emerges is something that no one willed. Thus history has proceeded hitherto in the manner of natural process and is essentially subject to the same laws of motion. But from the fact that the wills of individuals each of whom desires what he is impelled to by his physical constitution and external, in the last resort economic, circumstances. (either his own personal circumstance or those of society in general.) They do not attain what they want, but are merged into an aggregate mean, a common resultant, it must not be concluded that they are equal to zero. On the contrary, each contributes to the resultant and is to this extent included in it.

#766 In Global people-numbers the fifth-estate (the salary and wage workers and farmers - the producers) is the much larger estate. And has been observed previously the other estates in comparison to it are dwindling in people-numbers. One estate after another is reduced by competition and is in the course of a withering away. Such is the case of the first, clergy in the religious estates due to more enlightenment in the world. Whilst it may be that people give an outward show of religiosity they know deep down in their heart of hearts that there is no future in its whimsy and mythology. Or take another example the fourth-estate due to technological advances consolidation and so on the people in these estates are thrown one by one into the ranks of the fifth-estate.

#767 Whilst the salary and wage working fifth-estate is largest in people-numbers, in current global conditions it is the poorest in command of capital, all other estates on average have a per capita income much larger than those in the fifth-state. Even the sixth-estate Armed forces and Police on a global average surpass the incomes those in the fifth-estate in general. The seventh-estate thugs, due to blatant robbery drug money and the other ne'r-do-well lumpen-proletarians over 20 such as the hikikomori, and due to parental indlugement, all seem to be holding their own.

#768 In this period of social development the natural historical process is conditioned by objective causes and laws that exist outside peoples consciousness. Even when the fifth-estate, forced by the historical process becomes conscious of its role in society – even then subjectivism and arbitrariness may lead to negative results and their action to bring about cooperation, sister and brotherhood of man may lead to many negative results. Their glorious historic action for a better world will be crowned with success only if those actions correspond to objective social laws.

#769 Any law, as we know, expresses an objective, necessary, stable connection between phenomena, between processes. Similarly, the laws established by historical 2020 Materialism combined with other social sciences do and will further express a necessary, stable and recurrent connection between social phenomena and processes.

#770 Some social laws operate at all stages of social development. These include:-

#771 The law of the determining role of social existence in relation to social consciousness;

#772 The law of the determining role of the mode of production and distribution in relation to the particular structure of society, the determining role of the productive forces with regard to economic relations between the Estates;

#773 The law of the determining role of the economic basis in relation to the social superstructure;

#774 The law of dependence of the individuals' social on the totality of social relations and others.

#775 These are the general sociological laws, they operate at all levels of social development.

#776 Besides general sociological laws there are others that hold good only for certain social formations. These are primarily:-

#777 The law of the division of society into estates, which are characteristic only of certain modes of production and distribution.

#778 The law of the various estate's struggles for existence as a driving force of recent history, which remains valid only for those social economic formations that are based upon, now hidden, now open antagonism between estates.

#779 Some critics of historical 2020 Materialism will assert that a law is a relationship that exists always and everywhere. If the law of the fifth-estate's struggle to obtain dominion and say into how the 'added-value' that it creates (and that all other estates appropriate and squander) does not conform to this demand, it is not then a law.

#780 The laws of social life are, in general, shorter lived, and have a narrower sphere of application than the laws of nature. Nevertheless they are objective, real laws expressing intrinsic, relatively constant connections between social phenomena and processes. After all, even the laws of the biology of the earth do not operate on other planets of the solar system. But this does not lead anyone to doubt their reality, their objectivity. (but also this does not mean to say that there are not an infinite number of 'earth like' systems in the infinite universe.)

#781 Some third-estate apologist economists and sociologist will elevate social laws (for example, the law of the development and requirement for the existence of the third-estate) to the rank of eternal, natural, intransigent laws. By bourgeoisie standards all stages of development of society are seen through the prism of the development of third-estate principles and the necessity for its existence.

#782 Economic Laws are not eternal laws of nature but historical laws, which appear and disappear. And the code of modern political economy, in so far as it has been drawn up accurately and objectively by bourgeois economists, is to us simply a summary of the laws and conditions under which alone modern third-estate dominated society can exist. In short, its conditions of production, distribution and exchange is expressed in an abstract way and summarized. To Historical 2020 Materialism therefore none of these laws, in so far as it expresses purely third-estate rule, is older than modern society. They are laws which have been more or less valid throughout all hitherto existing history and express only those relations which are common to all forms of society based on class rule and class exploitation.

#783 Every law operates under definite conditions and its effectiveness depends on those conditions, which vary from one formation to another and within each formation, and from one country to another.

#784 As third-estate supremacy in every country has acquired certain features connected with the historical past of that country. It comes with a greater or smaller share of past feudal baggage so too the general laws of the development of the fifth-estate formation and development acquired in each separate country certain features and peculiarities connected with its historical past. (i.e. feudalism in America was historically weak while in Europe, especially Eastern Europe, it was historically strong.) But these peculiar features do not affect the main thing: they do not abolish and cannot abolish the general laws of the increase in the absolute people numbers of the fifth-estate and the increase in absolute money accumulation in the form of capital in the third-estate. There are no national laws of these developments, these laws are international in nature and scope. Here as in other fields, there is dialectical unity of the general and the particular, the national and the international. Ignoring this unity, overstressing the national to the detriment of the general leads to nationalist tendencies.

*****

Peoples Conscious Activity And Its Role In History. Freedom And Necessity >#785

#786 In regarding social development as a natural historical process do we not prevent ourselves from obtaining a correct understanding of the role of man's creative, revolutionary transforming activity? Does this not belittle the historical activity, the historical initiative of the progressive social forces, the role of the omega-subjective factor in human activity?

#787 Third-estate sociologists will claim that the 2020 Materialist approach to history regards the economic factor as everything, while ideas and various forms of social consciousness – philosophy, morality, religion – are nothing. This is how the critics of 2020 Materialism will present the case. Thus they will confuse historical 2020 Materialism with economic, vulgar materialism.

#788 Historical 2020 Materialism in no way ignores the significance of politics, of social consciousness, of various spiritual values put forth by the first-estate; on the contrary, as will be seen later on, it recognizes their tremendous role in social life.

#789 Reactionary ideas, those acting alone as bombers do and so forth, reactionary policy of the supremacist, racist ideology, militarism of the sixth-estate, nationalism and chauvinism play an extremely negative role in the progress of mankind. They poison people's minds and act as a brake on social progress. By contrast, progressive, revolutionary ideas and policies based on them play a great part, particularly when these ideas become widespread among the fifth-estate wherein they act as a mobilizing, organizing and transforming historical force.

#790 Third-estate critics of historical materialism will try to discover a contradiction between the revolutionary activity of the fifth-estate and the philosophers of 2020 Materialism and their views on historical necessity. They are particularly critical on the view of inevitable collapse of the Third Estate under the weight of increasing labor-token, capital-accumulation, financial crisis, and the dwindling people-numbers controlling it.

#791 Just as knowledge of the laws and processes of nature offers us the best chance of taming its spontaneous force, so does knowledge of the social laws, of the driving forces of social development, allow progressive people of all estates to consciously create history and social progress. By getting to know the objective laws of social development, with brother and sisterhood and cooperation as its aim the progressive elements in the world will be able to act, not blindly, not spontaneously, but with knowledge of what they are doing. And in this sense, freely (possibly with the tools of an enlightened fourth-estate, a universal language, and of computer aided plebiscite, initiative, referendum, and so on.) (computer aided plebiscite where in one person one vote might be possibly enhanced by palm print or iris identification)

#792 The laws of social development usually function as tendencies. They break their way through many obstacles, through a mass of chance events, through conflict with opposite tendencies supported by hostile forces, which have to be paralyzed and overcome in order to ensure the victory of the progressive forces and tendencies.

#793 Conflict between these various tendencies means that in every historical period there exists more than one possibility. Thus, expropriation and depredation of one form and another is always charged with the possibility of strikes and in extreme cases of war, often under the guise of religious war. And in certain conditions of profit in arms and in the forth-estates hunger for headlines 'scoops' and in its penchant for half-truths, yes and even critical silences, war can be foisted on an unsuspecting public. But as the world matures these measures of the third-estate to maintain itself are becoming less viable. Thus there arises and exists a growth in the forces of the fifth-estate, which forces another real possibility and that is of peace in the world.

#794 Historical necessity is, therefore, not the same thing as predetermination. In real life, thanks to the effect of objective laws of social development, far from freeing people of the need to act, demands their active, conscious participation in order to realize these laws. The teaching of Historical 2020 Materialism on social development as the natural historical process does not belittle the role of man, his conscious activity, but rather shows the significance of this activity, of the struggle of the progressive cooperative social forces. Ignorance of these laws and failure to take into consideration actual conditions and means of struggle condemns the fifth-estate to passivity or to adventurism and defeat.

#795 Freedom does not consist of any dreamt of independence from natural laws, but the knowledge of these laws, and the obligation of the fifth-estate to making them work for the brotherhood and cooperation of man. This scenario is opposed to the unremitting destructive private ownership of the public productive and distributive system – unmitigated competition – boom and bust – hoodism – and an anxiety system foisted on mankind by the third-estate through their mouthpieces in the fourth-estate. (This third-estate system requires a constant expansion, it cannot live in the new world of contraction, quietude and peace. It cannot exist on non-expansion.)

#796 This is how the philosophy of Historical 2020 Materialism must resolve the old philosophical and sociological problem of the relationship between freedom (freedom to exploit or freedom of the brother and sisterhood of man.) the relationship between freedom and necessity, the problem of free-will and determinism.

#797 Human history has not been a continuous and straight ascent, always and everywhere expressing the march of progress. It has known reverses, zigzags, disasters such as wars, barbarian invasions the decline and fall of powerful states, the disappearance of entire nations. But taken as a whole it has been an ascent, from one social-economic formation to another, from lower to higher forms.

#798 Nor has this movement of history been uniform. Its multiformity has incorporated much that is specific and connected with the peculiar features and conditions of development of various peoples. But in this lies the great significance of Historical 2020 Materialism, which will reveal in the seeming chaos and infinite diversity the law, the regular and recurrence in the main and most essential things that characterize the development of mankind.

#799 Is there any meaning in the history of mankind, in the development of society, or is this movement as meaningless and elemental as the flow of rivers that sweep away everything in their path? There is no grounds of course, for acknowledging any meaning imported to history from without, such as divine predestination, a pre-arranged program or supernatural destiny for the peoples of this globe. At the same time the history of society in every epoch has its own definite content. The peoples, the progressive social forces that make history, blaze the trail for new, more advanced economic political and other social relations, and fight to accomplish certain historical tasks. People may be more or less fully aware of these tasks, or they may misapprehend them, sometimes in a mystified religious, fantastic form. In the great transitional periods of history the conscious, creative activity of the masses, of the progressive salary and wage working fifth-estate, attain new heights. Thus the history of mankind is not entirely spontaneous but social consciousness also plays a large part.

#800 The content of the present epoch is the struggle between the forces of the fifth and third-estates. This movement will take place through the overcoming of various difficulties, profound contradictions and antagonism's; it therefore will not proceed in a straight line. Here, too, there will be zigzags and setbacks. But taken as whole, the future historical process is heading toward the elimination of the third-estate due to its moribund economic system and to it being finally overwhelmed by the far more numerous and advanced peoples of the fifth-estate.

*****

CHAPTER 6 >#801

MATERIAL PRODUCTION IS THE BASIS OF SOCIAL LIFE >#802

#803 As we have seen the subject matter of Historical 2020 Materialism is human society and the most general laws of its development. The first step towards discovering these laws was to establish the role of material production and distribution in the life of society. It will easily be understood that society cannot exist without producing the material goods needed for human life. But in the process of production people do not only create material products; production does not only provide people with the means of subsistence. In producing material goods people produce and reproduce their own social relations.

#804 The study of social production, its structure, its constituent elements and their interconnections, therefore, makes it possible to penetrate into the essence of the historical process, to reveal the deep-going social mechanisms that operate in the life of society.

*****

Society And Nature, Their Interaction >#805

#806 Material production and distribution furnishes the key to the interpretation both of the internal structure of society and its interrelationship with the external environment – surrounding nature. Production and the distribution of the products is above all the process of interaction between society and nature. In this process of interaction people obtain from surrounding nature the necessary means of existence. Labor, production, distribution, is at the same time the basis of the formation of man himself as a social being, his emergence from nature.

#807 From the simple use of objects provided by nature, which is sometimes observed among animals, our ancestors gradually passed on to making tools and this was the essential factor in the emergence of human labor itself. (and the gradual transition over many historical epoch to the work necessary for a modern society paid by salary and wages.) Labor activity had two decisive consequences. First the organism of man's ancestors began to accommodate itself not only to the conditions of the environment but to labor activity. The specific features of man's physical organization – upright walk, differentiation of the function of the front and rear limbs, development of the hand and brain – evolved in the long process of adaptation of the organism to the performance of labor operations. Second, because it meant concerted action, labor stimulated the emergence and development of articulate speech, of language as a means of communication, the accumulation and transmission of labor and social experience.

#808 Two important stages may be noted in the process of the formation of man. First stage of this formation is marked by the beginning of tool making this is the stage of man in Pithecanthropus and Neanderthal times. In recent times in south and east Africa the remains of man's oldest ancestors have been found in geological strata dating back 2.5 million years. Primitive stone tools were found with their bones. This confirms the intrinsic connection between the development of labor and human evolution. The second major qualitative stage was the replacement, about 100,000 years ago, in the middle Paleolithic age. The stage of Neanderthal man replaced by a modern type Homo Sapiens (rational man) Whereas the build of Neanderthal man still retained many features reminiscent of the apes, there have been no radical changes in man's physical type since the emergence of Homo Sapiens. In this period major changes took place in production, involving the making of various implements of labor (from stone, bone and horn). The stages in the evolution of man and his implements of labor were at the same time the stages in the formation of human society itself in its primary form, namely, tribal society. Man is a social being, he never lived and could not appear outside of society or before society. Nor, however, could society appear before man; the new form of relations between individuals developed only because man's ancestors were becoming people.

#809 There are many features distinguishing man from animals. The most important of them however, are production of the instruments of labor, articulate speech, and the ability of abstract thought. The first of these is primary. People begin to distinguish themselves from animals as soon as they begin to produce their means of subsistence.

#810 Taken in its most general form, the process of production and distribution is what man does to the objects and forces of nature in order to obtain and produce his means of subsistence; food, clothing, a place to live and so on. This process presupposes human activity or labor itself affecting the objects of labor.

#811 Unlike the instinctive forms of human activity, human labor, in the true sense of the word, is purposeful activity, which results in the creation and transportation of an object which existed in man's imagination, that is as idea. Comparing the behavior of the bees which so skillfully build their honeycombs of wax, with the activity of the architect – even the worst architect is superior to the best bee in that before he builds his house he has already created it in his own head.

#812 Wage, salary and consulting labor activity takes place with the help of the corresponding means of influencing the objective assistants of labor – tools – the instruments of labor.

#813 Tools bring about the transition from the immediate, direct actions, characteristic of the animals, which use their natural organs, claws, teeth, etc., to essentially human actions mediated by the instruments of labor. The latter continue, as it where, man's natural organs, performing at first the same functions as the natural organs, but intensifying their effect.

#814 Society may be described as a social organism. The biological organism has a system of natural organs performing certain specific functions feet and legs for walking and running, eyes for seeing, teeth for tearing and so on. The development of man, of human society involves the improvement of artificial organs. (Philosophers for thinking seeing and communicating, transportation for movement, wage and salary commodity producing workers for creation of a million objects for human consumption and above all creating tools – the means of labor.

*****

#815 **To sum up, human labor differs from the activity of even the most developed animals in that;-**

#816 **first, it exerts an active influence on nature, instead of merely adapting to it as is characteristic of the animals;**

#817 **second, it presupposes systematic use and, above all, production of the instruments of production;**

#818 **third, labor implies purposeful, conscious activity;**

#819 **fourth, commodity production is from the very beginning social in character and inconceivable outside society.**

#820 For these reasons social development differs from biological development. Man develops as a social being without any radical changes in his biological nature. Hence the difference in the character and rate of both processes. Radical changes in social life take place within the periods that would be quite insufficient for any changes to occur in the development of the biological species (not counting, of course, the changes that occur in nature because of man's activity). Biological development, moreover, is tending to slow down as certain species of organisms specialize and adapt themselves to the environment. On the other hand, the development of society shows a general tendency to accelerate despite its various twists and turns and temporary setbacks (Still there are certain anti-social tendencies carried along as baggage of the past that may take centuries of relearning to eradicate from the minds of men.)

#821 Thus there has been change largely due to the appearance of new mechanisms of continuity in social development compared with biological evolution. In the organic world the accumulation and transmission of information from one generation to another is effected mainly through the mechanism of heredity, which forms the basis of the inborn instincts, and in the higher animals also through parents' transmission to their progeny of certain skills. In social life a tremendous part is played by each generation's inheritance of the means of production created by the previous generation, and also by the continuing social experience embodied in language, thought, and cultural traditions. Whereas biological transmission of properties is limited by the information that can be stored in the apparatus of heredity (in the genes), the inheritance of social experience occurs constantly and has no limits. Viewed in the most general sense, culture is the embodiment of this experience, the sum-total of the material and spiritual values created in the course of human history. Each generation enriches culture with new achievements. In contrast to the biological world, where all changes take place spontaneously, unconsciously, human society is afforded ever-greater possibilities in the course of history of consciously and purposefully changing the conditions of its material life and interrelations with nature.

#822 Any material system presupposes a definite type of connection between its constituent elements. The specific nature of social life is determined by, commodity production, transportation, and economic connections. All forms of social relationships are made up in the final analysis on the basis of the relationships, especially between fifth-estate people, arising out of their wage, salary and consulting fee income in connection to the process of producing goods, services and the distribution of same. Thus the production relations cement the social organism and give it its unity.

#823 The qualitative new forms of connection that make up the social organism have corresponding specific laws of development that differ from biological laws. Biological laws do not regulate or determine the development of social phenomena. Society is governed by its own specific laws, which are being revealed more and more by Historical 2020 Materialism and all other sciences.

#824 This does not imply, however, that the fifth-estate develops in isolation from all the other estates and from nature. The development of the fifth-estate is inconceivable without certain social and natural preconditions. Chief among these are; the natural conditions surrounding society, usually called geographical environment, and the physical organization of people themselves who comprise the population.

#825 Various naturalistic theories in sociology have attempted to ascribe the determining role in history to those natural preconditions. Thus the exponents of geographical determinism (the French Philosopher Charles Montesquieu (1689 1755), the English historian Henry Thomas Buckle, (1821 1862), The French geographer Elisee Reclus (1830 1905) and others) tried to attribute the differences between the social systems and histories of various peoples to the influence of the natural conditions in which they live. In fact however, we find extremely different social systems in different geographical conditions and one and the same kind of social system in different geographical conditions (i.e. the tribal system was to be found at various times in Europe, Asia, Africa, America and Australia). Nor can historical succession of socio-economic formations be attributed to the influence of the geographical environment, if only because it occurs far more quickly than changes in this environment, which do not depend on the influence of society. (it might be noted that, in the present age however, society is more and more changing the environment by its actions requiring unmitigated growth under third-estate rule.)

#826 The basic methodological fault of the naturalistic theories in sociology is that they see the source of social development as something outside society. The influence of external conditions on any developing system, including society, cannot be denied or underestimated, of course. But change in such a system is not simply the imprint of changing environment, the passive result of its influence. A system has its own internal logic of development and in its turn exerts its influence on the environment.

#827 If we adopt the Historical 2020 Materialist classification system, society may be regarded as one so called open system, which exchange not only energy but also matter with their environment. Between society and nature there occurs, a constant metabolism, a constant exchange of substances, which take place in the process of labor, of production and distribution. From the vegetable and animal world man obtains his means of nutrition and raw material for making objects of use. Mineral resources provide him with the material for not only producing goods but also for the production of the means of production – tools. Production and distribution involves the use of various sources of energy: first of all, man's own muscular strength, then the strength of animals he tames, of wind and water, and finally the powers of steam, electricity, chemicals and atomic processes.

#828 The geographical environment influences the development of society in various ways at various stages of its development, but the direct influence of geographical conditions on Man's nature and his psychological make-up is never of prime importance (as Montesquieu and other geographical determinists maintain). The main thing is their mediated influence – through the conditions of production and intercourse. At the lower cultural stages, when man is mainly concerned with obtaining ready made products, more importance attaches to the natural means of subsistence: rich fauna and vegetation, fertile soil, an abundance of fish and so on. At the higher stages when industry develops, the means of production, are more highly developed and as industry develops man learns how to use nature more intensively in the use of navigable rivers, waterfalls, forests, metals, coal, oil and agribusiness. In the higher stages ships, railroads, roads, aircraft and spacecraft are added to the list of developments and while the old order still remains the new infrastructure is built upon it. Under the fifth-estate conditions free of incessant requirements to consume, to throw away, man will learn to preserve our spaceship earth.

#829 The direction of economic activity is not, of course, always the same among different peoples, it depends somewhat, but not entirely, on the geographical conditions under which they live. Uneven rates of development of production depend on different social conditions, on how relations took shape between different peoples – on their interconnection or isolation their mutual intercourse or conflict, and so on.

#830 Thus the influence of geographical conditions is always mediated by the social condition, primarily by the level of development of production and transportation. People make various use of the properties of their environment, more and more new material are brought into production, mankind penetrates new regions of nature (the depth of the earth and sea, the investigation of outer space) and masters them in order to serve his needs. This means that society's links with nature become increasingly widespread and many sided.

#831 Abundance of natural resources will never, of course, lose its significance; it constitutes an important element of a regions economic potential. It is true that harsh conditions may give an impetus to people inhabiting such regions to seek keener development. But where the conditions are either too severe or not severe enough then development may lag. But with the development of <u>rational</u> (not irrational and useless) production and distribution society's dependence on natural conditions is relatively diminished.

#832 The twin processes of the expansion of economic ties and the reduction of dependence on natural conditions are both predicated on the increase of man's influence over nature. Whereas natural conditions change comparatively slowly if left to themselves, their rate of change may be accelerated by man. Man's natural environment bears the stamp of his production and distribution activity.

#833 Geographical conditions on earth are to a significant extent the result of the activity of living organisms, which are responsible, for example, for the formation of limestone, dolomite, marble, coal fertile soil and so on. Man influences the vegetable and animal world, exterminates certain species of plants and animals and introduces and changes others.

#834 The scale of man's influence on the earth's crust and atmosphere is comparable with that of the most powerful geological forces. People have extracted and transported 60,000,000,000 tons of coal 3,000,000,000 tons of iron 25,000,000 of copper, 25,000 tons of gold and so on. Man's production activity brings to the surface not less than six cubic kilometers of rock per year. Man drives canals roads and railroads through continents, and wins back land from the sea. By watering deserts, drying marshland and altering the course of rivers he changes even the climactic conditions of his life. All of this makes man's condition on earth sometimes better and oft times poorer. The climate is also indirectly influenced by man's production activity because the burning of oil coal and peat annually returns to the atmosphere about 1,700,000,000 tons of carbon. The amount of carbon in the air is one of the factors affecting the temperature and climactic conditions on earth.

#835 The effect of nature on society is totally spontaneous, but the effect of society on nature is always the result of man's conscious activity and struggle for existence. Besides the intended transformation of nature, human activity also has unforeseen results, which in many cases subsequently cause tremendous losses. Huge areas of land may be eroded and become unsuitable for cultivation. The use of chemical pesticides and weed killers often destroys not only the insects and the weeds but may poison the water-table for man and microbes and animals.

#836 A particular feature of the contemporary stage of interaction between society and nature is the whole surface of the globe is becoming the scene of human activity; man is even venturing beyond the earth's bounds into outer space. Man is making use of nearly every substance that is to be found in the earth's crust and many sources of natural energy.

#837 However as the scale of man's activity increases, the danger of his uncontrolled influence on nature and the natural environment also increases. One of the side effects of man's activity, for example, is the upsetting of the balance between various processes in nature and pollution of air and water with so much industrial waste, radioactive material etc. The highest philosophical question that faces 2020 Materialist philosophers is the study and implementation of global systems and agreements on how to best to protect our own species from ourselves. Homo sapiens must be protected from Homo faber, Homo vendens, unqualified destructive competition that brings with it unmitigated growth, periodic crises, unparalleled anxiety and misery to all the estates devised and evolved by the economic mind of mankind. Yet it is not man per se who is to blame for all these tribulations, but his shortsightedness, the subordination of his activity to considerations of profit or narrow utilitarianism. The destruction of the natural environment has assumed such vast proportions that humanity is faced with the threat of an ecological crisis. But while warning of this danger, many third-estate ideologists, and we might even say apologists, are unable to offer any realistic way out of the situation. Some of them have proposed the idea of 'zero growth', that is to say, halting all growth of industrial production. Quite apart from the impracticability of this idea, we must remember that the great majority of mankind, particularly the populations of the developing countries, are suffering not from excessive growth of production but from too little of it.

#838 The attempt to shift responsibility for the ecological crisis on to technological processes, the scientific and technological revolution are obviously so misguided that even many liberal-minded authors, who are in no way advocates of revolutionary change, recognize the necessity for planning. For restricting third-estate private ownership of public property and the activities of the Multinationals and Transnationals, who are destroying the natural environment in the name of maximum profit – being driven thus by their own fear of ruin if they do not destroy the competition.

#839 Today it is becoming urgent for man to make wise use of the processes of nature on a global scale, which can alone make man the true master of his fate upon this earth. This necessity is also implied in the concept evolved by natural science of the nuosphere (from the Greek nuos (noos) = reason), as the sphere of interaction between nature and society organized by conscious human activity. The biosphere of the 21st century is becoming a nuosphere which presupposes the growth of science, of scientific understanding, and the social wage and salary commodity producing labor of the fifth-state which is based upon them.

#840 The creation of such a nuosphere presupposes the planned use of natural resources on the scale of whole countries and continents, and this is beyond the scope of the third-estate thinking. To achieve this there must be fifth-estate dominion over all production and distribution and not second and third-estate dominion who's only concern is with how can we denigrate the competition?, how can we maximize profit?, where can we find a safe haven for our value added accumulation (capital)? Fifth-estate use of nature is, above all, the use of nature in the interest of the whole of society, it is the planned transformation of nature, the integrated utilization of natural wealth. It stands to reason that the conditions of fifth-estate dominion does not come about automatically but demands rational production planned and managed in such a way as to protect the natural environment.

#841 If men are good masters of the Earth they must not tolerate a departmental approach; the work of transforming nature must be dealt with as a single whole. With economic development, the growth of cities and industrial centers the task of protecting the 'space ship earth' becomes ever more vast and complicated.

#842 To sum up, man's influence on nature depends on the level of the productive forces, on the character of the social system and on the level of development of society and people themselves.

#843 In principle the same is true of another natural precondition of human history – man's bodily organization, his biological properties. It is these biological properties that give him his need for food, clothing, and so on. But the means by which he satisfies these needs are determined not by biological but by social conditions. Procreation also proceeds according to human biological properties and yet the growth of population is primarily a social phenomenon, regulated by the laws of the development of society.

#844 From the naturalistic standpoint population growth is regarded as a factor independent of the laws of social development and even determining that development. Moreover, some sociologists treat it as a positive factor and regard the increase of the population as one of the causes that impel people to seek new sources of food supply and thus promote the development of production and transportation; others (the British economist Thomas Malthus (1766 1834) at the close of the 18th century and his followers today, the neo-Malthusians) see the rapid growth of the population as a social disaster.

#845 According to Malthusian 'law' the population increases faster than the food supply, and hence, so Malthus maintains, come the starvation, unemployment and poverty of the working people. His conclusion is that to improve their position the working people should control the number of births in their families.

#846 In reality the relation between the growth rate of the population and production of the means of subsistence is not something given once and for all. With a relatively conservative technical base and slow development in the pre third-estate social-economic formations there was pressure of excess population on the powers of production, which often led to large-scale migrations of population. On the other hand, in conditions of rapid technical progress the growth of production of the means of subsistence considerably outstrips population growth, as is seen for example, in the increase of per capita production.

#847 In the countries of developed capitalism it is not overpopulation that exerts pressure on the productive forces, but rather the irrational productive forces that pressure the population, and create a relative surplus of population.

#848 The conclusion is that every historically determined mode of production and transportation has its own specific laws of population, which are historical in character. An abstract law exists for plants and animal only, and only insofar as man has not interfered with them.

#849 Size of population, its growth, density, and territorial distribution undoubtedly exerts an influence on the development of society. At the same time the actual number of people that go to make up a society depends on the degree of development of production. At the beginning of the Neolithic age (i.e. about 10,000 years ago) the primitive tribes that had spread over all continents counted only a few million people. By the beginning of the present era the world's population was between 150 and 200 million people, while by the year 1000 it had risen to about 300 million. It reached its first billion in 1850, its second in 1930, its third in 1960, and its fourth in 1976. It is now at 6 billion.

#850 Acceleration in the rate of population growth is not a cause of change in the mode of production and peoples conditions of life; rather it is one of the results. Population increases depends on the ratio of death to births. Both these processes are influenced by a large number of social factors; economic relations, standards of life, housing conditions, medical development, health services, and so on. The types of reproduction of the population also depend on social and economic conditions.

#851 Though basically a spontaneous process, population growth can be influenced to a greater or smaller extent by state policy, legal and other measures aimed at encouraging or, on the contrary, limiting the birthrate. The neo-Malthusians maintain that the present 'population explosion' is no less dangerous than that of an atom bomb.

They compare the increasing numbers of the earth's population to a wildfire cancer growth and maintain that within the next ten years new extensive famine areas will make their appearance. And this is so, however they refuse to see the social causes of such famine.

#852 Scientific calculations show that a fuller use of agricultural land and increasing its yields would make it possible to feed ten times more people than there are at present in the world. There is no doubt that the use of the tremendous food resources of the seas and oceans and further advances in synthesizing food products will reveal possibilities of feeding even greater numbers of people. The realization of these possibilities, however, depends, not so much on finding more rational means of using the biosphere, as on solving social problems. The main one of which is overcoming economic and cultural backwardness in many countries, and elimination of third-estate domination and its requirement for ever more infinite expansion in a finite world.

#853 Historical 2020 Materialism's criticism of Malthusianism does not imply that for society in general there is no problem of regulating population growth and achieving a rational of reproduction. But it will be the historical duty for the fifth-estate to examine this matter in the light of conditions of the time.

*****

The Productive And Distributive Forces Of Society And Man's Place In Them. >#854

#855 Material production is the sphere of social life where the material product is created that afterwards is consumed by society as a whole, by further production or by individuals.

#856 No matter how high the level of development, a society cannot exist and develop without production and distribution. A complete cessation of production would spell disaster for society, which cannot exist without it.

#857 In the process of production people interact with nature and with one another. These two types of relationship constitute the inseparably connected aspects of any concrete mode of production – the process forces the production relations. Consequently, analysis of the mode of production in its general form entails discovering what productive forces and production relations are and how they are interconnected.

#858 The productive forces are the forces by which society influences nature and changes it.

#859 Nature itself cannot be included among the productive forces of society. Nature is the universal object of labor. Labor is the father of wealth and nature is its mother. Not all of nature, of course, is the immediate object of labor, but only that part of it which is drawn into production inasmuch as it is used by man.

#860 From nature man extracts the stuff, the raw material, from which things are made in the process of labor. But with the exception of the extracting industries, the plowing up of virgin land, and so on, production is usually concerned with the objects that have previously had some labor put into them. Thus the steel that goes into making a machine has previously been melted. Raw material and semi-manufactures are man-made objects of labor, but also creates them for himself. Industrial progress involves the use of more and more new materials. Modern industry uses various rare metals, new alloys and new kinds of synthetic materials – plastics, synthetic fibers, and so on. This is entirely natural since new materials widen man's productive powers.

#861 The means of labor are the things or complex of things that a man places between himself and the objects he creates – the objects of labor, and that serve as an active conductor of his influence upon that object. The objects and means of labor, that is, the material elements of the process of labor, constitute in their totality the means of production and transportation.

#862 The composition of the means of labor is extremely varied and changes from one epoch to another. Industrial and agricultural production today makes use of machines and engines and various subsidiary means of labor that are needed for transporting and storing products and for other purposes. Out of all the means of labor that have been applied in any particular epoch and are typical of it are those that directly serve as the conductor of man's influence on nature – the instruments of production – these constitute the bone and muscle of the system of production.

#863 But the means of labor become an active force that transforms the object of labor only in contact with living labor, with man. Men and women in the fifth-estate are a productive and transportive force thanks to their knowledge, experience and the skills needed to put production and distribution into practice.

#864 To sum up, the social productive forces of the Fifth Estate are the means of production created by society and, above all, the instruments of labor, and also the people who put them into operation, produce and distribute material goods.

#865 The means of labor are the determining element in the productive forces, inasmuch as they determine the character of man's relation to nature. It is not the articles made, but how they are made, and by what instruments, that enables us to distinguish different economic epochs.

#866 People of the fifth-estate with their knowledge and experience, are the main productive force of society. Since it is man who uses the existing machinery, creates new machinery, who operates the tools – the instruments of labor and carries on production and distribution, drawing on his skill, knowledge and experience. At the same time these human abilities depend on the available means of labor, on what instruments they are using. Without, lathes there would be no machinists, without schools, books and computers there would be no teachers, without ships there would be no sailors, without trucks, no drivers, without aircraft, no airmen. All of these aforementioned require capital to set them in motion but they do not require capitalists, who now have become a squealing brake upon it all.

#867 With the transition to machine production, education, culture and the scientific knowledge needed for working with machines and perfecting them assume ever increasing significance. The laborer cannot simply throw down his spade and start driving a bulldozer. He or she must master the new machine, even though the excavator performs the same work as they did albeit on a grander scale. At the same time machine production creates in its struggle of opposites a need for unskilled and semi-skilled labor. This is why the development of workers engaged in production has a contradictory nature.

#868 The fifth-estate, in becoming an element in the technological system of production, is not only compelled to obey its rhythm but themselves become an appendage in offices or of the machines themselves in the field and perform the simplest auxiliary functions in the overall scheme of things. So the appearance of machine production operated and superintended by the fifth-estate but owned by the third-estate sharpens the contradictions between mental and physical labor and does not lead to a harmonious rise in the cultural and technical level of the whole mass of the humanity. And although the third-estate conditions the sophistication of machinery it does not create a consistent demand for skilled labor, now garnering it here, now throwing it out there as profit occasion demands.

#869 The level of development of the productive forces is indicated by the productivity of social labor. A major factor in the growth of the productivity of labor is the creation of more productive instruments and means of labor, that is, technical progress. The improvement of the existing instruments and means of labor and the creation of new ones that are more productive, of new technology, the development of the power base and the corresponding re-equipment of all branches of the economy are, in fact, the mainspring of the development of social production.

#870 In the course of the existence of society the productive forces have achieved tremendous developments. Historically, production begins with the making and using of the most primitive stone, bone and wooden implements. The discovery of how to make and use fire was one of the great achievements of man's early development. This discovery finally set man apart from the animal kingdom. Another great step forward was the emergence of pottery. Man's capabilities were considerably expanded by the invention of the bow and arrow. People thus accumulated a collection of primitive implements that enabled them to engage in hunting, fishing and collecting. As tools improved, they tended to become more and more specialized for certain operations. At the earliest stage of primitive society man produced only instruments of labor, while taking his means of existence ready-made from nature which made him heavily dependent on natural conditions.

#871 The great revolution in the development of primitive production was the transition from appropriation to production of the means of existence, which was connected with the emergence of agriculture and cattle breeding. This transition occurred in the Neolithic period. The collecting of fruits and roots prepared the way for land cultivation, while hunting helped to introduce cattle breeding. The extremely primitive tilling of the soil with the hoe demanded an enormous amount of labor. But this was a fundamentally new step in development because it allowed man to use a new and powerful means of production – the soil. The development of agricultural implements led to the appearance of the plow and other means of cultivation and harvesting. Further progress involved the use of metal tools, at first copper and bronze, then iron, and tilling, cattle breeding, and metal tools raised production to a new level. There was now a basis for the division of social labor into cattle breeding, and soil cultivation, into craft and agricultural production, and later, into mental and physical labor. People began to produce more, it became possible to accumulate wealth. All this had its social consequences and prepared the transition from the primitive-communal system to a class society. We should also mention the tremendous importance that the invention of a written language had for the development of production and for human culture as a whole.

#872 In class society production developed at first on the basis of artisan's tools set in motion by man himself. Then it depended on the muscular power of animals this base is conservative in the sense that the instrument of the artisan is specialized and may achieve certain forms that set a limit to its development. For example, knives, axes, spades and hoes may change somewhat in being adapted to various forms of activity, but only within certain limits. Of course, these instruments improved and production developed on their basis, giving rise to various industries. Fairly soon, the power of water and wind began to be used, and more complex instruments were introduced. Mankind was enriched with the important inventions that were to play a great part in the development of technology: the mechanical clock, gun-powder printing and the production of paper, the compass, and so on. All this shaped the conditions for a new qualitative leap in the development of the productive forces – the emergence of machine production and transportation.

#873 It was manufacture that provided the immediate technical preconditions for the appearance of the machines. Cooperation in labor, that is, the joining together of people for the performance of various tasks, had always taken place on a certain limited scale – in quarries and mines, in workshops, in building, and so on. Manufacture differs from simple cooperation in that it is based on a detailed division of labor for the production of a certain kind of goods. The division of labor in manufacturing leads to specialization of tools and of the workman himself, in the course of which he becomes a performer of a particular function. Whereas a craftsman created the whole product, in manufacturing the production of an item is broken down into a number of specialized steps and operations, which creates preconditions for the replacement of the individual workman's operations by a machine or a series of machines.

#874 Machine industrial production began in the 18th century, when England became the scene of the first industrial revolution. The link of this revolution came with the appearance of working machines – the loom and the spinning machine. Such devices replaced a large number of workmen by performing operations that had been previously done by hand. But the working machine demands an 'infallible' and consistent prime mover, and such a motor was invented in the form of a steam engine. This motor, the transmission mechanism and the working machine constituted the first production mechanisms of machine production. The cycle of development was completed by the creation of an adequate technical base – the production of machines by machines. Thus a fundamentally new step was taken in the advance of the productive forces, introducing a new epoch in the development of production. The industrial revolution which had begun in England in the 18th century, spread during the 19th to other European countries, to North America, and by the end of the century to Russia, Japan and in the 20th century it spread throughout most of the countries of the globe. Along with this spread of production the primitive third-estate of the French revolution has progressed to a position where, in the 21st century it, in private ownership, owns and controls (all) the major portion of production, transportation, and information systems of the globe.

#875 In modern times technology is still developing on the basis of machine production. The rise of computer controlled machine production has led to an enormous leap-like growth in the productivity of the fifth-estate in developed countries. It has given over this time the process of wage and salary labor a social character. Bringing together as it does large masses of people 'under one 'flag'' in factories, mills offices and schools. It broadly develops various kinds of division and cooperation of labor, establishing close ties between specialties, facilities and branches of production. These ties are so vast, intertwined and convoluted that the individual wage or salary worker, unless he is very astute, cannot discern the extent of it in his company or in society as a whole. All this makes for such close interconnections between the various types of production that any change in one industry quickly affects others. And finally, in contrast to the artisan basis, the technical basis of machine production is revolutionary because the possibilities of its development are practically unlimited, while the conscious application of science to production makes recurrent technical revolutions inevitable. The development of machine production has revealed what tremendous forces that the fifth-estate and human labor can bring into operation.

#876 The advancement from the use of separate machines to the use of a system of machines and interfaces between one type of manufacture and another has moved on to the creation of automated production in which man is becoming more excluded from the direct process of material production. And his involvement is becoming more and more the task of controlling, adjusting and repairing machines and constructing new ones.

#877 Scientific advances and their technological application by the middle of the 20th century created the preconditions for a new grandiose leap in the development of the productive forces, for the 21st century scientific and technological revolution, which combines revolutionary changes in science and technology. This revolution introduces the age of automated production and leads to a fundamental change in man's place in production and distribution.

#878 The working machine and motor made it possible to transfer from man to technical devices the function of immediate influence on the object of labor. But man still retained control of the machine and the process of production. Thanks to computer techniques, the machine is today taking over the function of controlling production as well. The direct process of material production can now be carried out automatically, without human participation. This raises the productive forces to a qualitatively new level. At the moment we are still at the beginning of this process, but its prospects are already fairly clear. Development is moving from partial to full automation, when there will be not merely a tool, or even a system of machines, between man and nature, but a fully automated production process.

#879 The Scientific And Technological Revolution (STR) is also at work in the field of energetics where it involves peaceful uses of safe atomic energy, the storing and use of solar energy, the creation of space technology and in cybernetics and genetics.

#880 The STR changes the status of science in society, its relations to production. The industrial revolution of the 18th and 19th centuries took place with the participation of natural sciences, in the sense that production set science certain problems and the scientific solution of these problems made it possible to perfect production.

#881 This process goes even further in the 21st century. Here the development of science actually gives rise to new forms of production. Production still remains the final material basis of the development of science, but the social necessity is for science to anticipate the development of technology, in earlier times science followed industry; now it is tending to catch up, surpass, and lead it on to newer more exciting goals.

#882 With the development of machine production in general, and particularly in the context of the STR science becomes increasingly a direct productive force. And in becoming such a force science continues to be a system of knowledge and a sphere of intellectual production, especially when it is enlightened by the categories and philosophy of 2020 Materialism.

#883 The transformation of science into a direct productive force implies, first, that the means of labor, the technological processes are becoming a result of materialization of scientific knowledge. New technology cannot be created without science, and second, even the existing technology becomes an essential component of the experience and knowledge of the fifth-estate taking part in the process of production and distribution. Third, the actual control of production, the technological process, particularly in automated systems, becomes a result of the application of science. Fourth, the very concept of production is widened and comes to include not only production processes but also research and development, so that the spheres of science and production tend to penetrate one another.

#884 The overall effect is expansion of the human component of the productive forces, which already include not only manual wage workers but salaried engineers, technicians, teachers and even scientists who are directly concerned in production and transportation processes.

#885 Automation and 'scientification' of production create the basis for bringing together physical and mental work, lead to the intellectualization of the labor, evoke important changes in the professional structure of labor, and rapidly increase the proportion of skilled workers, technical and engineering personnel. Modern automated lines make special demands on the individual, on his ability to react quickly to contingencies, assess the situation correctly, and assume responsibility.

#886 Third-estate apologist writers will, in the future, spend a lot of time accusing fifth-estate philosophers in general, and 2020 Materialists in particular of regarding man merely as a 'productive force' and attaching no value to him as an individual. In reality however, it is not recognition of man as a productive force that belittles him, but the oppression of man by siphoning off all the value-added produced by the fifth-estate and throwing this away in a million different anti-social ways. And even what is much more frivolous creating boom and bust cycles with the resulting 'super rich'—'super poor' conflict and anxiety in global society.

#887 In the conditions of third-estate rule, where modern technical progress gives rise to increasingly acute social antagonisms, we find various kinds of 'technical mythology', which absolutes the role of technology and regard it as a force hostile to man. The authors of such concepts divorce technology from man, underestimate the role of the fifth-estate and ignore the significance of social conditions. Conditions on which the ultimate outcome of technical development primarily depends. If under the rule of the third-estate life actually is becoming more standardized and man is losing his individuality, the cause is not technological progress in itself but the domination of the third-estate over the irrational manipulation of the means of production.

#888 The development of STR in the hands of the fifth-estate implies the improvement of the individual's creative abilities and his liberation from boom, bust, war, frustration and anxiety. But especially it frees him from the 'every man for himself and the devil take the foremost' mentality that permeates present day society, this affliction leads to all manner of aberrations in mankind that now, due to its protracted and pernicious existence may take hundreds of years to nullify.

*****

Production Relations >#889

#890 In producing material goods people interact not only with nature but with one another, in the process of production certain relations necessarily arise between people. They are an inseparable aspect of every form of human productive activity, of all material production. These relations are a very component of any society and we shall consider their place and role in the vital activity of the social organism in more detail later. At the moment we must note that what made it possible to understand the functioning and development of production, not only as a technological but as a social process, was the singling out of production relations as the thing that determines both the social character of every element of the productive forces. And the social nature of the mode of production as a whole.

It is the production relations that tell us whether a workman is a slave, or a serf, or a wage or salary worker, whether a machine serves as the means of exploiting labor or, on the contrary as a means of making labor easier. Whether the factories and installations are working to enrich the exploiters of other men's labor or to satisfy the needs of the mass of people who produce the goods and transport them, and so on.

#891 Production relations are economic relations. They are studied in detail by the science of economics. What interests Historical 2020 Materialism is the question of their specific nature, their structure and the laws of their interconnection with the productive forces and other social phenomena.

#892 In what way do production relations differ from other social relations? First of all, like the production forces, production relations belong to the material side of social life. The materiality of these relations is expressed in the fact that they arise and exist objectively, independently of human will and consciousness. People are not free in the choice of the relations into which they enter in the process of production. In producing the material goods needed for their existence, they produce and reproduce their production relations according to the level the productive forces have achieved. In the process of the development of the material life of society, of economic relations there comes into being 'an objectively necessary chain of events, a chain of development which is independent of one's social consciousness, and is never grasped by one's own social consciousness completely.'

#893 As social relations, production relations should be distinguished from organizational, technical relations, which are determined by the technology of production, by the technical division of labor between the various trades and specialties. The character of these social production relations depends on who in the given society owns the basic means of production. Or, in other words, how the question of ownership of the means of production is decided, ownership being understood not simply as the legal right to own something but the actual totality of economic relations between people, mediated by their relationship to certain things, namely the means of production. Thus to define third-estate ownership of the means of production is nothing else than to expose the special social relations inherent between all the estates that have developed historically around the production of goods and commodities.

And it should be pointed out that when one talks about private ownership in this context one is not expressing the ownership of this or that chair, house or car but the special ownership in production that allows for the extraction of 'value-added' for personal private use.

#894 Ownership of the means of production may be either social or private. But both types of ownership vary in the degree of their development and the concrete forms they have taken, not to mention the existence of a number of transitional forms (joint stock companies and so forth). These must be taken into consideration even when problems are studied in their 'pure form', so to speak.

#895 If certain individuals or a part of society own the means of production while the rest of society is prevented from taking part in such ownership, this then takes the form of private ownership of public property. Private ownership of public property is the basis of a relation of an antagonistic struggle of opposites – of domination and subordination, relations of exploitation, that is to say the appropriation of other's labor – surplus-value or value-added. Three basic forms of exploitation – slave owning, feudal and capitalist third-estate – have been known so far in history. The slave is himself the property of the slave owner. Feudal property makes it possible to deprive the serf of a part of what he has produced to be given it up to the feudal lord. The most developed form of private ownership of public property is the capitalist.

#896 The economic structure of the domination by the third-estate is determined by two elements: the third-estate's private ownership of the basic means of production – factories, mines, mills, transportation and thus its power reaches downward and upward to influence all estates. It has three significant holds 1) Its most significant hold is the hold it has over 'free' labor power. 2) Another significant hold it has is over the state machinery 3) Another significant hold it has is over every other estate from the first to the seventh.

In the first we have people free to work in this or that establishment. Free to frequent the food bank. Free to sleep with the street people; (and! don't we need the street people to ensure that everyone else keeps their nose to the grindstone?) Economic necessity forces the wage and salary commodity-producing worker to sell his labor power to the owners ensconced in the third-estate. This free worker is a commodity and only in the form of a commodity is he able to sell himself and unite with the tools – the instruments of labor and begin the process of production. At various stages in history the workers themselves (peasants or artisans) have owned small private productive property based on personal labor. As a rule, such property plays only a subordinate role and in estate divided society small private productive property owners (i.e. consultants, welder's and their rigs, independent truckers, carpenters, computer technicians and so on and so forth) are themselves subject to exploitation.

#897 On the other hand in fifth-estate productive property ownership by groups of wage and salary commodity producing workers place people in an equal position in relation to the means of production. The exchange activity here takes the form of mutual assistance and cooperation and not as master and servant in a destructive unmitigated competition with its boom and bust frequency.

#898 Thus whether production is peaceful and un-stressful or antagonistic and anxiety prone depends upon the social character of production and distribution and depends directly upon the state of affairs between public ownership of public property and/or private ownership of public property.

*****

Dialectics Of The Development Of The Productive Forces And Relations Of Production. >#899

#900 The interaction of the productive forces and production relations obeys a general sociological law that has operated throughout history, the law of correspondence of the production relations to the character and level of development of the productive forces. This law characterizes an objectively existing dependence of the production relations on the development of the productive forces, and establishes the fact that the production relations take shape and change under the determining influence of these forces.

#901 When human beings had only just emerged from the animal state, the stone tool and other implements that they used were so primitive and unproductive that the individual armed with these tools would have been unable alone to obtain the material goods he needed for subsistence. People were compelled to work together, to support one another because of the weakness of the individual in the face of the mighty forces of nature. Thus the main productive force here was the strength of the collective itself, and it was on this basis that collectivist primitive communal relations arose.

#902 The appearance of agriculture and stock-raising, the transition from stone to bronze, and then iron tools raised the productivity of labor with the result that it became possible for people to engage in productive activity on an individual or family scale. The surplus product (i.e. the product remaining after the satisfaction of essential needs i.e. the father of value-added) made its appearance, along with the division of labor, the frame-work of the commune, and, as a result private property – the father of privately owned public property.

#903 The law of the correspondence of production relations to the character and the level of development of the production forces manifest itself at this stage of production in the fact that privately owned public property production relations correspond to the private character of the productive forces. It would seem that only small private property based on personal labor of the producers corresponds to the instruments of individual use. But this form of property never created a specific social-economic formation because it was incapable by itself of ensuring progress in the economic and cultural spheres. For this reason we find developing alongside it various forms of private property based on the appropriation of other peoples labor – other people's value-added, that is the exploitation of man by man, made possible due to the appearance of value-added and surplus product. (And eventually this state of affairs, in a higher society will lead to the mutual misery of both the expropriators and the expropriated in shared anxiety, frustration, disastrous boom and bust competitive cycles, and war.)

#904 When people were using simple implements of labor to cultivate the earth, or in artisan production, it was possible to appropriate the surplus product or 'value-added' over and above subsistence only by enslaving the person himself, by forcing him to work by the threat of the whip.

#905 The first and most primitive form of exploitation – slavery – was based on brute force, by means of which a person was turned into an instrument of labor, a right-less slave. Direct coercion, forced labor was widely used under feudalism in relations to peasants, who were themselves a step above slaves in that they were small property owners but at the same time constituted the main exploited class but they were also the main productive force of feudal society. These peasants were ruled either by the first or by the second estates.

#906 As the third-estate arises, the direct producer, the peasant is, gradually over hundreds of years, separated from his property and from the mean of production. One result of this process is the formation at one end of the scale of a market of 'free' labor power no longer tied to the land. It is free from the means of production and also free from its means of subsistence. And on the other hand a gradual concentration and ownership of the means of production into the hands of the third-estate who everywhere proclaim "You Can't Kill Capital – Capital is King!" (In other words you can't kill the expropriation of 'value-added'! Expropriation of 'value-added' is imbued with the divine right of kings!)

#907 Thus it has come about that salary and wage earners of the fifth-estate are deprived of the means of labor and the means of subsistence. And compelled (by the threat of falling into lives in poverty, into lives of pecuniary circumstance, yes and even (speaking globally) into lives of starvation) to sell their labor power to the third-estate. Thus there has come into being the fifth-estate, an estate totally separated from the means of production and creating by its labor all the wealth residing in its own and in of every other estate.

#908 In this society exploitation lies in the fact that the third-estate, calling it capital, appropriates the 'value-added' created by the fifth-estate. But owing to the development of the productive forces, the socialization of production, the product now becomes the result of the labor, not of a single producer but of an aggregate, collective of billions of people. So under the estate system nomenclature, with the dominant third-estate at the helm, there develops a contradiction between the social character of the process of production and the private third-estate appropriation of the all the value added created by the fifth-estate. This contradiction reveals itself in the cataclysms of the spontaneous destructive competition, in chaos of production, in irrational production, wars, crises of overproduction, strikes and in the now open now hidden struggle of the fifth-estate wage and salary commodity producing workers.

#909 The grouping of large funds in the hands of the third-estate amounting to many times the value-added by wage and salary workers in any given year washes around the globe at billions upon billions of dollars (labor tokens) on any given day. This is counter productive as it leads to anxiety in all sectors and in all estates including the third-estate itself as pointed out previously. Without going into the economics of it still one can imagine the manipulation, money laundering, money printing by various states and what is money but a labor token? The defilement is so stupendous that it stupefies the imagination.

#910 The development of large scale industry not only creates the material precondition but makes it imperative that the fifth-estate salary and wage workers take part in the just distribution of the value-added that they have created. But at this juncture in history the fifth-estate, is not yet conscious of this value-added and its magnitude of extraction are content to leave it to the whim of the few and ever fewer People who make up the third-estate. Who squander these vast riches on chicanery, destructive competition and boom and bust economies and war.

#911 Under the third-estate with the control of the state machinery and in its economy geared to their own narrow interests of profit. Automation reduces the number of workers required to be engaged in material production and throws large masses of people into the 'redundant' 'down size' category, awakening new conflicts and insoluble contradictions. The third-estate stands in the way of the true application of the great discoveries of science, technology and social psychology. Its ultra competitive, every man for himself philosophy has turned into a mass syndrome, thus the third-estate and their lackeys stands in the way of cooperation and brotherhood to achieve a better life for the vast majority and between different peoples of the globe.

#912 To sum up, each form of production relations exist for as long as it provides sufficient scope for the development of the productive forces. But gradually the relations of production come, through the struggle of opposites, into contradiction and antagonism with the further development of the productive forces and become a brake on them. They are then superseded by new relations of production, the role of which is to serve as the form of the further development of the productive forces. People never give up the productive forces they have brought into being but this does not mean that they do not give up the production relations with the owners of the means of production which up to the nodal point have served them well in their own development. On the contrary, in order that they may not be deprived of the results attained and forfeit the fruits of civilization they are obliged, from the moment when their mode of carrying on commerce no longer corresponds to the productive forces acquired, to change all their old traditional social forms.

#913 If the production relations change under the influence of the progress of the productive forces, then what may be asked, causes the development of the productive forces themselves?

#914 Here we must consider the action of a whole set of causes. In our examination of how geographical conditions and the growth of population interact with production we found out that their influence is considerable and may either stimulate or retard it. But they are not the basic source of development of the productive forces.

#915 This development has an inner logic of its own. The more complex instruments of labor arise on the basis of their simpler predecessors. The experience and knowledge accumulated by man find their material expression in the means of labor and man has to adapt himself to them. In any relatively developed economy an important change in one industry inevitably affects the others. For example, the development of industrial production leads to the technical re-equipment of agriculture, to the mechanization of construction: the intensification of agriculture demands production of fertilizers, which stimulates the development of the chemical industry, and so on. As technology develops and new and more efficient tools and machines appear, the existing machines become obsolete and demand replacement. Society is compelled to reckon with this logic of the development of production. But the internal needs of the productive forces still do not explain why production develops faster in some cases and slower in others, more or less evenly in some cases and through booms and crises in yet others. Nor can this be ascribed to the development of science. All technology is materialized knowledge, and without the development of human knowledge there could be no technical progress. Today research and development is a powerful source of technical progress. But the development of science itself, its actual growth rate depends in great measure on the development of production.

#916 The needs of society, of people, are an important factor in the development of production. Directly or indirectly, production always serves the purpose of satisfying certain human needs, and a complex dialectical interconnection between these needs and production establishes itself in society. The needs themselves are evoked by the development of production, the satisfaction of some needs give rise to new ones, and this is bound to influence production in some way or another. The relation of man's needs to production is mediated by production relations. The needs do not influence the productive forces directly, but do so through production relations.

#917 Every form of production relations subordinates production to a particular aim, this aim has certainly not always been the essential needs of humanity. The mass of the population in an estate divided society are motivated by various economic interests and corresponding stimuli, which are specific in every specific case. The first-estate is motivated by religion and the offering, The second-estate is motivated by hereditary right the third-estate by profit and so on. The active nature of the production relations shows itself in the influence they have on the development of productive forces as an economic form. This form is the basis for the emergence of objective regularities and stimuli characteristic of the society in question.

#918 The ruling classes in estate divided societies subordinate the development of production to their interests and needs. Thus with the third-estate in control the development of the productive forces cannot be attributed to the need of the salary and wage commodity producing worker for improvement of their material position. Here the decisive thing is the demand for the production of value-added, of profit for the third-estate. It is the objective laws of expanded production and reproduction, the laws of production of maximum profit through unmitigated mutually destructive competition, that have constituted and still constitute the driving forces of the development of irrational production and its productive forces.

#919 But what stimulates the actions of the fifth-estate, the direct producers? This depends on the position of the direct producer in the system of the given productive relations. A certain form of production relations is progressive inasmuch as it creates for the fifth-estate certain advantages as compared to their previous situation. The slave has no interest whatever in work, because he works under threat of the lash. Under feudalism the immediate producer – the peasant – has his farm, his family, and is therefore to some extent interested in work, in raising its productivity. The salary and wage worker of the fifth-estate confronts the owner of all the means of production – The third-estate – as a formally equal owner of commodities. He sells his labor power and generally the higher his skill the higher the wage and salary commodity producing worker receives, and is therefore compelled to some extent to develop the productive power of his or her labor. But working for the third-estate forces the salary and wage commodity producing worker to regard his work only as a source of livelihood. The whole mechanism is so constructed that it compels the salary and wage worker to strain every effort and ability. Their fear of being thrown out of production and becoming unemployed down-sized has no less force than the slave owner's whip.

#920 So, the causes of the development of the productive forces must never be considered in isolation from the social conditions in which this development occurs, that is, from the system of the given production relations. The development of the crude technology of primitive society and that of modern machine and computer technology cannot be ascribed to the same causes. Each historically definite mode of production has its own specific causes (sources) and economic laws of development of the productive forces that are valid for a given epoch, and the character of these laws of development depend on the character of the production relations.

#921 The effect of the production relations is positive when the production relations corresponding to the productive forces promote the development, and negative when the correspondence is upset and the production relations act as a brake on the development of the productive forces. What, then, is the braking effect of third-estate production relations upon all other estates? It shows itself above all in the fact that not all the possibilities of the level of production already achieved are used – Third-estate ownership of the means of production meets with barriers at a certain expanded stage which if viewed from other premises, would make it altogether inadequate. It comes to a standstill at a point fixed by a value-added extraction (and squandering) in the form of destructive competitive profit and not in the satisfaction of human need.

#922 This is where the limitations of third-estate control of the economy for its own misguided aggrandizement is revealed in universal anxiety, and by putting into effect a monstrous intensification of labor overstrains and exhausts people and creates an army of downsized unemployed, semi employed and street people. Chronic global unemployment goes hand in hand with periodic recession, chronic over loading and then under loading of productive capacities, and limited one sided use of scientific potential. Through the militarization and police-ization of some economies for profit the third-estate turns the productive forces into destructive forces.

#923 The effect of The ownership of the vast majority of the productive tools and factories in the hands of the third-estate is becoming a brake on the development of the productive forces – the wage and salary commodity producing workers

– is that the development of production proceeds extremely unevenly, in booms and busts downsizing and crises.

#924 Thus the active role of the production relations between the third and fifth-estates does not mean that the forms of private ownership of public property by itself holds back the development of production. Only people develop production or, on the contrary, are not interested in its development. People develop and change their mode of production, which constitutes the basis of their history.

LAW
The law of correspondence of the production relations to the character and development of the productive force determines not only the development of the given mode of production, but also the necessity for the replacement of the ownership of one mode of production by another. >#925

#926 As the productive forces develop in the womb of the old society new production relations are conceived that form a certain economic structure, the embryo, of the new mode of production. Slavery is conceived already in the womb of the old primitive communal system. The domination by the third-estate over the fifth-estate was conceived in feudal society dominated by the second and first-estates.

#927 The expanded productive forces come into conflict with the old production relations prevailing in society. This conflict cannot be resolved, that is the struggle of opposites ends in anxiety and bitter antagonisms, and the new production relations between third and fifth estates cannot prevail by means of a simple quantitative change. Here there must be a qualitative transition, the dismantling of the old obsolete and hidebound economic, social and political forms which opens the road for the establishment of a new mode of production. This 'dismantling' in the past has often taken the form of armed rebellion against oppression. i.e. The early clashes in the old Greek and Roman states to create feudalism out of slavery The English revolution (1642 1648), The American revolution (1775 1783), French revolution (1789 1799), the Russian revolutions (of 1905 and 1917), The Chinese revolution of 1949 and so on.

#928 Now a new qualitative change has taken place with the advent of a world body of the United Nations. This is the beginning of world government and a mechanism through which peaceful change 'can and may' take place but this body is only in its embryo state at this period in history and many States still oppose its tenets. One must remember that Fascism is a political philosophy which exalts the state. Nazism exalts the state when it is a land grabbing racial or religious state. But the UN's tenets do not exalt the state at all and this fact will eventually ensure the integration of the world economy and proportional development in all spheres of social, ecological and economic life of the peoples of the globe.

*****

CHAPTER 7 >#929

The Social Economic Formations Unity And Diversity Of The World Historical Process >#930

#931 The theory of social-economic formations is the cornerstone of the materialist understanding of history as an integral, law-governed natural historical process of social development. By singling out the various forms of society that constitute qualitative stages in its development, this theory allows us to place the study of history on a concrete basis. If history of society is built on the history of specific-social economic formations, we must study the laws of their development and transition from one formation to another.

*****

The Concept Of The Social-Economic Formation >#932

#933 We have seen that the basis of social life and historical development is the mode of production of material goods. No matter what social phenomena we take – the state, or nation, or the international, or science, or ecology, or morality, or language, or art, and so on – they cannot be understood on their own terms. But only as phenomena engendered by society and in the future it will be a global society corresponding to certain social needs. Just as people's way of life in a particular society is basically characterized by the mode of production, so are all other social phenomena dependent ultimately on the mode of production and proceed from it. The mode of production is the material and economic base of society and determines its entire internal structure The concept of social-economic formation primarily expresses this subordination of all social phenomena to the material relations of production.

#934 The study of society shows that all social phenomena, all aspects of society are organically inter-linked. The social-economic formation is not an aggregate of individuals, not a mechanically assembled set of unrelated social phenomena. But it is an integral social system each of whose components (that is, the various social phenomena) must be regarded not by itself, not isolated, but only in its connection with other social phenomena, with society as a whole. This is because each of them plays a definite and unique role in the functioning and development of society. This integrity is expressed by the concept of the social-economic formation.

#935 The history of society is made up of the histories of individual countries and peoples living in various geographical and historical conditions and possessing their own particular ethnic, national, international and cultural features. History is extremely diverse, and this has led philosophers and sociologists to maintain that it never repeats itself, historical science can only describe these individual events, and evaluate them from the standpoint of some ideal. Such an approach to history is bound to subjectivism because the very choice of ideals and values for judging history becomes arbitrary and loses the objective criteria that are needed to distinguish what is essential, paramount, determining in history, and what is derivative and secondary.

#936 The 2020 Materialist theory of society overcomes this subjectivism by singling out from the totality of social relations production relations as the most important and definitive. It was production relations that provided the objective criterion for distinguishing the essential and the inessential in social life. This also revealed the repetition and the regularity in the system of various countries, the general features in the history of individual peoples at one and the same stage of historical development.

#937 The concept of the social-economic formations – the Estate System (first brought to light by Plato and refined during the late 1700's and further refined in subsequent periods) makes it possible to single out the general features to be found in the systems of various countries. It is also able to distinguish one historical period from another. Every estate has its definite stage in the development of human society as a whole, a qualitative unique system of social relations exists between estates.

#938 The history of society is the history of the development and replacement of social-economic formations, one estate replacing another and becoming its dominant leader, Thus there were, and still are, religious dominated states – The first-estate.

#939 There were, and still are to this day, vestiges of feudal dominated estates, The second-estate. (Such estates are Kings, Sultans, Sheiks wresting a living from sharing in the spoils that their subjects produce or by the leasing of confiscated lands or other commodity revenues that once had belonged to their ancient peoples in common.)

#940 But the dominant estate that has taken over the ownership of the means of production globally is the third-estate. But, as was pointed out previously, this estate although growing in money power is dwindling in the number of people that actually operate and control it.

#941 The other estates such as the fourth-estate, the press and media has a mighty power because it is dominated by the third-estate in which a few very rich members largely own it. This estate feeds on itself in the sense that it reports out of all proportion on its own doings. It feeds, to a large extent, on itself, rarely reporting, in a constructive way, on producers of all the social wealth in this globe. It oft times denigrates the salary and wage worker and small subsistence farmers, his or her associations and their struggles and interconnections to value-added and its squander at the hands of all other estates.

#942 The fifth-estate, the wage and salary workers and professionals, teachers older people, those now in retirement who produce or had produced all of the world's goods is growing globally in people numbers. The large majority of this estate is living in fear of poverty, or actually living in poverty, anxiety, and unemployment.

#943 The sixth-estate, The police and the armed forces have the capacity to take over and rule the state machinery and in many cases have done so and are doing so to this day.

#944 Out of all the present chaos in the global economy comes the seventh-estate, The Street people, beggars, driven into thievery and economic criminal activity. These people (majority, but not all, driven there by the predatory operations of the third-estate) are also growing in number, but except for extreme circumstance have never been capable of attaining political power over the state. Although if one looks at the criminal activity of Nazi regimes based upon land grabbing racial or religious states one might be able to make a case that here too the criminal element is capable of controlling state machinery.

#945 The sequence of these formations is not a fixed pattern that the history of every people must obey, because some peoples are held in one development while others bypass whole formations. Needless to say History produces various transitional forms.

#946 The theory of the social-economic formations, by registering the basic stages in historical progress, reveals the main line of human development. And it shows that, varied though the paths of historical development of individual countries and peoples may have been, there is, in history a certain recurrence or regularity, a certain law.

#947 The social-economic formations is a definite type of society, an integrated social system functioning and developing according to its own specific laws on the given mode of production. The economic skeleton of the social-economic formation is formed by the historically determined production and distribution relations, but the whole body, its flesh and blood, as it were, comprises other social phenomena and relations, forming the complex structure that we now must investigate.

*****

Structure Of The Social-Economic Formations. Basis And Superstructure >#948

#949 All social-economic formations differ qualitatively but they do have certain general structural features that are inherent in all or, at least, in the majority of such formations.

#950 Every society is characterized by a definite type of social relations, one estate with another. Social relations are a special form of connection and interactions existing only in society and arising in the process of peoples work and social activity, and that is mostly in the sphere of production, politics, intellectual life, and so on. These relations are called social relations not only because they exist only in society, but also because they emerge from the interaction of large masses of people, in the various estates.

#951 Social relations are extremely varied. Their different types include: economic, political, legal, socio-psychological, organizational, moral relationships etc. To find any regular interconnection in this diversity we must make up our minds, which relations are essential, or primary, and which are derivative, or secondary. There is the ideological and there is the material. The ideological is the superstructure that is built upon the material.

#952 Material relations are above all economic relations that arise in the process of the production and transportation of material goods as the basic type of human activity. Also materials are the relations between man and nature, the relations between production and consumption, the initial, primary relations in the sphere of everyday existence, in the family. The concept of material social relations is therefore wider than the concept of economic relations.

#953 The feature common to all material relations is that they exist independently of social consciousness, that they are primary in comparison with all other forms of social relations. For example, let us take value. Value is just as objective and material as the thing produced the use-value. At the same time value is not something substantial that can be perceived by the senses. Value is the objective material relationship between producers of goods. This means that 'value' in materiality in this sense is of something substantial, something tangible in the mind of man. Of course, society cannot exist without the material substantial embodiment of the achievements of human labor (Thus the Parthenon is dead labor made manifest just as the car you are driving is dead labor made manifest although the laborer who built it may still be living and producing other automobiles.)

#954 The results of labor, buildings, ploughed fields, parks, canals, roads, commodities, the movement of man-made objects from here to there are all the creation of human hands – the materialization of man's activity and ideas. But these are not the only elements that constitute 'social' matter, the objective basis of all social relations.

#955 The superstructural relations, that is, secondary relations, derived from material relations, may be grouped under the general heading of ideological relations – association, unionization, political, legal, moral, and so on. The specific feature of these relations is that they arise only after the preliminary passage through the social consciousness. For example, (After the 'wake-up' call to the consciousness) Unions are formed on the basis of economic relations in a relatively small antagonistic relationship between employees and an employer. Political relations are formed on the basis of the economic relations and interests of various estates but in accordance with the political ideology of estates, that is to say, their awareness of their common estate interest and aims. It is the object of an estate to laud its own aims while remaining silent about, or suppressing, the aims of all other estates

#956 Now that we have drawn this distinction between material and ideological relations we can attempt to define the concepts characterizing the structure and specific quality of each social economic formation - base and superstructure.

#957 The basis is the economic structure of society, the sum-total of the production relations of the given society. The concept of basis expresses the social function of the production relations as the economic basis of social life.

#958 The superstructure comprises three intrinsically connected groups of phenomena. The First is social ideas, moods, social feelings that is, ideology and social psychology. Second, various organizations and institutions – the state, courts, church, and so on. Third the superstructure (ideological) relations. Consequently, the super structure is the sum-total of social ideas, institutions and relations arising on a given economic base.

#959 Historical 2020 Materialism methodology begins with the recognition of the priority and determining role of the material base in relation to superstructure (the ideological), with the fact that every social-economic formation has its own basis and corresponding superstructure. So both the superstructure and the basis have a historical concrete character.

#960 Depending on what kind of economic basis a society may have, its systems of political, legal, religious and philosophical views will correspond to that basis, as will the corresponding relations and institutions of that given society. A common feature of the economic structure of all estate divided formations is that they have relations which allow one part of society, the exploiting minority estate (with its substructure of vassal estates) to appropriate the labor of the rest. This state of affairs leads to an almost unbearable anxiety in the whole structure – in all estates – included in that, is the anxiety even felt by the peoples of the exploiting estate. On the other hand, societies differ in certain essential respects, depending mainly on the specific nature of their basis, that is to say, the prevailing forms of property and forms of human exploitation. For example, the basis of bourgeois society is the third-estate's ownership of the means of production, distribution and especially the Media – the forth-estate. (it is interesting to note that under the conditions of the 'internet' people have, and increasingly will have, the capability of inputting their voice in affairs which up to this point in history they have not had that powerful capability. And every one wills and 'flames' his own opinion on the internet and out of it comes that which no one wills.)

#961 The mechanism of third-estate exploitation is as follows:- all wealth that flows into the third-state individuals and into third-estate state machinery is by way of expropriated value-added produced by the wage and salary commodity producing labor of those in the fifth-estate. This expropriation is by way of taxes, profit, interest, and dividends etc. Thus domination in the economic sphere results directly in domination in all other spheres of social life including political, religious, and media. Through its ownership of the means of material production – unmitigated soul-less competition, the every man for himself – the third-estate takes possession of spiritual, intellectual production as well. Thus the third-estate shapes the superstructure, which protects and reinforces the conditions for its domination.

#962 Reflecting the nature of the given basis, the superstructure registers the contradiction that pervade the economic and judicial basis. In an estate divided society the economic contradictions inevitably manifest themselves in contradictions in the superstructure – in contradictions mainly between the third-estate and the fifth-estate and the movement of masses between different political parties, in the ideological struggle between the different estates.

#963 The superstructure's dependence on the basis is expressed in the fact that the changes occurring in the economic system of the society in question are reflected in its superstructure. It is characteristic of all estate divided, antagonistic social formations that the elements of the new basis and corresponding superstructure are conceived already in the framework of the economic and political structures of the old formation. This can be seen from the example of third-estate relations, which were conceived as a special structure within the framework of European feudalism. Their emergence was accompanied by deep-going changes in the intellectual life of the society, (i.e. Henry the VIII's fight against the church. (Second against First Estate.) The appearance of bourgeois ideology and a new culture, which arose in opposition to the feudal first and second estates at that time were progressive and in some cases even revolutionary. (i.e. infighting - Luther on the Protestant first-estate side against first-estate Rome. Thus preparing the ground for the infusion of bourgeois ideology.) (Washington and others of the third-estate against the opposition of the monarchy and the second estate residing in England.) All the anti-feudal social forces (the bourgeoisie, the mass of the serfs and working people) joined in the struggle against privileged sections of feudal society. This was a struggle that culminated in the third-estate revolution. Which revolution removed the obstacles of feudalism that the first and second estates had placed in the path of the development of capitalist production. All this action and reaction made the third-estate supreme in the sphere of political and economic ideology. It has subsequently blossomed from its first tentative beginnings in the Holland and English revolutions and is now global in scope.

#964 Further changes in the superstructure of third-estate society are connected with the transition from pre-monopoly capitalism to military imperialism to economic imperialism with the advent of the global Trans-nationals. Here it should be emphasized that the more the third-estate develops in its own economic way so it develops the wage and salary workers of the fifth-estate. It develops the productive forces, the more rapidly its economic system ages and the more reactionary it becomes in its political and ideological respects. Only the opposition of the fifth-estate, the drive of the salary and wage commodity producing workers for better global conditions, rights and so on, forces the third-estate to give little concessions here and there. But more often the third-estate uses the services of the sixth-estate that resort to methods of hidden and even open terror – to mask the reactionary nature of the superstructure, the one sided truths of the press are used to preserve an appearance of democracy, and so on. They even use the parliamentary processes to prop up failing banks and other institutions (most recently Japan etc.), then when they become healthy again they revert them back to private ownership. (witness the wholesale privatization of Russian and Mexican public institutions to a few oligarchs.) (Note too the expropriation of salary and wage workers unemployment funds and so on in Canada.) This is all tantamount to private profit and socialized losses the best of all worlds for the bourgeoisie.

#965 As we have noted, the fifth-estate cannot replace the third-estate until all the conditions are met for it to do so. It has been noted that the third-estate although building up and controlling tremendous numbers – trillions of labor tokens – itself, as far as people numbers are concerned, is a dwindling estate. The third-estate's stranglehold on production and distribution and unmitigated destructive competition that has engendered 'the every man for himself syndrome' and tremendous 'road-rage' anxiety, will gradually be replaced by world government wherein agreement and cooperation will be the by-word. This advance in history the third-estate fights at almost every turn. The UN or some forum like it with its off-shoots is destined to become what the old communists never could quite get going on a global scale and that was the International.

#966 At this time in history the superstructure of the third estate is relatively independent of the basis. The social system can never be as rigid and closely determined as a system of mechanical dependencies. The influence of the basis on the superstructure is exerted through an intricate system of mediating links between the various economies and various forms of ideology, etc. History is made by people especially the working people who produce all the goods. The salary and wage commodity producing workers through their organizations, associations and learned societies have the biggest role to play in this transition, although at the present stage of development they are not yet conscious of the role they are destined to play in it. They will, thorough a tortuous path it is admitted, change the superstructure, pursue policies, create new ideas and wage ideological struggle not only with the third-estate but also with the ideologically backward leaders of its own fifth-estate. For this reason the dependence of the superstructure on the basis should not be understood in an oversimplified way, as an automatically operating mechanism. All changes in the superstructure cannot be attributed solely to economic causes. The interaction of the elements of the superstructure themselves produces results that are sometimes not conditioned economically. It is only in the final analysis that the economy determines the social superstructure.

#967 The superstructure is always an active force influencing, in order to protect, reinforce and develop, all aspects of social life, including its own basis. In the present age the role of the superstructure as an active factor in history is sharply intensified. There are several reasons for this. The third-estate increasingly places its hopes on its increasing wealth derived by a decreasing physical number of them from the increasing number of people who globally make up the fifth-estate whose wage and salaried people pour their value added into third-estate coffers.

#968 The enhanced activity of the third-estate also shows itself in the state's extensive use of regulation of the economy. It's an economic control, its an application of increasingly sophisticated ways of shaping the social consciousness in order to subordinate the fifth-estate to its 'every man for himself, destructive competitive' will and retard any development of a cooperative will.

#969 The basis and the superstructure are the fundamental structural elements of any social-economic formation. They characterize its qualitative uniqueness, the difference between it and other formations. Besides the basis and superstructure a social-economic formation includes other elements of social life (everyday affairs, family relations and so on), but it is the basis and the superstructure that determine the specific nature of the formation as an integral social organism.

*****

Unity and Diversity Of The Historical Process. >#970

#971 The development and replacement of social-economic formations determine the progressive course of history. One aspect of the mode of production – the production forces – is the element that ensures continuity in the progressive development in society, determines the direction of this development from a lower to a higher stage in the spiral (coil). The other aspect of the mode of production and distribution – the production relations – expresses the discontinuity in historical development. Obsolete production relations are always abolished and replaced by a higher type of production relations and a higher formation. Consequently, the emergence and development of social-economic formations, the transition to a higher formation are due to the action of the law of correspondence of production relations to the character and level of development of the productive forces. This law manifests itself as a tendency in the development and replacement of formations.

#972 Former joint activity (division of labor based merely on age and sex), equally in distribution, strict tribal rules (taboos) and full compliance of the individual to them, and an elaborate system of conditioning the younger generation for the daily rigorous struggle for survival. This characterized the social relations of this period in the life of mankind, which lasted for thousands of years. Here the dependence of the way of life and the whole system of relations on the level of production stands out clearly in all its primeval simplicity. The primitive communal formation was universal. Nevertheless slowly, the productive forces developed within its framework. Man's labor became more and more productive, a division of labor developed between land-tilling and stock raising, between land tilling and the crafts; exchange. Thus arose a new form of economic relations, which took place between the tribes; the instruments of labor acquired an individual character and it became possible to store products, to distribute them and to accumulate wealth in the hands of a small part of society. One element of such wealth was man himself because it became economically profitable to exploit labor power. Land cultivation demanded a settled way of life; the development of crafts and the resultant appearance of a considerable variety of different products enabled people to form more extensive communities and create urban settlements. All these circumstances led to the decline in primitive communities and the breakup of their primitive relations of equality, which were superceded by economically stratified societies. These societies, with their public property now held in private hands, the inequality and exploitation of man by man was now able to enter upon the stage.

#973 Class societies did not spring up everywhere at once. They first appeared in the valleys of the Yangtze and Hwang Ho, the Nile and the Ganges, the Tigris and the Euphrates. The fertile and easily tillable soil of these areas yielded comparatively good harvests even with the use of only primitive implements of agriculture, and it was here that the primitive commune first began to decline and slavery appeared.

#974 The slave-owning formations arose where slavery became the basis of social production. It achieved its peak development and acquired classical forms in the Mediterranean (Greece and her colonies, Carthage, Rome and the Roman Empire). Slaves were obtained mainly by conquest, and the mass exploitation of slaves provided wealth for the slave owners. The whole social organization and culture of the ancient world developed on the basis of slave labor.

#975 Greece and Rome are usually taken as the 'model' by which we judge the whole formation, but this approach is not historically accurate. The development of India, China and a number of states of the Near East, assumed somewhat different forms. There, slavery did not develop so widely as in Greece and Rome. The system of relatively isolated agricultural communes and centralized despotic states which besides their political functions, performed the economic functions of building and maintaining irrigation works on which the system created a special type of society based on a mode of production that can be described as Asiatic. This type of society, which existed in Asia and also in some countries of Africa (Egypt) and Latin America (ancient Peru), was a class society divided into exploiters and exploited. But they retained significant traces of communal relations and certain communal forms, and this feature was specifically expressed in the low level of development of private ownership of land.

#976 Definitions of the specific features of the Asiatic mode of production and the society based upon it is a matter for concrete historical study. Whether this mode of production constitutes a special social-economic formation or not is a question that is being discussed by historians, but in any case it is clear that this was a change and development, which features sharply distinguishes it from the dynamic (for those days) world of the Mediterranean.

#977 Feudal society is a higher form of economic formation compared with the Asiatic mode of production and slave owning society. Land cultivation, stock raising and crafts constitute the material and technical base of this society, but they are developed to a higher level.

#978 Feudalism opened up a wider possibility for the development of the productive forces than had the previous formations. At the same time feudalism is a static society. The routine technology, local isolation and disunity, lack of communication and transportation facilities. Rigid ordering and control over all forms of activity, hierarchical divisions of the estates, heavy burden of traditions, strict regulation of spiritual life by the church and domination of religion in the ideological sphere put a brake on all progressive changes. Life revolved more closely to a circle than to the evolutionary and revolutionary spiral (coil). Life followed a set and almost unchanging rhythms.

#979 But slowly, deep inside the feudal system there evolved the material preconditions for the breakthrough to new social forms of life. The development of the division of labor, the growth of commodity-money relations, the appearance of new markets, then later machine production etc. brought into being new productive forces demanded new economic and social forms to provide them with scope for development. Thus feudalism was compelled to give way to a new economic formation capitalism. In its formative stage it held out great hope for cooperation but then within it were also the seeds that have grown into the threat we see today—great destructive competition, anxiety, boom and bust and war. While the fifth-estate in rich countries holds some of this capital it is not generally in the form required to extract value-added. The vast majority of capital that is capable of extracting value-added is now held in the third-estate and in its state machinery.

#980 Under the control of the Third Estate history becomes world history in the full sense of the term, the former isolation both of peoples and territories disappears and for the first time a single world system of economy, a single world market and transportation system comes into being.

#981 The source foundation of the development of capitalism are the productive forces connected with machine production largely now controlled by computer and Supervisory Control And Data Acquisition systems (SCADA). In this period the rate of economic and social development increases sharply, but the development itself proceeds in antagonistic forms because it is based on the third-estate's appropriation and squander of the fifth-estate's production of value-added. Competition is heralded as the be all and end all. Every person for itself is eulogized. Inflation (print Money print labor tokens) is kept ahead of the fifth-estate's capacity to absorb it. The scramble for profit, turmoil of production periodic crises, youth unemployment, seventh-estate (street people) and the great increase in the sixth-estate (police and armies) are the characteristic features of the development of this type of economy.

#982 In a comparatively short historical period capitalism passes through a number of stages. Beginning from early value-added expropriation and accumulation and proceeding through a system of free enterprise gradually replacing the first and second estates in economic importance to the age we are now in – the age of almost total domination by the third-estate in world affairs and in the global economy.

#983 Thus we see the transition from free competition especially in banking to monopoly conditions, to the omnipotence of finance capital, which brings under its control all estates, including its own third-estate. Already we see signs of the crumbling in this system as fifth-estate becomes more knowledgeable in the workings of these systems and under the aegis of the UN some banking machinations are now being exposed. Thus the intensification of all the contradictions, in the system are gradually being unveiled as global anxiety increases in all estates.

#984 We have examined the general trend in historical development to the extent that it is determined by the laws of movement of material production and the great role played by 'value-added' created by wage and salary commodity producing workers in such a system – in the movement of material production. But this does not imply that we have explained social development at every point of the historical process. Concrete history is much richer, and is affected by the great number of factors that vary and modify that process. We cannot therefore regard this process as something that proceeds in a single line, but as an upward spiral where changes are gradually made and the new history takes its lessons from the 'coils' below it that have gone before. Historical development springs from the interaction of many forces and to understand it in its concrete forms we must take into consideration all the essential factors contributing to the interaction. Historical 2020 Materialism provides the methods for studying concrete history because it reveals not only the unity of history and its general laws and direction, but also shows us how to perceive its diversity, how not to rely merely on economic history but on history in its totality. History when viewed from the 'Estate' point of view and armed with the fuller knowledge of its spiral paradigm shift gives a richer understanding of its inner deep going objective truths.

#985 The influence of one people on another is also an important factor in history. It has occurred in all kinds of forms, from wars and conquest to trade and cultural exchange. It may take place in all spheres of social life, from economics to ideology.

#986 The uniqueness of individual countries cannot be understood without taking into consideration the unevenness of world historical development. Some peoples forge ahead, others lag behind; for various concrete reasons some are able to leapfrog over whole social-economic formations. So, in every period throughout written history there existed not just one formation, but peoples at various stages of social development and there were complex interrelations between them. This means that we do not find the same sequence of formations of all peoples. Thus, among the Slavs and the Germanic peoples inhabiting Central and Eastern Europe the disintegration of the pre-Estate system occurred at the time when slave owning formations (Ancient Rome) had exhausted itself and was in a state of decline. For this reason the slave structure that had begun to take shape in Central and Eastern Europe did not develop into a slave formation and the peoples there passed straight from the tribal system to feudalism. (The great impetus to advance in capitalism in North America is that here hardly any feudalism existed to be overcome.)

#987 The character of the mutual influence exercised by peoples that are at different stages of historical development depends on the nature of their social systems. Thus it was in the nature of capitalism that third-estate Europe should have used its technical superiority to enslave the peoples of other continents and subject them to colonial oppression. The development of these peoples was not only held up by colonialism; in many cases they were actually thrown back both in their economic and cultural development.

#988 The present epoch; the Third Estate is in control of ever more billions of lives while at the same time the people numbers in this estate are dwindling due to the massive take-overs and consolidations of existing smaller 'weaker' companies. The fifth and sixth-estates are growing in people numbers but have dwindling control over any capital of significance. The third-estate has a vested interest in destructive and not constructive competition, it has a vested interest in foisting the every man for himself philosophy on society.

#989 The fifth, sixth, (remembering that the sixth-estate it-self comes from the people) and seventh estates of the present and future; their interests lie in cooperation and friendly competition; in lowering the anxiety levels that are so destructive to many lives in every estate. Their interest and every person's stake lays in doing away with the estate system altogether. (Ironically, the peoples of every estate will benefit by the demise of the estate system altogether.)

#990 While recognizing the progressive character of social development, the replacement of lower social formations by higher formations, Historical 2020 Materialism does not by any means regard this as a predetermined process ruling out the diversity of history.

#991 But, diverse though the history of various peoples may be, there are in every historical period certain leading trends of social development. In defining a period in world history according to its leading trends we use the concept of Estates and of Historical epochs. For example we speak of the epoch of slave society or the epoch of feudalism relating them to the time when these formations were dominant. In our own day vestiges of feudalism are still to be found in certain countries but it would be absurd to speak of the present day as the epoch of feudalism.

#992 Although the vestiges of every estate existed prior to the French revolution in late 1700's it was not till then that the people began to talk about and discuss the 'Estates' and relative positions of each. But many more divisions into estates are now required to accurately understand their roles in History. Almost every 'Estate' has had control of one society or another, we leave it to the scientific historians to identify these.

#993 Regarded from the standpoint of world history, our own time is also a transitional epoch. This transition is the leading trend of contemporary social development, reflecting the deep anxiety permeating the whole system. The every man for himself syndrome, the crisis in labor tokens (Money and its defilement by big bank money traders), the development of quasi-military groups, terrorist acts, the increase in the jail populations, decreasing fulfillment, rat-race, road-rage, shootings, and distrust of the 'system'. Deepening distrust of fourth-estate's dis-information and one sided truths, the increase of violent movies, pornography, distrust of the judicial system, the increase in numbers of lawyers visa a vis the total population. (lawyers driven to, in order to make a living, whipsaw their clients in tacit collusion with other lawyers, and over it all sits the judiciary nudge, nudging, wink, winking at the whole affair) and over it all presides the bourgeois state promulgating the laws to fit its master's agenda the third-estate outlook on things. This gives rise to a tremendous diversity of social problems.

#994 The trade unions and associations of salary workers are the front line defenders of the fifth-estate wage and salary commodity producing workers. Their efforts are largely in the area of trying to pry back at least some of their value-added that has been expropriated from them by the third-estate and their hangers on. It is well to note here that one of the first things that the Nazi regime in German did was to outlawed all such unions and associations and arrest their leaders. They replaced and nullified them all with the so called Nazi "Labor Front". Nowadays such leaders in some jurisdictions are simply ambushed and shot by right wing paramilitaries.

#995 Many unions are in disarray because their leaders do not understand or ignore their historical role, or suffused with the every man for himself syndrome they themselves use their organizations to make themselves rich at the expense of the wage and salary workers they represent. They are the 'crimps' that prey upon their own. Who, but a 'saint' or a martyr in a society such as this can be free of the temptation to cave in and go along?

*****

The Struggle Between The Estates >#996

#997 Unlike the general laws of development applicable to all social-economic formations The struggle between the estates is a law of development of only some of these formations. Mankind progresses from the primitive communal system, which knew no class division, through various formations until the present state where several estates can be found existing alongside one another. Possibly they may exist in a amicable way at one point and then in a hostile way at another. (i.e. depending upon the economic conditions prevailing at any given period, to the media spin doctors and also to the perception of the majority of citizens as to who is to blame for their plight – is it that foreign 'enemy' over there where the borders are, is it the immediate employer, is it the 'system' that is causing their acute anxiety? In this kind of atmosphere many seek the 'Doctor Of Nostrums' but others seek goals and action to relieve their anguish.)

#998 Many of these 'souls' believe they can beat the system and become themselves a bourgeoisie or some may attempt to change the system by direct and individual or small group action. The frustrations they feel result in some of them taking up individual or small group armed rebellion and, like Jesus, they are nailed to the cross by public indignation. There is a public out there not yet prepared enough by the vicissitudes, anxieties and frustrations of a life controlled largely by the third-estate. Their lack of 'Estate' consciousness prevents them entering into any action at all – due to their general lassitude and distrust of politicians of any stripe no matter how dedicated those politicians may be.

*****

CHAPTER 8 >#999

ORIGIN AND ESSENCE OF ESTATES >#1000

#1001 Estates are large groups of people into which society is divided. But there are many other large groups in society, divided on the principles different from that which divide Estates. There are age groups for instance (young and old generations, groups based on sex, race, nationality, profession, and so on. Some of these divisions have natural causes (age, sex, race), while others are social in origin. The natural difference between people do not themselves cause social distinctions and only under certain social circumstances may be connected with social inequality. Racial inequality is historical, not natural, in origin. Similarly the social inequality of the sexes is due not to natural but historical causes. At the early, matriarchal stages of history women held an honored place in society, which she subsequently lost owing to her changed role in production.

#1002 Estate divisions in general usually have nothing to do with natural differences; they exist within one and the same race, one and the same ethnic group, and so on.

#1003 Some third-estate sociologists seek causes of the division of society into estates in political factors, in coercion, for instance, in the subjugation of some people or peoples by others. Of course, the transition from a primitive communal society into an estate divided society did not occur without coercion. But coercion only accelerated and deepened social inequality; it was not its cause. Violence does not explain the origin of estates any more than robbery of value-added explains the origin of private ownership of the public means of production. Robbery (whether by gun or the mutual agreement to rob by stocks and shares) may result in the passing of some property from one owner to another, but it cannot create as private property the means of public production as such, nor, more importantly, can it create value-added. The division of society into estates is due to economic causes; it existed in a neophyte form, for example, even in places such as ancient Athens, where no conquest had taken place.

#1004 Its source is the division of labor within society which presupposes the separation of producers engaged in various forms of production, transportation and exchange between them of the products of their labor. First, stock-raising and land-tilling form special branches of work, then the crafts break away from land-tilling and finally mental work is separated from manual labor. The social division of the means of production, which supersedes the previous communal form of property, gives rise to social groups that have unequal standing in social production. Society is divided into global rich and poor, exploiters and exploited, a state of antagonism and inequality reigns and as a result anxiety and frustration runs rampant much of the time in both camps.

#1005 Estates are groups of people which differ from each other primarily by their place in a historically definite system of production. This means that each estate must be regarded in connection with the mode of production by which it is engendered, and that each antagonistic mode of production creates its own specific division of society into estates.

#1006 Within every system of production estates occupy different or even diametrically opposed positions, this being determined by their relationship to the means of production. This relationship also determines their role in the social organization of the Wage and Salary worker. Estates perform various functions in social production; in an antagonistic society some of them direct production, control the company and the state economy and all legal affairs of company and of state. And there are the salary and wage workers some of which are engaged predominantly in mental work in managing the company and in certain paid positions in the state structure, while others bear the burden of physical labor. This physical labor is more or less arduous depending upon the advancement of machine operation and production in a given society.

#1007 As social production and the whole life of society grows more complex various functions of administration become necessary. In the countries of the Ancient Orient, for example, large-scale irrigation works demanded a kind of centralized administration that was not needed in small individual farming. The large-scale machine production of today would be unthinkable without organizing activity, without management of production in all its fields. In an estate divided society the control and direction of social production is usually in the hands of the estate that owns the means of production. (In a religious state, it is usually the first-estate that takes on this role. In a feudal state it is the second-estate, in a dictatorship it may be the sixth-state that may take on the role – each situation has to be studied from an economic and historical perspective to reveal these interrelationships.)

#1008 When certain production relations begin to hold-up the development of the productive forces the role of the ruling estate in the social organization of labor also changes; it loses its organizing function in production and declines into a parasitic growth on the body of society. This happened with the land owning aristocracy in its time and the same thing is happening today with the third-estate (it is relinquishing its organizing functions to the managers, or the upper crust salary workers – to the technical intelligentsia. At the same time through unmitigated competition, banks, the stock market, and other institutions, speedups and layoffs it plays a disruptive role)

#1009 Estates also differ from one another according to their size and source of their social income. This distinction between estates is undoubtedly of great importance, but it still is not the defining factor. We can see this quite easily if we ask ourselves the question: why do various sources of income exist and consequently various conditions for the existence of estates? The chief reason lies in their position in the system of social production. At first sight it may appear that an estate is formed by people having a common source of income. But this view does not go to the bottom of inter-estate relationships; what it assumes to be the main and determining relationships are, in fact, a form of distribution that depends on the relations of production. If we consider only the sources and sizes of income we cannot correctly define estates and distinguish them from the multiple social strata and groups that also may receive their income from various sources. For example, civil servants receiving their salaries from the state, doctors, lawyers, performers, sports figures whose bills (Salaries) are paid by private clients (Agent and so on) have different sources of income. But this does not give us grounds for treating them as receiving funds directly from the extraction of value-added and treating them as members of the third-estate. (We shall study in more depth the value-added continuum and its ramifications on society in Moral Organon.)

#1010 All attributes of estates must be considered together in their organic unity. Estates are large groups of people differing from each other by the place they occupy in an historically determined system of social production, by their relation (in most cases fixed and formulated in law) to the means of production. By their role in the social organization of labor, and consequently, by the dimensions of the share of social wealth of which they dispose and the mode of acquiring it. Estates are groups of people which can appropriate the value-added produced by salary and wage commodity producing workers owing to the different places they occupy in a definite system of social economy.

#1011 Estate divisions run right through social life from top to bottom, affecting the whole system of social relations. These relations are divided into the material and the ideological. But what kind of relations become established between estates – material or ideological? The answer is both! Estates are connected by certain economic relations which enable the exploiting estate to appropriate the value-added of salary and wage labor and accumulate it, or distribute it to any estate in the hierarchy of estates as they see fit. The sum total of these relations forms the estate structure of society and constitutes the material, economic and class structure of society and constitutes the material and economic basis for the antagonistic struggle between Estates.

#1012 The relations between Estates, however are not confined to the economic field; they acquire their most concentrated expression in political life and in the struggle of unions and associations to win back some of the value-added produced by their members.

#1013 Besides estate distinctions in society, there are other social distinctions, such as the distinction between town and country, that is, in the final analysis between populations engaged in industrial and agricultural work, and the distinction, between physical and mental labor.

#1014 The division between town and country splits the whole population into two parts, one living in the town, the other in the country (although with mechanization in advanced states the countryside is being consolidated into larger and larger Agri-businesses thus whole country-sides are being gradually depopulated.) This division has unique features in every estate formation. For example, in feudal society the peasants and the feudal lords were concentrated mainly in the villages, whereas the towns were mainly the centers of the artisans, the traders, the emerging third-estate. Now however all social sections are represented to differing degrees in towns, villages and cities. This having been said and whereas previously the feudal lord lived alongside his toiling peasants nowadays there is a tendency for the third-estate peoples to move to, or trot on a global scale to, rich enclaves far from the sight of the ordinary citizen. (so too in later Roman times)

#1015 Within Estates are also considered social distinctions. For example, the bourgeoisie itself is divided into small, medium and large capitalists depending on the amount of the means of production they own and their individual ability to extract the maximum value-added from the global economy.

#1016 There exists in society more or less significant layers of people that belong to the seventh-estate those people who have lost connection with all other classes. Such of which consists of beggars, prostitutes, thieves etc. (lumpen proletarians) who have no definite occupation and have sunk to the lower depth of society.

#1017 Among all the various social distinctions the main are estate distinctions, the first three were identified and described during the French Revolution. Subsequent study has revealed several more. The first reason that identification of the class of estates in philosophy is important is that it gives a wider and deeper understanding of history, past, present and future. It gives a short hand methodology for the study and description of these sectors of class society. They spring from the deepest foundations of society, that is, directly from the relation of people to the means of production. They form the essence of the production relations, which determine all other social relations. Second, estate-classification is the most powerful tool because it reveals in history that in every estate there is the potential power to rule over all other Estates. It can be shown that in history every estate, in one jurisdiction or another, in one form or another, has taken the position of ruling the other estates. It, in other words, it shows that every estate given the proper historical conditions can rule and use the state machinery to further its own ends.

#1018 Estates are the most powerful and usually the most numerous social groups, whose interrelations and struggle exert a decisive influence on the history of society, on its entire social, political and ideological life.

#1019 First, second, third and fourth-estate sociologists often attempt to dissolve the concept of the philosophical class of estates into the more general concept of 'social groups'. To replace the division of third-estate ruled Society into classes by a division into social layers 'strata' (such terms as 'strata' and 'stratification' borrowed from geology to denote the division of society into various layers, usually imply a certain hierarchy). All kinds of criteria are used to determine the composition of the various strata. Such criteria as occupation, wealth, education, place of residence, middle class, and so on, but no emphasis is placed by these philistines on the main and decisive factor the relationship of each estate to the means of production.

*****

Social Structure And How It Changes >#1020

#1021 The sum total of the philosophical category of the classes – Estates – Social Layers – groups, yields a system of their relationship and form in the social structure of society.

#1022 When one mode of production is replaced by another the social structure is changed with the result that a certain class of estate is superseded in its role as 'ruler' by another. (In other words they take over the operation of the state machinery)

#1023 In slave-owning and also in feudal societies the social structure takes unique forms. In a number of Oriental countries society was divided into castes, isolated groups of people connected by the unity of an inherited profession. In other slave-owning societies (Ancient Greece and Rome) and also feudal society class distinctions were consolidated by the legal power of the state into division of the population into estates. The law laid down for every estate a special position in the state, and certain rights and obligations. The estates were formed on the basis of class division but did not entirely correspond to it since they introduced the element of the hierarchy of power and legal privilege.

#1024 In ancient Rome the population was divided into patricians and plebeians, who in their turn were divided into several grades according to their ownership of property. In feudal Europe the highest estates were the priests and aristocracy, who unlike the third, and lowest estate then 'known' (merchants, artisans, peasants etc.) enjoyed certain privileges. They at this time were freed from paying tribute, were exempt from physical punishment, could not be judged except by a court of their own estate and had the right to own land and the serfs who were bound to it.

#1025 The capitalist mode of production simplified the estate divisions of society and, at any rate, in principle, abolished the hierarchical privileges. Under third-estate control the direct producers – the wage and salary commodity producing workers in the fifth-estate, are legally free, but they are deprived of the ownership of the means of production (capital) and are economically dependent on the third-estate. Thus the antagonistic modes of production bring about various modes of exploitation and at the same time various divisions of society into estates.

#1026 Besides the present day basic philosophical classes i.e. third and fifth estates. Now the social structure comprises non-basic or transitional form either connected with the survival of parts of previous modes of production. (i.e. feudal Second Estate). The existence of embryos of a new mode of production in the form of special economic structures, or forms of estates that the third-estate requires to support its own structure, especially the fourth and sixth estates (Media, and Military and Policing). Consequently these are either old or new classes involving either obsolete or newly emerging forms in the economy.

#1027 There existed in slave societies, for instance, small free peasant farmers and also craftsmen. In feudal society, as the towns developed there arose a new social strata comprising craftsmen organized in guilds and corporations, merchants, and so on. Big landowners employing both capitalist and pre-capitalist modes of exploiting the peasants continued to exist for a long time in capitalist society and in countries where significant traces of feudalism still remain they exist to this day as one of the non-basic offshoot estates

#1028 In most countries controlled by the third-estate there is the non-basic estate of the petty bourgeoisie (a sort of watabe capitalist) comprising farmers, craftsmen, traders, shop keepers, and other small property owners – a numerically significant section of society which plays considerable part in the political struggle. Economically, they hold an intermediate position between the third and fifth estates. Although unlike the unearned private capitalist property of the third estate theirs is usually hard earned property accumulation by personal sacrifice and personal labor. The fact that they are owners of income producing private property brings their political thinking closer to the third-estate than to the fifth-estate.

#1029 These wantabe capitalist (petty bourgeoisie) identify themselves with the third-estate. But this attachment is tenuous as they live in a world of anxiety and frustration as newer and bigger agri-business and 'box stores' throw them out of business. They are constantly being cast off by the threat of bankruptcy default and actual bankruptcy. And in actual bankruptcy they often see the results of their hard labor blown away by economic conditions engendered by unmitigated competition and take over by the larger entities firmly ensconced in the third-estate. These entities eventually will kill most of these Mom and Pop operations. So it is that through these circumstances this non-basic class are linked to the fifth-estate by being workers themselves and experiencing the oppression of large capital who itself is being threatened by even larger capital. The watabees put in long and strenuous hours and with the depredation of big banks and the filchment by the stock market player's tacit agreement in mutual robbery often depletes their life savings.

#1030 The development of production alters the status of the various estates. In the middle of the 19th century the bourgeoisie was rather numerous because the instruments of labor were owned mainly by medium and small capitalists.

In England this class constituted eight percent of the able-bodied population; in other countries the proportion was even larger, while the army of hired labor accounted for only half of the able-bodied population; in other countries the proportion was even larger. The development of the third-estate, the fusion of multi-nationals with many states, the STR that began in the middle of the 20th century have brought about considerable changes in the mode of production. There is going on an unprecedented concentration of production and global centralization of capital, particularly since the second world war. All this is having the effect of building into the third-estate a powerful elite.

#1031 The number of this elite in relation to the numbers in the population has decreased owing to unmitigated competition, crushing and adsorption of many small and medium-sized capitalists. It now numbers between one and three percent of the able bodied population.

#1032 The army of hired wage and salary labor of the fifth-estate, the growing number of the dispossessed and destitute in the seventh-estate confronting the third-estate has grown considerably. The ranks of the former having been at first temporarily reduced by privatization of public property in the latter quarter of the 20th century then now once again being swelled mainly by numerical reduction of these petty bourgeoisie in town and country who are being driven out of business.

#1033 As the third-estate develops the petty bourgeoisie disintegrates. A small portion of it adds to its wealth and joins fully integrated into the 3E. The larger portion of it goes bankrupt and assumes the position of economically dependent property owners or wage and salary workers. Many petit bourgeoisie will even end up in the 7E and lowest estate, destitute, anxious and angry, many turning to religion, will hope for better times in the whimsical life in the hereafter. This is a regular process based on the advantages of large-scale production, on the law of concentration and centralization of capital into the hands of the 3E. (The reader will note that author has reverted to the symbolic notation required for deeper insights into these phenomena.)

#1034 But this process does not entirely oust the small producers. Of course technical progress in 3E controlled society does drive the small producers out of business. They cannot stand the pace, cannot keep on replacing old equipment with new. But it is not to advantage of monopoly capital to take over all the functions of production. The trans-nationals leave a number of such functions to the small businessman.

#1035 The trend towards forcing peoples into working for salary and wages, and living on the dole or into activities of the 7E does not lead to the conclusion that the lower strata of the 3E is completely eliminated. The development of production follows a contradictory and dialectical course. A number of new 'middle strata' are inevitably brought into existence again and again. Appendages to the factory people may work at home in small workshops scattered all over the country to meet the requirements of big industries. Such as the computer, housing and automobile industries etc. – These new small producers are just as inevitably being cast out as well as drawn into the lower echelons of the 3E.

#1036 The petty bourgeois survives in contemporary global development not because he is 'stable' but because he is needed by the large-scale capital which just as it needs him it also opposes him. Taken as a whole however, the small businessman is being steadily pushed out of the 3E into the 5E – into wage and salary work, or even unemployment.

#1037 The army of wage and salary commodity producing laborers 'liberated' by the 3E from any, even small ownership of the means of production, constitutes in the developed countries the overwhelming majority of the population. It rose from 66 percent of the able bodied population in the economically developed countries in 1940 to 80 percent in 1970 to over 90 percent at the end of the millennium.

#1038 In the past hundred and fifty years the numbers and proportion of the basic sections of the urban, industrial proletariat (wage and salary workers) has considerably increased, as against the decrease in the rural proletariat. At the turn of the century there were 29.9 million industrial workers in the US, Britain, Germany and France, but by the middle of the 20th century the figure had almost doubled to 58.1 million. The army of the salary and wage worker is now world wide and has become more mature and conscious and its political role in society has enhanced. The STR has altered the composition of the working class, the number of skilled workers having considerably increased as against a decrease in unskilled workers in the advanced capitalist countries.

#1039 The introduction of the assembly line and now computer operated robots supplemented the ordinary factory workers handling all-purpose tools and machines with a great number of specialized workers trained to perform both simplified operations on the line. This allowed for highly skilled workers to maintain the computer systems required to automatically control and operate the lines. Thus automation, is doing away with the 'one-skill' man and producing a new layer of highly skilled workers servicing, adjusting and repairing automated lines.

#1040 3E ideologists and philosophers often assert that in the context of the STR the salary and wage commodity producing worker is destined to disappear. First because of the decrease in the numbers of people engaged in production and the increase in those employed in the service industries, and secondly, because of the increase in intellectuals and white collar salary workers in general.

#1041 Similarly, there is rapid growth of the intelligentsia (themselves salary workers) and white collar workers. These considerably exceed that of the able bodied population as a whole, does not testify to the elimination of the salary and wage system in the general population or the emergence of a new so called 'middle class' not relying on a salary or wage absorbing them.

#1042 The term intelligentsia is generally used to denote the section of people professionally engaged in work of an intellectual nature. It may also include a considerable number of white-collar workers, but not all of them, of course, because many are not employed in intellectual work as such but perform various purely technical functions.

#1043 The intelligentsia never has been and never can be a separate estate class. It is not homogeneous in that sense because it is formed out of representatives of various estates and serves various estates.

#1044 Scientists and engineers form the most rapidly expanding section of the intelligentsia. But a large number of engineers and technicians are acquiring a status close to that of the working class i.e. they are salary and wage workers. In the last century the intellectuals and white collar workers were a comparatively privileged enclave but today they have turned into white collar proletarians. From the standpoint of working conditions and salary white collar workers are often not better but worse off than the wage worker. In the united States at the beginning of the 20th century the average salary of office workers in the processing industries was 2.3 times higher than the wage of the average manual worker; in the last quarter of the 20th century it is but 4/5 of that wage.. A large portion of engineers have lost their former supervisory functions which made them the so called industrial commissioned and non commissioned officers of the 3E. The rate of rhythm of these employees, are now increasingly determined by the actual technical process, many work overtime at no extra pay as they are on salary and there is a non existent social safety net to protect them. (Blow the whistle and in one way or another you're gone).

#1045 So the increased proportion of engineers, technicians and white collar personnel that some sociologists present as the 'de-proletarinization' of society actually means that an ever larger part of this stratum is placed by the 3E into living conditions resembling those of industrial workers. This, however, does not provide grounds for classifying all salaried technicians, engineers and other white-collar people engaged in production as working class because some of them may embrace socially different kinds of work, including that of intellectuals.

#1046 A certain part of the intelligentsia employed in the 'traditional' professions (doctors, lawyers, artists etc.) remains close in status to the middle section of society, and the upper class of the 3E intelligentsia. (A story is told that when there was only one lawyer in the town of '20th century' then that lawyer made only a meager living but when another lawyer came to town they both thrived beautifully. It might be noted that lawyers under 3E conditions must live in a world of tacit collusion using 'whipsaw tactics' to ensure they maximize their fees. But this sordid '21st century' law does not tell the tale of future of law. Which, in due course and under the appropriate conditions, is most probably, at some future time and under its own specific science of law, destined to supplant the dogma and mysticism of the 1E with truly scientific law making on behalf of the peoples of the globe.)

#1047 Thus we see that the class structure of society is remarkably complex, comprising various non basic classes and intermediate layers beside the basic estates classes. What is more, the classes are not closed groups of people like the hierarchical estates of feudal times. Individuals are constantly moving from one group or social strata to others.

#1048 Bourgeois sociologists try to present this fluidity in 3E dominated society as the disappearance of class divisions. Of course, there is far greater social mobility in 3E conditions than under the 2E or feudalism with its numerical hierarchical barriers. But class barriers do not disappear under 3E conditions and class contradictions increase. In the early stages of the development of capitalism some members of the nobility, village kulack (rich farmers) etc. were able to penetrate the ranks of the ruling class. Today it is no easier to enter the circle of the trans-nationals than it was in the age of absolutism for a petty bourgeois to gain admission to the nobility.

#1049 Although the class status of certain individuals may change this does not eliminate the distinction between classes and estates which form the structure of society. Moreover the changes occurring in the social status of global people only broaden the gap between the 3E and 5E.

*****

Estate's Interests and Class Struggle; Forms of Class Struggle and Organization >#1050

Note: for a re-look at the Estate system Matrix go to >#19

#1051 Estate's class struggle has persisted throughout the history of society ever since the collapse of the primitive commune. 'Freeman and slave, patrician and plebian, lord and surf, guild-master and journeyman, in a word oppressor and oppressed, stood in constant opposition to one another, carried on an uninterrupted, now hidden, now open fight, a fight that each time ended, either in a revolutionary reconstitution of society at large. (i.e. The British, US, and French revolutions and so on).

#1052 What is it that the causes the conflict between Estates? Is it historically inevitable? Certain historians and sociologists maintain that it is the result of 'misunderstanding', a mutual failure to communicate, the misguided policies of the ruling Estate, of 'incitement by evil minded elements', and so on. Many of them make an appeal for social and moral values capable of uniting estates. But to express that it is possible to unite estates with irreconcilable, antagonistic interests with the help of even the 'best' ideas or moral values implies a false, idealistic approach to the question.

#1053 What are estate interests? What is behind them? It is sometimes asserted that those interests are determined by the consciousness of the members of a given estate. This is incorrect. The 5E in any given country may for a certain time not be aware of the fundamental interests and restrict itself to fighting for certain particular interests. (for example for increased wages during inflation due to 3E state machinery money manipulation.) They may fight for shorter working hours, COLA, and a thousand other issues in the battle to maintain hard won gains of the past from being eroded in the present and so on.) But these little 'strikes' do not attack the root of fundamental 5E problems.

#1054 Any estate's interest is determined not by the consciousness of it but by its position and role in the system of social production. Since the wage and salary commodity producing worker is deprived of ownership of the means of production and subjected to giving up all the value added it produces. It will be interested in how it should go about obtaining this value-added that in large part plays, in the global role of things, so much havoc with its abuse. Abuse in the form of the anxiety it causes in all estates, unmitigated growth, destructive competition and world crises. It is in the interest of the people of the globe to control value-added for the good of mankind and not just for the privileged who exist in uneasy luxury in the 3E.

#1055 There may be antagonistic relations not only between the opposed estates of one socio-economic formation but also between contending estates of one of which is superseding the other. Such for example, were the relations between the 3E bourgeoisie and the 2E feudal aristocracy in the period when the bourgeois methods of extracting surplus-value as opposed to the aristocracy's methods. The result was that 3E methods of value-added extraction and 2E methods, after bitter clashes merged in the economies of several countries. And in the political field the 3E and the 2E landowners often formed a common front particularly when faced with a common enemy – the mass of the people in revolt under the conditions of the day.

#1056 There is an ongoing antagonistic relation between the necessity for unmitigated expansion required by the 3E and global ecology. Without continued expansion the system cannot survive, as severe unemployment is the result of stagnation in expansion. This is probably one of the most sensitive areas requiring further study to understand all the interconnecting relationships and ramifications as globalization grips the planet.

#1057 Whereas the opposition or divergence of estate interests form the basis of the struggle between them, coincidence of the interest of different estates creates the possibility of their also working together. In the situation created by contemporary life there are objective conditions for combined action on the part of the wage and salary workers, the farmers and the dispossessed. One might include some of the disgruntled members of the 6E, urban small shopkeepers, the bulk of the intelligentsia and white-collar workers, against the 3E expropriation of value-added. The First, or religious, estate may also see the poverty and anxiety that come through their door and may assist somewhat, but by and large their main concern is with 'out of world' matters of the soul after death. Thus there exists the possibility of an alliance between all these groups to expose the evils of value-added expropriation and the manipulation of all social life that goes along with this expropriation.

#1058 In the wage and salary commodity producing worker's struggle even radically different estates – even and including certain enlightened and conscious members of the 3E when faced by the common enemy – the huge problems associated with global expropriation of value-added, anxiety, boom and bust, unmitigated growth, unmitigated competition. In all of this they could come together in a body such as the UN to solve this basic problem. That is why certain 3E dominated countries neglect the UN and try to limit its scope of action or even try to overthrow it by various methods.

#1059 3E sociologists and philosophers, who think through the rose colored glasses of tenure based upon the cow-tow, that their present world is the be all and end all of social life, deny the necessity of change and the necessity of struggle. They assert that the driving force of progress is cooperation between estates and fail to see that the expropriation of value-added by the 3E on a ginormous scale is one of the major problems in the globe of today.

#1060 The 5E struggle of the wage and salary workers acts as a driving force of historical development primarily because it is the means by which an obsolete social system is transformed into a new and higher system. The conflict between the new productive forces and the obsolete relations of production finds its expression in an antagonism between estates. This struggle acts as the motivator of historical events not only in an epoch of social revolutions but also in so-called peaceful epoch. The reforms, the minor improvements lauded by the reformists are, in fact, a by-product of the struggle over value-added expropriation.

#1061 Contemporary ideologists argue that today the salary and wage commodity producing worker is 'integrated' into 3E and has a stake in that society, because it receives from it some of the good things of life. However, they conceal the fact that all these good thing have been produced by the wage and salary workers themselves and that only by its persistent struggle has it had restored to itself part of what it has created. They conceal the fact of the rampant anxiety that permeates the society.

#1062 Historically, political struggle developed after economic struggle, but it ranks first in importance because it is a higher form of inter estate struggle. The reasons for this are as follows;

1) In economic struggle action against the exploiters may be confined to separate contingents of wage and salary workers. (for example the personnel of an individual factory or concern.) Whereas in the political struggle under present condition the 3E Third Estate and the 5E are ranged against each other as classes in their entirety.
2) In the economic struggle the salary and wage workers defend their own immediate, daily interest, but in the political struggle they are defending their own fundamental 5E interest.
3) In the economic struggle, if it is conducted separately from the political struggle, the salary and wage workers acquire only a trade union type of consciousness, that is, an understanding of their own narrow professional interest. In the political struggle the salary and wage commodity producing workers evolve a truly 5E consciousness, an understanding of its fundamental historic mission.
4) The economic struggle provides the salary and wage worker with the organization it needs in the form of trade unions and associations. The political struggle demands the creation of a 5E political party.

#1063 The ideological struggle is also a highly important form of the 5E historical mission. To rouse the salary and wage workers for a broad economic and particularly political struggle which in the course of its efforts makes them aware of the nature of 'value-added' in all its carnations, incarnations and reincarnations. It requires the freeing of their mind from first, second, third, and fourth estate twaddle whimsy and mysticism. During this effort the true nature truth (i.e. absolute, objective, subjective and half-truth and lies) becomes evident in the consciousness of society.

#1064 Of course, the division of society into parties does not usually coincide with the division of it into estates. An estate is often represented not by one but by several parties expressing, along with the general estate interest, the interest of separate groups within the estate. (Serious wars of spheres of influence 3E Vs. 3E.) The contradictions between them may be and are often superficial (i.e. Republican, Democrat; Conservative, Liberal and so on) but sometimes they may reflect deeper differences between the various factions within the class. One might also mention that members of the salary and wage workers that operate the state machinery keep up the charade because of the strong ties between their professed affiliations and the good salaries and pensions they receive at the hand of the state.

#1065 The salary and wage workers of the 5E are themselves not in a homogeneous class. They include various inter-layers, such as recent arrivals thrown out of the 3E by bankruptcy. And also the upper crust of highly paid wage and salary workers that enjoy for a time some advantage in the supply and demand imbalance of their particular specialty.

#1066 The heterogeneous nature of the salary and wage commodity producing workers leads inevitably to divergence of views and aspirations among its different sections, and every turn in the fight to obtain value-added for global good evokes ultra right and ultra left wing deviations and trends. The dialectics of the 5E's historic mission to eliminate the expropriation of value-added for the 'good' of a few to its use for global good works, calming anxiety, stopping the unmitigated growth required by the 3E, stopping unmitigated destructive competition, ending boom and bust and so on.

#1067 These aims can be carried out through the new world body – the UN – the ILO the new international. It is the object of 2020 Materialism to bring the knowledge of truth (i.e. Absolute, Objective, Subjective, Half truth, and Lie) and the evil nature to which 'value-added' is being put while in the hands of the 3E. The object of 2020 Materialist Philosophy is to Guide the 5E on its historical mission.

#1068 If there is no meaningful productive work for millions of people, it is natural especially for youth to see no hope for themselves in the future. Many turn to petty crime and pot smuggling to earn a living and in this we see the total criminalization of certain sections of society driven there by the situation the 'value-added' expropriation of the 3E lauded on by their lackeys in the 4E. 4E CLEANSE THYSELF!. If the 3E makes work illegal by throwing millions in the global street then we will see global illegal work and the gradual criminilization of major portions of society.

#1069 Some ultra left theoreticians argue that the enhanced activity of certain groups such as students in time of crisis and they pin their high hopes on isolated instances of terror bombings and the like. Others pin their high hopes on the students whom they present as the most revolutionary force, the modern substitute for the allegedly 'conservative' proletariat wage and salary commodity producing workers. The student are indeed capable of great political activity. They hate the despotic, authoritarian 3E controlled system of higher education and do not want to become servants of business. But by and large students are unstable and come from different estates; they are not one of the productive forces of society and are therefore unable to undertake independently the historical mission of turning 'value-added' from a destructive global force into a force for good.

#1070 This value-added expropriation is on a global scale, is a global problem and can only be solved on a global scale by an organization such as the UN backed up by 5E governments that can effectively deal with it. If not solved globally then the 3E has the power to move its tools from jurisdiction to jurisdiction, withholding its productive tools from those jurisdictions that may try to devise social programs. The 3E, owning the productive tools thus bestow the 'honor' of placing them on the soil of the jurisdiction that bends to its needs (i.e. privatization, cheap labor and no taxes). Of course the writer understands that in the present epoch most UN delegates are representatives from the 3E but over time and with the knowledge of dialectical 2020 Materialism this matter will be resolved.

#1071 It is the historical mission of all thinking people especially union leaders and association of salary workers to ensure that this political agenda is transmitted to those most involved in this process. And, second, that that government sends representative to the ILO and the UN that will be instrumental, together with other national government representatives, in carrying out the historical mission of stopping 3E depredations on the globe.

#1072 Finally what may we put forward as an historical proxy for the necessity for the demise of the present State in capitalist countries? As this proxy we quote from Engels' "… the emperors or sub-emperors, who now lived in Constantinople, Treves, Milan. The Roman state had become a huge, complicated machine, exclusively for bleeding its subjects. Taxes, state imposts and tributes of every kind pressed the mass of the people always deeper into poverty; the pressure was intensified until the exactations of governors, tax-collectors, and armies made it unbearable. That was what the Roman state had achieved with its world rule. It gave as its justification for its existence that it maintained order within the empire and protected it against the barbarians without. But its order was worse than the worst disorder, and the citizens whom it claimed to protect against the barbarians longed for the barbarians to deliver them. " p135 The Origin Of The Family Private Property And The State. International Publishers New York

*****

Tsunami One.   Philosophy Organon

&

Moral Organon

Basics In
Moral Thinking, Ethical Codes,
Civil & Criminal Law

After almost a century we revisit Karl Kautsky and his 'Ethics And The Materialist Conception Of History'

In the course of this revisit we have modified his original work so extensively, that we would posit that we now have a new original work based upon Kautsky's skeletal framework. We leave the reader to judge as to the merit of this claim.

Dedicated To The Memory Of Karl Kautsky (1854 1938)

Note: Readers are requested to keep in the back of their mind's eye what the present author contends. That is that there are two portions to our moral inner self – First and innermost is the sturdy and almost indestructible qernel flame of morality and second is the more pliable outer envelope of morality, what we herein refer to as the rindlucent.

Together the 'Rindlucent' (R) and the 'Qernel' (Q) make up what we might call a RindeQern (RQ) or amalgam of morality. This rindeqern is under constant attack from perpetual bombarding attempts to beguile it. These attacks come by way of external ethical codes, civil and criminal laws. These latter are the reflection of the various regimes of life, one might well say, even the bizarre ideas that, from a person's birth, incessantly attempt to manipulate the rindeqern in this or that direction, for this or that cause, in this or that period in man's evolution.

But on close examination we find that, no matter how severe this tampering of the rindeqern, the qernel flame is <u>almost</u> never extinguished whilst the rindlucent is blown hither and thither by external ethical codes, civil and criminal laws impinging upon it. We go on to analyze this process and attempt to bring understanding as to the nature of that qernel flame of morality that can never be extinguished as long as we remain in the human and, I must say even, in the animal world.

We use the device of the moral eye
<•>
in searching for moral truth

Tsunami One   Moral Organon.

CONTENTS

~001< **TRACT 1:**
002<•>observes **The Ancient Split** Between Natural Philosophy And Mental Philosophy. Or, In Other Words, The Split Between The Physical Sciences And The Mental Sciences.

~028< **TRACT 2:**
029<•>observes **The Downfall Of Pleasure** As The Only Driving Force In Moral Thinking.

~048< **TRACT 3:**
049<•>observes **Ancient Ethical Codes Idealistic And Materialistic:** The Rise Of And Validation Of Idealistic (Written And Unwritten) Ethical Codes And Managing The Crowd.

~093< **TRACT 4:**
094<•>observes **Moral Thinking And Ethical Codes In The Period Of The Enlightenment:** From Whence, However, Is A Moral Ideal To Be Derived In A World Of Vice?

~146< **TRACT 5:**
147<•>observes **The 'Now' People Of The 21st Century** And Their Cry "Back To Kant!" We Say that Kant Is But A Sounding Board - a metaphysical foil that allows us to delve deeper into Materialistic Morality. This takes morality out of a mystic subjective realm and brings it into the real and the objective world.

~170< **TRACT 6:**
171<•>observes the **Critique Of God** And Immortality In Moral Thought And Ethical Codes engendered by the superfluous-ness in the ethereal world of whimsy, transcendence and Kant.

~198< **TRACT 7:**
199<•>observes that **The Happiness Maxim** Cannot Be Definitely Embraced In A Universal Rule. Kant, In This Too, is Our Sounding Board.

~211< **TRACT 8:**
212<•>observes **Freedom And Necessity.** We Straddle Two Worlds At The Boundary Line Between The Past And The Future. Humans, Animals and Kant.   Aims.

241< **TRACT 9:**
242<•>observes **The Regressive Philosophy Of Reconciliation** And Kant and neo Kant.

~259< **TRACT 10:**
260<•>observes **The Struggle For Existence**
Darwin: The Development And Change
In Plants And Animals.

~283< **TRACT 11:**
284<•>observes **Darwin: Self-Movement And Intelligence**
Consciousness, Space & Sequence In Time

~323< **TRACT 12:**
324<•>observes **The Motives Of Self Maintenance And Propagation** Darwin: The Individual Self Preservation Instinct.

~341< **TRACT 13:**
342<•>observes **The Social Instinct** Darwin: Sympathy: Conscience.

~412< **TRACT 14:**
413<•>observes **Ethics And The Materialist Conception Of History.** The Ethics Of Marxism. The Roots Of The Materialist Conception Of History. Cooperative Social Moral Thinking. The Role Of Statistics.

~475< **TRACT 15:**
476<•>observes **The Organization Of Human Society.** Technical Development.

~497< **TRACT 16:**
498<•>observes **The Development Of The Technical Consciousness Of humankind.** Technology And The Method of Life.

~514< **TRACT 17:**
515<•>observest that **A New Organism Arises –** Human Society: Animal & Social Organisms.

~537< **TRACT 18:**
538<•>observes **The Changes In The Strength Of The Social Instincts:** Language.

~557< **TRACT 19:**
558<•>observes **War And Property:** Military Moral Thinking.

~593< **TRACT 20:**
594<• >observes **The Rise Of Property:**
Custom & Moral Thinking.

~626< **TRACT 21:**
627<• >observes **The Influence Of The Social Instincts: Moral Thinking In Internationalism:** The Degree Of Strength In Which The Social Instincts Are At Work, Are Effective And Alter Themselves Person To Person Estate To Estate. Cohesion And Its Breakdown:

~641< **TRACT 22:**
642<• >observes **Class Division And Morality:**
Nomenclature Of The Estate Schema.

~660< **TRACT 23:**
661<• >observes **Women's Role.**
Gentile Cooperative Societies.
Venture Charities:- The Lowest Stage Of Capitalism.

~686< **TRACT 24:**
687<• >observes **The Tenets Of Morality**
The Basics Of Morality Is Not Changing but Portions of Morality Are Relative And Are Changing: Customary Elements: Custom and Convention.

~699< **TRACT 25:**
700<• >observes **The Dual Content In Moral Thinking.**
The Practical Roots Of Morality. (But Duty First.)

~720< **TRACT 26:**
721<• >observes **The System Of Production**
And Its Superstructure.

~750< **TRACT 27:**
751<• >observes **The Acid Test Of Morality:**
We Now Put Under The Scope Morality And Immorality.
We leave Karl Kautsky and enter a new phase

~771< **TRACT 28:**
772<• >observes that **The Moral Ideal.**
Understanding The Different Classes Of Property
And Their Connection To The Moral Ideal.

~ 843<• >observes that **TRACT 29:**
844<• >observes that **The laws of morality in Homo Sapiens**
Dialectics at work in such laws

~860<• >observes that **TRACT 30:**
861<• >observes that **Modes Of Operation Of Ethical Codes**
And Their Impact on Social Instinct. Moral Buttresses.

~906<• >observes that **TRACT 31:**
907<• >observes that **Moral Thinking In Regard To The Value-Added Continuum** Discussion Of The Value-added Continuum And The Aspects Of Life That Make It Up. Their Morality or Immorality. Capital in and of itself to be discussed in a following TRACT.

~001< **TRACT 1:**

002<•>observes **The Ancient Split**
Between Natural Philosophy And Mental Philosophy
Or In Other Words The Split Between The
Physical Sciences And The Mental Sciences.

003<•>observes that in the history of philosophy the question of the use **of Ethic Codes to modify Moral Thinking** comes to the fore soon after the Persian wars.

004<•>observes that the Persian Wars (492 - 449 BCE) were a series of wars fought by the Greek states and Persia over a period of almost half a century, and that fighting was most intense during two invasions that Persia launched against mainland Greece between 490 and 479 BCE.

005<•>observes that the Persian empire was at the peak of its strength, that the collective defense mounted by the Greeks overcame seemingly impossible odds and that they even succeeded in liberating Greek city-states on the fringe of Persia itself.

006<•>observes that the Greek triumph ensured the survival of Greek culture and political structures long after the demise of the Persian empire.

007<•>observes that in several blows the Greeks in the repulsion of Persian absolutism became a world power, ruling the sea which surrounded the Greeks and with that commanding its trade after the Persian wars. Greece and Athens in particular, became the command center of the 'known' world commerce of that time.

Tsunami One   Moral Organon.

008<•>observes that all this brings forth the philosophical thoughts of the great ancient philosopher and their ethical considerations born of slave times.

009<•>observes that fifteen hundred years later, in feudal religious times, those Ethical Codes (EC) had changed and had skewed Moral Thought (MT) more in line with feudalism's basic aims.

010<•>observes that two thousand years after Greek times third-estate capital concepts embraced the globe and dissolved all traditional relations, conceptions, and ethical codes which further skewed corresponding moral thinking.

011<•>observes that by many signs and relatively quickly the people found themselves transplanted from a slave holding society through a feudal society into a merchant capital milieu.

012<•>observes that this only took about 30 lives upon lives at 65 (L/L@65). And that it took only 10 more (L/L@65) for the individual to be thrust and transplanted into a third-estate capital controlled globe.

013<•>observes that ordinary people, keeping their heads down against the torrents in this world, find themselves now (by means of these new ethical codes) bereft of all traditional communal supports, in a world in which persons from all estates find themselves, more or less, wholly to themselves.

014<•>observes that despite all this seeming isolation in the new capitalist world, everyone feels, not only a need for distinct rules of conduct (Ethics). But they find, more or less clearly that, in their own inner being there works a regulator of their action which allows them to decide between good and bad, to aim for the good and to avoid the bad.

015<•>observes that this moral thought, this regulator, reveals itself as a highly mysterious power, that it controls the actions of many, but not all people, that its decisions between good and bad are given in most, without the least delay, and assert themselves with all decisions.

016<•>observes that if anyone asks, "What is the actual nature of this regulator - upon what foundation does it build its judgments, - are both the regulator, which dwells in the breast of every man, as well as the judgments which appears so natural and self evident, revealed anywhere as phenomena?" "And if so why are these phenomena harder to understand than any other phenomena in the world?"

017<•>observes that since the Persian wars, ethical codes impact on moral thought and the investigation of these mysterious regulators of human action first come to the fore in Greek philosophy and continues on in an upward dialectical coil through several layers of economic and social change.

018<•>observes that up to about 400BCE if there was any philosophy, even if it is religious philosophy, it is taken from the Greek idealistic philosophy and is considered by them as a 'nature' philosophy. (Now known as the Physical Sciences)

019<•>observes that early philosophy made it its duty to investigate and explain the laws which hold in the world of nature. But then it comes about that those philosophers lose interest with 'nature', and now instead, ethical codes and moral thought become the central point of their investigation.

020<•>observes that at that time 'Natural' (Nature) Philosophy now almost ceases to make further progress and natural philosophies (Physical Sciences) are split off from philosophy; All progress in ancient philosophy comes now from the study of the spiritual nature of man and his morality.

021<•>observes that a professional class of teachers appear in ancient Greece who give instruction in rhetoric, politics and disputation the Sophists despise the knowledge of nature. Still farther Socrates, is of the opinion that he could learn nothing from the trees, but certainly from the human beings in the town. Then next appears Plato who looks on 'natural' philosophy as play.

022<•>observes that at this juncture the method of philosophy changes for it is that natural philosophy is, of necessity, bound to rely on the observation of things and objects in nature. At this turning point philosophy is split between nature study and moral study. And nature takes a back seat.

023<•>observes that the reason nature study becomes secondary is that they think in those times that senses can be mistaken, other people can deceive us, but people themselves inwardly do not lie to themselves when they wish to be truthful. On peoples lip's is a question "How are moral thoughts to be recognized with more certainty than natural objective phenomena?" That is the question!

024<•>observes that some philosophers come up with the answer:- "Through the observation of our own personality! That alone is recognized as knowledge certain which people produce from themselves. It is this which must be wrested from the unknown and brought into the known."

025<•>observes that we now see that a shift in the method, but also the object of philosophy is now different. Standing alongside each other now are **1)** the philosophy of nature (Physical Sciences) and **2)** the philosophy of ethical codes and moral thought. (Also as we shall see these moral thoughts should all become portions of the Mental Sciences of History, Philosophy, Law, Economics, Statistics and so on.)

026<•>observes that natural philosophy aims at the examination of the necessary connection of cause and effect. Its point of view is that of causality. Moral thought which is internal to the individual and ethical codes which is external and attempts to modify that moral thought on the other hand deal with the will and duty of man, with ends and aims which he strives for. Thus its point of view is that of a conscious aim therefore the study of the evidence of design or purpose in nature. (teleology)

027<•>observes that these new conceptions do not always reveal themselves with equal sharpness in all the various schools of thought.

~028< TRACT 2:

029<•>observes **The Downfall Of Pleasure**
As The Only Driving Force In Moral Thinking:

030<•>observes that there are two methods of explaining the moral thought within us. One can look for its roots in the obvious motive forces of human action, and as such, appeared the philosophy of the pursuit of happiness or pleasure.

031<•>observes that under production and distribution of goods, the production of private producers externally independent of each other, happiness and pleasure and the conditions necessary thereto are also a private affair. Consequently people come to look for the foundation of moral thought in the individual need for happiness or pleasure. And they produce ethical codes to reflect this in order to pass this thinking along.

032<•>observes that under the foregoing it is what is good that makes for the individual's pleasure, and increases his happiness. And evil is that which produces the contrary. How is it then possible that not everybody under all circumstances wishes only the good? That is explained by the fact that there are various kinds of pleasure and happiness.

033<•>observes that evil arises when people choose a 'lower' kind of pleasure or happiness in preference to a 'higher', or sacrifice a lasting pleasure to a momentary and fleeting one. Thus evil is said to arise from ignorance or short-sightedness.

034<•>observes that accordingly Epicurus looks on the intellectual pleasures as higher than the physical because they last longer and give unalloyed satisfaction. He considers the pleasure of repose greater than the pleasure of action. Spiritual peace seems to him the greatest pleasure.

035<•>observes that in consequence all excess in pleasure is to be rejected and every selfish action is bad. This is because respect, love and the help of one's neighbors, as well as the prosperity and welfare of the community to which one belongs are factors which are necessary to a person's own prosperity. Such well being, however, one cannot attain if only looking out for oneself without any restraining force or inhibitions of action. (scruples).

036<•>observes that if this view of moral thought is put into an ethical code (verbal or written) it has the advantage that it appears quite natural. It is very easy to reconcile it with the needs of those who desire to content themselves with the knowledge which their senses give them of the knowable world as real and to whom human existence appears only a part of this world.

037<•>observes that on the other hand, this view of the ethical code was bound to produce in its turn a materialist view of the world. Founding ethical codes on the longing for pleasure or happiness of the individual (on egoism) and the materialist world concept, conditioned and lent each other mutual support.

038<•>observes that the connection of both elements comes most completely to expression in Epicurus (341-270 BCE). His materialist philosophy of nature is founded with a directly ethical aim.

039<•>observes that Epicureanism. The two great schools of the Hellenistic period were the Stoics and the Epicureans. The former founded by Zeno the latter by Epicurus, born in Samos in 324BCE. Both schools settled in Athens, where Epicurus taught that 'pleasure is the beginning and end of the happy life.' However, he was no sensualist and emphasized the importance of moderation in all things because excess would lead to pain instead of pleasure and the best of all pleasures were mental ones.

040<•>observes that he taught pleasures could be active or passive but the former contain an element of pain since they are the process of satisfying desires not yet satiated. The latter involving the absence of desire are the more pleasant. In fact, Epicurus in his personal life was more stoical than many stoics and wrote "when I live on bread and water I spit on luxurious pleasures."

041<•>observes that Epicurus disapproved of sexual enjoyment and thought friendship one of the highest of all joys. A materialist who accepted the atomic theory of Democritus, he was not a determinist, and if he did not disbelieve in the gods he regarded religion and the fear of death as the two primary sources of unhappiness.

042<•>observes that the materialist view of nature is in his view alone in the position to free us from the fear which a foolish superstition awakes in us and to give us that peace of conscious inmost material being (cimb) without which true happiness is impossible.

043<•>observes that on the other hand, all those elements who are opposed to materialism are obliged to reject this ethic code, and vice versa; those who are not satisfied with this code are not satisfied with materialism either. And this moral feeling of egoism, or the pursuit of the individual happiness, gives ample opportunity for attack.

044<•>observes that in the first place Epicuruism did not explain how moral feeling arose as a moral binding force, as an *in the guts* duty to do the right thing and not simply as advice, to prefer the more rational kind of pleasure to the less rational.

045<•>observes that the speedy decisive moral judgment on good and bad is quite different from the balancing-up between different kinds of pleasures or utilities. And in the foregoing it appears that morality is an individual imperative.

046<•>observes that finally it is possible for a group to feel a moral duty even in cases where the most generous interpretation can find no pleasure or utility from which the pursuit of this duty can be deduced.

047<•>observes that A group may refuse to lie, although by that means stirs up public opinion forever against itself, put its existence at stake, or even brings on the penalty of death. Then, in such a case, there can be no talk of even the remotest pleasure or happiness which could transform the discomfort or pain of the moment into its opposite. But what can the critics bring forward to explain this phenomenon? In fact nothing, even if according to their own view a great deal.

~048< TRACT 3:

049<•>observes Ancient Ethical Codes Idealistic And Materialistic:

The Rise Of And Validation Of Idealistic (Written And Unwritten) Ethical Codes And Managing The Crowd.

050<•>observes that since the dissatisfied were unable to explain the moral feeling by natural means it became to them the surest and most unanswerable proof that people lived, not only a natural life, but also outside of nature. That in them supernatural and non-natural forces work. That spirit is something supernatural. Thus arose from this view the written ethic codes of philosophic idealism and monotheism, the new belief in God.

051<•>observes that this new belief did not arise from the fact that the manifold gods were reduced to one God. This new belief in one God is quite different to the old polytheism; it differs from the latter not only in the number of the gods; but in the fact that there now arose a supernatural element.

052<•>observes that Polytheism is an attempt to explain the process of nature. Its gods are personifications of the forces

Tsunami One   Moral Organon.

of nature; they are thus not over nature, and not outside of nature, but in her and form a part of her.

053<•>observes that the manifold gods here and there maintain a traditional existence – for a time even in philosophy. But only as kinds of supermen and superwomen who no longer play any active role. Even for Epicurus, in his materialism, the gods are not dead, but they are changed into passive spectators. ("We should enjoy life while we can," said Epicurus, "superstitious beliefs cause needless suffering.")

054<•>observes that natural philosophy supersedes the belief in manifold gods in the degree in which it discovers other than personal causation in the processes of nature, and develops the idea of natural law, of the necessary connection between cause and effect.

055<•>observes that even the non-materialist ethical school of philosophy, such as is most completely represented by Plato (427-347 BCE), and whose mythical side is far more clearly developed by the neoplatonists. Especially by Plotinus (204-270)—In the Enneads 6 sets of 9 treatises in the chain of being – even this school does not find the gods necessary to explain nature, and deals with them in no other way than do the materialists.

056<•>observes that their idea of God does not spring out of the need to explain the natural world around us, but to explain the moral feeling and spiritual nature of man. In order to create an ethical code requires them to have a spiritual being standing outside of and over nature, thus outside of time and space. Thus to have a God which can validate the ethical code (usually formed by the ruling Estate) a code which is a quintessence of all that ruling estate's desire to change morality. Thus with such a duly validated ethical code in hand they can manage the crowd who work both with their hands and minds.

057<•>observes that just as the 'ethical philosophers' conceived themselves as noble, and the 'natural materialist philosophers' appeared to them common and vulgar, so does nature become mean and bad, the spirit on the other hand elevated and good. People are unlucky enough to belong to both worlds, that of matter, and that of spirit. Thus they are half animal and half angel, and they oscillate between good and evil.

058<•>observes that in some minds God rules nature and she also places the moral feeling in the mind of adults, thus she gives persons the force to overcome nature and the desires of the flesh and to triumph over them. BUT more complete happiness is nevertheless impossible for folks so long as they dwell in this vale of tears, where one is condemned to bear the burden of one's own flesh and the predators in society. Only with death when the so-called soul is free from life can the spirit return to its original source — God — can one enjoy unlimited happiness.

059<•>observes that with the foregoing it will be seen that God or Allah plays a very different role to what she does in the original Polytheism. This one God is a minimal personification of nature, but it is an overwhelming creation in people's mind of an independent existence on the part of the spiritual (or intellectual) nature of man.

060<•>observes that the Godhead tends to no multiplicity. And in its most complete metaphysical (idealistic) philosophic form, the one God, has no other function than that of validating the ethical code produced by the temper of the times and that is to be inserted into the moral thinking and the moral feeling of the people at large.

061<•>observes that for God to interfere in the course of the world in the manner of the ancient Polytheistic gods is not God's business. Now God serves, at least for idealistic philosophers and theologians, to validate the manipulated ethical codes as a methodology of changing moral thinking of the people into binding laws.

062<•>observes that Idealists know full well that binding moral laws *do exist* and are thus easily accepted by human reason. But these laws are to be found not in idealism but are in fact found in natural materialistic scientific laws of cause and effect.

063<•>observes that the more Godhead becomes popular and grows into the religion of the people, the more does a higher, all embracing and all ruling spirit take on again personal characteristics. God now takes part in human affairs, but the old gods smuggle themselves in. (at least in the Christian religion and somewhat less in Islamic and Judeo Religions)

064<•>observes that the old gods come in as intermediators between God and man, as saints and angels. But even in this form the contempt for nature holds true. For this belief, and its corresponding faith, brings with it a general view that the spiritual and especially the moral thinking of man is of supernatural origin and affords an infallible proof of the existence of a supernatural sigma metaphysical and idealistic world.

065<•>observes that between the two extremes -idealism of Plato and the materialism of Epicurus, there are many intermediary positions possible. Among these the most important is that of the Stoic philosophy, founded by Zeno of Citium (341-270 BCE).

066<•>observes that just like Platonic philosophy Zeno attacks those who seek to derive moral thinking or feeling from pleasure or egotism in a single individual. Zeno recognizes in a person a higher power standing over the individual. A power which can drive them to action, and which may bring them pain, grief, even death.

067<•>observes that in fact Zeno and the other Stoics noticed that a lot of the problems and hardships people undergo seem to disappear when they simply decide not to be bothered by them.

068<•>observes that also, different from Plato, Zeno sees in moral thinking and feeling nothing supernatural, only a product of nature. Virtue arises from the knowledge of nature; happiness is arrived at when man acts in accordance with nature, that is, in accordance with the universe or universal reason.

069<•>observes that Zeno thinks that to know nature and act in accordance with her, reasonably, which is the same as virtuously, and voluntarily to submit to her necessity, disregarding individual pleasure and pain, that is the way to happiness which the wise must go.

070<•>observes that in Zeno however, the study of nature is only a means to the study of virtue (morals). Nature is itself explained by the Stoics from a moral point of view. The practical result of the Stoic moral thinking is to provide ethical codes, which are but the contempt of pleasure and the disdain of the good things of the world and are not the search for mere happiness.

071<•>observes that this contempt of the world by Stoics is to serve the same end, that which appeared to Zeno as well as Epicurus as the highest state of repose for the individual ever living soul (see Cimb). Both systems of ethics arose out of the need for the 'soul's' eternal rest.

072<•>observes that the intermediary position of Stoic between the Platonic and the Epicurean corresponded to the view of the universe which Stoicism drew up. The explanation of nature is by no means without importance to them. But nature appears to them as a peculiar kind of monotheistic materialism, which assumes a divine original force from which, in the believers, the human soul springs.

073<•>observes that the Stoics thought that this original force, this original fire, is material, it exists in and not outside of nature, and the soul is not immortal (see Cimb), even if it survives the human body. Finally it will be consumed by the original fire.

074<•>observes that thus materialist Epicureanism is overcome in those ancient times and that Stoicism and Platonism finally become elements of at first a revolutionary and then later an ossified Christianity.

075<•>observes that materialist Epicureanism can now only prove satisfactory to a social class which has been subjected to a billion hypocrisies by such religious thinking. A class that is not satisfied with things as they are, which does not find in these things any pleasure and happiness, and has need for another state of affairs.

076<•>observes that thus we see that Epicurean materialism is necessarily rejected by all people to whom the world-as-it-is seems bad and full of pain. They are the decaying second estate of the old aristocracy and with them their peasants and serfs, (and more recently the decaying third estate and with them their salary and wage workers of the fifth estate.)

Tsunami One   Moral Organon.

All of the mentioned herein for whom present and future happiness in this world can only be equally hopeless.

077<•>observes that if the Epicurian material world, that is the world of experience, is the only plausible one, then no reliance can be placed in it to control people through ethical codes in class divided society. Now in order to control ethical codes in that divided society there must arise a reliance on an almighty spirit who can validate such codes and if the code is not followed, has it in her power the ability to bring this world to destruction. Now then, with only the idealistic sigma metaphysical world to worry the mind, a better life in the hereafter is made possible.

078<•>observes that finally ancient materialism is bound to be rejected by the whole society as soon as that society had degenerated to the point that even the ruling classes suffer under the economic state of affairs. So that even these classes come to the opinion that no good can come out of the existing world, but that this spaceship earth only brings forth evil. To despise the world with the Stoics, or look for a redeemer from the other side with the Christians and other such idealistic religions, that has become the only alternative.

079<•>observes that a new element comes into Christianity with the invasions of Rome by the Barbarians. The outsiders substitute for the decadent society of the Roman empire another in which the decrepit remains of the Roman system of production and their views of life is swept away. Now old Rome combined with the youthful German society, and a people of simple thought, content to enjoy life, these elements combined to produce a strange new formation.

080<•>observes that on the one hand the Christian Church became the bond which held the new state together. Here once again the theory is apparently confirmed that the spirit is stronger than matter, since the intelligence of the Christian priesthood showed itself strong enough to tame the brute force of the Barbarians.

081<•>observes that this brute force, springing as it did from the material world, appeared to the representatives of Christianity, as the source of all evil if it was not ruled and held in check by a holy spirit.

082<•>observes that the new social situation only contributed to strengthening the philosophic foundation of Christianity and its system of ethical codes and their impact on moral thinking. And so too there comes, through this new situation, the joy in life and a feeling of self confidence in the organism of society which had failed to be fully enjoyed at the time of the initial rise of Christendom.

083<•>observes that even to the Christian clergy – at least in the mass – the world no longer appeared a vale of tears and they acquire a capacity for enjoyment – a happy Epicureanism, in a coarser form and one which had nothing in common with a now ancient philosophy.

084<•>observes that nevertheless the Christian priesthood was obliged to hold to the Christian ethical codes no longer as the expression of their own moral feeling, but as a means of maintaining their rule over the people.

085<•>observes that everything forced the priesthood to recognize the philosophic foundation of this system of ethics (both written and unwritten), namely the independence and the mastery of spirit over the real world. And of course these ethical codes were silent in many aspects that were to haunt mankind in the years to come (the most salient ones being the silence on interest and profit)

086<•>observes that this spirit cannot just dismiss the material world. Thus the new social situation produced on the one hand a tendency toward a surreptitious materialist moral feeling, while on the other this led to a series of reasons to strengthen the traditional Christian ethical code and thereby twist moral thinking in individuals towards a sigma metaphysical Christianity.

087<•>observes that this is how the double morality arose, which becomes characteristic of Christianity and all religions in general. The formal recognition of a system of codified ethics which is only partially the expression of people's moral feeling and will, whilst the materialist part of moral thinking is more or less obscured, consequently there is a combined morality (one formal and the other surreptitious) which controls people's action.

088<•>observes that in other words ethical codes in these epochs lead to moral hypocrisy which becomes a standing social institution, which is never so widely spread as under religion. Morality and religion appeared now as inseparably bound together. Certainly the ethical code is the logical creator of the new God; but in religion God appears as the author of the ethical code. And this code is often found not just as a religious code but is often found embedded in Civil & Criminal Law.

089<•>observes that thus they believe that without a belief in God, without religion, no morality. Every ethical question becomes a theological one.

Tsunami One   Moral Organon.

090<•>observes that this brings into existence a form of social indignation, a moral indignation, bound up with the feeling by the mass of the people of the immorality and hypocrisy of any existing social institutions that are in decay.

091<•>observes that so does every social uprising commence in the form of a theological criticism to which vitriol comes as an additional factor in the life of Church, Mosque or Synagogue.

092<•>observes that in the middle ages the Christian church is the foremost means of class rule and the Roman priesthood are the worst exploiters, so that all rebellion against any form of exploitation always affects the Church in the first place. Even after the renaissance at a time when philosophic thought again arises, questions of moral thought and codified ethics remain bound up in theology.

~093< TRACT 4:

094<•>observes that **Moral Thinking And Ethical Codes In The Period Of The Enlightenment:** From Whence, However, Is A Moral Ideal To Be Derived In A World Of Vice?

095<•>observes that after the renaissance the study of nature again begins to arouse interest, and with it also its philosophy, which from then till well into the 21st century became principally the physical sciences. During the enlightenment economic philosophy, which was part of the mental sciences progressed rapidly until the end of the 19th century. (in the broad community and broadly speaking thought in these mental sciences has remained locked into this time period ever since). But still, as such, raises people's knowledge of the world far above the level reached in the ancient world.

Tsunami One   Moral Organon.

096<•>observes that between the 14th to 17th centuries philosophers set out from the progress over the Greeks which the Arabs have made in natural science during the middle ages. The high-water mark of this development is certainly formed by the theory of Spinoza (1632-1677): Also of note we see F. Bacon, (1561 1626): Hobbes, (1588 1679): La Mettrie, (1709 1751): Holbach, (1723 1789): Helvetius (1715 1771): & Diderot (1713 1784)

097<•>observes that ethics takes second place with these thinkers. Attention to the study of ethic codes and their impact on internalized moral thinking is subordinated to the study of natural science, of which ethics forms only a part. But ethics comes again to the fore as the rapid, but neophyte development of third estate capitalism (3E) in west Europe in the eighteenth century creates a similar situation to that which had been created by the economic awakening which followed on the Persian wars in the Greek environs.

098<•>observes that it is now that philosophers begin to speak in modern language, a reassigning all new values, and therewith a zealous thinking-out and investigation into the foundation and essence of all morality.

099<•>observes that with that investigation on morality goes an eager research into the nature of the new method of production. Simultaneously with that study comes a reappearance of the study of the moral thinking of the masses as well as of individuals and the ethical codes that go along with it. And the question is, are ethical codes capable of modifying and controlling moral thinking and to what degree?

100<•>observes that at this point there arises a new science of which the ancients were ignorant, politics and economy and political-economy thus are born the special children of the capitalist system of production, whose explanation it serves.

101<•>observes that in ethics in this period, however, we find three schools of thought running along side each other. The moral thoughts now often run parallel to the three systems of the ancients, i) the Platonic, ii) the Stoic, iii) Epicurean. Now it becomes 1) anti-materialist: 2) the traditional religio/quasi materialist, and: 3) the materialist.

102<•>observes that now there comes an optimism and joy of life in the rising Bourgeoisie, at least in their progressive elements, especially their intellectuals. This intellectual torrent feels strong enough to flow openly and to throw aside all hypocritical masks that had hitherto been forced upon them by the ruling second estate aristocracy armed with religiosity. (mainly Christianity and latterly not limited to that religion alone.)

103<•>observes that as miserable as the present might be, yet the uprising 3E bourgeoisie and their philosophers felt that the best part of reality – the future belonged to them! And they felt the ability in themselves to change the vale of tears into a paradise, in which 3E capital could follow any inclination that possessed them. Including the overthrow of the second estate (2E) aristocracy.

104<•>observes that in reality and in the natural impulses of folk their thinkers see the germs of all good and no evil. This new school of thought finds a thankful public not only among the more progressive elements in the bourgeoisie, but also in the court nobility. This 2E now have acquired such an absolute power in the state that even they think that they can dispense with all religious (Christian) hypocrisy in their life of pleasure. This comes about all the more successfully as they are now divided by deep chasms with the first estate

Tsunami One   Moral Organon.

(1E) religion on one side and the life of the people on the other.

105<•>observes that even though serfs were not free but tied to the land the 2E aristocrats looked on 'free' citizens, serfs and peasants as being of a lower order to whom their philosophy is incomprehensible. This brings about their thought that they can freely and undisturbedly develop it without fear of shaking their own means of rule over the rising 3E bourgeoisie, the 1E church, and the people.

106<•>observes that even this Philosophy of Enlightenment has a conservative root, it regards contemplative enjoyment as happiness so long as it serves the needs of the court nobility, which draws its living from the existing autocratic regime.

107<•>observes that despite that, and what the aristocrats do not quite grasp at first, in the main, is the real content of the philosophy of the most intelligent and farthest developed as well as the most courageous elements in the 3E bourgeoisie. They give it a revolutionary character.

108<•>observes that from the very beginning the 3E were in the most absolute opposition to traditional religion, ethical codes and civil and criminal laws and the rindlucent in moral thinking that are backed by the nobility's state machinery and force. And the more the bourgeoisie increased in strength and class consciousness, the conception of a fight – a conception which would have been quite strange to the old Epicureans – the fight against priests, hereditary nobility and tyrants; the fight for new ideals.

109<•>observes that the nature and method of the moral views and the height of moral passions are determined by the conditions of human life, especially by the constitution of the state as well as by education. <u>It is always self interest that</u>

Tsunami One   Moral Organon.

<u>determines the actions of people; it can, however, become a very social interest, if society is so organized that the individual interest coincides with the interest of the community, so that the passions of individual men and women serve the common welfare.</u>

110<•>observes that true virtue consists in the care for the commonweal, it can only flourish where the commonwealth at the same time advances the interests of the individual, where a person cannot damage the commonwealth without damaging himself.

111<•>observes that it is the incapacity to perceive and ignorance which renders a state of affairs possible which of necessity brings the individual interest into conflict with that of the community and the more durable interests of mankind as to the best form of government, society and education.

112<•>observes that it only remains to make an end of this ignorance, to find a form of state, society and education corresponding to the demands of reason, in order to establish happiness and virtue on a firm and eternal foundation.

113<•>observes that now then here we come on the revolutionary essence of French materialism, which accuses the existing state (controlled by 2E nobility) as the cause of immorality. With that accusation French Materialism raises itself above the level of Epicureanism – because now it becomes no mere question of inventing the best form of state and society; Morality now becomes an imperative that must be fought for. And the breast of every person knows now the powers that must be confronted and overthrown in order to establish an empire of virtue.

114<•>observes that arriving at the forgoing state of affairs requires, however, great moral zeal, and where is that to come from if the existing society is so bad that it prevents altogether the growth of virtue and a new morality? Must not that new morality be already there in neophyte form in order that the higher society may arise?

115<•>observes that is it not necessary that the new morality should be alive in the people before the new ethical codes, new moral thinking and then the new laws can indeed become a fact? Whence, however, is a moral ideal to be derived from in a world of vice? (we shall show answers to these questions as follows)

116<•>observes that we obtain no satisfactory answer in the period under observation. In very different fashion to the French, the Englishmen of the eighteenth century endeavor to explain 'moral law'. They show themselves less audacious in general and more inclined to compromise, in keeping with the history of England since the reformation.

117<•>observes that in England their insular position was especially favorable to their economic development during this period. They were driven thereby to make sea voyages which in the seventeenth and eighteenth centuries, thanks to the colonial system, forms the quickest road to fortune.

118<•>observes that their insular position keeps England free from all the burdens and the ravages of wars on land, such as exhausted the European powers. Thus England acquires in the seventeenth and eighteenth centuries more wealth than all the other nations of Europe and placed herself (so far as her economic position is concerned) at their head.

119<•>observes that new classes and new class antagonisms and with them the new social problems, arise in England at an earlier date than elsewhere. (Except in a small way in Holland) The new classes only attain a small degree of class consciousness, and still remain to a large degree imprisoned in the old methods of thought, so that the class antagonisms only appear in a very undeveloped form. (thus the aristocracy in England, adopting bourgeois methodology of blending in, is still to this very day in positions of some power.)

120<•>observes that in such a land as England is at the time it does not at once come to a final and decisive struggle in the class war. There it comes to no decisive overthrow of the old classes. They there continue to rule with only token limit and remain at the height of their power until the middle of the first world war when a new colossUS arises in the form of a super 3E power in the United States. A power not fettered by a feudal past.

121<•>observes that based upon this meager evidence it seems to be a general law of social development, that countries which are pioneers in economic development are tempted to put compromise in the place of radical solutions.

122<•>observes that at this time and since the reformation England, together with Scotland, has taken the place of France and Italy as the pioneer of economic development. And thus compromise and integration of second and third estate interests has become, for both England and Scotland, the form of the solution of their class struggles.

123<•>observes that this sequence of events came about because in England, in the seventeenth century, capital acquired power more rapidly than elsewhere. Because there, earlier than in other countries, it came to a struggle with the feudal aristocracy. And this fight ended in compromise, and that compromise ended in a 'combination' which explains the fact that the feudal system of landed property in the period under observation is stronger in England than in any other country of Europe – Austro-Hungary alone excepted.

124<•>observes that for the same reason, that of her rapid economic development, the class war between wage labor and bourgeoisie 3E first blazed up in England of all countries in the world. It blazed up at a time when wage labor and industrial capitalists had not yet got over the small bourgeois methods of thought. It blazed up when many, and even clear-sighted observers, mixed up the two classes together as the industrial class. It blazed up when the type of the wage labor, self-conscious and confident in the future of his own class, as well as that of the autocrat and unlimited ruler in the state – the industrial and finance capitalists – had not yet fully developed. It blazed up when the capitalist class were merely bourgeoisie wantabe capitalists

125<•>observes that thus we can say that historians of the time failed to see that in the womb of the 3E was growing the fifth-estate (5E) salary and wage worker and the reality of this separation had not yet made itself manifest on peoples minds.

126<•>observes that thus the struggle between the second and third estates landed, after a short and showy flare-up, in a compromise and assimilation with one another which for many years to follow gave unlimited rule to the bourgeoisie of England. This rule in England was thus far greater than in any other land with a modern system of production.

127<•>observes that thus we see that it is not always true that the land which takes the lead in the economic development invariably also brings the corresponding forms of the class war to the sharpest and most decisive expression. Even materialism and atheism as well as ethical codes were subject, in England, to the spirit of compromise, and assimilation, which has ruled since the sixteenth century.

128<•>observes that the fight of the democratic and rising class against the governing power, independent of the bourgeoisie and subject to the feudal aristocracy with their court nobility and their state church, commences in England more than a century before that in France. It developed at a time when only a relatively few have gone over, in England, from Catholic to Protestant thought. Thus in England the revolution manifests itself as only a struggle between sects – special Protestant sects, the state-church-organized, and a portion of the nobility – the Catholic sect.

129<•>observes that more than a century later in France the fight, however, against the state church now has advanced and becomes a fight between Catholic Christianity and atheistic materialism.

130<•>observes that in France in the period of the enlightenment, the majority of new thought and the classes that came under its influence thought as materialists and atheists, while English thought however still looks, during this period, for a compromise between materialism and Protestant Christianity.

131<•>observes that in some people materialism certainly finds its first public form in England in the theory of Thomas Hobbes (1588-1679) (Leviathan). And of course materialist sentiments were to be found in English thinkers on ethical code questions, whose courage surpassed that of the most courageous Frenchman, such as Mandeville (1670-1733) (The Fable Of The Bees. Private Vices Public Benefits) the English physician and satirist (born in Holland) who declared morality to be a means of ruling. Thus ethical codes were fashioned and promulgated to keep the wage workers of the

Tsunami One Moral Organon.

time in subjection, and who oddly enough looked on vice as the root of all social good.

132<•>observes that such ideas had little influence on the thoughts of the many. A Protestant Christian profession remains the sign of respectability, and even if this morality is not internally felt in every person, still to pretend to feel it becomes the duty of every person of learning, who did not wish to come into conflict with society.

133<•>observes that thus Englishmen remained very skeptical of the new materialistic morals and their ethical codes, which wished to found new moral thoughts based on self love, or on the pleasure and the ability of the individual.

134<•>observes that as the intellectual circles of the rising bourgeoisie in France and even in England sought to explain moral thinking as a natural phenomenon they see that compulsory ethical codes cannot be fashioned from simple considerations of utility. And they see that any such constructions are too artificial which are required to unite moral thinking with the motives of utility – let alone to think of making ethical codes based on utility as energetic motive forces to change moral thinking.

135<•>observes that thus these people come to finally distinguish very nicely between the sympathetic and the egoistic interests in man. They discuss a moral thinking which drives man to be active for the happiness of his fellows. After Hutcheson (1694-1747), the most distinguished representative of this theory is Adam Smith the economist (1723-1790). The sympathetic (Theory of Moral Sentiment). The economic egoistic (The Wealth Of Nations).

136<•>observes that Adam Smith says, amongst other things, Quote. "In every civilized society, in every society where the distinction of ranks has once been completely established, there have been always two different schemes or systems of morality current at the same time; of which one may be called the strict or austere; the other the liberal, or if you will the loose system. The former is generally admired and revered by the common people; the latter is commonly more esteemed and adopted by what are called people of fashion." End quote p746 Modern Library Edition.

137<•>observes that thus in his two principal works he investigates, what your observer would call his two mainsprings of human action. In the "Theory of Moral Sentiments" (1759) he starts out from sympathy as the most important bond of human society; his "Wealth of Nations" (1776) assumes that egoism – the material interest of the individual – to be the mainspring of human action. Adam Smith uttered orally in Glasgow as early as 1752 or 1753. His theory of egoism and his theory of sympathy were not mutually exclusive, but were complementary the one of the other.

138<•>observes that if these Englishmen set moral thinking on the one hand and egoism (basically economics) over against each other, so how is that to be compared to 1) materialism, 2) the approach to Platonism and, 3) the approach to religion especially the Christianity of the time?

139<•>observes that since, while according to Christianity, man is bad by nature and according to the Platonic theory our natural impulses are the source of evil in us, so for the English school of the eighteenth century, moral thinking of sympathy was opposed certainly to economic egoism. But overriding this feeling of sympathy they feel that all the economic forces of egoism are natural impulses. (on sympathy we will expand further on)

140<•>observes that this economic egoism appears to them not as a bad, but as a fully justifiable impulse which is as necessary for the welfare of society just as sympathy for others is necessary. Moral thinking, especially economic egoism is elevated by them to a sense just as any other human sense, and in a certain degree was their sixth sense. (so in this we see the code in their thought unconsciously impacting greatly on the rindlucent).

141<•>observes that certainly with these assumption, just as in the case of the French materialists, the difficulty was only postponed and not solved. To the question, whence comes this 'economic egoism sense' in man, the Englishmen have the answer – It is given by nature to man. (That might suffice for those who trade in a faith in God. But is it scientific?)

142<•>observes that thus the task for the further scientific development of ethical codes and civil & criminal law, to modify moral thinking is required. The French, as well as the English, schools have by this time achieved much for the psychological and historical explanation of moral feelings and views. But neither one nor the other can succeed in making quite clear that morality is an outcome of causes which lie in the realm of economics (or what some like to call egoism) and human experience.

143<•>observes that for progress to take place the English school must be surpassed and the causes of moral thinking, must be updated and ethical codes and civil & criminal laws investigated. It is also necessary to go beyond the French school and to lay bare the objective causes of the moral ideal in people's thinking.

144<•>observes that moral development goes in no straight line – it moves in contradictions. The next step of philosophy in regard to ethics codes takes the opposite direction. Instead of investigating the moral nature of man in order to bring this under the general laws of nature, this 'going beyond the French school' comes to quite other conclusions.

145<•>observes that this next faltering step is achieved by German philosophy with Kant (1724-1804) and others. Certain people like to cry now, "Back to Kant!" But those who mean by that the Kantian ethic, might just as well cry "Back to Plato!"

~146< TRACT 5:

147<•>observes that **The 'Now' People Of The 21st Century** And Their Cry "Back To Kant!" Your Humble Author Says that Kant Is But Our Sounding Board.

Note: Why must we go way back to Kant? Because although many have progressed way beyond Kant our present day apologists have not even reached the level of Hegel let alone Marx and others. Neo-Kantian thought is rife in our snarled society. Many cling to Kant and such sigma metaphysical philosophies as do drowning men to any life preserver no matter how decrepit it may be.

148<•>observes that Kant takes the same ground as the materialists. He recognizes that the world outside of us is real and that the starting point of all knowledge is the experience of the senses. (This is Kant's opening statement in Critique of Pure Reason (CPR) but then come the pages and pages of smoke and mirrors that modify this fundamental concept and twist it out of shape.)

149<•>observes that and here comes part of that modification. "knowledge of which we acquire from experience is partly composed of that which we acquire through the sense impressions and partly from that which our own intellectual powers supply from themselves; in other words, our knowledge of the world is conditioned not simply by the nature of the external world, but also by that provided (RER out of thin air) by our organs of knowledge."

150<•>observes that Kant says that for a knowledge of the world the investigation of our own intellectual powers is equally as necessary as that of the external world. This investigation of this subjective intellect is the duty of philosophy – this to him is the science of science.

151<•>observes that there is, in this Kantian view, a content which even some, if not most, materialist of the day could subscribe to, or that, perhaps has also been previously said by materialists. But certainly only in the way in which certain sentences from the materialist conception of history had already been uttered before Marx, as conceptions which had not borne fruit.

152<•>observes that it was Kant (even though he was off base due to the historical period in which he found himself) who first made the detached-from-objects-mind the foundation of his entire theory. Still it is through him that philosophy first becomes the science of science, a Mental Philosophy Science as opposed to the purely Physical Sciences.

153<•>observes that thus Kant, even though he leads us astray, has identified the Mental Philosophies and sciences whose duty it is **not** to teach a distinct philosophy, but how to philosophize, the process of knowing, methodical thinking, and that by way of a critique of knowledge.

154<•>observes that Kant went farther than this, and his great philosophical achievement, the investigation of the faculties of knowledge, became itself his philosophical stumbling block – since our sensual experience does not reveal to us the world as it is in itself, but only as it appears to us. (i.e. Sun around earth; Earth around sun; hidden from view value-added; and other such appearances, arguments and dialectics and in the coil of progress in human knowledge. (epistemology))

155<•>observes that Kant did not take into account, that the constitution of our faculties of knowledge, our sense perceptions, are but a mirror image of the objective world, and as in all mirrors there is distortion in that reflection. So that the world as it is in-itself must be different to that which it at first appears to us. (billions of misperceptions held at large.)

156<•>observes that as a consequence of this Kant distinguishes between the world of phenomena – the world of things in themselves – and the "noumena," (the idea itself inaccessible to experience) or the 'brain' world. Certainly this latter is for us unknowable, it lies outside of our experience and is nothing but fluff. (we shall soon see further on that the world of advertising has an 'in' to this stuff of fluff and whimsy.)

157<•>observes that one might simply take the foregoing as a method of designating the fact that our knowledge of the world is always limited by the nature of our intellectual faculties, is always relative, that for us there can only be relative (objective truth) and no absolute truths. There never was or never can be a final and complete knowledge only an endless process of knowing.

158<•>observes that Kant was not content with this nagging question. He felt an unquenchable longing to get a glimpse into that unknown and unexplorable world of things in themselves, in order to acquire at least a notion of it. And indeed he got so far as to say quite distinct things about it.

The way to this world he saw in the critique of our powers of thought.

159<•>observes that the question is how do we get knowledge from experience? Kant, in order to solve his problem came up with the idea of 'a priori knowledge.' That is we get experience from knowledge, (a completely silly about-face concept but accepted by millions) and that, according to Kant, all experiences are contained in our 'feelings'

160<•>observes that in this manner he discovered the ideality of time and space. According to him these are not conceptions which are won from experience, but simply the forms of our conception of the world, which are embedded in our faculties of knowledge.

161<•>observes that Kant believes that only under the form of conceptions in time and space can we recognize the world. But outside of our faculties of knowledge there is no space and no time. Thus Kant got so far as to say about the world of things in themselves, that world is completely unknowable, and something else, very distinct, namely, that it is timeless and spaceless.

162<•>observes that this is a logical feat of the human mind of the time. But now with greater knowledge and the development of control of society by the 3E it now comes open to criticism and there is great deal to be said against it, and in fact there are very weighty objections which have been brought to bear in this matter.

163<•>observes that the assumption of the ideality of space and time in the Kantian, and sigma metaphysical sense leads to inextricable contradictions. There can certainly be no doubt that the conceptions of time and space are conditioned by the make-up of people's faculties of knowledge, but sticking to this concept only amounts to saying, that no other connections to events in the universe can be recognized. The adoption of this concept is to call forth mythical events in nature which only exist as ideas in peoples minds. In this context one must be reminded that ultra-violet and ultra-red rays are imperceptible to our vision but we know they do exist.

164<•>observes that despite Kant there are relations and distinctions of the things themselves, so that the different things appear in nature as, hard or soft, big or small, near or far, sooner or later. And these are real relations and distinctions of the external world, these are real relationships whether my mind is conscious of them or not. My mind becomes conscious of them through the organs of vision, hearing, smell, touch, and taste. (and also by instruments that enhance these faculties)

165<•>observes that there are, for example, things of 'vision' and concepts of 'time' (i.e. sooner or later) that people cannot see but man through his ingenuity has produced instruments that aid the senses in detecting ranges in the real world. Those are the things beyond the ability of the limited ranges of people's senses.

166<•>observes that Kant, on the other hand, is of the opinion that not simply are space and time forms of conception for us, but that even the temporal and spatial differences of phenomena spring solely from our heads, and indicate nothing real. (this then is pure Berkeley)

167<•>observes that if what Kant espouses is really so, then all phenomena spring simply from our heads, since they all take the form of temporal and spatial differences. Thus, by inference, we can know absolutely nothing about the world outside of us, not even that it exists.

168<•>observes that when it comes to ethics and morals. If an overwhelming number of theologians and idealists of the present day should abandon Kant and finally admit that there exists a world outside our minds mankind would not be mired in an imperfect, one-sided mechanism, which communicates to us only a one-sided idealistic knowledge of the world.

169<•>observes that, going back to Bishop Berkeley for a moment, Kant can attack ever so energetically the "mystical" idealism of Berkeley, which he hopes to replace with his "critical" idealism. Kant's criticism takes a turn, which nullifies his own opening salvo in The Critique of Pure Reason – "That all our knowledge begins with experience there can be no doubt." Then the rest of the tome is devoted to the idealistic approach and as Kautsky says "thus mysticism cast out from the one side finds on the other a wide triumphal doorway open, through which it can enter with a flourish of trumpets."

~170< **TRACT 6:**

171<•>observes that **Critique Of God And Immortality In Moral Thought And Ethical Codes.** Superfluousness In The World Of Transcendence And Kant

172<•>observes that Kant assumes as his starting point that the world is really external to us and does not simply exist in our heads, and that knowledge about it is only to be attained through our senses over time (experience). Then he wavered as we have seen.

173<•>observes that just this very examination becomes for him an incitement to discover an unknowable world, of which he felt sure was of quite another nature than the world of reality and fact, that it was completely timeless and spaceless, and therefore causeless as well.

174<•>observes that this break-neck leap over the boundaries of reality caused him to lose all firm ground underfoot, the ground from which he springs is logical, but the leap lands him into a jungle of contradictions, into swamps of super-sensuous worlds all of which nullify his own opening assumptions.

175<•>observes that we must understand that between German and English philosophy of the time there is a great difference. The English philosophized at a time of great practical advance, of great practical struggles – the opening of the new bourgeois outlook on things and how to bring about a world of 3E capital out of the 2E aristocratic world.

176<•>observes that the English practice captured their entire intellectual force; even their philosophy was entirely ruled by practical considerations. Their philosophers are greater in their achievements in economics, politics, natural science, than in the moral philosophy of capital.

177<•>observes that thus in the history of the moment the German thinkers found no practice which has not been raked over by English philosophers, which, as we have seen, was steeped in the practical considerations of physical sciences and the economic philosophy of the rising 3E. This state of affairs left the Gordian knot of moral thought conditioned by ethical codes to the German thinkers of the time and leads them into concentrating their entire mental power on the deepest and most abstract problems of a sigma subjective moral philosophy.

178<•>observes that thus these German philosophers in this respect are without their peers outside of Germany. This state of affairs is founded, not on any race quality of the Germans, but on the circumstances of the time. In the sixteenth and seventeenth centuries when the deepest physical philosophic thinkers are to be found in Italy, France, Holland, England, leaving this moral philosophy the only avenue open to the Germans.

179<•>observes that Kant, despite his sympathy for the English, could find no satisfaction in their philosophy. He is just as critical towards it as towards materialism. In both cases these foregoing ethics are bound to strike him as the weakest point from which to launch his philosophy.

180<•>observes that it seems to him from his 'hindrance point in history' quite impossible to bring moral thinking and ethic codes which might control such thinking into a necessary connection with nature, that is, connect them with the world of phenomena.

181<•>observes that Kant's explanation of morals and ethics requires another world, a timeless and spaceless world of pure spirit, a world of freedom in contrast to the world of phenomena which is ruled by the necessary chain of cause and effect. (but as we shall soon see such a 'world' unconnected to the reality of the senses can lead to gods, hobbits, angels dancing on the heads of pins, whimsy, and fantastic virtual reality computer games - such 'worlds' may be entertaining but are they regressive or progressive in human evolution?)

182<•>observes that stuck on the horns! On the one horn, the world of phenomena and on the other horn Kant's experience in Christian feelings. The feelings, an outcome of a pious education, were bound to awaken in him the need for the recognition of a world in which God and immortality were possible in his 'old way' of thinking.

183<•>observes that God and immortality were there locked up in his Cimb and were somehow pure objects in the world of his experience. Thus Kant had to go around them in his 'new' philosophy and allow that God and immortality were completely superfluous in the world of transcendence. But such a philosophy must still prove they still somehow exist.

184<•>observes that he is obliged to look for a world "beyond" phenomena and experience for them, and thus the spaceless, timeless and causeless world of mind in itself corresponds most completely to his needs.

185<•>observes that Kant obtains the best proof for the existence of God and immortality in this world of the "beyond" from the moral laws. Thus we find with him, as with Plato, that there is a repudiation of the materialist explanation of the world thus Kant brings about a neo-rehash of belief in a special world of spirits. (Or if it is preferred a world exclusively of spirit. Thus Kant, leaning on Plato, lend each other a mutual support and render the world of spirit a necessity.)

186<•>observes that the question now must be asked – How, however, does Kant manage to obtain farther insight into this spirit world? The Critique Of Pure Reason only allowed him to say of it, that it was timeless and spaceless. Now this spacelessness has to be filled up with a content. Even for that Kant has an idea.

187<•>observes that in Kant's unknowable world of things in themselves (minds in themselves) becomes at least partly knowable directly one succeeds in getting a hold of a thing in itself. And Kant finds this 'thing in itself' for us. **It is the**

personality of man. I am for myself at once phenomenon and thing in itself. "My pure reason is a thing in itself."

188<•>observes that one must remember when one studies Kant that 1) Thing in itself = the personality of wo/man. or 2) Thing in itself = One's Pure Reason.

189<•>observes that as a part of the sensuous world we are subject to the chain of cause and effect, therefore to necessity; as a thing in itself (one's pure reason). I am free, that is, my thought actions according to Kant are not determined by the causes of the world of the senses, but by the moral law dwelling within me. Which moral law Kant says, springs from one's pure reason and calls out to me not 'Thou must,' but 'Thou shalt.' This shall is an absurdity if there does not correspond to it an, 'I can! If I was only free from of all this sensuous objective stuff that surrounds me!'

190<•>observes that we can now say that moral thinking of people is certainly a complicated thing. It brings along with it contradictions since this moral thinking comes in the form of little inputs to the brain over time (experience) from the sensual world. And output from the brain as is expressed in action (or even inaction) which attempt to change the world of phenomena, and thus they fall into the chain of cause and effect.

191<•>observes that from all the foregoing Kant draws the following "Fundamental Law of the Pure Practical Reason." "Act so that the maxim of thy action may be a principle of universal legislation." And we discover that this principle is by no means startlingly new. It forms only the philosophic translation of the ancient precept, to do unto others as you would have them do unto you.

192<•>observes that the only new thing in this declaration is that this precept forms a revelation of an intelligible world. A revelation which with the greatest application of philosophic insight was to be discovered as a principle which applied not only for humanity, "but for all finite Beings who possess Reason and will even including the Infinite Being as the highest intelligence."

193<•>observes that unfortunately for Kant the proof for this law which applies even to the Supreme Intelligence shows a very serious flaw. It ought to be independent of all conditions appertaining to the world of the senses – the objective world that surrounds us, but that is easier said than done.

194<•>observes that just as it is impossible with an air pump to create a completely airless space. (Even the addition of the 'Getter' in old vacuum tubes could not accomplish this feat entirely.) Thus it is to be recognized that in a similar way a thought cannot possibly work in a vacuum, we cannot possibly grasp a thought, which is independent of all conditions appertaining to the world of the senses. Our moral thinking, our ethical codes which try to modify such morality, and especially our civil & criminal laws do not escape this fate of being tied to reality.

195<•>observes that as we shall see fully developed further on, moral thinking already includes conditions which belong to the world of the senses. Moral thinking is not an isolated thinking in the consciousness or the detached power of control the mind has over its bodily actions in itself. Moral thinking is an electo-chemical process conditioned over billions of years. It is reconditioned to fit and be modified by ethical codes, social instinct, and mores imposed on it which is brought to us by mutual contact with our fellow humans and animals, and even by inanimate nature, by touch, sound, smell, taste, and sight.

196<•>observes that Kant refutes his own premise that there can be pure reason outside the senses when he says "act so that the maxim of thy action may be a principle of universal legislation." This statement assumes not only people outside of me, but also the wish that these kinsmen should behave themselves in a particular manner to one another.

197<•>observes that according to the forgoing these kinfolk are to behave themselves and morally think and so react to a billion situations as, the ethical code their mores and the civil & criminal laws, of their time prescribe them to act.

~198< TRACT 7:

199<•>observes that **The Happiness Maxim –**
Cannot Be Definitely Embraced In A Universal Rule.
Kant, In This Too, Is Our Sounding Board.

200<•>observes that as we shall soon see, the inner moral thinking of an individual that 'goes along' with external ethic codes and laws of the given society may be far different than what that code and the law prescribe.

201<•>observes that when philosophers speak about moral thinking and pleasure, it is surprising that they should think of calling the 'desire for happiness' a universal law. This on the ground that the desire for happiness is universal and therefore also the maxim by which everyone's moral thinking should be, willed, should be externalized on this desire alone.

202<•>observes that whereas, in other cases a universal law of nature makes everything harmonious, here, on the contrary, if we attribute the 'happiness maxim' to a universal law the extreme opposite of harmony will follow.

203<•>observes that for, in the 'happiness maxim', the will of all has not one and the same object, but everyone has his own (his private welfare), which may only accidentally accord with the purposes of others which are as equally selfish.

204<•>observes that thus the 'happiness maxim' while it may satisfy an individual who is thinking it, is far from a sufficiency for a law, because the occasional exceptions which one is permitted to make under it are endless and cannot be definitely embraced in a universal rule.

205<•>observes that thus pleasure is not to be a maxim which can serve as a principle of universal legislation because it can call forth social disharmonies. Moral thinking, ethical codes and universal laws have thus to create a harmonious society. And such a harmonious human globe must be possible, otherwise it would be absurd to wish to create it.

206<•>observes that Kantian Moral Thinking assumes:
1) in the first place, a harmonious society as desirable and is possible, so far so good. But it also assumes,
2) in the second place, that this moral thinking must take place in the vacuum of pure reason untainted by sensual experience, and that,
3) thirdly this pure reason is the means to create such a harmonious society and
4) fourthly, that this result can be achieved through a rule which the individual sets for himself.

207<•>observes that we see now how thoroughly Kant is deceived, when he thought that moral thinking, ethical codes and laws are to be found in the realm of a 'mythical world of pure reason' and are independent of all conditions appertaining to the world of sense. And that Kant purports to form a principle which would apply to all causeless, timeless and spaceless spirits, including God Almighty himself.

208<•>observes that Kant works in a time in history wherein his writings have the stamp that are conditioned and determined by the condition of the state and society in which he lives. Accordingly Kant posited that moral thinking in society which exists in time and space is determined by ethical codes standing outside of time and space.

209<•>observes that this Kantian 'pure reason' purports to direct and command the individual in right morals divorced from sensual input and output. This is a morality of the individual imperfect; senses, objectivism and society have no place in it.

210<•>observes that in a society in which people are used by other people simply as means to their, mostly economic, ends the Kantian Moral 'Law' (Moral Thinking) is a protest against a very concrete feudal society. A feudal society with its personal relations of the aristocracy depending upon tied-to-the-land serf production and for this reason Kant is progressive – 'his out of this world philosophy' gives us, if nothing else, a sounding board in which to test-off further development in thinking.

~211< TRACT 8:

212<•>observes that **Freedom And Necessity**
We Straddle Two Worlds At The Boundary Line Between The Past & The Future. Humans, Animals & Kant. Aims.

213<•>observes that people straddle two worlds, in which they live – Past and Future, the present forms the boundary of the two. People's whole experience lies in the past, all experience is past, and all the connecting links at the boundary for the future which past experience shows them, lie with inevitable necessity behind them.

214<•>observes that also at the boundary the immediate past is clouded with misconceptions, distortions, mal-information and propaganda. What is left for people to do at the boundary is clear up and sort out the source of intrigues and bring light to bear upon the true nature of the immediate past as quickly as possible. This is so that the mistakes of the past are not repeated over and over again. And the prime tool in this quest for knowledge is WHY! who, what, when, how are also essential tools but the prime tool is WHY!

215<•>observes that once this information is more or less sorted, facts and objective truth laid bare for all to see there is nothing left to alter, people can do nothing more in regard to these past facts and objective truths than recognize their necessity. Thus the world of experience, the world of knowing, and the world of necessity is laid bare for people so that they may step on firmer ground for future decisions.

216<•>observes that of the future, people have not the slightest experience. Apparently they are free to mould the future as it lies before them. But it is as a world, which people cannot explore as absolutely knowing it, but only in conjecture, in which they have to assert themselves as active agents.

217<•>observes that certainly people can extend the experience of the past into the future, yes indeed they can conclude that these experiences will be even necessarily determined for the future but even if they recognize this future world it is only on assumption. Yet people are required to act in it these assumptions.

218<•>observes that even if compulsion is exercised over their actions, there remains the choice, whether they shall yield to it, or not. There remains only, as an extreme last resort – the possibility of withdrawing themselves by a voluntary death.

219<•>observes that action implies continual choice between various possibilities, and that of doing or not doing. It means accepting or rejecting, It means defending, abandoning or opposing.

220<•>observes that choice in moral thinking, however, assumes in advance the possibility of a distinction between the acceptable and the unacceptable, the good and the bad. Moral thinking and judgment is a structure and a configuration from the world of the past, the world of experience, the world of personal autonomy and freedom of action.

221<•>observes that as well as moral thinking there is also the world of ethical codes and civil & criminal laws in which there is, at first sight, nothing to choose, where it appears that iron necessity rules. But as we shall soon see that whole of morality (rindeqern) embodies two things 1) The Social Instinct (qernel) and 2) the mores of a society.(rindlucent). If any of the ethical codes and laws do not embody a social instinct they will be eventually overthrown by codes and laws that do embody such social instinct.

222<•>observes that in the world of the past, the sequence of cause and effect (Causality) rule. In the world of action of the future the thought and aim (Teleology) rule. For this future the feeling of freedom of action and social instinct are an indispensable psychological necessity, which is not to be got rid of by any degree of knowledge.

223<•>observes that even the sternest fatalism (the doctrine that every event is subject to fate), even the deepest conviction that people are a necessary product of their circumstances, cannot vanquish the struggle of opposites in its billions of guises especially in love and hate; defend and attack.

224<•>observes that people have no monopoly on all the forgoing for it holds also for the animals. Even these have freedom of the will, in the sense that people have, namely a subjective, idealistic, inevitable feeling of freedom, which springs from ignorance of the future and the necessity of exercising a direct influence on it.

225<•>observes that in the same way as the foregoing animals have command of certain insights into the connection of cause and effect. Finally, if you've visited a slaughter-house, then you will know that the conception of an end is not quite strange to them either.

226<•>observes that some animals in respect to insight into the past and the necessity of nature on the one hand and in respect of the power of foreseeing the future on the other hand, and the setting up of aims for their action therein. It is the observer's opinion, that some of the lowest religiously brain-seared and propagandized specimens of humanity hold more in common with the more rapacious animals than with civilized peoples.

227<•>observes that the setting up of aims is not, however, anything which exists outside the sphere of necessity of cause and effect. People may set up aims for themselves for the future and seem to be traveling into a sphere of apparent freedom. The very act of setting up the aim itself (from the very moment when they set up the aim) belongs to the past, and in its necessity the aim must be recognized as the result of distinct causes.

228<•>observes that the setting up of aims is not in any way altered by the fact that the attainment of the end is still in the future – in the sphere of uncertainty. Let the attainment of the end be assumed as ever so far distant, the setting up of the aim itself lies in the past. In the sphere of future autonomy there lie only those aims which are not yet set up, of which we do not even know anything as yet.

229<•>observes that the realm of conscious aims is still in the world of necessity. The cause is already given for each one of the means we apply to achieve the aim. To those who brought about the aim it is <u>under certain circumstances</u> recognizable, and they determine the way in which the aim is to be achieved.

230<•>observes that if we look at nature in the narrower sense – apart from society, and then look at aims in their relation to the future in society, we find at once a big difference. Natural conditions usually change much slower than social. And now we need very rapid social change indeed if we are to survive our depredations on the natural - the ecology.

231<•>observes that Social aims are now at a period in history when ordinary people commence to philosophize. They are at the period in history in the production of wares of a highly complicated nature, and people are working for salary and wages, barter taking a back-seat. But also they are in a period where social laws are unclear to them, much being camouflaged and bound up and obscured in society by the fourth estate (4E) media. Whereas in nature there are a large number of complex processes, whose subjection to law from the micro to the macro processes can be relatively easily perceived and such knowledge can be freely disseminated. This is because this type of knowledge does not have any immediate connection to knowledge of the methodology of surplus-value (value-added) extraction and all that that entails in society.

232<•>observes that the consequence is, that despite our apparent freedom of action in the future, this action, nevertheless, as far as nature is concerned, comes to be looked on as determined at an early period. As the future lies before people, they know of a certainty that summer will follow winter. That to-morrow the sun will rise, that to-morrow they shall have hunger and thirst. That in winter the need for warming themselves will occur to them, and that people's action and aim will never be directed to escaping these natural necessities, but only with the idea of satisfying them.

233<•>observes that thus people recognize, despite all apparent freedom in facing nature their actions are necessarily conditioned. The constitution of nature external to people and of their own bodies produce necessities which force on them a willingness to action which, being given according to experience, can be reckoned with in advance.

234<•>observes that the situation is quite otherwise with people's conduct to their fellows in their social actions. In this case the external and internal causes, which necessarily determine their action, are not so easy to recognize. Here they do not meet with the overpowering forces of nature, to which they are obliged to submit. In the realm of social action people are faced with factors on a level with themselves, people like themselves, who by ordinary nature have no more strength than they.

235<•>observes that each of these people may feel themselves to be free of obligation, and may also appear, to the casual observer, to be free in their moral conscience to their fellows. But in reality each individual will feel love, hate or indifference and in their relations to one another they make moral judgments.

236<•>observes that the realm of moral thinking, is certainly other than that of recognized necessity, it is also not timeless, spaceless, and it is no transcendental world, but it is a particular portion of the world of sense seen from a particular point of view.

237<•>observes that what is today the future, will to-morrow be the past; thus what today is felt to be freedom of action for tomorrow will be recognized tomorrow, on looking back, as necessary action.

238<•>observes that thus moral thinking in people, which regulated this past action ceases only to reappear as an uncaused cause, it falls into the sphere of experience and can be recognized as the necessary effect of a cause—

239<•>observes that only in such a cause are people at all able to recognize moral thinking, or can moral thinking become an object of science. In that people transfer moral thinking from the "this side," the sensual world, to the "other side," omega metaphysical world, (See definition of sigma and omega metaphysics)

240<•>observes that Kant in his sigma metaphysical world has not advanced the scientific knowledge of moral thinking, but has closed all access to it. This obstacle must be overcome before people can make progress in moral thinking. People must rise above Kant if they are to bring the problem of it, ethical codes, civil & criminal law nearer to a rational understanding.

~241< TRACT 9:

242<•>observes that Regressive Philosophy Of Reconciliation And Kant

243<•>observes that French materialism had been a philosophy of the fight against the traditional methods of thought, and consequently against the institutions which rested on them. An irreconcilable hatred against Christianity made it the watchword, not only of the fight against the church, but of that against all the social and political forces which were bound up with it.

244<•>observes that Kant's 'Critique Of Pure Reason' equally drives Christianity out of the temple by bringing to the fore sigma metaphysics to replace God. Thus Kant's philosophy, instead of a weapon in the fight against the existing methods of thought and institutions, becomes a means of reconciling the antagonisms.

245<•>observes that the way of development is that of struggle. The reconciliation of antagonisms implies the stoppage of development. Thus Kantian Philosophy and any other philosophy that relies on sigma metaphysics becomes, not only a conservative factor, but a positive brake on the science behind the understanding of moral thinking.

246<•>observes that the greatest advantage thereby was drawn by theology. It emancipates religion from the quandary, into which traditional belief has fallen because of the development of the physical (natural) sciences, in that it renders it possible to reconcile physical science, but not the mental sciences, with religion.

247<•>observes that just after the outbreak of the French revolution a specially strong need arose for a theology, which was in a position to hold its own against materialism, and to drive it out of the field amongst educated people.

248<•>observes that Zeller writes further. "Kant's religious views corresponded exactly both to the moral and intellectual need of the time; it recommended itself to the enlightened by its reasonableness, its independence of the positive, its purely practical tendency; to the religious by its moral severity and its lofty conceptions of Christianity and its founder."

249<•>observes that Zeller writes further as German theology from now on took Kant as their authority, "His Moral Theology became after a few years the foundation on which Protestant theology in Germany almost without exception, even the Catholic to a very large extent, was built up. The Kantian Philosophy, exercised for that reason, that the majority of German theologians for close on fifty years took their start from it, a highly permanent and far-reaching influence on the general education. Thus the development of the method of knowledge by Kant implied at the same time a practical rebirth of Protestantism.

250<•>observes that the great French revolution created the soil for the influence of Kant, which was strongest in the two decades after the Terror. Then this influence became paler and paler and even more pale. The 3E bourgeoisie acquired after the eighteen thirties, even in Germany, strength and courage for more decided struggles against the existing forms of state and thought, and to an absolute recognition of the world of the senses as the only real one.

251<•>observes that thus through the Hegelian dialectic there arise new forms of Materialism. And it comes about in its most vigorous forms in Germany, for the very reason that their Bourgeoisie are well behind that of France and England. Why? Because in Germany people had not yet conquered the existing 2E aristocratic state machine; because they had still to upset it, they required a fighting philosophy and not one of reconciliation.

252<•>observes that But in the last decades of the 19th century, however the 3E's desire to replace Kant and Hegel is greatly diminished. Even though they have not attained all that they wish, yet they have all which is necessary for their development, and wish no further 'Mental Philosophy'. But they still continue to want go gung-ho in the philosophy of the Physical Sciences.

253<•>observes that Further struggles on a large scale and energetic fights in the mental philosophy field against the existing rottenness, is of much less use to them than to their great enemy, the salary and wage working proletariat, (The fifth-estate 5E). To them the 5E, which they themselves created by their requirement for salary and wage labor, grew in a most menacing fashion to them. And now, for its part, that 5E took up the requirement for a new fighting philosophy.

254<•>observes that 5E salary and wage work is more susceptible to the influence of materialism and development of the world of senses showed the absurdity of the existing order and the necessity of change.

255<•>observes that the 3E Bourgeoisie, on the other hand, became more and more susceptible to a philosophy of reconciliation, and thus Kantism was aroused to a fresh life. This resurrection was prepared in the reactionary period after 1848 by the then commencing influence of Schopenhauer.

256<•>observes that in the 19th century the sounding-board-influence of Kant has found its way into economics and socialism. The laws of 3E bourgeois society, which were discovered by the classical economists, now showed themselves more clearly as laws which made the class struggle and the eradication of the capitalist's incessant requirement for growth, destructive competition, and order of things necessary. The bourgeois economists now take refuge in Kantian and neo-Kantian moral thinking influenced by bourgeois ethical codes. Such codes being independent of time and space must now be put in a position to reconcile the class antagonisms and thus thwart and prevent the 5E from promulgating new civil laws and ethical codes which do take place in space and time.

257<•>observes that side by side with the 3E ethical school in economics we get a so called ethical socialism, and a so called social democracy which endeavors to play down class antagonisms, and the role of destructive competition, war and mutual robbery in the market place. The bourgeoisie (wantabe capitalists) and capitalists themselves play down the vast social problems engendered by the 3E rule over the affairs of the globe. Thus they cry in certain circles of the intelligentsia "Back to Kant!" with all its repudiation of materialism.

258<•>observes that the categorical moral imperative of Kant's ethic cries to the individual for reconciling the antagonisms in the globe, not of coming to grips with them through struggle.

~259< TRACT 10:

260<•>observes that **The Struggle For Existence**
Darwin: The Development And Change
In Plants And Animals.

261<•>observes that Kant, like Plato, had divided mankind into two parts, a natural and a supernatural, an animal and an angelic. But there was strong desire to bring the entire world, including our intellectual functions, under a metaphysical unitary conception. This sigma metaphysical unity was devised to exclude all factors except the subjective from it. But the materialist method of thought, was too deeply grounded in the circumstances of history for Kantian or neo-Katian sigma metaphysical concepts to be able to paralyze it for any length of time.

262<•>observes that the splendid progress made by the natural or physical sciences, which began just at the very time of Kant's death began to make a spurt forwards. The physical sciences brought a series of new discoveries, which fills up the gap between mankind and the rest of nature, and among other things reveals the fact that the apparently 'angelic' in people was also to be seen in the animal world, and thus was of an animal nature.

263<•>observes that the materialist ethics of the nineteenth century, so far as it is dominated by the conceptions of the

Physical Sciences, came in a bold and outspoken form. It took in German, English, and French versions.

264<•>observes that Feuerbach founded morality on the desire for happiness, Auguste Comte, the founder of Positivism, took on the other hand from the English the distinction between moral or altruistic feelings, and the egoistical, both of which are equally rooted in human nature.

265<•>observes that a great and decided advance over Kant's, Feurebach and Compte's position was first made by Darwin, who proves in his book on "The Descent of Man", that altruistic feelings form not just in mankind but they are also to be found in the animal world.

266<•>observes that in the animal world, just as in mankind, altruistic feelings spring from similar causes, which are in essence identical and which have called forth and developed all the faculties of higher beings endowed with the power of moving themselves.

267<•>observes that to any thinking person it can be seen that the 'angelic' was almost the last barrier between man and animal to be torn down. Darwin does not follow up his discoveries any further, and yet they belong to the greatest and most fruitful of the human intellect, and enable us to develop a new critique of knowledge.

268<•>observes that when we study the organic, it shows us, in contrast to the inorganic world, one very striking peculiarity: We find in the vital world adaptation to meet ends. All organized beings are constructed and endowed more or less with a view to an end. **The end which they serve is nevertheless not one which lies outside of them or outside of society.**

269<•>observes that the universe, the cosmos, as a whole has no aim. The aim lies in the individuals themselves, its parts are so arranged and fitted out, that they serve the individual particular and society as a whole (Universal in that sense).

270<•>observes that as far as the universal (society) is concerned purpose and division of labor arise together. The essence of the organism is the division of labor just as much as adaptation to an end. One is the condition of the other. The division of labor distinguishes the organism from inorganic individuals, for example, crystals.

271<•>observes that even crystals are distinct individuals with a distinct form. They grow, when they find the necessary material for their formation under the requisite conditions, but they are through and through symmetrical. On the other hand the lowest organism is a vesicle whose external side is different, and has different functions to the inner.

272<•>observes that the division of labor is one which is suitable for the purpose, that is, one which is useful to the individual, renders its existence possible, or even ameliorates it. But what is the work which the organs of the organism have to accomplish? This work is the struggle for life, that is, not just the struggle with other organisms of the same kind, as the word is occasionally used, but the fight with the whole of nature.

273<•>observes that nature is in continual movement and is always changing her forms, hence only some individuals are able to maintain their form for any period of time in this eternal change. Some individuals and society as a whole, are in a position to develop particular organs against external influences which threaten their existence as well as to modify some, or even most, of those parts which the individual, or even society, is obliged to give up continually to the external world.

274<•>observes that quickest and best are those individuals and groups who assert themselves, whose weapons of defense and instruments for obtaining food are the best adapted to their end, that is, best adapted to the external world, to avoid its dangers, and to capture the sources of food.

275<•>observes that the uninterrupted process of adaptation, and the selection of the fittest, by means of the struggle for existence produce, under such circumstances, an increasing division of labor. This also happens in many species other than man and animals. (bees and ants come to mind in the insect world and so on)

276<•>observes that in fact the more developed the division of labor is in a society, the more advanced does that society appear to your observer. The continual process of rendering the organic world 'more perfect' is thus the result of the struggle for existence in it – and that probably, for a long time to come, will be its future.

277<•>observes that development need not always proceed at the same rate. From time to time periods can come, when the various organisms, each in its way, arrive at the highest possible degree of adaptation to the existing conditions, that is, are in the most complete harmony with their surroundings. (sharks come to mind in this respect there basic outline, function, content and form, were laid down millions of years ago.)

278<•>observes that so long as conditions endure they will develop no farther, but the form which has been arrived at will develop into a fixed type, which procreates itself unchanged. A further development will only then occur when the surroundings undergo a considerable alteration, when either the external inorganic, the external organic or both may be subject to such changes which, in their turn, disturb the balance of the organism.

279<•>observes that other changes, however, will take place from time to time either single, sudden and violent, or numerous and unnoticed. The sum total and effect of this, however, brings on new situations. Examples of this are alterations in irradiation, the ocean currents, surface of the earth, perhaps even in the position of the planet in the universe, which bring about climatic changes, transform thick forests into deserts of sand, cover tropical landscapes with icebergs and so on.

280<•>observes that these alterations render new adaptations to the changed conditions necessary, they produce migrations which likewise bring the organisms into new surroundings. They produce fresh struggles for life between the old inhabitants and the new comers, exterminate the badly adapted and the unadaptable individuals and types, and create new divisions of labor, new functions and new organs or transform the old.

281<•>observes that it is not always the highest developed organisms which best assert themselves by this new adaptation. Every division of labor implies a certain one-sidedness. Highly developed organs, which are specially adapted for a particular method of life, are for another far less useful than organs which are less developed, and in that particular method of life less effective, but more many-sided and more easily adaptable.

282<•>observes that thus we see often 'higher' developed kinds of animals and plants die out, and 'lower' kinds take over the farther development of new higher organisms.

~283< TRACT 11:

284<•>observes that Darwin: Self-Movement And Intelligence
Consciousness, Space & Sequence In Time

285<•>observes that at an early period the organisms divided themselves into two great groups – those which developed the organs of self motion, and those animals and plants which lacked such locomotion.

286<•>observes that it is clear that the power of self-movement is a mighty weapon in the struggle for life. It enables the organism to follow its food, to avoid danger, to bring its young into places where they are secure from dangers and which are provided with food.

287<•>observes that also self-motion, however, necessarily implies an intelligence, and vice versa. The one of these factors without the other is absolutely useless. Only in combination do they become a weapon in the struggle for life.

288<•>observes that the power of self-movement is completely useless, when it is not combined with a power to recognize the world in which the organisms have to move themselves. What use would the legs be to a stag, if it did not have the power to recognize its enemies and its feeding grounds? On the other hand, for a plant intelligence of any kind would be useless.

289<•>observes that if a blade of grass is able to see, hear or smell the approaching cow, that would not in the least help it to avoid being eaten. Self-movement and intelligence thus necessarily go together, one without the other is useless.

Wherever these faculties may spring from, they invariably come up together and develop themselves jointly.

290<•>observes that as a means to life organs and especially sense organs are developed and perfected in the struggle for life. There is no such thing as transcendence or an imaginary sense capacity which, for obvious reasons, is useless as weapons in the struggle for existence. Thus is explained the one-sidedness and the peculiarity of, especially mankind's, intelligence.

291<•>observes that to get their mind around the never never world of the sigma metaphysical transcendental 'world' of the imagination may appear to many theologians and their so called philosophers an important task. BUT for mankind's existence it is highly indifferent to a 'true understanding' of having such one sided idealistic thoughts.

292<•>observes that on the other hand for every being endowed with power of movement it is of the greatest importance to rightly distinguish the objective things in nature and to recognize their relations to one another.

293<•>observes that the sharper the organism's intelligence in respect to life the better will it serve the organism. For the existence of a singing bird it is of paramount importance to understand objective things which appear to it, as a berry, a hawk, or a thunder cloud.

294<•>observes that this objective world as seen or felt through its senses is indispensable for this little bird's existence. The bird must distinguish exactly berries, hawks, and clouds from the other things among its surroundings, since that alone puts him in a position to find his food, to escape the enemy, and to reach shelter in time. It is thus inevitable that the intelligence of an animal should give it the power of distinguishing things in space.

295<•>observes that also just as indispensable to this bird's life is for it to recognize the sequence of the things in time, and indeed their necessary sequence as cause and effect.

296<•>observes that understanding cause of movement will aid in the maintenance of existence. The understanding of effects of movement is much easier to learn the closer such movement is to cause and visa versa.

297<•>observes that it is not just sufficient that our bird should know how to distinguish berries, hawks, and thunder clouds from the other things in space, it must also know that the enjoyment of the berries has the effect of satisfying its hunger. It must know that the appearance of the hawk will have the effect that the first little bird, which the hawk can grasp, will serve it as food. It must further know and understand that the rising thunder clouds will more than likely, produce storm, rain, and/or hail as a result.

298<•>observes that even the lowest animal, as soon as it possesses a trace of ability to distinguish self-movement, develops an inkling of causality. If the earth shakes, that is a sign for the worm that danger threatens (possibly from the little bird) and that it has incentive to burrow deeper. Thus if the intelligence is to be of use to an animal in its movements it must be organized so that it is in a position to show it the distinctions in time and space as well as the causal connections.

299<•>observes that the organs in our bird must do even more. All parts of the body serve only one individual, only one end, maintenance of the individual. The division of labor must never go so far that individual parts become independent, because that would lead to dismemberment of the individual. Organs will work efficiently, the tighter the parts are held together, and the more uniform the word of command. From this follows the necessary unity of the consciousness.

300<•>observes that if each part of a body has its own intellectual organs. Or if each sense which contributes to a knowledge of the outer world has its own impression to its own consciousness - then the integrated knowledge of the objective world and the cooperation of the various members of the body, in such a case, are much impeded.

301<•>observes that in the forgoing case, advantages in the division of labor will be abolished, or be changed into disadvantages, and support which the senses or the organs of movement mutually give to each other will cease and there will come instead a mutual hindrance. Finally, however, the consciousness must possess, in addition, the power to gather experiences and to compare them.

302<•>observes that To return once more to our bird, it has two ways open to it to find out what food is best for it and where. Under the principle of the conservation of energy it takes the easiest route to be found. It must find out what enemies are dangerous for him; how to escape them and when to run for cover. In these matters it first, turns to its own near life threatening experience, and second it turns to the observation of other and older birds, who have already incorporated into their conscious life those experiences that help it survive.

303<•>observes that every animal finds it easier to maintain itself in the struggle for life by increasing its living experiences – if such maturity is well arranged in the consciousness then better are its chances for survival.

304<•>observes that to the foregoing, however, belongs the gift of memory and the capacity to compare former impression with later, and to extract knowledge from first the common and, second the universal elements, to separate the essential from the unessential, that is: to think. (which only goes to refute Descartes' "I think therefor I am." And for organisms at least it is in reality – I am therefor I think.)

305<•>observes that all these dualities of the intellectual powers, we find developed in the animal world, even if not to such a high a degree as in people. They are often difficult to recognize, since it is not always easy to distinguish conscious actions springing from intelligence, from the involuntary and unconscious actions, simple reflex actions and instinctive movements, which in every animal play a great role in its life.

306<•>observes that so we find, in deep retrospection on the subject, that all these qualities discussed about the senses, the consciousness and the intellectual faculties are a necessary for the power of self movement – the power of locomotion in the animal world. So too do we also find the same qualities, as discussed, imbedded in mankind's own animal origin.

307<•>observes that it is important to note that the forces and capacities, just discussed, which are acquired as weapons in the battle for existence can naturally be made available for other purposes as well.

308<•>observes that an animal can employ the muscles, which were developed in it for the purpose of snatching its booty, or warding off the foe, as well for dancing and playing. But the muscle's particular character is obtained by the more primordial capacities all the same. Muscles exist because they develop from the struggle for life. Play and dance engender no particular muscles although such activity may enhance those that do exist.

309<•>observes that what is good for the muscles also holds good for intellectual powers and faculties. Each was developed as a necessary supplement to the power of self-movement in the struggle for life in order to render it possible for the organism to have the most suitable movement for its own preservation. But this evolution also allows all of these muscles and intellectual powers to serve other purposes.

310<•>observes that also our intellectual powers have not been developed by the struggle for existence only to be an organ which regulates our movements in conformity with their evolved purpose. The brain has not been developed as some kind of organ that recognizes 'pure knowledge' outside the objective world which surrounds it.

311<•>observes that from the very beginning pure knowing is most intimately connected with the power of movement, it develops itself completely only in its mutual dependence on movement and is only brought to perfection in this connection.

312<•>observes that also the power of the human faculties of cognition and human knowledge is most intimately bound up with human practice, as we shall see.

313<•>observes that it is practice which guarantees to mankind the certainty of its knowledge. As soon as people's knowledge enables them to bring about distinct effects, the production of which lies in their power, the relation of cause and effect ceases for them to be simply chance or simple appearance.

314<•>observes that the knowledge of this relation of cause and effect becomes, through practice, a knowledge of something real and is raised to the level of knowledge certain.

315<•>observes that also theory and practice are dependent on one another, and only through mutual absorption, one by the other is the highest result attainable. Only through the struggle of opposites can this highest result be obtained, and all this is the outcome of the fact that movement and intellectual powers, from their earliest beginnings, are bound up together.

316<•>observes that thus we have shown that even in knowledge there is the requirement for movement and in the necessary course of the development of human society there is movement.

317<•>observes that but there have arisen in society on the side of movement – the materialist philosophers; and on the other side the non movement theologians of thousands of sects and the idealist philosophers. (although they may profess acknowledgement of movement just as Kant did in his opening page of his CPR)

318<•>observes that the division of labor has brought about the natural unity of two factors in nature – practice and knowing.

319<•>observes that But there are those in society who would destroy this unity by creating classes in philosophy, the first to whom principally the understanding of movement fell, and the other class of idealistic philosophers to whom principally fell all that phantom 'knowing'.

Tsunami One   Moral Organon.

320<•>observes that even the deepest, most abstract knowledge, which apparently is farthest removed from the practical, eventually influences practice, and are influenced by practice, and bring in its wake an impact on our consciousness.

321<•>observes that as stated before, knowledge remains, in the last resort, always a weapon in the struggle for existence, a means to give to our movements, be they movements in nature or society, the most suitable forms and directions and becomes the duty of a critique of human knowledge. (Epistemology)

322<•>observes that "Philosophers have only interpreted the world differently," said Marx. " The great thing, however, is to change it."

~323< TRACT 12:

324<•>observes that **Motives Of Self Maintenance And Propagation** Darwin: The Individual Self Preservation Instinct.

325<•>observes that both the powers of self-movement and of knowing belong inseparably together as weapons in the struggle for existence. It is a relationship of mutual symbiotic development.

326<•>observes that self-movement and knowledge, combined in themselves, do not form sufficient weapons in the struggle for life. Of what use is merely the strongest muscles, the most agile joints, the sharpest senses, the greatest understanding, in this struggle, if the organism does not feel the impulse to employ them to its preservation? Of what use are they if the sight of food or the knowledge of danger leaves them indifferent and awakes no emotion in them?

327<•>observes that the first weapons in the struggle for existence is the combination of self-movement and intellectual capacity. Then, if with them, there arises a longing for self-preservation in the organism it will elicit the knowledge (consciousness of the movement in time and space) which is of utmost importance for the organism's existence. And it will produces in it the will to carry out the movement necessary for its preservation, and therewith call forth this defensive movement.

328<•>observes that thus we see that self movement and intellectual powers are without importance for existence alone if the individual is left without its instinct of self preservation, just as this latter again is of no importance without both former factors. All three are most intimately bound up with each other. (self-movement, intellect, instinct for self preservation.)

329<•>observes that the instinct of self-preservation is the most primitive of the animal instincts and the most indispensable. Without it no animal species endowed in any degree with the power of self-movement and a faculty of intelligence could maintain itself even a short time. The foregoing things thus rule the entire life of the organism.

330<•>observes that in social development of a society which may ascribe the care of the intellectual faculties to a particular class, and the productive movement to other classes, this is bound to bring about in society an elevation of the subjective over the objective. This state of affairs goes far in the process of isolating the intellectual faculties of society from objectivity.

331<•>observes that this kind of subjective knowledge has never as yet been able to overcome the instinct of self-preservation in a society. Often this idealistic philosophy, this theological subjective outlook, has caused mankind to regress into dark ages in history but it has never 'yet' come to completely paralyze the objective productive forces which serve for the maintenance of life.

332<•>observes that although many an individual suicide may be philosophically grounded, we always (in every act of denial of individual life) finally meet with disease or desperate social circumstances as the cause but not, in the overwhelming number of cases, a philosophical theory. Mere philosophizing, as some would have us believe, cannot overcome the instinct of self-preservation.

333<•>observes that self-preservation is the most primitive and widely spread of all instincts. It serves for the maintenance of the individual. If the individual does not reproduce itself, it disappears without leaving any trace of its individuality behind. (sympathetic impact; discussed further on)

334<•>observes that it is only those species of organisms with will that assert themselves in the struggle for existence, who leave a progeny behind them. Now then with the plants and the near-animal organisms reproduction is a process which demands no power of self-movement and thus no faculty of intelligence. (thus no will)

335<•>observes that that situation changes, however, with the animals endowed with locomotion (self-movement and thus some form of consciousness). As soon as reproduction becomes a sexual act, in which two individuals are concerned, who have to unite in order to lay either eggs and seeds (sperm) on the same spot outside of the body, or to incorporate the sperm in the body of the individual carrying the eggs.

336<•>observes that self-movement and thus some form of consciousness demands a will (desire), an impulse, to find a mate, to unite. Without will and desire sexual propagation cannot not take place, the stronger the will and desire is in the periods favorable for reproduction, the sooner it takes place and better are the prospects of a progeny for maintenance of the species.

337<•>observes that on the other hand the greater the complexity of organs, the more complicated the organism, then such a situation will require a longer period for its development and its attainment to maturity.

338<•>observes that from considerations of space in certain species the mother's body is not in a position to bear an organism as big as itself. It must expel the young long before that stage of development.

339<•>observes that in young animals, however, the capacities for significant self-movement and/or cognition are the latest achieved, and they are very weakly developed as they leave the protecting cover of the egg or the maternal body. The progeny expelled by the mother has limited motion and limited cognitive acumen and because of the lack of experience has also limited intelligence, but the potential for all these to develop in the healthy offspring is fast and vast.

340<•>observes that shortly after birth the care for the progeny becomes an important function of the mother: the hiding and defense of the eggs of the young, the feeding of the latter, etc. As the impulse for reproduction, so is it with the love for the young, especially in the animal world the maternal love is developed as an indispensable means, from a certain stage of the development on, to secure the perpetuation of the species.

~341< TRACT 13:

342<•>observes that **The Social Instinct**
Darwin: Sympathy: Conscience.

343<•>observes that Besides the individual preservation instinct there is the migratory instinct which for the purposes of this dissertation we will not go into further.

344<•>observes that besides the individual preservation instinct which are common to all animals, the struggle for life develops in particular ways in particular kinds of animals. In the context of moral thinking, ethical codes, civil and criminal law we are interested in another kind of instinct which is of very great importance for our subject: the social instinct.

345<•>observes that the cooperation of similar organisms in larger crowds is a phenomenon which we discover in their earliest stages: the microbes. It is explained alone by the simple fact of reproduction. If the organism has no self-movement, the progeny will consequently gather round the producer, if they are not by any chance borne away by the movements of the external world, water currents, winds, body fluids and phenomena of that sort.

346<•>observes that the apple falls not far from its tree and when it is not eaten, and falls on fruitful soil, there grows up from its pip a young tree, which lovingly keeps the old mother tree company. But even in animals with power of self-movement it is natural that the young should remain with the old, if no external circumstances supply a ground for them to remove themselves.

347<•>observes that the living together of individuals of the same animal species is the most primitive form of social life, is also the most primitive forms of life itself. But it is important to note here at the outset that the division of organisms, which have a common origin, is a later development.

348<•>observes that the separation of original source organisms can be brought about by the most diverse causes. The most obvious, and certainly the most effective, is the lack of sustenance. Each locality can only yield a certain quantity of food. If a certain species of animals multiplies beyond the limits of their food supply, the superfluous ones must either emigrate or starve.

349<•>observes that, depending upon the species, the numbers of organisms cannot go above a certain aggregate number living in one place. But there are species of animals, for whom the isolation and division into individual pairs, who live mostly by themselves, for whom such a life almost alone affords an advantage in the struggle for existence. (The importance of these and the following observation will soon be made manifest in moral thinking.)

350<•>observes that thus, for example, some (not all) cat species, which lie in wait for their prey and take it with an unexpected spring. This method of acquiring their sustenance would be made more difficult, if not impossible, if they circulated in troops or prides. The first spring on the spoils would drive game away for all the others.

351<•>observes that for wolves which do not come unexpectedly on their prey, but worry it to death, the foregathering in packs affords an advantage; one or many wolves frightens the game to the others. The domestic cat, by stealth, nevertheless hunts more successfully alone.

352<•>observes that there are other animals who choose isolation because in this fashion they are less conspicuous and can hide themselves to escape foe. The traps formerly set by man have, for example, had the effect that many animals which formerly lived in societies, are now only to be found isolated, such might be said of the beavers in Europe. That is the only way for them to remain unnoticed.

353<•>observes that however, there are numerous animals which draw advantage from their social life. They are seldom beasts of prey. We have mentioned the wolf above. But even they only hunt in packs when food is scarce, usually in winter. In the summer when food is easier to get, they live in pairs. The nature of the beast of prey are always inclined to fighting and violence, and consequently thus they do not agree well with one another – one taking dominance over the others.

354<•>observes that herbivores are more peaceful from the very manner in which they obtain their food. That fact of itself renders it easier for them to herd together, or to remain together, because they are more defenseless alone. These animals win a right to life usually through their greater numbers until weakened by sickness or old age.

355<•>observes that thus the union of many weak forces in common action can produce a new and greater force and through union the greater strength of certain individuals is used for the good of all.

356<•>observes that when the stronger of these animals fight for themselves, they also fight for the good of the weaker. When more mature and experienced animals in the herd look out for their own safety they also automatically do so for the inexperienced and the weaker.

357<•>observes that now we see it becomes possible to introduce a division of labor among the united individuals, fleeting though it may be in herbivores, yet it increases their strength and their safety. It is impossible for one animal to watch the neighborhood with the most complete attention and at the same time to feed peacefully. Naturally during sleep all observation of all kind comes to an end. But in a herd one watcher suffices to render the others safe during sleep or while eating.

358<•>observes that through the division of labors the union of individuals becomes a body with different organs to cooperate to a given end, and this end is the maintenance of the collective body. Thus it becomes a many sided organism of individual organisms. This is by no means to say that the new organism is a body in the same way as an animal or a plant, but it is an organism of its own kind – a social organism.

359<•>observes that one type of organism is made up of collectives of cells and organs without power of self-motion and without consciousness of their own. It is only in the individual collective of organs especially those of touch, sight, smell, hearing and taste wherein the animal is made manifest and whole individual has self motion and consciousness.

360<•>observes that the other type of organism is a society of individuals each with their own power of movement and consciousness. Even if, however, the individual animal in the herd has the power of self-motion and consciousness and the herd, in and of itself, has motion, yet the herd is lacking an overall social consciousness.

361<•>observes that the individuals which form the herd-society can entrust individuals among their members with functions through which the social forces are submitted to an instinctive regular will, and thus uniform movements in the society are produced.

362<•>observes that on the other hand the individual and herd-society are much looser connected than the cell the organs and the whole organism. The individual can separate itself from one society and join another as emigration proves.

363<•>observes that usually (if we leave certain cells of a particular kind out of account i.e. sperm and eggs etc.) emigration is usually impossible for a cell or an organ; for it the separation from the whole usually results in its death.

364<•>observes that thus we see here a difference in a society. The society can usually withstand the separation of an individual from it without causing death, can forthwith impose on new individuals any change of form, without any change of substance, which is impossible for an animal body.

365<•>observes that finally the individuals who form a society can, under certain circumstances, change the organs and organization of society, while anything of that kind is quite impossible in an animal or vegetable organism.

366<•>observes that if, therefore, society is an organism, it is no animal organism. To attempt to explain any phenomena peculiar to society from the laws of the animal organism is not less absurd than when the attempt is made to deduce peculiarities of the animal organism, such as self-movement and consciousness, from the laws of vegetable being. Naturally this does not go to say that there is not also something common to the various kinds of organisms.

367<•>observes that just as in the animal, so also will any social organism survive better in the struggle for existence if its movements are more unitary, the stronger the binding forces, the greater the harmony of the parts.

368<•>observes that unlike an animal organism, society has no fixed skeleton, which supports the weaker parts. It has no skin which covers the whole, no circulation of the blood which nourishes all the parts, no heart which regulates it, no brain which makes a unity out of its consciousness, its knowing, its working, and its movements.

369<•>observes that society's unity and harmony, as well as its coherence can only arise from the actions and will (desire) of its members. This unitary will (desire), however, will be much more assured if it springs from strong impulses.

370<•>observes that among some species of animals, in whom the social bond becomes a weapon in the struggle for life, this strong social impulse encourages a consequent individual pressure. When individuals in such a social bond come into conflict with external forces that would destroy them, this social pressure kicks in. Such is the social pressure, which in many species and many individuals grows to an extraordinary strength so that they will, more often than not, even overcome the impelling force of individual self-preservation and reproduction.

371<•>observes that to the commencement of the social impetus we can look for in the simple fact of living together in society which produces in individuals the shared aims of their colleagues, to whose society they are accustomed to from youth.

Tsunami One   Moral Organon.

372<•>observes that reproduction and care for the progeny already render relations of a more intimate kind necessary between different individuals of the same species. Thus the corresponding nurturing emotion easily give a point of departure for the development of social instinct.

373<•>observes that these instincts themselves can vary according to the varying conditions of the various species, but a sequence of favorable impulses forms the requisite conditions for the growth of any kind of society. In the first place naturally comes altruism, self sacrifice for the whole. Then comes bravery in the defense of the common interests; fidelity to the community; submission to the will of society; then obedience and discipline.

374<•>observes that then comes truthfulness to society whose security is endangered or whose energies are wasted when they are misled in any way by false signals. Finally comes ambition, the sensibility to the praise and blame of society. These then are all social impulses which we find expressed already among animal societies, many of them in a high degree.

375<•>observes that these social impulses (instincts) are nevertheless nothing but the highest virtues, they sum up the entire consciousness and moral thinking. At the most instincts lack the love for justice, that is, the impulse for equality.

376<•>observes that For the development of the social instinct of justice and equality there certainly is no homestead in animal societies, because they only know natural and individual inequality. They know not of those inequalities called forth by social relations in mankind. Animals know not of ethical codes, civil & criminal laws which may manifest themselves in social inequalities.

377<•>observes that what appears to a Kant, the neo-Kantians, the theologians and the idealistic philosophers as the creation of a higher world of spirits, is actually a product of the animal world. How narrowly the social instincts have grown up with the fight for existence, and to what an extent they originally were useful in the preservation of species, can be seen from the fact that their effect often limits itself to individuals whose maintenance is advantageous to the species.

378<•>observes that quite a number of animals, which risk their lives to save younger or weaker comrades, kill (or at least fail them herd-protection) sick or aged comrades who are superfluous for the preservation of the race, and are become a burden to society. The feeling of sympathy in this regard, does not extend to these animals.

379<•>observes that in the foregoing an animal impulse is the law of raw nature. Then, in people, whence comes sympathy's mysterious nature – this voice in us – which has no apparent connection with any external stimulus, or does it have such a connection?

380<•>observes that sympathy is certainly a mysterious impulse. But it is not more mysterious than sexual love, maternal love, instinct of self preservation, being of the organism itself, and so many other things, which belong to the world of phenomena and which no one of thought looks upon as products of a sigma metaphysical spirit world.

381<•>observes that sympathetic vibration in the physical non-organic world takes place for example in the case of a bell and glass when the bell is rung the glass can be made, under certain conditions, to vibrate in sympathy with the bell. So it is with all physical vibrations (fluorescence and so on.) The five senses in animals and in human beings are also so affected by such sympathetic vibrations and movements in the material world.

382<•>observes that because the universal animal instinct is of equal force to the instinct of self-preservation and reproduction thus its force and power which people may obey without contemplation, thence their rapid decisions, in particular cases, whether an action is good or bad, virtuous or vicious. When however upon contemplation and reflection people begin to analyze instinct's fundamentals, they have difficulty in explaining it.

383<•>observes that if then the individual finally finds that to comprehend all means to pardon all, that everything is necessary, that nothing is good and bad.

384<•>observes that not from our organs of knowing, but from our animal impulses and sympathetic vibrations comes some of our moral thinking that has been an input upon our brain. Couple this with the input to that organ of knowing is a conditioned feeling of duty, and our consciousness (or even distorted consciousness) of the particular situation results in our judgment as to action.

385<•>observes that in many kinds of animals the social impulses attain such an overwhelming strength, that they become stronger than all the rest. When social impulses come in conflict with, let us say reproductive impulses, with commands of duty – <u>the social instincts may even overcome the impulse of self-preservation with an overpowering strength.</u>

386<•>observes that nevertheless this situation may not always hinder the impulse of self-preservation or of reproduction. Preservation and reproduction may be temporarily stronger than the social instinct and overcome it. But if the perceived danger to the social milieu is once again made manifest by events, then the strength of the self-preserving and reproductive instincts usually shrivel up. (Similar to the reproductive instinct that shrivels up after completion of the act.)

387<•>observes that in people the social instinct however always remains just below the surface, and under certain conditions, regains dominion over the individual and works on one as the voice of conscience and of repentance. (even though this consciousness may be flawed by, say a manipulation of it or by the lack of knowledge of external global circumstance. In people public opinion, praise and blame are also certainly very influential factors.)

388<•>observes that we would find it difficult to find social consciousness in mankind if everyone did not feel its effect on himself. Conscience is certainly a force, which does not obviously and openly show itself, but works only in the innermost being.

389<•>observes that nevertheless many investigators have gone so far as to posit even in animals a kind of conscience. Thus to paraphrase Darwin 'Besides Love and Sympathy the animals show other qualities connected with the social instincts, which we should call moral thinking in men' He goes on to describe dogs' behaviors etc.

390<•>observes that if conscience and feeling of duty are a consequence of the social instincts in many species of animals and if many impulses are subject to great oscillation so too is it with the social instincts which, in the individual, is also in constant vacillation.

391<•>observes that one peculiar phenomena is that social animals, when united in greater numbers, also feel a stronger social impulses. It is for example a well known fact that an entirely different spirit reigns in a well filled meeting then in a vacant hall, the bigger crowd alone has an inspiring effect on the speaker.

392<•>observes that in a crowd, individuals are more bold, this could be explained by the greater support which each believes he will get from his fellows; they are also more unselfish, more self- sacrificing, more enthusiastic. And the opposite is true when they find themselves alone.

393<•>observes that (Auguste-Henri Forel 1848 - 1931) Forel found: that the courage of every ant increases in exact proportion to the number of its companions or friends, and decreases in exact proportion the more isolated it is from its companions. Every inhabitant of a very populous ant nest, is much more courageous than a similar one from a small population.

394<•>observes that thus we see that strong social feeling need not necessarily be bound up in a higher faculty of intelligence. In general every instinct probably has the effect of obscuring in the organism exact observations of the objective world. It would appear that what animals and people wish, they readily believe, but what they fear they easily exaggerate.

395<•>observes that instincts have the effect on organisms of disproportionately magnifying things that are relatively big or near, while others, maybe even death dealing things, are pushed to the background.

396<•>observes that the fact is well known that in many organisms reproductive instincts often render animals blind and deaf to danger. However social instincts usually do not effect the intellectual faculties unless those faculties are damaged by massive defective input. Thus we see that in many organisms, including mankind, the social instincts do not make themselves manifest as a rule so intensely as others.

397<•>observes that take another example in the animal kingdom. Sheep; the social instinct can influence the flock very considerably – a faithfulness so strong that the flock will follow the leader blindly wherever it may go.

398<•>observes that Moral thinking in people can lead intellects astray. In itself moral thinking is neither a product of wisdom nor does it produce wisdom. Even though moral thinking in people may be, or can be, modified yet it is still of the same nature as the instincts for self-preservation or reproduction. This does not infer however, that mankind can, or ought to, follow all its instincts without check.

399<•>observes that we must – ask what is the nature of such a check? The answer is that instincts restrain one another. However a further question must be asked and that is; Which instinct becomes the dominant one and which restraint at a given moment wins the day? And further to this struggle, we must ask; what may be the consequences that a victory in any of them brings for the individual and his society?

400<•>observes that in order to answer these questions we must understand that there is no moral thinking, no ethical code, no civil or criminal law standing in the camp of the supersensous, sigma metaphysical, subjective, idealistic world.

401<•>observes that if, however, moral thinking is recognized as a social instinct, which like all the impulses is brought out in people by the struggle for life, the super-sensuous religious world has lost a strong support in human thinking.

402<•>observes that as we know the simple gods of Polytheism, while still a force in the masses minds, were already dethroned in thinking-men's-minds by natural philosophy. Then a resurgence of religion starting in ancient times arises with Plato and a new philosophy. A little later a revolutionary Christian movement, arises to overthrow an already decaying Roman slave system which in due course awakens feudalism and the belief in a single God existing as a figment in some sigma metaphysical world.

403<•>observes that All the problems associated feudalism, Christian theology and religion accumulate over time. And by the time leading up to the French revolution it is seen that an even newer philosophy is required. This new philosophy rejecting a single God and putting a world spirit in its place. This new philosophy is provided by Kant amongst others. (And for the purpose of this dissertation we use Kant and neo Kantians of whatever stripe as our sounding board of that movement.)

404<•>observes that it is thought that then, (and even now for those stuck in this world spirit morass) that moral thinking, arises from some mysterious world of sigma metaphysical super-sensual feelings. This explanation could not be deducted either from the pleasure hypothesis or from the some innate moral sense, and yet these offered the only "natural" causal explanation which seemed possible to the minds frozen in those times.

Tsunami One   Moral Organon.

405<•>observes that Darwin, amongst others of his time, are the first to make understood there is no real separation between objective reality and moral thinking in mankind. Thus are overthrown the philosophy of Plato and hundreds of others right up on through Kant and Hegel, and all the religions, all of whom rendered the necessity, of 1) a natural and animal world on the one hand and 2) a supernatural heavenly realm, on the other.

406<•>observes that an understanding of the forgoing misconceptions now brought to light by Darwinian insight there was yet to be solved how it was that from the real world the entire moral thinking of individuals and mankind as a whole came into being.

407<•>observes that however brilliant Darwin - the questions of moral thinking, ethical codes and civil & criminal laws – the entire understanding of morals is not yet solved. The question of morals outside of sexual and protective instincts have yet to be solved – i.e. How are social instincts like morals, in duty, in conscience and in virtue to be explained from the sexual and protective instincts?

408<•>observes that of the last there is not the least sign in the animal world. Only people themselves can set ideals and follow them. Whence come these ideals; are they prescribed to the human race from the beginning of all time as an irrevocable demand of nature, as commands which people themselves do not produce but which however confront people as a moral ruling force in their life?

409<•>observes that the answer to these questions is, in the main:- that it is viewed by many thinkers of the 18th and 19th century (materialists as well as atheists, theists and idealists) that moral thinking is primordial and is prescribed for the human race for all time!

410<•>observes that the 'new' evolution idea which recognizes the descent of man from the animal world makes the foregoing primordial moral idealism absurd in a materialistic mouth.

411<•>observes that even before Darwin founded his epoch-making work that theory had arisen which revealed the secret of the moral ideal. It was the theory of Marx and Engels. The study of Darwin only helps us to better understand their theory of the moral ideal.

~412< TRACT 14:

413<•>observes that **Ethics And The Materialist Conception Of History.** The Ethics Of Marxism. The Roots Of The Materialist Conception Of History. Cooperative Social Moral Thinking. The Role Of Statistics.

414<•>observes that Physical sciences were formerly referred to as the natural sciences because they are not placed on a really solid base until the period now under observation. There now arose a rapid progress of the physical sciences (as opposed to the slow progress in the mental sciences of philosophy, law, history and dialectical political economy etc.) from the French revolution on is intimately connected with the expansion of capitalism from this time on.

415<•>observes that 3E capitalist big industry rests entirely on the application of physical science and consequently has every reason to supply itself with. 1) 5E salary and wage workers 2) fixed capital and 3) circulating capital - 2 and 3 being the means by which to put 1 to work in production. Production not only of goods and commodities, but also of value-added which is expropriated by the owner of 2 and 3 (The private ownership of the social tools required to put labor to work). (your observer apologizes for so many digressions in these last two paragraphs. It is necessary to point out facts that the reader in moral investigation may not have in his mind unless such reader has studied the ramifications of dialectical political economy, which as will we shall see has a great impact on the 'new' moral thinking of mankind.)

416<•>observes that modern techniques gives to the physical sciences, not only new objects of activity, but also new tools and new methods. Its global reach and international communication drives new material for exploitation to it.

417<•>observes that physical science has given a great stimulus to many thinkers thus so too does the French revolution (3E Bourgeois Revolution) now become an epoch of importance for the development of the Science Of Society, the mental sciences, and in moral thinking

418<•>observes that the means the rising 3E bourgeoisie had of fighting the 2E aristocrats were to become the mental sciences of philosophy, law, history, political-economy. Whereas the 2E had its roots in the past, 3E capital had its dreams, its aims and its means were the new social and political agenda of the future.

419<•>observes that once firmly in their gasp these sciences are only used by 3E bourgeois to discredit the past, to paint a new up-and-coming redeeming future in contrast to that past. This then, in this epoch, forms the principal occupation of these sciences.

420<•>observes that this state of affairs gives the 3E bourgeoisie the essence of what they want. But it also reveals to them

<u>what they do not want</u>. It reveals to them, and to mankind as a whole, social forces that push beyond their selfish bourgeois boundaries. These new forces begin to be more dangerous to the 3E than the relics of the old deposed 2E aristocracy.

421<•>observes that thus it comes about that an alliance is forged between third and second estate directed at suppressing the up-and-coming proletariat – the 5E salary and wage workers of the globe.

422<•>observes that the aftermath of the 3E bourgeois revolutions when the Nirvana has not been reached has brought a great disillusionment to the ideologues themselves. (the peoples of the world living in poverty, and many in actual slavery, and in constant revolution and war, battling over the assets and who produces them.)

423<•>observes that great as were its revolutionary achievements for the 3E bourgeoisie, they were not up to the expectations of a harmonious empire of "morality," general well being, and happiness, such as had been looked for from the overthrow of the old.

424<•>observes that disillusioned by the social failures of the 3E to bring about the hoped for nirvana. Terrifying is the reminiscence of the most recent past and now no one dares to build hopes on the future;

425<•>observes that people began thinking about how bright the pre-revolutionary past seemed to be. And the further back people hanker the brighter the farther past seems to be. Thinking like that brought about romanticism in art.

426<•>observes that this atmosphere produces movements in the mental sciences. People begin to study the past, not in order to condemn it, but to understand it; not to show up its absurdity, but to understand its reasonableness.

427<•>observes that the industrial revolution had done its work too thoroughly for people to dream of re-establishing what had been set aside from the ancient past, Thus arose the concept of the future and social evolution.

428<•>observes that in Germany revolutionary thought had never penetrated so deeply as in France. In America the young community and the industrial revolution of the United States was already so far advanced, that there a separate class of intellectuals had already developed a real American literature and science.

429<•>observes that what especially distinguished America from Europe, was, however, the close contact of 3E capital controlled 'white' civilization with the still existing aboriginal indigenous hunting and gathering societies. And also to be mentioned was the absence of a regressive feudal aristocracy putting a brake on progress.

430<•>observes that those facts are the objects which especially attracts literature and sciences. Soon after the German romanticism there arises the American Indian romance and the introduction of aboriginal lore. Fairy tales, the world of legends, and their ethic codes which bring with them a comparative study of written records. Their authenticity and their meaning (philological) research in Germany, the scientific theory of the social, linguistic and other conditions of the native peoples in America. (Morgan)

431<•>observes that at an earlier period, however, the settlement of the English in India has afforded the necessity, of a study of the languages, the customs, the mores, ethical codes and the civil & criminal laws of these territories.

432<•>observes that at the commencement of the nineteenth century the knowledge of Sanskrit has penetrated as far as Germany, which lays the foundation for the comparative study of languages, which in its turn affords the most valuable insight into the life of the Indo-Germanic peoples in primitive times.

433<•>observes that all the forgoing renders it possible to study the accounts given by civilized observers on primitive peoples as well as the discoveries of weapons and tools of disappeared races. And it now comes about that these things are seen differently than they had been formerly when they were simply looked upon as curiosities.

434<•>observes that up to this time the entire writing of history was based upon the individual, historic, protagonist, martyr, hero. In the written sources of the past, from which formerly the knowledge of human history was exclusively culled, only the extraordinary had been related, because it was that only which seemed noteworthy to the chronicler of the events of his time.

435<•>observes that who in the past cared to describe what was everyday, what everybody knew! The extraordinary man, the extraordinary event, such as wars and revolutions, alone seemed worth relating. Thus it was that for the traditional historians, who never got beyond writing up from the sources handed down to them with more or less criticism, the big man was the motor power in history. In the feudal period the king, the military commander, the religious founder, the priests, and later philosophers and quasi-philosophers arose such as Neitzsche, Heiddigger, Ayn Rand that espoused the supermen in history.

436<•>observes that in ancient times some concepts of social history are in the written record but the time of the victory of the Greeks over the Persian invasion, is the culminating period of the ancient social historical writing. From that time on society in the lands round the Mediterranean began to decay, and so too did its social history ending up in the dark ages of the Barbarian immigration. But all is not lost for scholars of today glean much of social history from their digs.

437<•>observes that in so far as development socially is concerned, and even though there has been an evolution from Slave to Feudal society in Europe, the people have not risen far above the lead of classical antiquity in politics, philosophy, and art even by the 18th century.

438<•>observes that to your observer, looking upon these times, with popular written history as a 'guide', especially written European history appears simply to rise and descent, a repetition of the same old circle. With the odd exception, there seems to be no coil of progress, and especially no dialectic, in human thinking.

439<•>observes that but the foregoing is, upon closer scrutiny, otherwise when one examines individual university departments. History of Law, Comparative Philology, Ethnology, we now find in the material which they work up, some of the extraordinary and the individual but, now at least, the everyday and commonplace is beginning to be described.

440<•>observes that by way of a questioning technique poses the question can the study of primitive history trace with certainty a line of continuous development? Can it produce a social law of development and unfolding panorama of moral thinking?

441<•>observes that the historical material which is at mankind's disposal is two sided 1) facts of the technical side of life, and 2) historical speculation and even hard evidence of law, custom and religion through the ages. And as a further observation the second of these are the means by which the technical side of life is controlled without relying on the help of extraordinary individuals.

442<•>observes that in order to understand the ordinary in history people need the aid of a new science and (your observer coins the phrase 'necessity is the mother of invention') thus was born the science of statistics.

443<•>observes that as long as the parish was the most important economic institution, statistics were hardly required. In the parish it was easy to get a view of the state of affairs. But even if statistics were revealed there, they could scarcely suggest rigor in scientific observations, as with such small figures the law had no chance of making itself manifest.

444<•>observes that this situation is bound to alter as 3E capitalist control over the method of production creates the modern states, which modern states are nowhere near the earlier, simple bundles of communes or parishes and provinces, but have evolved into unitary bodies with global economic functions. The effect of all of this is that capital produces highly complicated connections which cannot be perceived without the means of the science of statistics.

445<•>observes that statistics was originally founded for the practical purpose of tax gathering and raising of recruits, for customs, and then for the insurance societies. Statistics gradually embraces wider spheres and produces a mass of observations on a large scale, which show laws which must impress themselves on observant compilers of the statistical material.

446<•>observes that in England this happened at the end of the 17th century, when Petty (1623 1687) arrives at a political arithmetic, in which, estimates play a very big role. At the beginning of the nineteenth century the method of statistical inquires is so complete and its sphere so varied that it is possible to discover with the greatest certainty the laws governing the actions of great masses of people. The Belgian Astronomer and statistician Quetelet (1796 1874) makes an attempt in the 1830's, to describe in this manner the functions of living organisms and their parts (the physiology) of human society.

447<•>observes that Petty and Quetelet see in their statistics that the determining element in the alterations of human action is always a material change, usually an economic one. Thus decrease and increase of crime, of suicide, marriages, shows to be dependent on the prices of grain and so on.

448<•>observes that they are careful to note that economic motives are, for instance, not the sole cause that a marriage is made between individuals, they did not declare the sexual passion to be an economic motive. But in large numbers the alteration in the annual number of marriages is called forth by changes in the economic situation.

449<•>observes that besides all these new sciences there is finally to mention a change in the character of the modern writing of history. The French 3E revolution comes to the fore so clearly as a class-struggle, that not only its historian must recognize that, but a number of historians were inspired to investigate in other periods of history the role of class wars.

And to see in them the motive forces of human development and moral thinking.

450<•>observes that classes are a product of the economic structure of society, and from this spring antagonisms and therefore the struggles of class against class, estate against estate.

451<•>observes that it is necessary to find what holds every class together, what divides them from other classes and what determines class opposition to the 'opposite' class and what is the particular class interests that each brings to the fray.

452<•>observes that it's an ancient, not a new kind of interest, but, just like statistics it is only becoming conscious to the mass of mankind and it is about that which no moralist of the eighteenth century has any idea whatever in which class he might belong.

453<•>observes that with all these advances and discoveries which certainly often enough are only piece-meal and by no means quite clear but by the 1840's all the essential elements of the materialist conception of history and moral thinking lay there to be uncovered. The beginnings of that manifestation of these events is brought forth and laid bare in all its brilliance by Engels and Marx.

454<•>observes that only to deep, dedicated, thinkers such as they, in their personal work and sacrifice is an achievement of that nature possible. But no Engels, no Marx could have achieved it in the 18th century, before all the new sciences have produced a sufficient mass of new evidence, new statistics, and new urgency.

455<•>observes that finally, however. Even Engels and Marx despite their genius and despite the preparatory work, which the new sciences had achieved, would not have been able, in the time of the 1840's to discover it. But they had understood the tremendous contribution to mankind that is given to it by the little person. Every person the unsung heroes of all production and transportation – the salary and wage workers, the farmers, the slaves and the serfs – the laborers of the globe.

456<•>observes that also it was absolutely necessary to the discovery of this materialist conception of economy and history and moral thinking that they understand the philosophies and morals of The First, Second, Third, Fourth, Fifth, Sixth And Seventh Estates. (although they did use this nomenclature).

457<•>observes that the rise of the idea of evolution not only of organisms but of society took place during a period of political reaction in Europe, when most people think that they are at the epitome of human development sordid as it was for the majority. Thus the conceptions of evolution of society are for past societies, (thus the idealist think that there <u>was</u> development but that there is no longer development.)

458<•>observes that as soon the reality, that is the reality of capitalist controlled society, had sunk-in the idealist conception of the evolution of society becomes entirely non-sensical.

459<•>observes that thus this fantastic idealism is superseded by a more or less open materialism. But only from the salary and wage workers point of view was it possible to translate the social development into a materialistic one – in other words to recognize that now we can understand that the evolution of society was proceeding in accordance with specific natural laws.

460<•>observes that with the discovery of this evolution of society comes the great reaction. The third-estate bourgeoisie is obliged to close its eyes to all ideas of a further social evolution, and repudiate every philosophy of evolution, to halt it, and even by the force of arms and terror to throw it back.

461<•>observes that that which they attempt to throw back can only be a philosophy of the salary and wage worker and other laborers, that proletarian philosophy and along with it almost all of the mental sciences are more or less repudiated and belittled by 3E capital. While at the same time the physical sciences are lauded and strengthened. And, no matter what, now all the sciences lay under the influence of 3E bourgeoisie controlled society.

462<•>observes that the idea of evolution, generally accepted for the physical sciences, (and certain specialized branches of mental science), remains dead for the mental sciences as a whole as taught by Bourgeois controlled universities. Bourgeois intellectuals, stuck in bourgeois funded universities, and stuck in Kantian and neo-Kantian philosophy could not even get further ahead even to Hegel in their philosophy.

463<•>observes that they try to turn back to Kant, try to purify it of all the defects which have been made manifest by subsequent events and by certain advanced thinkers. Here we have these bourgeoisie using blatant materialism in every day life but they want no truck with a materialist salary and wage labor's historical, economic or moral philosophy. They want no truck with any philosophy or science of the Group of 6 Billion who make up the fifth-estate.

464<•>observes that Bourgeois moral thinking, bourgeois ethical codes, and bourgeois civil & criminal laws are now brought to bear against materialist philosophy, against all the other mental sciences, and against the theory of social evolution and against the very 'group of 6 billion' itself.

465<•>observes that Assets man! They are fighting over the assets and the 'Freedom man!' to expropriate value-added and that is what it's all about! Your observer must ask; wherein lies the morality behind all of that?

466<•>observes that many opine that "You can't kill Bourgeois money! Bourgeois private capital is king!" Your observer must ask; if you understand money as labor-tokens wherein lies the morality behind all of that?

467<•>observes that many opine that "You can't modify market economy! market economy is king.!" When you see not only small business but even large corporations being killed by antagonistic competition; Your observer must ask; wherein lies the morality behind all of that?

468<•>observes that many opine that "You can't kill destructive warring antagonistic competition! destructive warring antagonistic competition is king!" Your observer must ask; wherein lies the morality behind all of that?

469<•>observes that many opine that "You can't change individual moral thinking into cooperative social moral thinking! Individualism in morality is king!" Your observer must ask; wherein lies any scientific moral thinking behind all of that?

470<•>observes that when you finally get down to it you can't kill terror! Terror is king! Multi-billionairs and millionairs paying factions in the Sixth and Seventh Estate's to carry out the killing of salary and wage labor the globe over. In their supreme ignorance attempting to drive society into a neo-dark age where all salary and wage labor is in grave danger of becoming paupers for centuries to come. Your observer must ask; wherein lies the moral thinking behind all of that?

471<•>observes that dialectical materialism of the mental sciences, history, economics, moral thinking, is a materialism of its own kind, which is quite different from the materialism of the physical sciences. Disliking the word 'materialism' many people wish to change it. Smoke and mirror euphemisms are in vogue nowadays. (deregulation for privatization. collateral damage for killed civilians in a war and so on.) But your observer and humble reporter refuses all of that.

472<•>observes that if Marx and Engels held on to the word materialism it was based upon the same ground that they refused to rename their manifesto of the Communists into a manifesto of the Socialists. The word socialism carries such adverse connotations, why even Hitler called himself a National Socialist. One cannot bandy about with the word Communist. (Even though it has been twisted by the red directors, the apparatuchuks, and the fourth-estate out of all recognition to its real content.)

473<•>observes that despite distortions in Communism of the past it, in essence, can be said to be:- salary and wage workers in large enterprises, farmers and aboriginal people and small shop keepers joining together in a harmony, each individual giving and taking a moral equal share in social production and in private consumption under the aegis of a deep-going grass roots democracy. It also entails the elimination of gross exaggerations in expropriation and in balloon incomes which bring with them all the lice and cliques and apparatuchuks of this world.

474<•>observes that therefore dialectical materialism comes into disrepute with the euphemism-loving 3E bourgeoisie. But for that very reason followers of the proletarian salary and wage worker philosophy have every incentive to hold fast to this very name, which is also justified in fact. The conception of moral thinking, ethical codes, and civil & criminal laws which arise from this philosophy outrank subjective idealism and appear as objective materialistic ones.

~475< TRACT 15:

476<•>observes that **The Organisation Of Human Society.** Technical Development.

477<•>observes that we may now regard mankind from the standpoint of the materialist conception of history at the stage at which we left people in the foregoing paragraphs, for example at the boundary which divides mankind from the rest of the animal world.

478<•>observes that the question must be asked:- What is it that raises mankind above other animals? Do there exist between people and animals only gradual differences or is there also an essential difference?

479<•>observes that neither as a thinking nor as a moral being are people essentially different from animals. Perhaps the difference lie in the fact that mankind *produces*, that is, adapts material found in nature by means of change of form or of place to his purposes? This activity is, however, also found in the animal world.

480<•>observes that we find this behavior in insects, such as bees and ants. We find it among birds, among many warm blooded animals and even among fishes we find a type of productive activity, namely, the production of refuges and dwellings, with nests, underground and underwater homes, and so on.

481<•>observes that however, much of this productive activity food finding and so on is also the result of inherited instincts but they are often suitably adapted to various circumstances, and that means that consciousness – the knowledge of causal connections – must also play a part.

482<•>observes that the question must be asked: is it the use of tools which raises mankind above animals? But also we note that among animals we find at least the beginnings of the application of tools, of branches, of trees for defense, of stones for cracking nuts and so on. This intelligence as well as the development of its feet and hands enables the apes to do that.

483<•>observes that thus not the production for means of consumption, and not the use of tools distinguishes humans from the animals. What, however, alone distinguishes the mankind from animals is the making of tools, which serve for the making of other tools and the goods and commodities for exchange in general.

484<•>observes that animals can, at the most, find their tools ready-made in nature: They are not capable of inventing them as such. An animal may produce things for its immediate use, prepare dwellings and collect provisions.

But it is not able to think to produce anything which will not serve for direct and almost immediate consumption.

485<•>observes that with the production of the means of production the 'animal man' begins to become the 'human man'. And with that he breaks away from the animal world to found his own empire, an empire with its own kind of development, which is wholly unknown in the rest of nature, in which nothing similar is to be found.

486<•>observes that with organs provided by nature and the tools provided by the natural environment the animal cannot rise above those means provided for it by nature.

487<•>observes that the animal's development only occurs as his own organs unfold and evolve of themselves – the brain included. This is a slow and unconscious process carried on by means of the struggle for life, which the animal can in no way hurry on by its conscious activity.

488<•>observes that on the other hand the discovery and production of 'tools' means that humans (Homo sapiens) consciously and purposely give themselves new organs. Or discover new ways to strengthens or lengthens their natural organs, so that now they are not only capable of producing the same that these organs produced, but besides that they are in a position to produce astounding results now which were formerly unattainable.

489<•>observes that as man is not simply an animal endowed with higher intelligence, hands and productive tools but also must have been from early-on a social animal.

490<•>observes that even if a certain degree of intelligence and the development of the hand forms the necessary condition for the capability to produce tools. So to the social character of man affords the conditions for continual additions of new improvements to old handicrafts which are handed down through social interaction, thus leading to a continual development of technical skills of mankind as a whole.

491<•>observes that there is a 'slow' unconscious process of development of individuals through the struggle for life that rules the entire organic world. This process of course also goes on in the human world, but in the world of people there comes into play a conscious transformation that may produce advancements 'quicker' than natural development.

492<•>observes that conscious transformation in mankind takes on two forms **1)** Conscious technical transformation in the technical sciences, and **2)** Conscious mental transformation especially in the mental sciences. In the era of your observer's existence people's thinking and consciousness in the mental sciences have lagged far behind their technical consciousness.

493<•>observes that technically people now have the ability to destroy themselves and the known world. But the majority of people do not understand the underlying causes of antagonistic competition which cognition has been slow to develop in the human brain. With only a few outstanding exceptions people's collective moral thinking in regard to this subject is almost non-existent as things now stand.

494<•>observes that If the mental sciences are 'forced' to atrophy by the powers that be, as they have been for over a century, this state of affairs may well throw humankind back to a very dark age indeed.

495<•>observes that if the foregoing indeed does occur then the 'unconscious' natural progress of social development will lay bound beneath the feet of 'conscious' technical development of mankind. It is the object of your observer to bring this unconscious progress of mankind into consciousness and thus hopefully help to unbind it.

496<•>observes that the police states required by conscious technical developments which are uncontrolled by a conscious mental science can only lead to disaster. Thus mass grass roots deep informed ethical codes, and civil & criminal laws, that lead to a progressive moral thinking and away from police-states are the necessary tools now required for the advancement of humankind.

~497< TRACT 16:

498<•>observes that **The Development Of The Technical Consciousness Of humankind.**
Technology And The Method of Life.

499<•>observes that the great leap forward when primitive people (Homo faber) first discovered that they could go beyond the ape's stone or stick and join stone to stick to make a hammer or an ax: - bone to vine to make a fishing instrument and so on.

500<•>observes that as soon as primitive people possessed the spear, they were in a position to hunt still bigger animals. People's food up to then must have come principally from tree fruits and insects, as well as probably birds, now with the spear, people could kill even bigger animals, meat became more important for food.

501<•>observes that the majority of the bigger animals, however, live on the earth, not in the trees, hunting thus drew primitive people from their airy regions down to the earth. People now gradually became hunters, thus they could emerge from the forest and tackle the grassy plains. This is but the barest of outline of what probably happened in human development.

502<•>observes that thus many people adapted themselves out of the tree-fruit stage and were now obliged to seek for animal food, and could no longer in the same degree feed themselves from tree-fruits. We see clearly the close connection which exists between new means of tool production and new methods of life leading to ever newer needs.

503<•>observes that we see that one factor necessarily produces another factor, each becomes of necessity the cause of further changes, which in their turn elicit new fresh changes. Thus every discovery produces inevitable changes, which give rise to other discoveries, and therewith brings new needs and methods of life which again call forth new discoveries and so on – a coil of endless development.

504<•>observes that let us consider the consequences which the rise of hunting as a source of food for people and their emergence from the primitive forest was bound to draw with it. Besides meat, man took in place of the tree-fruits, roots and fruits of the grasses, corn and maize into his bill of fare.

505<•>observes that in the primitive forest a cultivation of plants is not easy and to clear the primitive forest is beyond the power of primitive people as they lived from plentiful fruits and hunting and gathering in general, people could not even arrive at this idea of 'farming'.

506<•>observes that also to plant fruit trees which would only bear fruit after many years assumes that a high degree of culture and settlement has already been attained. On the other hand, the planting of grasses in meadows and steppes is much easier than in the primitive forest and can be brought about with much simpler tools.

507<•>observes that planting grasses, which often bear fruit after only a few weeks, is, however, easier to conceive than that of planting trees. Cause and effect are so nearly connected in this case that their dependence is easier to see. Even unsettled primitive people might hope to be able to hold out against beasts and elements for a short period between seed-time and harvest in the neighborhood of the cultivated ground.

508<•>observes that people when they left the primitive forest are far more at the mercy of climatic changes than in their original home. In the thick forest the changes of temperature between day and night are much less than on the open plain, which during the day a burning sun rules and by night a radiation and loss of heat.

509<•>observes that storms are also less noticeable in the forest than on a plain, and against rain and hail this latter offers much less protection than the almost impenetrable foliage of the forest. Thus the mutual evolution of people, tools and habitat are bound to make people feel a need for shelter and clothing which the primitive man in the arboreal forest never felt.

510<•>observes that it was certainly the need for protection against cold which allowed mankind to aspire for the possession of fire. The technical ability to use fire for other means people could only gradually learn after eons of evolutionary time. The warmth which fire gave out was on the other hand at once evident.

511<•>observes that not in the damp forest but only in a drier region, where greater quantities of dry fire material were to be found at intervals, moss, leaves, brushwood, lightning, flints and so on could conditions arise which gave people an acquaintance with fire.

512<•>observes that we see how the entire life of peoples, their needs, their dwellings, their means of sustenance were changed, as one discovery finally brought numerous others in the coil of development.

513<•>observes that in all these transformations consciousness played a great part. But even greater was that the consciousness of the people was handed upward to their progeny.

~514< **TRACT 17:**

515<•>observes that **A New Organism Arises – Human Society:** Animal And Social Organisms

516<•>observes that the division of labor by the various organs in a living thing has its limits. For instance it is highly unlikely that the same limb can serve equally well for the various functions of grasping, flying, or walking. Tools, however, can be changed by people to suite their needs. If the hand for example (which is limited in its function for grasping) can manipulate innumerable tools – the limb is limited but the tools are innumerable.

517<•>observes that sticking to the example of the hand the force with which it can be moved is limited (but in theory at least) it can be made. by means of tools, to control infinite power.

518<•>observes that in addition to the foregoing, the potential in tool movement is by no means confined to one individual, many individuals can unite to operate them. Thus beasts of burden, water, wind, steam, ships, nuclear capability are instances where many hands come together to operate these powers.

519<•>observes that the separation of artificial organs (tools) of people from their personality has, however, still other effects. If the organs of the animal organisms are bound up with it, that means that every individual has the same organs at his disposal. The sole exception, the psychological excepted, is formed by the organs of reproduction.

520<•>observes that only in this region of tool manipulation is a division of labor to be found among the higher organisms. But we must also recognize at this point that there may be certain functions in society which do not require the manipulation of 'hard tools' for example leaders, who may use 'soft tools' (to be discussed later.)

521<•>observes that the discovery of the tool makes it possible that in a society certain individuals exclusively use certain tools oftener than others and in that they understand its use far better than any one else.

522<•>observes that thus we come to see a form of division of labor in human society, which is of quite another kind from the modest beginnings in animal societies. In the animal society there remains individual organs these being the only division of labor (bound up in its hide) which are sufficient for its self-support.

523<•>observes that whilst in human society the individual also has his personal organs but there has evolved through the coil of progress a supra division of labor through tools. (extensions to the natural organs).

524<•>observes that the farther the division of labor advances in society the greater are the number of the organs which society has at its disposal.

525<•>observes that society now has evolved to a place which gives it a greater power over nature but this renders the individual helpless outside of society.

526<•>observes that a virtually tool-less animal society (the herd etc.), which arises as a natural growth, can never raise its members above nature. Tool making division of labor in human society, on the other hand, forms for/in its individuals and in society as a whole a nature which is a quite apart from mankind's animal origins and the animal world as it is today.

527<•>observes that thus we see from the foregoing that there come into account two distinguishing features when speaking of societies. 1) the animal organism itself possesses all the organs which it requires for its own existence. 2) while the human individual under the advanced division of labor cannot live by itself without society.

528<•>observes that a Robinson Crusoe, who without any means to produce for himself is only to be found in children's story books and 'scientific works' of bourgeois economists. Many of these philosophers and economists believe that complete isolation and individualism is the epitome of human progress, that it is every man for himself and the best way to discover the laws of society is to completely ignore society.

529<•>observes that the peculiar nature of society is, however, in a continual state of change, because, as opposed to animal society, human society is always subject to development in consequence of the advancement in technology and the sciences, especially will it be so when the mental sciences of philosophy, history, political-economics and law are finally freed up from the clutches of the 3E and their sycophants in the 4E.

530<•>observes that a one sided advancements in the physical sciences without advancement in the mental sciences of history, economics, law, ethics, and philosophy (and general learning of these by the majority of mankind) can only mean an end to progress, and may even lead in human society's complete extinction.

531<•>observes that thus we see the struggle for advancement against reaction and revanchement as a struggle between the forces that would bury the mental sciences in moral obfuscation.

532<•>observes that the world now stands on the brink of a new dark-age with ethical code manipulation for profit. This is carried out by the insertion of for profit anti-social ideas in the moral thinking of people. The use of propaganda and regressive civil & criminal laws is used and the hampering and killing of those forces which would bring the mental sciences up to, and in line with, the tremendous advancement in humankind's tools and in the physical sciences.

533<•>observes that reactionary movements can, however, to speak historically, never last long. Sooner or later these fetters of society are burst, either by internal movement, revolutions, or, and what is oftener the case, by shock from without by wars, or by even internal wars that enervate the guts of a people.

534<•>observes that wars nowadays always have the potential of spinning out of control into nuclear biological or chemical wars. Thus the tools of war, the advancement in the physical sciences and the subtle machinery of propaganda, and the loss of civil liberties in support of war are very dangerous to mankind. And all the while, the mental sciences, it seems by your observer, have lapsed into some decay at the time of this observation.

535<•>observes that in spite of the foregoing pessimism society changes from time to time, its members, its boundaries, its names, its economics, its moral thinking.

536<•>observes that it can seem to the casual observer as if society is showing traces of old age, and is now near death. In reality, however, if we want to take a simile from the animal organism or from human history, one type of organism or society may suffer from a disease from which it will emerge as a new organism or society; changed forever with renewed strength.

~537< TRACT 18:

538<•>observes that **The Changes In The Strength Of The Social Instincts:** Language:

539<•>observes that since human society is continually rapidly changing in contrast to a slower animal evolution, for that very reason the people in society must be also changing relatively rapidly. The alteration in the conditions of life must react on the nature of people and upon their moral thinking.

540<•>observes that since the discovery of tools the division of labor necessarily extends some of peoples natural organs in a greater degree and transforms many thought processes.

541<•>observes that many animals are subjected to manifold and rapid changes by the incursion of people and their tools. The encroachment is so rapid that many animals have no time to evolve defensive mechanisms and they become extinct. But having said that, people are confronted with even more and ever growing problems of adaptation to their surroundings, but fortunately people can use the power of their intellect to adapt, that is if the mental sciences have not been blunted too severely by conditions of their time. (in later development by bourgeois 3E capitalist moral thinking and their immoral operations.)

542<•>observes that thus we see that the changes in society are able to transform the organism of mankind, not only their hands and feet etc. but their brains. It is the duty of the mental sciences to make people conscious to enable them to change their views and consciousness in the following broad areas. That which is useful, that which is harmful, that which is good, that which is bad, that which is possible, that which is impossible, that which is moral and that which is immoral. And it is through language that the higher forms of consciousness are brought about. (your observer needs to cover certain ground prior to discussion on the universal criterion of morality and what it is based upon.)

543<•>observes that thus it is the duty of the mental sciences to uncover the coil of progress and the laws governing these aspects of life and to promulgate this knowledge. This despite the tremendous pressure and present state of affairs that go a long way to suppress this knowledge by the 4E, silence, half truth and propaganda machine operating

Tsunami One   Moral Organon.

largely in the hands of the 3E. (Whilst the individual reporter wants to be honest his copy must be bent to fit his boss and profit. Or at least to fit the morality of the so-called 'free' market which is touted to be the epitome of human progress.)

544<•>observes that we have previously noted that the animal world had already developed social impulses and that the first advent of tools elevated human society slightly above the animal. In this scenario all social animals could get by in life, with a few means of mutual understanding, cries of persuasion, of joy, of fright, of alarm, of anger and sensational noises (a sort of 'grunt' language) and so on.

545<•>observes that sensational noises do not, however, suffice, if there is to be labor having different tasks which are to be allotted using different tools for creating and consuming different products. Thus 'Grunts' do not suffice for individuals, who are helpless without the help of other individuals, in cooperative labor.

546<•>observes that in order to effectively and cooperatively use tools a richer communication now becomes necessary – a new instrument of social intercourse and understanding for communication between individuals, thus the 'grunt' language of the social animals gradually evolves into a full blown language of communion by Homo sapiens. (and is still rapidly evolving)

547<•>observes that division of labor is impossible without a language, which describes, not merely sensations, but also things and processes, it can only do that to the degree in which language is perfected and developed alongside of the development of tools and the higher technical processes.

548<•>observes that go, come, get, climb, sleep, make, kill, fish (fishing) and so on –the verbs are older than the nouns, verbs form the roots from which the nouns are derived. (although lately even nouns have evolved into verbs i.e. fishing, paperize, digitize, rubberize and others seen in print)

549<•>observes that the development of language is not surprising if we grasp the fact that the first duty of language is the mutual understanding of people engaged in common activities and common movements. This role of language was first as a help in the process of production and later it came into the process of, ethical code generation, writing, art and so on.

550<•>observes that the development of language is not to be understood without the development of the various methods of production. From this latter it depends whether a language remains the dialect of a tiny tribe or a world language, which a billion people speak.

551<•>observes that with the development of language there may be an uncommonly strong means of social cohesion. A freeing up of the mental sciences from their dormancy can lead to an enormous strengthening and a clear-cut consciousness of the social instincts.

552<•>observes that in addition language certainly produced quite other effects; it is the most effectual means of retaining acquired knowledge, of spreading this, and handing it on to later generations; it first makes it possible to form concepts, to think scientifically.

553<•>observes that thus language starts the development of both the mental and physical sciences and with that brings about the understanding of nature by science. But people need to go further than that they need to understand society itself and language is in the forefront of that understanding.

554<•>observes that the capacity for abstract presentations depends again on language. People describe things which are similar to each other with the same word at the same time they unconsciously undertake a 'scientific work' – the collection of the similar, the separation of the unlike.

555<•>observes that language is then not simply an organ of mutual understanding of different men with each other but has become an organ of thinking. Even when we do not speak to others, but think to ourselves, the thoughts must be clothed in certain words.

556<•>observes that the higher animal gathers experiences which utilizes and impulses which, under certain circumstances, it can hand on to its descendants. But it is only through language, that renders it possible to communicate ideas to others, as well as abstract conceptions, scientific knowledge, and convictions.

~557< TRACT 19:

558<•>observes that **War And Property:**
Sixth Estate Military Moral Thinking:

559<•>observes that a further means beside community in work and language to strengthen the social impulses, it is stated by bourgeois writers, are formed by the social development through the rise of war.

560<•>observes that we have no reason to suppose that primitive man was a warlike being. Herds of ape-men who gathered together in the branches of trees with copious sources of food, it is true, can have squabbled and driven each other away.

561<•>observes that if this got so far as killing their opponents, of that there is no example among the living apes of today. Of male gorillas it is reported that they occasionally fight each other with such fury, that one kills the other, but that is a fight for a mate, not a fight for feeding grounds.

562<•>observes that the foregoing changes as soon as man becomes a hunter, who has command of tools, which are directed to killing, and who has grown accustomed to killing by the shedding of 'strange' blood.

563<•>observes that also another factor comes into account, which Engels points out to explain cannibalism which often comes up at this period possibly occasioned into custom by the uncertainty of the sources of food. (The moral imperative to cannibalism).

564<•>observes that vegetable food is in the tropical forest in abundance. On the grassy plains, on the other hand, roots and fruits are not always to be found and the capture of game is, for the most part, a matter of chance. The beasts of prey have thus acquired the capacity of being able to fast for incredibly long periods. The human stomach has not such powers of endurance.

565<•>observes that thus this necessity easily forces a tribe of savages to a fight for life or death with another neighboring tribe, which has got a good hunting territory. In this way technical progress lets loose struggles, which the original ape-man probably did not know.

566<•>observes that thus arose primitive people's fights not only with animals, but fights with the members of their own kind.

Such struggles, often more bloody than those with the leopard and the panther, against which at least the tribes understand very well how to defend themselves when united in greater numbers.

567<•>observes that nothing is more fallacious than the idea that the progress of culture and increase of knowledge necessarily bring also higher humanity with them. We could far better say therefore that the ape is oft times more 'human' than mankind itself.

568<•>observes that the progress in division of labor assigns the tasks of; **1)** workers killing animals Hunters, Butchers and **2)** the killing of people by many fractions and categories within the various other estates, military men, executioners, soldiers of fortune, arms merchants, torturers, terrorists, gumshoes, spies etc., who then occupy themselves with brutality and cruelty either directly or indirectly as a lucrative business or livelihood or profit all carried out within the boundaries of civilization. Thus with the latter, we see a moral thinking quite different from those of the former.

569<•>observes that murder and slaughter in the numbers of humans for economic motives are products of a culture and of a technology that plays up the physical sciences in arms and warlike pursuits while at the same time it continually downplays and scoffs at the mental sciences in humanism. (or blankets its immoral acts in the cloak of 'self defense.)

570<•>observes that now, in our own age, the perfection of the physical sciences and technology is ranked as the greater part of the intellectual labor of mankind. We have reached a point at which, only under special circumstances, and in special classes will there be any farther progress of culture and a refinement of manners.

571<•>observes that armies relieve the ordinary citizen of the necessity of killing just as butchers do but they are on a different level. Thus people in many other estates are entirely relieved of the necessity of shedding blood. Especially the intellectuals who have been for centuries so unused to the spilling of actual blood that many confine themselves to their writing desks spewing out justification for other's going off to wars in order to spill it.

572<•>observes that a techno slaughter is taking place. No longer is war a hero knight's war but it is become a war against the wage and salary people and other types of labor – global in scope. And, with that, refinement of armchair manners among our intellectuals pundits, and apologists, will soon reach its end for they too can become, not just theoretically, but actively and intimately embroiled. Why? It is because in this period of history, many of them too are usually misguided wage and salary workers.

573<•>observes that wars have become, since the hero knight's age, considerably more brutal. The death penalty which even in the fifty years of last century was generally condemned by most states, meets with hearty applause nowadays, and the cruelties of colonial wars, has been replaced by 'conflict diamond' wars, terrorist wars, ignorant intelligence wars, sell the armaments wars. The glorification of profit from war comes from many quarters.

574<•>observes that in any case war or even lesser conflict comes between the 3E of one country or faction against the 3E of another. Or even, let us say, conflict between the 3E of one country against the salary and wage workers of the 5E in the same country. Conflicts play, among modern peoples, a similar role as was once between the nomadic pastoral and hunting peoples, but on a highly intensified scale.

575<•>observes that if it is hate and animosity and killing on the one hand, it shows itself on the other as a powerful impetus to strengthen the bonds within the family, or the bonding of the various individuals to the estate to which they belong.

576<•>observes that the greater dangers to mankind as a whole comes from the constant bombardment of half truths from the 'popular' for 4E press which is almost totally controlled by the 3E at the time of this observation.

577<•>observes that the greater the dangers which threaten one – the more does one rely upon his/her society, class, estate, or family, to which they think that they, with their distinctive or their joint forces, can ostensibly protect one from the perceived danger.

578<•>observes that in the beginning the first cause of conflict must have been the uncertainty in the food sources and the consequent battle over them. But this cause almost ceases as soon as agriculture and breeding of animals are developed.

579<•>observes that then begins a new cause of war: the possession of wealth, (assets) and not private property at this time, but tribal property. Side by side with tribes in fruitful regions we find others in unfruitful. War and conflict now become robbery and defense against robbery, and it has remained in essence the same in tribal society until today. (Assets and who owns them and who wants them.)

580<•>observes that this kind of ancient tribal war and conflict had a strengthening effect on the social instincts, so long as the property in the tribe is in the main communal.

581<•>observes that on the other hand the strengthening of the social instincts through war and conflict ceases as soon a classes are formed in the tribal community.

582<•>observes that now with classes formed in the tribe intertribal war, while it still exists, recedes somewhat and conflict becomes between the chief who has usurped (at first by acquiescence of his tribes-people then by force of arms) communal property and made it his own personal property. Thus from millions of these small filtchings arose the even bigger and more organized plunder that was to take place under slavery then under 1E religion and later by 2E aristocracy and even later by 3E capital.

583<•>observes that by the simplest of mechanism it came – the best talker; the best 'looker'; the best hunter; the best at artifice becoming the head of the tribe and the tribe itself heralding this leadership. Soon however this condition hardened into heredity right for the chief's progeny.

584<•>observes that For those who care to look; this aspect of the process of the splitting of the tribe into classes can be seen in the life of some of our own aboriginal peoples of today.

585<•>observes that with the development of heredity right came the development of the old wink-wink nod-nod and with these came a split in the moral thinking between the Chieftain and that of ordinary peoples.

586<•>observes that thus we see that this simple affair of the ruling chieftain and his dukes, earls and sheiks. All whose ever waking endeavors are aimed towards an increase in their sphere of exploitation; or to thrust themselves by war into the place of another ruling class in a neighboring land has gradually changed society.

587<•>observes that now it becomes for the subject classes that such wars – inter-tribal and internecine – are often enough, not about the subject of their very existence, not about a better standard of life, but about only who will 'forevermore' be their lord and master.

588<•>observes that now on top of all this social development comes the army (of the Sixth Estate 6E) which becomes either an aristocratic army, in which the mass of the people have no part, or in the situation where ordinary people cooperate it becomes a paid army. In certain states it becomes a compulsory army, in others it becomes a mercenary third party army.

589<•>observes that such armies are commanded by the ruling classes. And the tribes people, the plebeians, the serfs, the peasants and the citizens (motivated, not by objective reason but by the development of smoke and mirrors) must put their lives at stake. They fight, not for their own property, their own wives and children, but to champion the interests of other, often hostile, interests.

590<•>observes that written ethical codes begin to appear and with them come the civil & criminal laws in their billions, many of which are directed at coercing the moral thinking of ordinary people in support of the hostile interests mentioned.

591<•>observes that this development of armies is no longer derived from social instincts but solely from fright of a remorselessly cruel penal code, by which military and civil laws are such armies held together. And in latter day developments the 4E media comes fully equipped to either to remain silent on issues of to disseminate and bludgeon truth, with half-truths. And half-truths repeated often enough become lies. Often cover-up and outright lies are part of their daily fare. So much for the moral thinking of journalists of the 'popular' 4E paid by the 3E.

592<•>observes that more often than not at this stage war ceases to be a school of social feeling for the mass of the people. In the ruling, 6E warrior classes it becomes a school of a haughty, overbearing demeanor towards the people. It teaches, through the press, to treat people just as they do the common soldiers in the army, to degrade them to blind subordination to an absolute commander, to dispose of their assets by means of taxes and even their life without any scruple toward their perceived enemy. Thus has arisen 6E military moral thinking

~593< TRACT 20:

594<•>observes that The Rise Of Property:
Custom & Moral Thinking:

595<•>observes that this development of war, as discussed previously, is as a consequence of the development of privatization of public-property, which again comes from the technical historical development of society.

596<•>observes that Every object, which is produced in society or with which production is carried on in it must be at the disposal of some entity and this being can either be a single individual, a group, or the entire society.

597<•>observes that the nature of this disposal is determined by the nature of the things, and the nature of the method of production and that of the products.

598<•>observes that a person who, in tribal times, made his weapons used them. Who made the garment used them, who made the ornament or mask used them, on the other hand it was equally natural that the house which was built by the common labor of the tribe should be inhabited in common by them.

599<•>observes that the various kinds of enjoyment of the various things for utility was always set, and repeated from generation to generation became the fixed custom.

600<•>observes that thus arose a law of custom, which was then extended still further when quarrels arose. Who had the right was put before the assembled members of the tribe who then decided.

601<•>observes that law in those times did not arise from any thought-out legislation or social compact, but from a custom resting on the technical conditions, and where these did not suffice, the individual decisions of the society were decided case by case. Thus arose over time a complicated right of property in the various means of distribution of the products of society.

602<•>observes that common property, however, preponderated in the beginning, especially in the means of production, a soil worked in common, water apparatus, houses, also herds of animals and other things besides. Even this common property was bound very largely to strengthen the social impulses, the interest in the common good, and also the subordination of individuals to the common good and the dependence on the common good.

603<•>observes that private property of single families or individuals as soon as it arrived developed at such a pitch that it began to usurp the place of common property.

604<•>observes that the foregoing began as a consequence of the growing division of labor. The various branches of hand work began to separate themselves from agriculture in which they had hitherto found employment, when crafts became, not only independent from agriculture, but also separated into various branches themselves.

605<•>observes that this development means an extension of the realm of society through the division of labor. This heralds an increase in the number of crafts by those people who form a society because they, not only work devising tools for the herders and agricultural peoples, but they work for each other and thus are mutually dependent for their existence on each other.

606<•>observes that but this extension of social labor does not develop on the lines of an extension of work in common, but towards a separation of individuals from common work, and to making their work the private work of independent producers.

607<•>observes that those who produce that which they themselves do not consume, trade that produce to obtain, in return, the goods of other branches of craft industries in order to consume them. That is production, not for their own use, but for sale in the market.

608<•>observes that with that there arises side by side with private property, which had already existed at an earlier period, even if not to so great an extent, an entirely new element in society. This new element is the competitive struggle of the different producers of the same kind, who struggle against each other for their share of the market. This competitive struggle is occasioned by the fact that the artisan has now been cut of from communal food and shelter.

609<•>observes that war and market competition are often regarded as the only forms of the struggle for existence in the entire natural world. In fact both arise from the technical progress of mankind and belong to mankind's special peculiarity.

610<•>observes that both of the foregoing are distinguished from the struggle for existence of the animal world. In the animal world there is a struggle of individuals or entire societies against surrounding nature, a fight against living and nonliving forces of nature in which those best fitted out for the particular circumstances can best maintain themselves and reproduce their kind.

611<•>observes that in the animal world there is no fight for life or death against other individuals of the same kind, with the exception of a few beasts of prey, especially in the struggle for sexual natural selection. Even this does not usually end in death of the defeated individual.

612<•>observes that it is with mankind alone, thanks to the perfection of tools especially tools of war does the struggle against individuals of the same species come to the fore, oft times ending in death and billions of times ending in misery. In a world devoid of communal ties deep down this struggle is always over the assets and who gets to control and use them.

613<•>observes that if a struggle breaks out between two different human societies (Let us say ruling 3E in country QQ over the ruling 3E in Country RR) over the assets it means an interruption of domestic production and this can never be a permanent aspect of the struggle.

614<•>observes that the foregoing presupposes, however, at least that there is no internal great class antagonisms that exist in either QQ or RR at the outset of the conflict. Now it is either QQ or RR must eventually succumb to absolute ruin, but in any case they mutually drag themselves down to a point where revolution in one, the other, or both becomes a possibility.

615<•>observes that competition on the other hand is a struggle between individuals, and indeed between individuals of the same society. This struggle is, in normal times, a regulator, which keeps social cooperation of the various individuals going, and arranges that, in the last resort, these private producers shall always produce what is socially necessary. (this is the Adam Smith approach)

616<•>observes that during the stress of war and also antagonistic competition divisions in the society come to the fore and then we may have class conflict within the society (country). Exacerbation of relative poverty forces the contending estates to fight it out for supremacy. (such was the case for example during the French Revolution when 3E bourgeoisie capital wrested control of the French state machinery out of the hands of 2E aristocracy.)

617<•>observes that just as war does, so does antagonistic competition mean a tremendous waste of human assets. Competition (as long as it does not degenerate into antagonistic competition) is also a means of obtaining the highest degree of proficiency of all the productive forces and their most rapid improvement.

618<•>observes that competition is consequently of great economic importance until it creates such gigantic productive forces that the frame-work of commodity-production and the global market economy that it engenders becomes too narrow – become choked. This development is similar to what happened in the frame-work of primitive social, or cooperative production, it became too narrow for the growing division of labor.

619<•>observes that we must understand here that primitive social production had somewhere to go – it had an infinite world with which to work out its destiny. This is not the case with modern commodity production and global markets, for it; the world is no longer infinite but merely a 'global village'.

620<•>observes that antagonistic competitive struggle between individuals of the 3E and 3E has, now under all circumstances, an absolutely deadly effect on social and ecological progress in the globe.

621<•>observes that overproduction, and no less the artificial limitation of production by employers' associations. As well as the propensity to create war-needs by 3E capital shows that the time is long past when healthy competition can make its return as a spur to production and help our social evolution.

622<•>observes that for people under a developed system of production of commodities and global markets it seems that egoism is the only natural impulse in mankind. Those apologists in the 4E would have us believe that the social instincts are only a refined egoism. The religious 1E would have us believe that all of this including moral thinking comes from a supernatural mystery.

623<•>observes that if in society of today the social instincts have kept any strength, it is only due to the circumstance that general commodity production and global markets are only quite a young phenomenon, hardly 200 years old.

624<•>observes that but the social instincts are being bombarded hourly by the forces of radio, screen, and TV, that put forward that individualism and the every person for his or her self is the ticket to paradise. This is a cold paradise where the individual is cut off from the warmth of society. This can never happen, for if it does, humankind will cease to exist just from the very fact alone that there can no longer be social intercourse or social production and mankind will disappear, not from some natural disaster, but by its own ignorant folly.

625<•>observes that thus we see a special moral thinking coming out of, and during of the rise of, private commodity producing property.

~626< TRACT 21:

627<•>observes that **The Influence Of The Social Instincts:** Moral Thinking In Internationalism The Degree Of Strength In Which The Social Instincts Are At Work, Are Effective And Alter Themselves Person To person Estate To Estate. Cohesion And Its Breakdown:

628<•>observes that traditional ethical codes try to modify moral thinking into a force which regulates relations of person to person.

629<•>observes that since such ethical codes start with the individual person (or company) and not with the society as a whole. They overlook the fact that the moral thinking of, let us say, a person of the 3E may not correspond with the moral thinking of a person from the 5E.

630<•>observes that the foregoing merely points up the fact that moral thinking in each of the seven estate differs from every other estate. Which only means to say that the moral thinking of the first, second, third, fourth, fifth, sixth, and seventh estates, while they may exhibit some things in common still not all moral thinking from every estate will be the same.

631<•>observes that As an example of this let us take the 3E moral thinking on the necessity for war and killing, (Ethical Code that leads to Moral Thinking in this 3E; 'Kill the competition'). That thinking will be quite different than 1E thinking upon the same subject matter. (Ethical Code that leads to moral thinking: in the 1E 'Thou shalt not kill') (although your observer is well aware of the fact of history that the 1E might well, and usually does, go along with the ruling class and war – blend in)

632<•>observes that we come to the point when we must recollect the origin of the social instincts. They are a means to increase the social cohesion, to add to the strength of society. But as is illustrated in the foregoing in an economically class divided society we have a breakdown in cohesion.

633<•>observes that on the other hand, the animal rarely comes into conflict in its social instincts for members of his own herd, because the herd is not economically class divided.

634<•>observes that the various degrees of moral thinking in each of mankind's estates is by no means fixed once and for all. This thinking changes with the progress of productivity and the conditions under which human labor works and the elements, extent and depth to which propaganda, war, unemployment, economic conditions, ethical codes, and civil & criminal laws are embraced. And it may be noted that it is important to understand that all these conditions may be relative and not concrete, in other words there is what might be called a delta aspect to them.

635<•>observes that in an economically divided society there are manifold moralities but the foundations of a general human moral thinking is being formed. It is not formed by this or that faction that has an economic stake in the outcome of the particular moral thinking that may suits its narrow purpose. But by the development of the salary and wage workers in production, communication, and transportation – the productive forces of mankind on a global scope – by and for mankind and not for any narrow faction alone. The 3E especially has no future in it.

636<•>observes that certainly it is capital which creates the material foundation for a general human morality, but it only creates the foundation by treading this morality continually under its feet. The wink, wink, nod, nod of 3E controlled private capital must be transformed into grass roots 5E publicly controlled capital, only then will morality be free to seek its true goal of making the world a better place.

637<•>observes that 3E capital continually wants privatization of public property. But when the chips are down caused by its predatory techniques and when it is under bankruptcy it always calls on the public purse to drag it out. If it's to be public purse, then it's got to be public control. (not bureaucratic but grass roots public control). That should be our watchword which finally leads to a rational morality for all.

638<•>observes that it is important to note here <u>that Public Control does not mean a bureaucratic Red Director, Apparatuchuk control</u> as took place in the old Soviet Union. That is the lesson to be learned from recent history.

639<•>observes that thus we create the foundations of a future universal solidarity in morality of all nations and relieve them of the terror of the worst and most forcible weapons of a most brutal barbarism.

640<•>observes that the group of 6 billion, small business people, entrepreneurs, farmers, aboriginal hunters and gatherers and salary and wage workers of the globe alone have no share in the 3E capitalist exploitation; they suffer from it and they fight it and must fight it!

~641< TRACT 22:

642<•>observes that **Class Division And Morality:**
Nomenclature Of The Estate System:

643<•>observes that 3E capital economic development tends to make the circle of society wider within which the social instinct and virtues in order to fight it come into being. This process continues until they finally embrace the whole of humanity. BUT

644<•>observes that at the same time 3E capital creates not only private interests within society which are capable of considerably diminishing the effect of these social instincts.

645<•>observes that capital also creates special domains in society, which it can materially control. Some domains it fosters others it injures at the entire expense of global society.

646<•>observes that the formation of classes is also a product of the division of labor. Of these your observer has noted the following divisions of which he has named (from an historical nexus) the following:-

647<•>observes **Estate Nomenclature**
There are generally two classes in present day society. Bourgeoisie class and the salary and wage labor proletarian class. But it is essential to understand the historical motions of the various domains in society. Each and every one of these domains is capable, given the right conditions, of assuming state power in any given country.

648<•>observes that **First-estate Domain: 1E** Those (in their millions) who live off the avails of Religion.

649<•>observes that **Second-estate Domain: 2E** Those (in their thousands) who live off the avails of hereditary right, (Leasehold; Nobility).

650<•>observes that **Third-estate Domain: 3E** Those (in their hundreds of thousands) who live off the avails of the extraction of value-added. Divided into – Capitalist; who's primary income is from Profit, Stocks, Bonds, Rent, Interest and financial instruments. Bourgeoisie; the wantabe capitalist, the pernicious little 'capitalists' who work for themselves in long extended hours for small incomes and identify themselves as capitalists. They can be further categorized into Small medium and large who's primary income is from shop-keeping and merchandising and the like who hire one, two or more workers. Apparatuchuks;

entrenched, bloated, self-aggrandizing, bureaucratic labor and socialist leaders receiving inordinate salaries and perks, the cause of which twists them to eventually identify with, and collaborate with, Third-estate (Capital) against the very Fifth-estate (salary and wage workers) they are elected to represent. Upon this obscenity (and other historical distortions) the Soviet Union did fail.

651<•>observes that **Fourth-estate Domain: 4E** Those (in their millions) who live off the avails of income from media and entertainment. Divided into Newspapermen (Written word), Electronic wo/men (Electronic word and depiction) Motion Picture wo/men and entertainers of every sort and description including sports figures. Forth-estate Media TV and sports superstars have largely now replaced the religions of yesteryear. Except that the Fourth-estate's internal operations, unlike the First-estate's, through regulation is a public matter.

652<•>observes that **Fifth-estate Domain**: **5E** (in their billions) Salary and Wage Commodity Producing Labor, the producers of all 'value-added.' in this world. Those who live by salary, wages, fees and commissions in the production of commodities etc. giving up the value-added they produce to maintain all the other estates. They include Entrepreneurs, Farmers, Proletariat (Students, temporarily unemployed, the infirm and retired people who are willing to participate but due to their historic condition are unable to do so due to their present circumstance in life). The true leaders of the Fifth-estate bind themselves to a life of study, oratory, leading and educating the salary and wage worker, and rejecting bloated pecuniary reward for their efforts:- 'Supeerio', the hero, in the hour of his peoples' distress, sets his own life lower than that of the totality.

653<•>observes that **Sixth-estate Domain: 6E.** Those (in their millions) who live off the avails of the application of force; policing and military pursuits. (Also Dictators, Terrorists, 'Freedom Fighters' and the like)

654<•>observes that **Seventh-estate Domain: 7E** Those (in their hundreds of millions) who live off the avails of Begging, Prostitution, Hikikomori, Thievery, Spies and gumshoes – all usually referred to as the lumpen-proletariat. The mob etc. Its conditions of life prepare it for the part of a bribed tool of reactionary intrigue.

655<•>observes that It is well to note some things about each estate system of nomenclature. 1) Each such Domain (Estate) in itself is not a monolithic structure but is itself divided into many, hierarchy, fractions, strata, categories, parties, apparatuchuks, and status groups, of the foregoing much has been written by Marxist and non Marxists. 2) The estate system of nomenclature is itself in historical transition. The first Estate in Plato's time was that of the learned or wise. 3) Engels dismissed the Estate system of nomenclature. As follows: Quote "Estates here in the historical sense of the estates of feudalism, estates with definite and limited privileges. The revolution of the bourgeoisie abolished the estates and their privileges. Bourgeois society knows only classes. It was, therefor, absolutely in contradiction with history to describe the proletariat as the 'fourth estate'. (Note by F Engels to the German edition of Value Price and Profit 1885) It is, however, the author's contention that the estate terminology has advanced, is now the subject to dictionary definitions, that the 'fourth-estate' has by definition become the media and the 'fifth-estate' the proletariat. The author has added the sixth and seventh estates. Every 'estate' in this schema is capable of taking state power and many have done so, and are still doing so. The 'estate' 'tool' to facilitate and enlighten about class structure in society is so priceless that the author has maintained and elaborated upon this schema. Further, every 'estate', at the time of this writing, exists in society and none have been abolished by the 3E's emergence and subsequent dominance as Engels contended over a century ago. 4) It is to be noted also that while a person may move from estate to estate in his lifetime the estates themselves are objective and are concrete.

656<•>observes that even an animal society has no homogeneous formation, (it is not a monolithic structure.) In its bosom there are already various groups, which have a different importance in and for the community. Thus it can be seen that the foregoing estate schema, whilst being much more elaborate for mankind, is fully consistent with the natural world in the animal kingdom. BUT, it must be observed that the natural world of the animal kingdom is much simpler because it is not controlled or divided by economic interests.

657<•>observes that in human societies of all description there are handers up of knowledge and in the early verbal stages this sufficed for the beginning of the physical sciences, the mental sciences, mathematics, law, economics political science, and especially history. Thus the elders through vast life experience were then honored as the bearers of a higher, more balanced wisdom.

658<•>observes that verbal heritage soon evolved into hard copy writing and printing and other forms of communication with a continual revolutionizing and storing of almost all experience, which is the characteristic feature of the modern system of production.

659<•>observes that in the past, the 'old' held the key to the rich verbal heritage of the village they lived in. In North America wampum was used as money but it was also a store of knowledge each shell or bead had an historical meaning and the owner of the chain could recollect past occurrences by referring back to his powerful wampum. But with the advent of virtually universal communication the older citizens now, it would appear, only receives sympathy, many no longer enjoy any prestige. There is now no higher praise for an old person than to say that: "still young at heart and still capable, from the standpoint of history, of taking in and refining new ideas."

~660< TRACT 23:

661<•>observes that **Women's Role.**
Gentile Cooperative Societies.
Venture Charities:- The Lowest Stage Of Capitalism.

662<•>observes that technical progress, division of labor, the separation into trades was limited till the last century almost exclusively to men; the household and the woman having been only slightly affected by these changes.

663<•>observes that the separation by sex in the workplace while still at the time of this observation is not perfect, (women have not completely become integrated) there have been great strides over the past century in regard to the emancipation of women in the salary and wage workplace.

664<•>observes that as the separation into different professions and trades advances the social organism becomes more complicated in nature and in the methods of women's cooperation in the fundamental social process.

665<•>observes that social change is quite independent of the will of the individual male and female that are submerged in it and is necessarily determined by the given material conditions of their time. Among these the technical factors, the physical sciences and the mental sciences are again very important in those phases where their development affects the methods of production and distribution.

666<•>observes that differences, not simply between individuals, but also between individual groups within the society existed already in the animal world as we have remarked already, distinctions in the strength, the reputation, perhaps even of the material position of individuals and groups. Such distinctions are natural and will be hardly likely to disappear even in a 'true' socialist society.

667<•>observes that the discovery of tools, the division of labor, and its consequences – economic development – contributes still further to increase such difference or even to create new ones. In any case, they cannot exceed a certain narrow limit, so long as social labor does not yield a surplus over that necessary to the maintenance of the members of the society.

668<•>observes that as long as the foregoing is the case, no idlers, (or in socialist society; no war machines, no shadow governments, no intrigues and no plunder) can be maintained at the cost of society, none can get considerably more in social products than another.

669<•>observes that this does not mean to say that the possibility exists for small jealousies, differences arising between families, different ages, different callings can bring little splits in the community just as well as that between individuals.

670<•>observes that in primitive society, despite beginnings of the division of labor which are to be found there, human society was never more closely bound up together or more in unison than at the time of the primitive gentile cooperative societies which preceded the beginning of class antagonisms.

671<•>observes that things, begin to alter as soon as social labor begins to produce a surplus as a consequence of its tremendous productivity. Under those conditions it now becomes possible for single individuals and professions to secure permanently for themselves a greater share in the social product than others can secure.

672<•>observes that property in the products is narrowly bound up with property in the means of production, who possesses the latter can dispose of the former. Endeavors to monopolize the social surplus by the privileged class produce in it the desire to monopolize and take sole possession of the means of production.

673<•>observes that it becomes possible in the latter stages of this process in a world population of six billion, for five or six hundred individuals to control the globe, in one or two colossus nations, by the process of 3E capital accumulation into a very few hands. Intensification is engendered by the system of capital expropriation in and from the Hinterlands. And to back it all up puppets, intrigue, Quislings, agents-provocateur, shadow governments, threat of, or actual use of sippenhaft and force of arms to demand and receive the tribute of the world into these few hands.

674<•>observes that it should also be noted that in those colossus nations much of the population can be blinded as to the true facts of the problems of the globe and their origin by the deluge of sops that fall upon them. But the sops often have the habit of a periodic drying up.

675<•>observes that it is by this methodology, in a billion different ways that the salary and wage workers and farmers – the mass of the working people of the globe – become disinherited, degraded to slaves, serfs, pauper wage and salary laborers. Thus it has evolved that the strong bond in common property in the means of production and their use in common which held primitive society together is torn asunder. (and this process happened in the twinkling of the eonic eye; 80 (L/L@65) men's lives placed on top of one another)

676<•>observes that and whereas the social distinctions which managed to form themselves in the bosom of primitive society wavered within narrow limits, now the class distinctions which form themselves have evolved into seven broad domains as mentioned.

677<•>observes that these domains (estates) can grow lopsided on the backs of the 5E salary and wage workers, aboriginals, and farmers. This occurs through the technical progress which increases the surplus of the product of the social labor over the amount necessary to the simple maintenance of an environmentally healthy and antagonistically free society.

678<•>observes that in the degree in which this lopsided development and the corresponding expropriation of value-added advances in society the more it becomes antagonistically divided: the class struggle becomes the principal, most central and continuous form of the struggle of the individuals for life in human society.

679<•>observes that many of the factions in this struggle lose sight of the fact that the whole aim of the true direction of the struggle is masked by the many contending parties to it. Each estate having its own agenda, but the one glaring fact that comes out of it all is that the salary and wage worker, farmers and other laborers produce all the value-added that is expropriated and squandered. No other estate but the 5E can produce this value-added.

680<•>observes that also in this antagonistic struggle the social instincts towards society as a whole lose strength. Although eventually over a period of time it becomes evident, even to the intellectually blind, that individuals cannot pursue their own one-off aims at the cost of society and must eventually identify with the commonweal.

681<•>observes that it is specially the exploited, oppressed and uprising classes in whom the class war thus strengthens the social instincts and virtues. Due to the circumstance of being forced into unemployment, brigandage, and war are obliged to put their whole personality into these social instincts with much more intensity and more moral thinking and reasoning than the ruling estates.

682<•>observes that these ruling estates are eventually left in the position of leaving their defenses, the weapons of policing, the weapons of war, the management of their affairs, the weapons of the intellect, to hirelings. Often these hireling are salary and wage workers and have their roots in the 5E itself.

683<•>observes that besides that, however, the ruling estates are often deeply divided internally through the struggles between themselves for the social surplus and over the means of production. The moral thinking of the 3E is a far cry from that of the salary and wage worker and farmer. One of the strongest causes of those kinds of division we have learnt is the battle of destructive competition.

684<•>observes that the factors mentioned above work against the social instincts. But some loam is left to provide the basis for a luxuriant growth of the social instincts and this is evident by the volunteers, the number and amount of contributions to charities that are provided by the fifth estate. (Venture Charities excepted)

685<•>observes that the more that the salary and wage workers of the globe are forced back on their own strength and there ever increasing knowledge, the stronger their members feel in their solidarity against the ruling estates.

~686< **TRACT 24:**

687<•>observes that **The Tenets Of Morality**
Rindlucent Morality Is Relative And Changing Whilst Qernel Morality Is More Stable: Customary Elements: Custom and Convention:

688<•>observes that We have discussed that economic development introduces into the human world a moral thinking that is partially transmitted from the animal world. This brings with it an element of pronounced mutability, in that it gives a varying degree of force to the social instincts, moral thinking, and virtues in different periods of time, and also at the same time it introduces different types of moral thinking in different estates.

689<•>observes that that in addition to the foregoing, over time in several waves, it widens and then again narrows the scope within which the social impulses can take effect. i.e. on one side expanding its influence from the tiny tribe till it embraces the entire humanity. And on the other hand, as economic society evolves, limiting it to certain estates within that entire humanity and so on.

690<•>observes that we may now note the animal instinct in morality that has been handed down for millions and maybe even billions of years is what we refer to as the qernel of morality. We also note as well, that human economic development creates in addition a special moral thinking, which did not exist at all in the animal world. This latter is what we refer to as the rindlucent (R) of morality. The rindlucent and the qernel (Q) go to make up the rindeqern (RQ) that is the total all encompassing morality of an individual person. The rindlucent is the most changeable, since not only its strength but also its contents are subject to far reaching changes as estates evolve appear and disappear. These are the Ethical Codes (written and unwritten) which, operating over time, in the various estates which again, over time, tend to change moral thinking in any one individual depending upon those ethical codes that impact upon it.

691<•>observes that in the animal world we find only strong moral feelings, but no distinct moral precepts which are addressed to the individual. That last assumes that a language has been formed which can describe not only impressions but also things or at least actions.

692<•>observes that we note that this animal is in an existence in a world were there are very few signs compared to the human world. The plethora of human signs, millions upon millions of them, first arise as the development of human common work arises, and as the necessity for common division of labor arises.

693<•>observes that because of the plethora of signs, in the foregoing context, this language in humans then takes on esoteric dimensions by division of the various methods of work and as the physical sciences arise. The esoteric language in the mental sciences have however not been so rich due to the fact that under present 3E control of things the mental sciences have been pushed into a backwater or it is bent for their own purpose.

694<•>observes that in the beginnings of society, where the development is very slow, thousands of years pass under particular social conditions. The social demands in the individual repeat themselves so often, and so regularly that they become a habit, of which the outline need not be laid down in written symbols but is finally 'inherited'. i.e. Passed on upward in hardly any changed content or form from generation to generation.

695<•>observes that we see from the foregoing that certain suggestions suffice to arouse the habit in the ascendants (old term descendants) as well, also for instance the feeling of shame, the habit of covering certain portions of the body whose nude state appears immoral.

696<•>observes that we see extreme throwbacks in many of the 1E religious beliefs today, wherein it is immoral for women even to show their face to the crowd. At the other extreme we have sixth estate bomb droppers who have 'grasped' the moral conviction (under various justifications and even under written ethical codes) that makes it perfectly acceptable to blow these customs apart. The latter's intent is to 'liberate' people from their assets who do not want this kind of 'liberation' of this we can see millions of like examples in history.

697<•>observes that thus we see demands on the individual in society as a whole, which become numerous the more complicated society becomes. At first the 'fixed' demands on the individual in primitive society need no consideration, they have become recognized as moral commands. But as we see from the foregoing these 'fixed' moral commands become more mixed and transitory as society divides into classes and into estates.

698<•>observes that in the Bible (Genesis 38:10) Onan is killed by Jehovah, because he allowed his spermatozoa to fall to the ground instead of attending to his duty and having intercourse with the wife of his dead brother, so as to raise up children. We may infer from this, that in that society, the society could only exist by having a critical mass of people for its survival and continuation. The ethical codes to bolster such commands could only, for this reason, become customs because they met deep-lying, ever returning social needs. (But what of the society that has an overabundance of children:- how does that now affect the promulgation of ethical codes and thus impact on the rindlucent (R) in moral thinking?)

~699< TRACT 25:

700<•>observes that The Dual Content In Moral Thinking.
The Practical Roots Of Morality. (But Duty First)

701<•>observes that a simple custom cannot explain the force of the feeling of duty, which often shows itself more powerful than all the instincts of self-preservation.

702<•>observes that the customary element in social moral thinking only has the effect that certain rules are forthwith recognized by 'all' as truisms. But individual social instincts may override some moral thinking precept in an individual which may compel the performance of an action or duty by that individual that lies outside this moral thinking.

703<•>observes that the force of the social instincts can bring it about that a moral thinking person in one context will almost never allow that thinking to interfere with peer pressure thinking and may even prefer death itself to that which the person regards as shame in other contexts.

704<•>observes that thus we see (even fleetingly) new conventions, fashion, custom, once stamped upon the peer group take its effect upon the individual. (take for example all the that twisted moral thinking of persons in Nazi Germany who killed off all the salary and wage working population of one group in particular in Europe, any person in that group who could see ahead and who could pay for it escaped, thus many in the 3E and in this group escaped the horror, whilst the 5E people in this group of population was annihilated. This annihilation is a blot on the record of the majority of 5E Germans who did not come to their comrades rescue. (An aside; sitting on this philosopher's stone far from the fray and the terrible social milieu of the times it is easy to criticize without the fear of immediate arrest torture and death. Your humble author understands the dilemma faced by all parties in this terrible blot on human history.)

705<•>observes that We see emerging from this state of affairs a dichotomy in moral thinking and as will be explained later this dichotomy is made up of two elements. 1) the 'bedrock' of social instinct - the qernel and 2) the ever shifting social mores of the times and the estates - the rindlucent.

706<•>observes that now we have multibillionaire group of people today, although the rulers under a regime that claims to be highly 'Moral' under their god they have no compunction in carrying out odious practices under cover of various masks (Through Deception We Will Win) that override social moral thinking. The rindlucent has almost completely snuffed out the qernel in this group. Thus we see, in this 3E, blatant distortions in the progress to a better world. And we see now the 5E, in this special group, except for a few brave individuals, almost paralyzed by their own 3E. But mankind is a social animal and these problems will be overcome. The salary and wage working population in this too, will eventually take the controlling hand and bring a new social instinct morality to bear upon this problem.) Similarly in the opposing group their 5E lays dormant whilst bombers emanate from their environs. On deeper examination one will find property relations at the heart of this problem. The problem of so called redeamed and unredeamed lands could be made the subject of a whole moral study in itself. (Your philosopher understands the danger he brings himself under by expressing these observations but what is the use of a moral dissertation without concrete examples?)

707<•>observes that some 'moralists' carry the idea that 'moral regulation in individuals' is simple custom and described them as simple conventional fashions. They base this on the phenomenon that every nation, each class, and each estate has its own particular moral conceptions which often stand in absolute contradiction to each other, that consequently absolute concrete universal moral thinking has no validity.

708<•>observes that it is concluded from that that morality is only a changing fashion, which only the thoughtless philistine crowd respect, but which the superman can and must raise himself above as a thing that appertains only to the ordinary herd.

709<•>observes that the social instincts are not conventional, but something deeply grounded in human nature, the nature of man as a social animal; even the universal moral tenets are nothing arbitrary but arise from social needs.

710<•>observes that it is certainly not possible in every case to fix the connection between certain moral conceptions and the social relations from which they arise. The individual takes moral precepts from one's social surroundings without being aware of their social causes.

711<•>observes that Moral thinking becomes a habit to people, and appears to them as an emanation of their own spiritual being, given a priori to them, without any practical root.

712<•>observes that only can the mental sciences, with proper scientific investigation, gradually show up a series of cases elucidating the relations between particular forms of society. Investigation will show up the differences between their estates, and their particular moral precepts. Until then these investigations remain hog-tied and much work remains to bring them the light of day.

713<•>observes that social forms, from which moral principles arise and which still hold good at a later period, often lie far back, in very primitive times. Besides that, to understand the connection between ethical codes, civil & criminal law and moral thinking, not only the social need must be understood which called them forth, but also the peculiar thought and productive methods of the society their connection to the estate which created those moral precepts.

714<•>observes that every method of production is connected not only with particular tools and particular social relations, but also with the particular content of knowledge, with particular powers of intelligence, a particular view of cause and effect, a particular logic, in short a particular form of thought. To understand earlier modes of thought is, however, uncommonly difficult given the overriding supremacy in funding of the physical sciences over that of the mental sciences at the time of this observation.

715<•>observes that the connection between the tenets of moral thinking and social needs has been discussed above and practical examples given, if we accept these foregoing observations then we must accept them as a general rules. If these connections indeed exist then, if there is to be an alteration in society, this must necessitate an alteration in any moral thinking precepts, especially those in the rindlucent envelope.

716<•>observes that Moral thinking changes are nothing strange, it would be much more bizarre that if with the change of cause the effect itself did not also change. These changes in moral thinking are necessary because every form of society requires certain moral precepts suited to its condition. How diverse and changing is moral thinking is well known. Hence we give from Karl Kautsky's paper one example that suffices to illustrate a morality differing from our time and in late 19th century European thought.

717<•>observes that the quote is given unchanged from the electronic version. (except for numbering and for breaking up into alphabetical paragraphs.) It might be also noted that your observer has spent many years working in the Arctic Environment with the native peoples during oil exploration. And your observer has a good feel of what is indeed in the quote.

718<•>observes that Start Quote:-
AAA 'Fridtjof Nansen gives us in the tenth chapter of his "Esquimaux Life" a very fascinating picture of Esquimaux morals, from which I take a few passages.
One of the most beautiful and marked features in the character of the Esquimaux is certainly their honorableness. ... For the Esquimaux it has especial value that he should be able to rely on his fellows and neighbors.

BBB 'In order, however, that his mutual confidence, without which common action in the battle for life is impossible, should continue, it is necessary that he should act honorably to others as well... For the same reasons they do not lie readily to each other, especially not the men.

CCC 'A touching proof of that is the following incident related by Dalager: "If they have to describe to each other anything, they are very careful not to paint it more beautiful than it deserves. Nay, if any one wants to buy anything which he has not seen, the seller describes the thing, however much he may wish to sell it, always as something less good than it is.

DDD 'The morals of advertising are unknown to the Esquimaux as yet. Certainly that applies to their intercourse with each other. To strangers they are less strict.
"Fisticuff fights and that sort of ruffianism is not to be seen among them. Murder is also a great rarity and where it happens is not a consequence of economic quarrels but of love affairs. They consider it dreadful to kill a fellowman.

EEE 'War is hence quite incomprehensible to them and abominable; their language has not even a word for it, and soldiers and officers who have been trained to the calling of killing people are to them simply butchers of men.

FFF 'Those of our commandments, against which the Greenlanders oftenest sin is the sixth. Virtue and chastity do not stand in great esteem in Greenland. Many look on it (on the west coast) as no great shame if an unmarried girl has children. While we were in Gothhael, two girls there were pregnant, but they in no way concealed it, and seemed from this evident proof that they were not looked down upon to be almost proud. Gut even of the east coast Helm says that it is there no shame if an unmarried girl has children."

GGG 'Egede also says that the women look on it as an especial bit of luck and a great honor, to have intimate connection with an Angekok, that is, one of their Prophets, and wise men, and adds—even many men are very glad and will pay the Angekok for sleeping with their wives, especially if they themselves cannot have children by them.

HHH 'The freedom of Esquimaux women is thus very different to that appertaining to the Germanic women. The reason certainly lies in the fact that while the maintenance of the inheritance, of the race and family has always played a great role by the Germans, this has no importance for the Esquimaux because he has nothing to inherit, and for him the main point is to have children...

III 'We naturally look on this morality as bad. With that, however, is by no means said that it is so for the Esquimaux. We must absolutely guard against condemning from our standpoint views which have been developed through many generations and after long experience by a people, however much they contradict our own.

JJJ 'The views of good and bad are namely extraordinarily different on this earth. As an example I might quote, that when this Egede had spoken to an Esquimaux girl of love of God and our neighbor, she said 'I have proved that I love my neighbor because an old woman who was ill and could not die, begged me that I would take her for a payment to the steep cliff, from which those always are thrown who can no more live. But because I love my people, I took her there for nothing and threw her down from the rocks.'"

KKK 'Egede thought that this was a bad act, and said that she had murdered a human being. She said no, she had had great sympathy with the old woman and had wept as she fell. Are we to call this a good or bad act?" We have seen that the necessity of killing old and sick members of society very easily arises with a limited food supply and this killing becomes then signalized as a moral act.

LLL 'When the same Egede at another time said that God punished the wicked, an Esquimaux said to him he also belonged to those who punished the wicked, since he had killed three old women who were witches.

MMM 'The same difference in the conception of good and bad is to be seen in regard to the sixth commandment. The Esquimaux puts the commandment: 'Be fruitful and multiply' higher than chastity. He has every reason for that as his race is by nature less prolific.

NNN 'Finally a quotation from a letter sent by a converted Esquimaux to Paul Egede who worked in the middle of the 18th century in Greenland as a missionary and found the Esquimaux morals almost untouched by European influence. This Esquimaux had heard of the colonial wars, between the English and Dutch and expresses his horror over this inhumanity.

OOO 'If we have only so much food that we can satisfy our hunger and get enough skins to keep out the cold, we are contented, and thou thyself knowest that we let the next day look after itself. We would not on that account carry war on the sea, even if we could. We can say the sea that washes our coasts belongs to us as well as the walruses, whales, seals and salmon swimming in it; yet we have no objection when others take what they require from the great supply, as they require it.

PPP 'We have the great luck not to be so greedy by nature as them....It is really astonishing, my dear Paul! Your people know that there is a God, the ruler and guider of all things, that after this life they will be either happy or damned, according as they have behaved themselves, and yet they live as though they had been ordered to be wicked, and as if sin would bring them advantage and honor.

QQQ 'My countrymen know nothing either of God or Devil and yet they behave respectably, deal kindly and as friends with each other, tell each other everything and create their means of subsistence in common.

RRR 'It is the opposition of the morality of a primitive communism to capitalist morality which appears here. But still another distinction arises. In the Eskimo society the theory and practice of morality agree with one another; in cultivated society a division exists between the two. (RER The reason for that we will soon learn.)

End Quote

719<•>observes that your observer has quoted the above for he knows by personal experience of its validity, and it is especially important in the face of the vanishing hunting and gathering societies that this, once again, be brought to attention.

~720< TRACT 26:

721<•>observes that The System Of Production And Its Superstructure.

722<•>observes that Moral thinking alters with the society and with the various estates in it, yet not uninterruptedly and not in the same fashion and degree as social needs. It become promptly recognized and felt as rules of conduct because it has become habit. Once they are taken root for a relatively long period of time morals lead an independent life, while

Tsunami One   Moral Organon.

technical progress advances, developments in the methods of production, and thus the transformation in social needs go on.

723<•>observes that The consequence of social development are an anathema to the 3E who are stuck in their private ownership global market system as being the ne plus ultra in the advancement in mankind. Thus 3E apologist philosophers are stuck in Kantian moral thought, they have not even advanced to Hegel, let alone Marx. These third estate philosophers like to smuggle in the spirit as an independent driving power in the development of the social organism.

724<•>observes that like other ideological factors morality can also advance economic and social development, in this lies its social importance. Moral thinking is adapted to the society which creates it the smoother it reacts on social life the better. Since certain social rules arise from certain social needs then in tandem with them morality renders social cooperation easier.

725<•>observes that when moral thinking begins to lead a life independent of society, and if such morality is no longer controlled by society, reaction of the individual (with such a morality) to society takes on another character. The further such a morality is cut off from society any development in it now becomes purely ideological.

726<•>observes that as soon as moral thinking is separated from the influence of the outer world it can no more create new objective conceptions, but only rearrange those already attained so that the contradictions between society and morality become highly subjective ones. Such contradictions cannot be resolved outside of society, especially economic society.

727<•>observes that getting rid of contradictions, winning a unitary conception in moral thinking, solving all problems which arise in the real world from contradictions, that is the work of the thinking essence laboring on objective societal problems.

728<•>observes that in the thinking essence of the objective world can, however, only remain in an intellectual superstructure already set up. Thinking essence which is not objectively based cannot raise something superior to itself.

729<•>observes that only with the appearance of new objective contradictions, new problems can new development in moral thinking take place. Human essence and thinking does not, however, create contradictions from out of its own inner being. Contradictions are produced in moral thinking only by the influence of objective contradictions in the surrounding world upon it.

730<•>observes that if for any reason moral thinking grows independent of the objective world, such thinking ceases to be of any consequence in social progress and may even damage such progress. In this case the rindlucent portion of moral thinking ossifies, become a conservative element – an obstacle to progress.

731<•>observes that the foregoing can happen in human society which is impossible in the animal world. Morality under these conditions can become instead of an indispensable social bond, the means of an intolerable restraint on social life. This indeed becomes the case when we are influenced by anti-materialist moralists.

732<•>observes that the contradictions between distinct moral principles and distinct social needs can arrive at a certain development in primitive society, but such contradictions become very deep with the appearance of class antagonisms.

733<•>observes that in a society without classes, the adherence to particular moral principles is only a matter of habit, their disappearance only requires that the force of habit be overcome.

734<•>observes that in distinction to the above once class antagonisms enters the fray maintenance of a particular way of moral thinking becomes a matter of interest, often of the very powerful in the ruling classes and their estates.

735<•>observes that with the advent of 'modern times', now appear on the stage weapons of force, of physical compulsion, to keep down the exploited classes. And this means also of compulsion placed at "morality's," gate in order to secure obedience to moral thinking which are in the interest of the ruling estates.

736<•>observes that any classless, estate-less, society needs no such compulsory weaponry. In such a society, the social instincts may not always suffice to achieve the observance by every individual of every item on the ethical code. But the strength of social instinct on moral thinking is very different in such a society as a whole as well as in the various individuals that make up that society.

737<•>observes that even if we leave weaponry out of the equation public opinion created by a 4E press controlled by 3E capital works in a class society as an efficient weapon of policy to secure the public obedience to 3E ethical codes. The individual is so weak compared to the press, that he has little strength to defy their 'unanimous' voice.

738<•>observes that this has so crushing an effect, that it needs no further means of compulsion or punishment, to secure the course of social life laid out for it by the 3E. But then come those powerful contradictions again - unemployment, small capital gobbled up by large (the struggle of capitals), war, wastage and ecological disaster. The cover-ups, half-truths, intrigue and hypocrisy cannot live on forever.

739<•>observes that in 3E controlled society weaponry is at first turned outward to the external enemy (competition), then as conditions worsen internally this weaponry is turned inward against its own people. The 6E controlled by the 3E even brings the police state down to the abhorrent level of state surveillance. Thus are files made upon the persons of three year old children, (see Calgary Herald 01 11 25 pA14) this together with 'state sanctioned assassinations' and 'Venture Charity' is carried out in countries at the lowest stage of capitalism. Where is the 5E morality in all of that?

740<•>observes that as these conditions deepen and worsen prison, poverty, suicide and death are preferred by people to shame at the hands of the 3E. These conditions cannot live on if human kind is to flourish.

741<•>observes that even public opinion fails where it is other than the individual against society but 3E against 3E. Thus the ruling class must apply other weapons of compulsion if they are to prevail, means of superior physical or economic might, of superior organization, of superior intelligence or even politically uncontrollable shadow governments and intrigue.

742<•>observes that soldiers, police, and judges are joined to the Priests, Imams, Rabbis etc. as an additional means of 3E dominion over all other Estates in the 21st century,. And it is just the ecclesiastical organization of the 1E to whom the special tasks fall of conserving 'traditional' morality.

743<•>observes that this connection between religion and morality was first achieved as new religions appear at the time of decay of primitive communism and the gentile society. Now in modern times the 1E in the 21st century stand in strong opposition to the ancient nature religions and mythology, whose roots reach back to the old classless period, and which then knew no special priest caste.

744<•>observes that in the old religions Divinity and Ethics (thus morality) are not joined together. One god religions on the other hand grow on the soil of that philosophy in which ethic codes and belief in God are most intimately bound-up together one factor supporting the other.

745<•>observes that now we have religion and ethic codes intimately bound together as a instrument, even a weapon, to maintain 3E rule. But as they saying goes, "Times they are a changin'" as humankind advances upward along the coil of progress then new, other than sigma metaphysical religious, ethical codes are emerging.

746<•>observes that the qernel of morality burns ever steadily on. Yet almost every salary and wage 5E organization, union, association, advocacy group, government and non governmental organization has devised its own ethics code, The combined rindlucent in those mentioned all lead to a new, and hopefully better, moral thinking in all of mankind.

747<•>observes that certainly moral thinking, ethic codes, civil & criminal law are a product of the social nature of mankind. In them there is no room for the individualistic loner, forlorn, blowing-things-up, superman creed of the 3E and which is so much espoused by 4E media and often carried out by the 6E. The foregoing is especially true in the film industry which profits from young people's exuberance and inexperience. The mayhem that many of them invent for profit leads to degradation of the social instinct and a twisting of the young people's rindlucent side and of humankind's moral thinking in general.

748<•>observes that certainly the moral thinking of the time is the product of particular social needs; assuredly old time moral thinking and understanding, old time social needs have everything to do with religion. But in the modern world, based on faith alone, religion now has failed us.

749<•>observes that that mayhem is the kind of moral thinking which must be maintained in the interests of the ruling 3E, that requires 1E religion and the entire ecclesiastical organism for its support.

~750< TRACT 27:

751<•>observes that **The Acid Test Of Morality:**
We Now Put Under The Scope Morality And Immorality

752<•>observes that as mankind advance in its fits, starts and even sometimes regression so do the contradictions become greater between the minority ruling party's morals in regard to society, economics life, action, and moral thinking and that of its overwhelming majority.

753<•>observes that the great brake on development of a better world is outlived moral thinking, and ethical codes and standards that remain in force, while economic developments advance and create new social needs which demand new ethical standards.

754<•>observes that we need to scientifically examine and throw out those old standards which contain no social instinct factor in them. We need then to put in their place new ethical codes which do contain social instinct factors, all this in order to sustain continued human growth and development.

755<•>observes that it is well to note in this regard that we now have billionaires and multimillionaires, and whole state apparatuses which are able to purchase the tools of destruction, killing off salary and wage workers. Killing off farmers, aboriginal peoples and small business people the globe over, and the justification of all this is backed up by the kind of anti-social instinct in moral thinking and ethical codes emanating from 3E requirements for ever increasing profits, market-share destructive competition and other antagonisms.

756<•>observes that these antagonistic contradictions show themselves in different estates and in different manners. The 3E, whose existence rests on old social conditions, cling firmly to the old morality, not only in theory, but in practice.

757<•>observes that still even the 3E rule over all other estates cannot escape the influence and reality of new social conditions brought about by the operations of the 3E itself.

758<•>observes that individuals in estates, and estates as a whole, more often than not transgress secretly against the moral thinking and ethical codes, which they publicly preach. We then have, especially in the decaying estate, in its blatant hypocrisy, a deep-rooted cynicism rising up in the general global population.

759<•>observes that the power of the social instinct almost disappears in this decaying estate in consequence of the growth of contending and antagonistic private interests. Such decay is further exacerbated by allowing apologists, Quislings and hirelings to be proxies, agents, that partially mask their own direct action. Actions, that if broadly known by the public, would pose a danger to their operations. We can sum up the last few observations as 'the growth in immorality'.

760<•>observes that idealist moralists and theologians conclude from the foregoing, that if there are entire immoral classes, estates, and societies there must be moral thinking and ethical codes eternal and independent of human beings, their economic life, and even of 'time & space' itself. There must be, according to them, a standard independent of the changing social conditions on which people can measure the morals of every society and class and estate that ever was – or will ever be.

761<•>observes that in order to refute the foregoing idealist position we observe that social instinct is that element in human moral thinking which is much older than the more recent changing social and economic relations. It is just that very fact (social instinct) alone which gives human morality its common ground with the animal kingdom.

762<•>observes that what, however, is specifically human in morality? The answer is – It is the ethical codes (written and unwritten) which are subject to continual change and thus coupled with the <u>almost</u> solid bedrock of social instinct bring in their wake, advanced renewal in moral thinking. (And this renewal can be regressive just as well as progressive.)

763<•>observes that that does not go to say that a class, estate, or social group cannot be immoral. It proves simply that so far at least as ethical codes and moral thinking are concerned, immorality is a relative idea. Mankind has inherited social impulses and virtue from its beginning as a social animal and it is that only the lack of social impulses and virtues, in a person or an estate, and no other thing that can be regarded as an absolute concrete immorality.

764<•>observes that if we take any civil or criminal law and/or ethical code that lacks the essence of social impulses, instincts, and virtues then those laws and codes are a very big divergence from a very distinct standard. In other words every law and ethical code must contain at least some pith of social impulse, instinct and virtue for it to be really moral, and a strict adherence to this concept in making laws and codes will, eventually show up in peoples practice and in their moral thinking. (the inner qernel must be kept alight, no matter how its surrounding rindlucent may be blown about for a code or law to be brought into the realm of validity.)

765<•>observes that in other words any law or code that does not contain this pith of social instinct will eventually peter out and will be ignored or ridiculed in people's practice, thus over time their moral thinking will eventually diverge from such virtue-less law or code. And this despite how vigorously the powers of regression try to shoe horn people into prison.

766<•>observes that thus ethical codes and civil & criminal laws must contain two aspects **1)** the solid bedrock of social instinct, and built upon that, the ever changing **2)** mores of a specific society (or an estate) as a whole.

767<•>observes that when viewed from the foregoing aspect we can see that there is great difficulty, for all except the individuals that make up the producing 5E, to meet such high ethical social standards. (whether they have met them or not depends on the historical circumstance they find themselves in.)

768<•>observes that as an example: it is thus nonsense to declare particular moral principles of any individual, people, class or estate, to be immoral simply because they contradict our present day moral thinking. Only when the particular codes or laws under comparison are subjected to the acid test of social impulse, instinct or virtue and found lacking therein can that particular code or law be declared immoral.

769<•>observes that your observer must make a point here in regard to 4E blood and guts films in particular. These filmmakers like to say it is only society they are portraying but this will not stand the acid test as outlined above – it is only labor tokens (money) they desire the social impulse is completely missing in many of these films. So from this point of view they are highly immoral. (Especially when they are viewed by the young and innocent but I digress to make a point, still such a point can be expanded scientifically in the effort to understand a million different situations, laws and codes.)

770<•>observes that it is well to note that under this acid test that the particular mores in any society, as long as they do not contradict the social instinct and while they my have very significant investigative interest, they have no place in the declaration or morality or immorality.

Tsunami One   Moral Organon.

~771< TRACT 28:

772<•>observes that **The Moral Ideal.**
Understanding The Different Classes Of Property And Their Connection To The Moral Ideal

773<•>observes that Growing contradiction between changing social conditions and stagnating and regressive moral thinking of the 3E and its lackey estates, which goes hand in hand with a weakening of the social instincts tends to a growing immorality in those estates and in their growing hypocrisy. This fact shows up as cynicism in the population as a whole.

774<•>observes that 3E interests which created the ruling morality and that were once, many moons ago, an almost complete progressive force in society are now, in the 21st century, as good as an outright antagonism to social foundations.

775<•>observes that in an upward spiral comes the salary and wage workers, aboriginal peoples and farmers of the globe with a new moral ideal, which grows ever bolder and the more they are hobbled, shackled, killed, terrorized and pauperized they win in new moral strength.

776<•>observes that at the same time the power of the social instincts in the 5E are being especially developed and strengthened by means of the struggle between estates. And in that struggle they are armed with the daring new moral ideal based on social instincts and other aspects of their ethical code.

777<•>observes that at the same time the same evolution produces increasing immorality in the 'neo ancient regime', the 3E in the case of the 21st century, just as increasing immorality had done in the 2E of Holland, England, France, and Russia commencing over four hundred years previously. In those times past it was only counties, countries or regions involved now 3E immorality is global in scope.

778<•>observes that the 3E increase in immorality produces in the 5E's intellectuals a phenomena which we can only call Ethical Code Idealism which is not, however, to be confused with philosophical idealism. (see below)

779<•>observes that the 5E intellectuals are inclined to philosophical materialism which the declining first, second and third estates oppose from the moment that they become conscious that reality, by their own depredations, has spoken the sentence of death over them.

780<•>observes that these regressive estates believe that they are there for all time and have divine right. They feel that they can only look for salvation by the infusion in the belief in supernatural powers from on high divine or from on earth ethical codes into the global mass of the 5E salary and wage workers.

781<•>observes that the content of the new ethical codes is not always very clear. It does not emerge from any scientific knowledge of the social organism, which is often quite unknown to the authors of the ideal. But it comes from a deep social need, a burning desire, an energetic will, for something other than the existing, for something which is the opposite of the existing. And thus also this moral ideal is fundamentally only something purely negative, nothing more than opposition to the existing hypocrisy.

782<•>observes that thus we see in the bowels of this historical negative aspect of morality a progressive element – an idealism that is progressive as opposed to philosophical idealism which is purely regressive in nature.

783<•>observes that as long as class rule has existed, moral thinking of the ruling class has been imposed upon the under class and this thinking is guarded and enhanced by propaganda and especially in the 20th and 21st century by the rise and power of the 4E press.

784<•>observes that thus we see that wherever in history a sharp class antagonism has been formed, slavery, serfdom, wage and salary inequality, exploitation, the moral ideal of the uprising classes has always taken on the same appearance, which the participants in French Revolution summed up with the words, Freedom!, Equality!, and Fraternity!.

785<•>observes that it would seem as if this Freedom! Equality! Fraternity! is an ideal implanted in every human breast independent of time and space, as if this were the task of the human race to strive from its beginning for the same moral ideal, as if the evolution of mankind consisted in the gradual approach to this ideal which continually looms before them.

786<•>observes that if we examine this more closely, we find that the agreement of the moral ideal – Freedom! Equality! Fraternity! – in the various historical epochs is there – but behind it there lie great differences of social aims. Social aims which correspond to the differences in the social, technical and economic situations in the various epochs in humankind's advancement up the coil of progress.

787<•>observes that if we take some of the major epochs and compare Christianity, the French Revolution, the Socialist movement today, we find that Liberty and Equality for each of them meant something quite different according to their attitude towards property and production.

788<•>observes that the primitive Christians demand equality of property in that they ask for its equal division for purpose of consumption by all. They want emancipation from slavery and they get, as time progresses, Feudalism which becomes a step above it. Under 'Freedom' they want an emancipation from all work. They imagine heaven and paradise as the condition as is lived by their masters, who neither toil nor spin and yet enjoy their life.

789<•>observes that the French Revolution again understood by equality, the equality of property rights. 'Private property' it declared to be sacred. And true freedom was for it the freedom to apply property in economic life, according to pleasure in the most profitable manner.

790<•>observes that we must distinguish between the various types of property. There are, in essence, four
BREEDS OF PROPERTY

1) Epsilon Property i.e. Non productive publicly-owned-property i.e. parks, city hall, lakes, rivers and so on.

5) Iota Property:- personal-private-property i.e. socks, book, house and car etc.

3a) Kappa (p) Property:- productive privately-owned-property used as the means of production to create profit and all other forms of value-added i.e. Privately owned factory or utility.

3b) Kappa (n) Property:- non-productive for-profit property i.e. Interest, Rent and Lease.

4) Mu Property:- productive publicly-owned-property used as the means of production to create value-added. i.e. Publicly owned factory or utility.

791<•>observes that the Socialists neither swears by kappa private property nor does it demand its division. It demands its socialization, it demand that Kappa property be converted into Mu property and the EQUALITY which it strives for is the equal rights of all the globe in the products of social labor.

792<•>observes that they strive for a property right wherein all produce their moral equal share and subsequently take part in consumption of their moral equal share.

793<•>observes that we have in society today in the 21st century a move afoot to privatize public property: that is to move it from Mu property to Kappa property. But what this amounts to is privatization of profits and socialization of losses. Where is the social instinct morality in all of that?

794<•>observes that when things are going well – then take the profit, when things turn sour due, to antagonistic competition and even war then – lay those losses off on the tax payer – socialize the losses. This amounts to - let the people pick up the tab in unemployment and tax allocation of huge sums to bail out private investors and pay for war ventures. Where, one might ask, is the social instinct morality in all of that?

795<•>observes that imbued as they are with 3E morality of the 'every person for themselves' 3E politicians, have a gut feeling that the foregoing is really outside of social instinct morality. They cover up the foul deeds by using all kind of euphemisms to fool the public and even themselves. i.e. deregulation = privatization. War preparations = defense.

Tsunami One   Moral Organon.

Money labor token manipulations = fiscal policy and so on. Where is the social instinct morality in all of that?

796<•>observes that These same politicians create laws to hamper salary and wage workers at every turn. i.e. taking from their cheques unemployment premiums, compensation premiums and health premiums which at every turn they frustrate the 5E in thousands of ways from ever collecting upon any meaningful 'insurance' from the premiums the 5E in their billions have paid into such funds. Where is the social instinct morality in all of that?

797<•>observes that now then one might ask what's wrong with privatization – well privatization in the hinterlands of the world enriches the colossUS by a methodology to be later explained. And where is the social instinct morality in all of that?

798<•>observes that the social freedom which true socialists asks for is freedom from the expropriation of the value-added which they produce and that is used in a billion misadventures. This value-added (of which profit is only a small part) amounts to the forced expropriation of tremendous sums of labor-tokens, sums undreamed of by 3E apologist economists who think that this is a natural infinite historical process. Value-added goes to taxes for war machines, profits, competitive infighting, bank interest, dividends, support of terrorist groups and every other imaginable 'cost of doing business' in the twisted antagonistic world of 3E necessity and making.

799<•>observes that Mu property run by the salary and wage worker themselves means that the necessary labor to operate society which cannot be 'free'. But must be socially ethically and morally regulated so that work and the impact on the environment can be reduced to a minimum while at the

498

same time enriching the group of 6 Billion and the flora and fauna of this globe.

800<•>observes that the foregoing leaves, for all, sufficient time for freedom. Free artistic and scientific activity. Free enjoyment of life. Freedom from antagonistic competition. Freedom from war. Freedom from anxiety. Freedom from worry about health. Freedom to ensure that all society's undertakings are ecologically sound. Freedom from the profit motive. Social freedom – that is what is meant by real freedom. But with all these freedoms come moral obligations too.

801<•>observes that thus it can be seen that the same moral ideal of Freedom and Equality can embrace very different social ideals. The external agreement of the moral ideals of different times and countries is, however, not the result of a moral law independent of time and space, which as some would have it, springs up in mankind from a supernatural world.

802<•>observes that but that the external agreement of moral ideals of different countries, and now the globe, are only the consequence of the fact that despite all social differences the main outlines of class rule in human society have always been – to exploit and despoil.

803<•>observes that even so a new moral thinking ideal cannot simply arise from class antagonism. Even within the 3E there are thinking individuals who develop only loose ties with this estate socially and sit there with no class consciousness whatsoever but they see antagonism all around them.

804<•>observes that with that, however, they possess strong social instincts and virtues, which makes them hate all hypocrisy and cynicism, and they have a great intelligence which shows them clearly the contradiction between the traditional ethical codes and moral thinking and the crying social needs of the day.

805<•>observes that such individuals are bound also to come to the point of lifting up the new moral ideal. But whether this new ideal obtains social force, depends upon whether they result in 5E ideals or not. Only the motive power of the class struggle can work fruitfully on moral ideals.

806<•>observes that not the single-handed endeavors of enlightened people, but only the struggle between Estates possesses the strength to develop society farther. And to meet the needs of the higher refinement in the mental sciences, philosophy, history, economics, law and in the enlightened refinements in the people engaged in various methods of production and distribution.

807<•>observes that many now think that this new moral ideal cannot ever be reached. But moral ideals are nothing more than the complex of wishes and endeavors which are called forth by the opposition to the existing state of affairs.

808<•>observes that the motor power of the class struggle is a means to collect the forces of the salary and wage workers, the aboriginal, the farmers and small businessmen pushed into bankruptcy – the 5E and its allies in the struggle against the existing hypocrisy, and to spur them on. This combination together with the intellectuals is a powerful lever in overturning of existing extremely rotten state of global affairs.

809<•>observes that the new social conditions, which are coming into place of the old, do not only depend on the form of the moral ideal but also come from changing material and technical conditions. The natural milieu, the nature of its neighbors and predecessors of the existing society, and the complete and utter contempt with which the 3E and their shadowy shadow governments hold global society up to ransom. But they must now be well aware that society is better educated and most people see through the smoke and mirrors of immoral deceptions.

810<•>observes that we have seen above how, in the 'beginning', the 3E held the moral high ground when it was in opposition to 2E. We have examined how the dichotomy between moral theory and practice arises, so that now morality appears as thing which everybody demands but nobody practices – something which is beyond anyone's individual strength – morality, it seems to many, is only given to supernatural powers to carry out.

811<•>observes that now we see in the rise of the educated salary and wage worker of the 5E a different kind of antagonism arising between moral theory and practice; the antagonism between the moral ideal and the reality created by a social revolution. For a period of time during this revolution morality appears as something which everybody strives for but nobody can obtain – and it seems to them for a while that it is in fact unattainable for earthly beings.

812<•>observes that but from this heavenly height morality is drawn down to earth by the facts of life and it is there analyzed by people having the mental sciences and the tools of dialectical and historical materialism at hand.

813<•>observes that we have made acquaintance with social instinct morality's animal origin and see how its changes in human society are conditioned by the changes in mores which people and their ethical codes (written and Unwritten) are going through, driven ever on by developments in technology.

Tsunami One   Moral Organon.

814<•>observes that we see now how the new moral ideal is revealed in its purely negative character as opposition to the existing moral order. And the importance is recognized that the motor power of the class struggle as a means to collect and inspire the forces of the 5E which will change the negative into the positive in moral ideals.

815<•>observes that at the same time, however, the 3E's moral ideas by negativity alone will not give the 5E power to direct its own political policy.

816<•>observes that it is not only from the 5E's own moral ideals, but from the distinct material conditions of salary and wage workers, farmers, small businessmen's, and aboriginal people's lives and the deplorable economic conditions going on in the globe, does the policy depend.

817<•>observes that we ask, upon which road will society take to clear the swamp, get rid of the all those pesky muscats, in its efforts to further social development? What was once largely unconscious morality must become, in the hands of the 5E, a conscious social instinct morality.

818<•>observes that there has been a weak conscious directing social knowledge at hand, in the last four hundred years, but it worked unsystematically and inconsistently in the formation of social aims.

819<•>observes that it is the materialist conception of history which first deposed morality as the sole or even the major directing factor of social evolution. And it has taught us to deduce our social aims almost solely from the knowledge of its material foundations and in the understanding of the struggle of opposites.

820<•>observes that having said that the 5E's ethical codes and moral thinking – its moral ideals – will never be deprived of its influence in society; this influence will simply be given its proper dimensions.

821<•>observes that the social instinct coupled with the mores and ethical codes of revolutionary times give the salary and wage worker of the 5E through their unions, associations, and advocacy groups a new moral ideal. Such a new moral ideal is not an aim but a force or a weapon in the social struggle for life.

822<•>observes that no quasi collaborative social democracy but real Social Democracies as organizations of salary and wage workers in their struggle with the 3E cannot do without the moral ideal, the moral indignation against smoke and mirrors and intrigue and exploitation and class rule.

823<•>observes that the student always endeavors, and rightly, to put the moral ideal in proper perspective this is necessary because moral thinking, must be stripped into its constituent parts – **1)** social instinct (qernel) and **2)** mores of the times (rindlucent). Unless the student is not careful in this matter it becomes a source of error in science. Thus once stripped and studied they then can be modified and brought together once again to form a true ethical code and true civil & criminal laws that will reflect the lofty moral thinking for the group of 6 Billion.

824<•>observes that the physical sciences of the future will not be able to reject social instinct in moral thinking. But it must be able, in its rigor to reject the mores of the times. (Therein lay the moral dilemma of the atomic physicists for example or nowadays the geneticists.)

825<•>observes that but the mental sciences must take full account of the two aspects that make up moral thinking and incorporate them into its science in a meaningful way. (Thus rindlucent plus qernel must equal an all rounded rindqern.)

826<•>observes that all the same even in winning and making known physical scientific knowledge morality is not got rid of. New scientific knowledge implies often the upsetting of traditional and deeply rooted conceptions which had grown to a fixed habit.

827<•>observes that in societies which include class antagonisms new scientific knowledge, especially that of all the mental sciences and even more especially in the science of social conditions becomes suspect. For this research often points up 'damage' to the interests of the particular class, thus, as such, an estate that has a vested interest in the suppression of such research may not provide funding to a university. Thus the university usually suppresses such knowledge under the present state of affairs in the globe. As a consequence of the forgoing we see the salary and wage workers, even those with tenure, in the mental sciences of the scientific community hobbled by current conditions.

828<•>observes that to discover and propagate the mental sciences and knowledge which is incompatible with the interests of the ruling third estate, is to declare war on them. If such research findings are indeed carried out it assumes not simply a high degree of intelligence, but also ability and willingness to fight as well for independence by the university from that estate mentioned. (Although this is only partially possible in present global conditions.) And above all it would show a strong moral feeling, strong social instincts, a ruthless striving for knowledge and to spread the truth with a warm desire to help the oppressed 5E of which all professors and administration etc. in the university are a part. Which condition, if they really look at themselves, becomes evident on deeper reflection.

829<•>observes that the conscious aim of one aspect of the class struggle is an elevation of the mental sciences to take in and embrace Scientific Socialism.

830<•>observes that over the last couple of centuries this struggle, which had been previously on a more or less moral basis, has been largely transformed from a moral into an economic aim but in the recognition of this fact the struggle loses none of its greatness.

831<•>observes that what appeared to all previous social innovators as a moral question, we can now recognize as a necessary result of the economic development of mankind in an ever upward spiral reaching for the eventual abolition of all economic classes. The use of scientific understanding of morality alone could never attain this lofty aim for mankind.

832<•>observes that the aim is not for the abolition of all professional distinctions; Not for the abolition of the division of labor, but for the abolition of all social distinctions and antagonisms which arise from kappa private property in the means of production. The aim is the abolition of the present system of extraction of value-added for personal use of a few super rich families, and abolition of their use of state terror on the peoples of the globe to maintain this extraction. We will show further on that this does not mean, however, that the 5E wishes to abolish the extraction of value-added completely.

833<•>observes that the means of production have become so enormous, that they burst the frame of kappa private property. The productivity of labor is grown so huge, the war machine so great, the gumshoe and soldier of fortune 6E is so extensive, that if all this was turned into productive instead of destructive purpose, we would be able to alleviate all abject misery, anxiety, poverty and ecological damage in the globe.

834<•>observes that along with the forgoing the ecological system of the globe would not have to bear the brunt of the depredations mentioned. Thus the antagonisms of rich and poor, exploiters and exploited, wise and ignorant, will be eliminated as the coil of economic development proceeds.

835<•>observes that along this main path, and with the help of all the mental sciences, especially materialist philosophy we can burst the chains of Kantian neo-Kantian and other mysticisms. Thus in due course humankind will develop new moral thinking, new ethical codes, new civil & criminal laws all of which proceeds in peace to its inevitable human destiny.

836<•>observes that such solid scientifically based moral ideals which open such splendid vistas are won from sober economic considerations.

837<•>observes that although progressive songsters singing the praises of Freedom! Equality! Fraternity! Justice! Humanity! May help a bit along the way it is the unemployed, the salary worker, the wage worker, the farmer, the transportation worker, the aboriginal, the farmer, the small businessman and the transformation of Kappa property into Mu property etc. in the economic struggle that is really the power behind progress.

838<•>observes that these foregoing outlooks are no mere expectations of conditions which only ought to come, which we simply wish and will to come, but they are outlooks at conditions which must come, which are necessary.

839<•>observes that these conditions are certainly not necessary in the fatalist philosopher's sense – that a higher power will present them to us of itself. But they are necessary, unavoidable in the sense, that the inventors improve technology and the 3E capitalists in their desire for profit revolutionize, not only the technical aspects, but the whole economic life of mankind.

840<•>observes that just as the foregoing is true in the struggle of opposites, so is it true, and also as inevitable that the salary and wage workers aim for shorter hours of labor and higher wages, that they organize themselves, into unions, into associations, into advocacy groups. Many however, taken on a global scale, are often unemployed and more often than not in a constant state of anxiety.

841<•>observes that with all of the foregoing they are also in a constant fight somewhere in the globe with 3E capital, its state, its war machine, its hirelings and its Quislings. As well as this they are constantly being bamboozled by half-truths (and discrete silences) emanating from the 4E press.

842<•>observes that it is inevitable, as the crisis develops, that the salary and wage worker's aim for the conquest of political power and the overthrow of 3E capitalist depredations and war. Socialism and the brotherhood of man is inevitable because the class struggle and the victory of the salary and wage 5E is inevitable.

Tsunami One Moral Organon.

~ 843<•>observes that **TRACT 29:**

844<•>observes that **The Laws Of Morality In Homo Sapiens**
Dialectics at work in such laws

845<•>observes that **The Law Of Morality**·
Thus we have arrived at the following law: Moral Thinking and action in an individual is made up of five distinct and separate elements:-

1) The Eternal Social Instinct. (Qernel) Q. This element of morality has been conditioned over eons of time, and for all intents and purpose is innate in all Homo Sapiens and is to be found in many animals.

2) The Ephemeral Envelope Of Mores Of The Age. This element of morality is conditioned by Ethic codes civil & criminal law and is further conditioned as to Place, Time, Estate, Or Situation. This (Rindlucent) R is to be found in varying degrees only in Homo Sapiens.

3) The eternal Q and the ephemeral R in Homo Sapiens are combined in varying proportions and degrees to form the Rindqern. RQ. That is, to form the overall combined moral-outlook of the individual.

4) Internal private Moral Thinking in an individual is irrelevant to society and only becomes relevant to society as a whole when it expresses itself in some form of external action.

5) Such external action may operate at a very narrow level of intensity or it may be combined to form a whole network of social action at a very high level of intensity.

This pentapartite law of morality is examined in more detail in the following.

846<•>observes that **Corollary 1:** While the eternal social instinct Q varies little in intensity it is oft time blown hither an thither by the enveloping rindlucent R. R in its turn is influenced by the ephemeral mores of the era and by propaganda, ethical codes, civil & criminal laws.

847<•>observes that **Corollary 2:** In order to be morally 'correct' every ethical code, civil law, criminal law or act must contain an element of social instinct. If it does not then it is suspect as being immoral.

848<•>observes that **Corollary 3:** If social mores overwhelm and sink social instinct then the thinking, code and/or law promoting such mores is probably immoral. On the other hand if the social instinct overrides a more such a condition most likely brings about morality in moral thinking. What indeed is to be aimed for:- to achieve at least some semblance of social instinct in every ethical code, civil & criminal law to nurture the social instinct and in all people's moral thinking. This will bring about a feeling of general well-being in all of society's members – it will generally kill anxiety.

849<•>observes that **Corollary 4:** Every individual has his own way of moral thinking, which is a complicated mix of 1) social instinct and 2) mores or social views. Often in 2) these mores and/or social views, are evoked by use of extensive subjective criteria and propaganda, news-speak and PR puffery in ethical codes and in the civil or criminal laws of their epoch, of their class, of their estate, or of their time.

850<•>observes that Observation 1: Morally every 'Physical Philosopher' (Physical Scientist) must never ignore the social instinct in his work but must be very circumspect as to the Mores of his time. Otherwise the conclusion made in physical sciences themselves lead into error and become suspect.

851<•>observes that Observation 2: To those who study Law, History, Psychology, Political Economy, etc. in short the Mental Philosophers, if their work is to be of any lasting benefit to mankind must be aware of, and take into account in their work the dual nature in the make up moral thinking and actions in Homo Sapiens.

852<•>observes that We will now look into objectifying the subjective in a dialectical world.

853<•>observes that There is a dialectical contradiction in almost every moral system. This dialectic manifests itself as a struggle between social instinct Q and the mores of its time R. Every ethical code promulgated is itself conditioned by some moral thought that emanates from the realm of 'spirit'.

854<•>observes that The question then arises. But does this realm of spirit emanate from the sigma subjective or from the omega subjective world? From definitions we find that **The Omega Subjective** relates to or of things in the mind occasioned by the objective world or by the omega metaphysical world. **The Sigma Subjective** relates to or of things in the mind occasioned by the sigma metaphysical whimsical world.

855<•>observes that Thus we can say that many ethical codes might arise from the whimsical world of individuals unattached to the objective material world around them. This state of affairs leads to a Nietzcheian - Heiddeggerean, private superman 'will to power' or to a Sartreian world of gloomy individualism.

856<•>observes that These worlds that are sigma subjectively based, having been produced by a plentitude of speculative, convoluted, gases in the brain are soon exploded by a touch of the eternal flame of objective social instinct. This touch-gas takes place when people crawl out of their individualism and act together in estates and classes for particular aims in collective life.

857<•>observes that Preliminary Remarks On Social Instinct And The Mores That might Override Them.

858<•>observes that We shall now show that a Society's 'universal' ethical codes (in a perfect world without classes and estates and defective mores) would correspond exactly to moral thinking in the individual. If such a occurrence ever came about we would have a perfect social system. But we do not live in a perfect world!

859<•>observes that We shall also show that mores may have some affect on the social instinct and in some cases completely override and bury that instinct. In that case moral thinking in the individual is distorted and blighted from the social instinct point of view. If the majority of individuals in the society hold these blighted moral thoughts then the society as a whole has a distorted outlook on things.

~860<•>observes that **TRACT 30:**

861<•>observes that **Modes Of Operation Of Ethical Codes** And Their Impact on Social Instinct. Moral Buttresses.

Tsunami One   Moral Organon.

862<•>observes that let us now move on to give some thought on specific subjects and to the ideals in moral thinking about them, the social instinct behind them, and the mores that might override the social instinct for individuals in many areas in ordinary everyday life.

863<•>observes that Ideals: above all come the social impulses which should be embodied to some extent in every ethical code civil & criminal law to produce moral thinking in Individuals (I) and in Society (Σ) as a whole.

864<•>observes that Let ethical code, civil law & criminal law = e
Rem. this is a portion of (R)

865<•>observes that Let mores, custom and praxis =m
Rem. This also is a portion of (R)

866<•>observes that then, in four a mix can be made up in ethical codes that might influence a person's moral thinking.

867<•>observes that There are Four possibilities in any mix of them and they are:- **i)** -e-m, **ii)** -e+m, **iii)** +e-m, **iv)** +e+m These symbols are here included to expose the fact that mores civil and criminal laws do not present themselves as a monolithic structure but are themselves diverse in nature. (i.e. R is many faceted)

868<•>observes that Now then further. Let call Social Instinct qernal (Q)

869<•>observes that Let us call Mores (R) as previously. In society one could have a situation wherein the following might apply Q > R then in this case one would have a just ethical code. If the situation was reversed Q < R one might still have a ethical code that fit some modicum of morality. But if the situation was such that Q was completely extinguished, blown to death, smothered, as it where, by R then the Ethical Code devised for this situation would have little or no validity in morality. And is therefor unjust and should be expunged from any ethical code.

870<• >observes that **Now Consider Further i)**
-e-m
Ethical codes that do not fit social instinct combined with mores that do not fit Social Instinct. i.e. many of the Ethical codes and laws of Nazi Germany, the practice of the majority of the people that go along with especially religious custom and mores often built up over years that go along with so called 'ethnic' cleansing all leading to great injustice with very little modicum of social instinct. Let us call this condition. -e-m.(minEminM) (Pronounced min E min M)

871<• >observes that **Now Consider ii)**
-e+m
Ethical codes that do not fit social instinct. (Immoral Code) combined with mores that do fit social instinct or at least do not distract from social instinct this leads to mixed moral thinking in an individual. This situation may lead the individual to act outside of such immoral ethical codes (and laws). Example: In certain societies there is a great body of civil law that contends that profit and interest are ethical but as we shall soon see such 'laws' do not have a modicum of social instinct in them. This causes some individuals in this type of society to act in a peculiar way. Such might be the case where a capitalist works all day to kill the competition which the immoral code allows. Such a person might then work all night in the soup kitchen assisting the destitute in order to assuage his social instinct. -e+m (minEpluM)

872<• >observes that **Now Consider iii)**
+e-m

Ethical code that fit the social instinct combined with mores that do not fit the social instinct. This state of affairs brings with it frustration in moral thinking of an individual. An example of this sort might be given in the case of émigré (Royalists, White Russian, Cuban Exile and so on). Such people's moral thinking might be lost in the past and, as such, take place post revolution when the ethical codes and civil & criminal laws of the revolution are made to fit more closely with social instinct. The old mores of the émigré diaspora population persist in acting out using the old anti social pre revolutionary codes in their moral thinking. +e-m (pluEminM) (Note aside: we are not saying here that all revolutions produce better social instinct in their laws. Or better conditions on the ground)

873<•>observes that **Now Consider iv)**

+e+m
Ethical codes that fit the social instinct and Mores that also fit the social instinct: This nirvana on any scale has not yet been reached in human society. Example: of the social programs of the utopian socialists of the 19th century +e+m. (pluEpluM) or even possibly the situation in the old gents of the gentile society of pre slavery days.

874<•>observes that Jigging By Advertising And Propaganda Of Ethical Codes, Civil & Criminal Laws And Mores

875<•>observes that If the ethical codes and the civil & criminal laws do not meet the criteria of a least a modicum of social impulse then they are unethical. And no amount of jiggery repeating half-truths propaganda aimed at force fitting either the above or of customs, mores, praxis, and will put them to right in a global context.

876<•>observes that If the ethical codes and civil & criminal laws do not have at least a modicum of social instinct bound up in them then such a situation in society can only lead to immorality in society as a whole, might lead people carry out unjust wars and so on. Some people in this situation might try to force-fit some modicum of social instinct into their moral thinking that assuages their Social Spirit (Cimb) Or attempt to modify, their actions and practice in that society they find themselves bound to. Such becomes the case of civil disobedience. (Case in point - the brave German's who worked in their country to ameliorate the situation caused by their own Nazi Juggernaut) (And again here we are not saying that all civil disobedience has a social instinct component to it. Also think of the case of Charities that are required in capitalist society. Charities assuage the human heart in a society without it. But a whole section on Charities, their 'good' and 'bad' faults, will be subject to scrutiny further on.)

877<•>observes that   If ethical codes and civil & criminal laws fulfill the content criteria of the social impulse, and if then deviant custom mores and praxis lead into a thinking in individuals that is out-side of, and overrides the ethical codes civil & criminal laws that do fit those social instincts then the content of such a 'moral' thinking in the individual is said to be 'immoral thinking' or just Immoral. **While it is in its thinking stage** there can be no external impact. It is only when thinking is turned into external action that it has an impact on other individuals or society as a whole, it then becomes a moral or an immoral act or utterance.

878<•>observes that A divergence between the ethical code and moral thinking thus shows up as a mores difference – a class divergence. Thus between such classes there exists misinformation, a different reality, a different praxis, different mores and a different world-view.

Tsunami One   Moral Organon.

879<•>observes that Contents Of The Ideal Ethical Code. That would Buttress Social Instinct In Moral Thinking.

880<•>observes that Ideal Universal Ethical Code Buttress 1: Trustworthiness:

881<•>observes that Ethical codes, civil and criminal law should contain some social instinct of Trust: When we are trusted we are given greater leeway by others, this is because they don't feel they need contracts to assure that we will meet our obligations. They believe in us. Thus there is a duty: we must constantly live up to the expectation of others and refrain from destructive competition and self serving behavior that tarnishes if not destroys relationships, person to person, group to group and society to society.

882<•>observes that This fits the social instinct but in a world of classes and estates is it attainable? Of this more later. Deviation from this ethical code leads to bad moral (Immoral) thinking and to a breakdown in cohesion of the social instinct. (Note: And as stated previously this:- thinking is only relevant to the external world of action is taken upon that thinking.) Problem: when the situation is beyond our control then we may not be able to meet our obligation to morality i.e. loss of job leads to default on debt pay-down.

883<•>observes that Ideal Universal Ethical Code Buttress 2: Truthfulness & Openness

884<•>observes that Ethical codes civil & criminal law should contain the obligation of truthfulness precludes intentional misrepresentation of fact (lying or repeated half-truths.). Intent is the crucial distinction between fact and truthfulness. (See Note To Buttress 1)

885<•>observes that Ideal Universal Ethical Code Buttress 3: Honesty:

886<•>observes that Ethical codes, civil & criminal laws should all contain the obligation in an honest manner, in probity and integrity. Honesty is a predisposition to tell the truth and inspire trust, honesty implies a refusal to lie steal or deceive. (See Note To Buttress 1)

887<•>observes that Ideal Universal Ethical Code Buttress 4: Anti-deception:

888<•>observes that Ethical codes, civil & criminal law should contain the obligation of sincerity. It precludes all acts of out of context statements, and even silences that are intended to create beliefs, or leave impressions that are untrue or misleading. (a thousand facts may not make a truth. i.e. what if we are bombarded with propaganda giving only one-sided facts – are these kinds of facts leading to truth?). Also civil & criminal law is silent in many aspect of Buttress 3 and 4. For example using jailhouse informants and even torture to obtain convictions because the policeman's and the lawyer's reputations (and income) depends upon the number of convictions they can place on their CV. (See Note To Buttress 1)

889<•>observes that Ideal Universal Ethical Code Buttress 5: Candor:

890<•>observes that Ethical codes, civil & criminal law should contain candor that requires trust forthrightness and frankness. Cheating is a vile form of dishonesty and takes advantage of those who are not cheating. (See Note To Buttress 1)

891<•>observes that Ideal Universal Ethical Code Buttress 6:

Integrity:

892<•>observes that Ethical codes, civil & criminal law should contain integrity so that there are no divisions in public life, and in individual life there are no self interest, self deception or self righteousness and or an end justifies the means attitude. (See Note To Impulse 1)

893<•>observes that **Ideal Universal Ethical Code Buttress 7:**
Respect:

894<•>observes that Ethical codes, civil & criminal law should contain an aspect of respect. While the universal social instinct is common in the mores of another person or society and as long as those mores do not completely over-ride the social instincts then those mores should be respected by others (See Note To Impulse 1).

895<•>observes that **Ideal Universal Ethical Code Buttress 8:**
Fairness:

896<•>observes that Ethical codes, civil & criminal law should contain an element of decency. It is unfair to handle similar matters inconsistently. Punishment must fit the offenses. All decisions should be made without favoritism or prejudice. (See Note To Impulse 1).

897<•>observes that **Ideal Universal Ethical Code Buttress 9:**
Caring:

898<•>observes that #2051 Ethical codes, civil & criminal law should contain genuine concern for the welfare of others. (See Note To Impulse 1).

899<•>observes that **Ideal Universal Ethical Code Buttress 10:**
International Citizenship:

900<•>observes that Ethical codes, civil & criminal law should contain an element of citizenship. The good citizen knows the laws of humanity and obeys them, and works on a grass roots International basis to change those laws that are not consistent with the social instinct (See Note To Impulse 1).

901<•>observes that **Ideal Universal Ethical Code Buttress 11: International Duty:**

902<•>observes that Ethical codes, civil & criminal law should contain the obligation to act or refrain from acting on any issue which does not contain at least a modicum of social instinct. We shall soon see that war is one act that the citizens of a country might have to partake of, but is it ethical from the global international point of view? It is the duty of all to seek the social instinct in this matter, for many wars attempt to extinguish the social instinct while others are fought to maintain or obtain them. (Note To Impulse 1).

903<•>observes that **Thus the 11 Buttresses of the International Universal Ethical Code Are:** Trustworthiness, Truthfulness, Honesty, Anti-deception, Candor Integrity, Respect, Fairness, Caring, International Citizenship, International Duty. These are the hallmarks of social instinct that should be embedded in the ethical codes, criminal & civil laws that lead to instinctive moral thinking and instinctive moral action.

904<•>observes that **Moral Thinking. (both Σ and I)**
i.e. for all the peoples and for the individual. We have seen above that moral thinking in human beings is usually comprised of two main components.
1) The Social Instinct. (Q). 2) The Mores of the times. (R)

905<•>observes that We have also shown that every moral thought in individuals that leads to moral action, in order to be valid for society as a whole, must contain at least a modicum of 'Social Instinct'. This despite how much the 'mores of the times or of the estate' influences an individuals moral thinking.

~906<•>observes that **TRACT 31:**
907<•>observes that **Moral Thinking In Regard To The Value-Added Continuum** Discussion Of The Value-added Continuum And The Aspects Of Life That Make It Up. Their Morality or Immorality. Capital in and of itself to be discussed in a following TRACT.

908<•>observes that **What is the value-added continuum?** To fully understand this economic concept, please consult Tsunami Two. In order to understand its ramification in so far as ethics and morals are concerned stay with Tsunami One and study on.

909<•>observes that **1) What is Off The Value-added Continuum** Euthanasia, GMF, Suicide, Abortion, Marriage and other like social issues. This second aspect of ethics and morals will not be discussed in the present volume.

910<•>observes that **2) What is On The Value-added Continuum** Profit, Interest, Dividends, Expenses, Taxes, Medical Insurance, Unemployment Insurance, Social Expenditures and the like. The discussion to follow in this tract will revolve around these.

911<•>observes that **Critique in regard to the aliquot parts on the value-added continuum by salary and wage work:-**

Tsunami One   Moral Organon.

Remembering from Economics Organon that the price of a product or a service is made up of the following sets with all their relevant items of division and sub-division that go to make up each set:-
Depreciation on capital +
raw material +
power (fuel) +
expenses +
salary and wages +
Value-added.

912<•>observes that **Now just examining the** Subsets On The Value-added Continuum For social instinct and mores (qernel and rindlucent) leading to Morality. Those Major Subsets For Value-added Are:- Profit, Interest, Dividends, Derivitives of the forgoing, Advertising, Taxes for war Taxes in general, Expenses (Transportation etc.), Charities, Child Welfare, Health Care, Pensions.

913<•>observes that An aside comment: Where do funds for war come from? They come out of Value-added! And they are usually extracted in the form of taxes.

914<•>observes that **In General What are the methods of value-added (Surplus Value) extraction?** Historically, in ancient times slavery and in more recent times the Serf system was used to extract value from the labor of the many for the aggrandizement of a few. The methodologies used in this extraction had very little or no social instinct component to them, this extraction was purely for the use of the individual and not for society as a whole. Nowadays this extraction has been by private capital hiring salary and wage workers at their competitive subsistence rate and having those workers produce much more than their substance. The purchaser of that labor then has the 'right' of selling what has thus been produced for much more than the cost of production, and thus pocketing the difference. But it must be said at the outset that not all value-added extraction comes at the cost of killing the social instinct. We will launch into a critique insofar as the social instinct is concerned of each one of the subsets involved in value-added (some-times referred to as surplus value)

915<•>observes that Critique Of Value-added Extraction & Its Subset: Profit

916<•>observes that many of the present world's ethical codes and moral thinking problems revolve around value-added extraction and antagonistic local and global competition.

917<•>observes that this state of affairs leads to unemployment, poverty, criminality and war. Because of these problems we will first discuss the morality of profit. A discussion of profit first is in order to facilitate our discussion in the whole subsequent litany of items on social instincts on the value-added continuum. The discussions revolve around mores, moral and immoral thinking that takes place in the various estates and also on such moral thoughts that take place in the individual persons that go to make up such estates.

918<•>observes that **How Is Profit Derived?** Profit Extraction is only part of value-added extraction form salary and wage work. Profit in-and-of-itself has no social instinct component to it. It is purely an individual extraction usually (but not always) in the money form of commodities. In this system the work of others is converted, by a convoluted mechanism, (see Economic Organon) into this money form and ends up in the hands of a few. Private gain is its sole and only reason for its existence. The group of six billion who produce it get no good part of it but that group does get to compete in the labor market, the unemployment, the poverty, the wars, the many illegalities and adulterations and other forms of competitive antagonism that the drive for profit creates.

919<•>observes that **What arguments are put forward by Philistines about the necessity for Profit?** The Third Estate says "The world needs profit and competition for efficiency!" Yes but this efficiency-competition comes at the price of antagonistic competition. Kill the competition is the word often heard around capital's offices. We would ask the reader to think about the following areas where much acrimony in ethics is concerned. And think about the problem if there was no Profit involved. Plagiarism, Abortion, Cloning, GMF, Slavery, Strikes, War, Terrorists, Freedom-fighters, Product-adulteration, Pharmaceutical production, Advertising and Ecological degradation.

920<•>observes that What does the first estate religion think of Profit? We have only to go to St. Luke 19: to find that the extraction of profit (labor tokens, money) from one's fellow man is to be tossed out of the temple.

921<•>observes that So herein we have a progressive passage even in the new-testament of the Bible. The old-testament is silent upon this matter. **Profit extraction in the hands of individuals fails to meet the following Social Instinct in Ethical Code Standards:-**

922<•>observes that Profit extraction fails to meet the Social Instinct of Trustworthiness. Comment; in the struggle for profit the combatants cannot be trustworthy for the simple reason that the trustworthy one is, in the eyes of all of the others, a fool. Such a blockhead has no business acumen, and so the trustworthy one must go down to the impact of the shrewd and the thousands of the untrustworthy. Many odious and untrustworthy practices are used in the pursuit of profit. discrimination, adulteration, price-gouging, pornography-for-profit, dumping, hazardous material, bribery, compromising worker safety and so on.

923<•>observes that Profit extraction fails to meet the social instinct of Honesty: Comment: in the struggle for profit the combatants cannot be really honest and open about their products for it is the shrewd puffery in advertising that sells products that make profit. They cannot reveal their take-over plans, they cannot be open about their upper management and even in many cases upper management uses all manner and means to be less than honest to their smaller shareholders. The IPO (initial public offering) is a most horrendous method of foisting off on the people at large dud companies and above all in the last instance capital cannot be completely open with salary and wage workers – it's a maelstrom of dishonesty in a whirlpool of immorality.

924<•>observes that Profit extraction fails to meet the social instinct of Truthfulness. Comment: no combatant in the antagonistic race for profit can be really truthful about the affairs of his individual company there are thousand of lies promulgated by capital. Off balance sheet accounting, take-overs, scooping of pension plans, plant closures and movements to cheaper jurisdictions, tax avoidance, tax fraud to name a few.

925<•>observes that Profit extraction fails to meet the social instinct of Anti-deception, Comment: in the struggle for profit deception is the name of the game. Deceive the competition, deceive the government, deceive the salary and wage workers, deceive the customer. If not deceiving then be deceived by the competition.

Tsunami One   Moral Organon.

926<•>observes that Profit extraction fails to meet the social instinct of Integrity, Comment: Every society including a socialist society requires integrity. Integrity is being at one with the situation, no dichotomy in acts insofar as the social instinct is concerned. In seeking profit at the expense of society this oneness with social instinct is completely overridden by the mores of the times. The social instinct must be almost completely buried or else the antagonistic competition will bury it for you. In the ideal society ethical codes, civil & criminal law should contain elements of integrity so that there are no divisions in public life, and in individual life there are no self interest, self deception or self righteousness and or an end justifies the means attitude.

927<•>observes that Profit extraction fails to meet the social instinct of Respect: Comment: 3E capital is no respecter of the social instinct, it cannot be, if it tries to be, it is doomed to extinction at the hands of other 3E Capitals. Power is the ability to initiate your own program while at the same time crippling the power of your adversary in initiating his/her program – we see no social instinct in this type of power. Thus, once again, we see the mores of the profit system completely submerging the social instinct.

928<•>observes that Profit extraction from the value-added continuum fails to meet the social instinct of Candor: Comment: Candor is the social instinct that leads to frankness, openness sincerity and freedom from bias. 3E capital cannot possibly attain this lofty goal for if it practiced all of these it would go down to defeat at the hands of other capitals.

929<•>observes that Profit extraction under 3E private control fails to meet the social instinct of Fairness: Comment: Fairness is the ability to be objective relative to ones own self-interest and to treat the self-interest of others justly and equitably.

Tsunami One   Moral Organon.

Impartiality to ones own needs is the hallmark of fairness. When, in the battle for 3E profit, can this lofty social instinct be carried out?

930<•>observes that Profit extraction fails to meet the social instinct of Caring: Comment: Caring is to be genuinely concerned with the welfare of others. Only insofar as it affects its own individual bottom line does 3E capital care. It is not possible for the social instinct of universal caring to come to the fore when competing capitals are locked in an antagonistic battle for survival.

931<•>observes that Profit extraction fails to meet the social instinct of International Citizenship: Comment: Capital sees heavy boundaries in citizenship and it touts the patriotic card at every turn. It is only the patriotism of the bottom line that in reality counts for them. In the global scheme of things 3E nationalistic capital wants to and must kill other 3E nationalistic competing capitals in the drive for accumulation. The social instinct of global citizenship (international solidarity) is completely extinguished its goal is strategic alliances, war alliances, and police alliances as capital's depredations on the UN will attest. Capital's laws, as promulgated by its mouth-pieces in the parliaments of the globe, require citizens to follow the mores of capital while at the same time many of those mores and laws completely override any social instinct factors altogether.

932<•>observes that Profit extraction fails to meet the social instinct of International Duty: Comment: There are two aspect to duty. The first is (a modification to) Kant's Categorical Imperatives it will show up in every ethical code, civil or criminal law that is unconditional for all agents and has a social instinct component to it and also to which its validity or claim does not depend on any ulterior motive. Thus it is the duty of every citizen to check the mores of his society and if they completely override the social instinct then those mores must be suspect and, if needs be, changed. There is always an ulterior motive in 3E capital and that ulterior motive is private gain at the expense of public good. As the reader can see 3E capital cannot attain this lofty goal of international duty – for its ulterior motive is always profit at any cost.

The other aspect is the hypothetical imperative an example of which is 'Do not steal of you want to be popular!'

933<•>observes that thus we see that the mores of profit taking overrides all aspects of social instinct in every item that buttresses moral thinking. Much 'moral thinking around profit' thus ends up as immoral thinking and so results in subsequent immoral acts and actions such as unjust war. i.e. 3E capital's war on other 3E capital, or 3E capital's war on 5E salary and wage workers.

934<•>observes that **Let us now examine the other items along the value-added continuum.**

935<•>observes that **Critique Of Value-added Extraction & Its Subset: Interest:** The extraction of various forms of interest from the value-added continuum item for item is the same as that for profit extraction.

936<•>observes that Here we have the Islamic 1E faction that condemns interest and, in a perfect world rightly so, saying in the Quran. Quote, Al Rum (the Romans) Para: 40: Whatever you pay as interest that it may increase the wealth of the people it does not increase in the sight of Allah: But whatever you give in Zakat (Charitable Tax with a variable rate RER) seeking the favor of Allah – it is these who will increase their wealth many fold. But how does Islam get around interest? Islam gets around interest by the use of usufruct; for which see definitions Tsunami Two.

937<•>observes that **Moral Critique Of Value-added Extraction & Its Subset: Dividends:** The extraction of dividends from the value-added continuum item for item is the same as that for Profit Extraction.

938<•>observes that **Moral Critique Of Value-added Extraction & Its Subset: War:** The extraction, from salary and wage work usually by taxes for war purposes, from the value-added continuum item for item is even more horrendous than that of profit extraction. This type of extraction generally leads to devastation of the lives of salary and wage working people and in the destruction of their property. To make the contrast -- mere profit, interest and dividend extraction does not destroy wealth it merely transfers it from one class of people to another, whilst war actually destroys lives as well as wealth.

939<•>observes that **War** and the preparations for war in the modern world are a totally immoral acts and no amount of ethical code, civil & criminal law can justify them, although many justifications for them are tried. They are foisted upon the 5E by smoke, mirrors, and national patriotism at every turn.

940<•>observes that while the extraction for war purposes can be by direct marketing of goods and products it is by the extraction of taxes that is the usual methodology of paying for war in the modern state. War has to be separated out from taxes for its special place in the depredations on salary and wage labor and upon international mankind as a whole.

941<•>observes that war extraction of value-added fails to meet the social instinct of Trustworthiness: All the intrigue and special agents, secrecy surrounding war leads to immorality and corruption.

942<•>observes that war extraction fails to meet the social instinct of honesty: In struggles even between allies let alone the 'enemy' it is obvious that a national state cannot be open and honest about its intentions. Thus it does not meet the social instinct of honesty and in fact the subterfuge required for this activity leads to immorality and dishonesty.

943<•>observes that war extraction fails to meet the social instinct of truthfulness. In war and in the preparations for war truth is the first victim and thus in war it is necessary for the people engaged in its upper echelon to resort to the anti-social instinct of the big dissemble and the even bigger lie.

944<•>observes that war extraction fails to meet the social instinct of Anti-deception: It is obvious that deception is the main means of advancing war aims (i.e. 'Through Deception We Will Win' is the actual motto of one war group)

945<•>observes that war extraction fails to meet the social instinct of Integrity: In seeking war aims at the expense of the salary and wage workers of the globe the social instinct is completely overridden. Integrity is buried beneath the mores of corruption bred by the necessity of the struggle.

946<•>observes that war extraction fails to meet the social instinct of Respect: In bolstering up their side the other side must be belittled by the use of all kinds of disrespect for the enemy. Gooks, Sand Nigger, and a million other epithets are used to belittle the opponents, this military unwritten ethics code completely overrides social instinct, its immorality is palpable.

947<•>observes that war extraction fails to meet the social instinct of Candor: Candor is the social instinct the leads to frankness, openness and sincerity and freedom from bias. It is obvious that in war situations one must be biased toward the enemy and further than that the 3E must be secretive as to war aims to the 5E salary and wage workers on both sides of the struggle.

948<•>observes that war extraction fails to meet the social instinct of Fairness: Fairness is the ability to be objective relative to ones own self-interest and to treat the self-interest of others justly and equitably. Impartiality to ones own needs is the hallmark of fairness. Thus we see the war party's ethic code of perfidiousness completely overrides the social instinct of fairness and is thus leads to immoral thinking and thus to immoral acts.

949<•>observes that war extraction of value-added fails to meet the social instinct of International Duty: We see the nation states preparations for war and actual war overrides the international duty to provide for a safe globe. The war party always depends upon an ulterior motive and its unwritten clandestine ethic codes reflect this. Their duty is to their own self-interest and not to global salary and wage workers their children and the to the sick and the retired.

950<•>observes that having said the foregoing there are just wars and there are unjust wars but in the long run all wars are immoral. It is the 5E and only the 5E that can determine if a war is just or unjust. This last fact is for the simple reason that almost every other estate has a vested interest in the perpetuation of war.

951<•>observes that **Moral Critique Of Value-added Extraction & Its Subset: Advertising:** The extraction from the value added continuum for advertising and selling have some social instinct components. Illustrations on the two aspects of this item are discussed for the student's thoughts.

952<•>observes that **Trustworthiness in Advertising. A) The immoral case.** It is immoral to lie in advertising, when personal gain and profit are at stake, then this immorality can permeate society. In the immoral case obviously a situation can arise where no trust can be placed in the advertiser. Ethical codes civil & criminal laws and Better Business Bureaus try to ensure that there is a modicum of truth in advertising and its cohort selling. Under this scheme of things Caveat Emptor – let the buyer beware.

B) The moral case is best illustrated by the little story about the Eskimo. A touching proof of that is the following incident related by Dalager: Quote "If they (the Eskimos RER) have to describe to each other anything, they are very careful not to paint it more beautiful than it deserves. Nay, if any one wants to buy anything which he has not seen, the seller describes the thing, however much he may wish to sell it, always as something less good than it is."

953<•>observes that thus we can go through the other item in the Buttresses of Ethical Standards leading from the social instinct through ethical codes, civil & criminal laws needed in the peoples guidance to right moral thinking. In this particular area of advertising there are always immoral and moral precepts involved surrounding Honesty, Truthfulness, Anti-deception, Integrity, Respect, Candor, Fairness, Caring, Citizenship and Duty.

954<•>observes that we would ask the readers to flesh out for themselves the other buttresses of social instincts that lead to moral or immoral thinking in the matter of advertising.

955<•>observes that **Moral Critique Of Value-added Extraction & Its Subset: Taxes:**

956<•>observes that **Trustworthiness:** It is obvious that taxes are required for the human social imperative to survive. But we also know that taxes are used for nefarious purposes. The question then becomes for what purpose is the tax being used and can society trust the people who are administering the just and transparent extraction of it?

957<•>observes that **Immoral use of Tax: Example:** If 'Leaders' of a nation state incur national debts, for example to bolster private banks and other private enterprises dedicated to the extraction of value-added. Then under 3E rule this is an immoral extraction. Such debt in a 3E milieu must attract interest which must in turn be paid out of the public purse in the form of taxes.

958<•>observes that **Moral use of Tax: Example:** Taxes to increase publicly owned capital. The operation of a modern infrastructure and a modern industry require vast amounts of capital. It is a legitimate extraction from the day to day production of value-added by the 5E to augment and to accumulate social capital in public hands. There is no private gain over the public good in such extraction.

959<•>observes that Thus by the two examples given above we can see that there is an unjust and a just methodology for tax extraction from the value-added continuum. I am sure that the reader with the knowledge thus gained from this Tsunami One can fill in many more blanks in regard to taxes for war and other nefarious private gain activities undertaken at the expense of the 5E. Such a list would be too extensive and require a depth of detail too onerous to comment upon in a work of this nature.

960<•>observes that then too future people using the well stocked armory of social need would be able to list many of those items of tax that would be of value to and enhance those

Tsunami One   Moral Organon.

social instincts that would lead to the betterment of humankind in their future time. Also it might be pointed out that only future peoples, in the light of advancement in the human condition, will only then, be able to identify such needs.

961<•>observes that We have many and numerous 3E pundits, ministers, prime ministers, senators, COO's, presidents, that say the lofty goals as outlined herein are naive simple-minded and as such will never be achieved because of rapacious, penurious human nature. But you author has shown that the eternal flame of social instinct can never be extinguished. Otherwise, if it was to be completely snuffed out, human beings would no longer be human beings and thus the whole of society would collapse.

962<•>observes that The excuse for their own ignorance is that they are so brain-seared that they think that the only human progress can be a destructive competitive market orientated progress. These ignorants have observed wars, have viewed mighty capitalist empires collapse, have witnessed the collapse of whole countries economies, have watched the intrigue, have beheld the depredations of uncontrollable monsters and shadow governments but still locked in a brain-seared mist they intone their mantra.

963<•>observes that If, on the other hand, the 'Leaders' who fight for the social items (infrastructure, housing, child, disabled, adult, worker, and senior welfare etc.) that also go to make up the value-added extraction continuum. They are to be trusted and we have a moral thinking in these leaders that are consistent with the social instinct.

964<•>observes that Truthfulness, Honesty, Anti-deception, Candor Integrity, Respect, Fairness, Caring, International Citizenship, International Duty – in all these morals buttress social instincts. They in turn are vital to creation of ethical codes, civil & criminal laws leading up to a moral thinking (both Σ and I) that must be met to achieve a truly just system in the matter of taxes.

965<•>observes that **Moral Critique Of Value-added Extraction & Its Subset: Expenses:**

966<•>observes that Trustworthiness: In the matter of expenses all people, all public and private concerns must incur expenses in order to survive, to carry on any enterprise. Once again, in discussing this matter, we are faced with the possibility of immoral and/or moral uses of the labor tokens extracted from the value-added continuum. It is obvious that in these matters that the Buttresses of Morality:- Truthfulness, Honesty, Anti-deception, Candor Integrity, Respect, Fairness, Caring, International Citizenship, International Duty Must be met in this area of peoples activity and practice for it to meet the social instinct in the matter of incurring and reporting expenses.

967<•>observes that There are mores in this area that run very counter to the social instinct such as kick backs, back handers, padding, short changing, short weight and measures, dilution, debasement of currency, adulteration, packaging, and other practices that in the long run can shrewd an economy to death. These rindlucent mores are so prevalent in the globe that in many jurisdictions they override and sink social instinct altogether.

968<•>observes that **Moral Critique Of Value-added Extraction & Its Subset: Charity:**

969<•>observes that Trustworthiness, The donations to charities under 3E rule on things is tremendous, we see at every turn the salary and wage workers of the globe donating to charities through their own funds and through the tremendous size of the extraction of value-added from them.

970<•>observes that Through smoke, mirrors and constant propaganda the 3E capitalist organizations (who make a world that requires charity) make the pitch that it is out of their pockets that charity is given. If they were truthful and Trustworthy they would own up from whence the labor tokens (money) really comes from – the salary and wage workers of the globe. This deception amounts to immorality.

971<•>observes that Then there are other deceptions in charities. Some, not all, people at the head of charities pay themselves first, garnering big salaries out of all proportion to their contribution to the effort to relieve the people's suffering under the scourge of 3E capital's rule. Such deformity amounts to immorality.

972<•>observes that there is the other distortion and that is running big operations with many levels of bureaucracy — a bureaucracy that must be paid out of value-added from somewhere.

973<•>observes that we now have the concept of 'Venture Charities' – for profit charities – this is the lowest stage of capitalism an immorality heaped upon an immorality the mores of which override and completely sink the social instinct.

974<•>observes that we then have the true social instinct Charity of the ordinary salary and wage workers helping ordinary people. These are the real heroes in Charity giving but what little they have to assist their fellows and they do it in Truthfulness, Honesty, Anti-deception, Candor Integrity, Respect, Fairness, Caring, International Citizenship,

International Duty. This kind of charity has the true social instinct ring about it.

975<•>observes that with charities there is so much smoke and mirror about them – in a profit system thrall how does one distinguish which charity has a true social instinct about it and which rings hollow? If the globe could rid itself of profit, interest, dividends, their derivatives and all the antagonism and war they cause then true charity would not be hobbled by immorality and could rise into the lofty realm of a true social impetus.

976<•>observes that **Moral Critique Of Value-added Extraction And One Of Its Subsets: Child Welfare:**

977<•>observes that Child Welfare: Is another element along the value-added continuum. Value-added extraction for child health and welfare is a very large part of the social instinct. Those misanthropes who would privatize and thus profit from this social goal have gradually to be rooted out as society changes over the next millennia. The world's children need imperative support from the salary and wage workers and your observer lauds extraction for this lofty goal. We will let the thinker ponder on the buttresses of Trustworthiness, Truthfulness, Honesty, Anti-deception, Candor, Integrity, Respect, Fairness, Caring, International Citizenship, International Duty. And all that requires value-added extraction a pure necessity for this item in human progress.

978<•>observes that **Moral Critique Of Value-added Extraction And One Of Its Subsets: Health Care:**

979<•>observes that we now have Politicos of the right that want to throw Health Care completely off the Value-added continuum and instead extract it from the Salary and wage worker's income, leaving this portion on the value-added continuum solely to profit. A profit system that we have hitherto shown is completely immoral, why because profit has no social impulse to it has only a purely private motive behind it. If there is any good that comes out of such a system it is only as an adjunct, a requirement to mask the true nature of its business which is profit.

980<•>observes that Trustworthiness, we now have politicians that want to ensure that health care is a private matter, a for profit matter. Both these aims as we have seen are anti-social instinct in nature. By means of the big dissemble the politicos of capital see only profit, markets and antagonistic competition as the great social movers of the age.

981<•>observes that but these regressive movements are the cause of much distress in the globe and are completely out of touch with the social instinct and lack in any modicum of Truthfulness, Honesty, Anti-deception, Candor Integrity, Respect, Fairness, Caring, International Citizenship, International Duty.

982<•>observes that **Moral Critique Of Value-added Extraction And One Of Its Subsets: Pensions:**

983<•>observes that Trustworthiness: The politicos of the day want to throw Pensions off the Value-added continuum and force their premiums from the individual salary and wage worker themselves. Often they attempt and succeed in giving this over to private for profit organizations, a procedure that, as we have already seen is an ant-social act. We would ask the reader to consider the place of pensions which have been so badly mismanaged at the hand of the 3E capitalists in the past. We would ask the reader to think about the Truthfulness, Honesty, Anti-deception, Candor

Integrity, Respect, Fairness, Caring, International Citizenship, International Duty embodied in for profit pensions.

984<•>observes that **Let us now reiterate what we have thought about Moral Thinking** up to this point. Social Instinct is an objective concept in Moral Thinking. Mores is a subjective concept in Moral Thinking.

985<•>observes that **The possibility exists for Social Instinct (Q) without a Mores (R) component may show up in a Moral Thought. (RQ) Thus** = Q>R = +QR

That also both Social Instinct and Mores may show up in a Moral Thought. **Thus** +Q+R = ++QR

That where the Mores actually override and blots out the Social Instinct in a thought then that thought is most likely, but not necessarily, an Immoral Thought
Thus +Q<R = - QR

That these are not the only possibilities the examination of which is left to the philosophical devices of the reader. We will discuss dilemmas in a separate volume (i.e. lifeboat and prisoners dilemmas and other dilemmas etc.)

986<•>observes that **thus we have arrived at what the social community** should aim at is to completely derail those items presently ensconced on the value-added continuum such items as profit, interest, dividends and all their derivatives, and regressive taxes. And the social community should retain all the social instinctive items on the continuum such as Progressive Taxes, Expenses, Child welfare, Health care, Pensions and the like.

Tsunami One   Moral Organon.

987<•>observes that **What the politicos of the right**, in their ignorance, are aiming at is the support of those minority people in the retention of profit, interest etc. for private use. And thus they do all of those nefarious things to maintain and retain those items which we now see are of an immoral nature. They want to retain these immoralities on the value-added continuum and they want to throw out all those items on which the peoples depend for social progress.

988<•>observes that **What this then amounts to** is foisting all those social instinctive items which the right have been able to expunge from the continuum down upon the individual. This of course amounts to every person for him or herself. It is a concept of the hero, cowboy, loner, hood, with no social instinct component in its makeup whatsoever.

989<•>observes that **We leave the section** of value-added ethics and morals' with one more organon that gives us, together with previous symbols other possibilities of short hand. A symbolism in moral thinking that might be used for a deeper more penetrating examination of ethics codes civil & criminal law that lead to a higher moral thinking in mankind.

Ethics Codes
Group Ethic Codes are (sigma Ethics) (ΣE)
Group Moral Thinking is (sigma Moral Thinking) (ΣMT)
Individual Ethic Codes are (Iota Ethics) (IE)
Individual Moral Thinking is (Iota Moral thinking) (IMT)

Moral Thinking
We have already discussed The rindlucent (R) and The Qernel (Q) in Moral thinking
Overall Moral Thinking = a varied combination of the mores of the times of class, or of estate and eternal social instinct.

Moral Action
Moral Thinking leads moral action. MT~MA

990<•>observes that whatever society exists, capital is required as the mainspring of all economic social action. What then is the vital question? Does capital stand in the camp of the individual or does it stand in the camp of society as a whole?

991<•>observes that Capital itself does not appear on the value-added continuum. But it is vital for the philosopher to understand just where capital accumulation does stand in regards to its morality.

992<•>observes that Note to reader. It is the intent of the author to discuss those ethical codes and moral items that do not lay in a realm of the value-added continuum. Such items might be, but not limited to: Marriage, Family, Abortion, Cloning, Crime & Punishment, Euthanasia, GMF, Homosexuality, Sex, Suicide and such items that are extremely subjective. As seen from this present analysis in the Tsunami we do have a methodology of bringing the both the sigma subjective and the omega subjective into the realm of objectivity.

End.

Tsunami One   Moral Organon.

ISBN 1553958574-8